Cultural History and Material Culture

Everyday Life, Landscapes, Museums

For
Magdalen Roos Schlereth
1886–1973
Horticulturist and Historian

Contents

Graphic Evidence

Foreword

Say the words "material culture" and someone will probably respond "Tom Schlereth." And rightly so. No other person in America has been as fully or as frequently identified with the study of material culture. No other person has done so much to publicize and promote material culture scholarship. Tom Schlereth has simultaneously served as chief chronicler of the material culture movement and as one of its major actors. Few events focusing on material culture have taken place without his presence. Few who work in the field are not in some way in his debt. In fact, I have grave doubts that there even would have been a material culture movement if Schlereth had not turned his energies and insights in this direction.

I am delighted that UMI Research Press and series editor Simon Bronner decided to add this volume to their list of material culture titles. Here we finally have "the concise Schlereth," "the Schlereth reader," pulling together in one place an informative and provocative selection of the writings of one of the most influential cultural historians of our time. This collection of Schlereth's shorter pieces provides a valuable introduction to and summary of his work. From this sampler readers can gain an accurate understanding of his interests, his methods, his purposes.

There is no need to recapitulate the contents of this book. Schlereth makes his case with clarity and grace. He is, at the same time, characteristically modest about his achievements. I can speak without restraint. I can say straight out that these essays are admirable, that they provide valuable models for emulation. I can state that I am impressed by the sense of purpose, the authenticity, the integrity, the commitment that pervade these writings. And I can say that the more I think about it and the more I compare Tom Schlereth's work to that of others, the more I am convinced that he provides an inspiring role model for those who would be humanist scholars in a democratic society.

What makes Schlereth exceptional? Perhaps most of all, his dedication to teaching. Throughout this book, Schlereth is constantly teaching, always teaching. He believes in education and this belief constantly informs his essays.

Schlereth's style of teaching is Socratic. Each of his texts generates ideas, insights, and questions, questions, and more questions. For Schlereth the material world is full of questions—as well as clues to answers to those questions. Schlereth's most engaging writings move from question to question, from the known to the unknown, opening more of the world to inquiry. His studies spiral outward, generating new recognitions, realizations, conceptualizations, and always questions, more questions.

No one can read much of Schlereth's writing without noticing that he is an irrepressible bibliographer. His pages are packed with references to other scholars, other works. Footnotes abound. I selected one of the chapters in this book at random; it had fifteen pages of text—and seven more of footnotes. Most of these contained multiple references which, in turn, led to more suggestions, more connections, more explorations.

Schlereth's commitment to teaching is apparent both in his accessibility and in his method. There is nothing secretive or evasive about his writing. There is no mystification, no jargon, just plain talk. Schlereth's goal is communication. He achieves it admirably. Likewise, there is nothing elusive about his method. It is always clear, always explicit. In fact, method is usually a large part of the point in Tom Schlereth's essays. He speaks of lesson plans, of providing techniques for research and teaching. He offers an array of methodological exercises. His purpose is to send readers off on their own paths of inquiry. He does all he can to give them the tools they need.

Schlereth's impact as a teacher is enhanced by personal qualities and stances that are apparent to those who know him or read him: awareness, decency, populism, activism, and commitment to the intellect. These coalesce in and give power to his work. All are apparent in this book.

Schlereth prefaces each of these essays with a few paragraphs explaining the contexts in which they were originally written. These comments are often heavily biographical. This series invites such reflective commentary but I suspect that Schlereth would have provided it anyway. Schlereth's subject matter, his style, and his dedication to teaching are all consciously grounded in his own values and experiences—in awareness, in other words. Schlereth works to promote a similar awareness in his students, whether narrowly defined as those in his classes at Notre Dame or, more broadly, as all who read his books or hear his lectures. Behind his work seem to stand the twin directives: know thyself; know thy world.

It may appear old-fashioned to talk about an author's character but it seems appropriate when character pervades work as fully as it does here. Tom Schlereth's scholarship has always been marked by a fundamental decency. He is authentically human and humane, consistently gracious, supportive, and encouraging. He is famous for acknowledging others, for offering positive reinforcement. I have never seen him take a cheap shot. Schlereth makes important points, takes tough stands, without attacking, without wounding. Respect for others is a constant in his scholarship. And he uses humor effectively. Tom Schlereth's populism informs nearly every page of this book. We see it in his attention to many voices, to rural folks, children, women, laborers, history's losers. Schlereth's emphasis on teaching method is part of his populism, for this teaching holds out the promise of intellectual enfranchisement to all who can read. Populism shapes his choice of subject matter as well. The avenues Schlereth opens are not limited to the affluent but accessible to all who may be attracted to them. He shows how people can find history in such everyday artifacts as landscapes, cityscapes, plants and trees, highways, place names, mail-order catalogues, photographs. All material culture holds clues to the human past. Schlereth shows how we need only an inquiring mind to start to make meaning from it.

Academics sometimes speak in obscurities to privileged audiences, then fancy they are making bold political gestures. Maybe they are, but such attitudes and activities seem effete when compared to Schlereth's straightforward attempt to create a more democratic history. His teaching, lecturing, and writing all focus on that goal. Schlereth has definite ideas about the importance of education in American society and has devoted his life to encouraging education on all levels. Schlereth's activism is also manifest in his continuing efforts to expand the educational role of America's history museums by improving the quality of their products. Schlereth has lobbied energetically to establish a regular program of reviewing history museum exhibits. As consultant and speaker he has been much sought after by institutions anxious to draw upon his visions and insights. Tom Schlereth has had a positive impact on the history museums of America.

Schlereth's activism is grounded in a profound faith in the liberating power of the mind. I have never heard Schlereth put it in exactly those terms but the lesson is implicit in his work. It is clear that he is deeply committed to learning and understanding. It is also clear that he accepts the risks and responsibilities these bring. Schlereth respects his audience and reality enough to embrace complexity and ambiguity. In Schlereth's writing there is no reductionism, no oversimplification. On the contrary, he cautions us that "it wasn't that simple," then demonstrates why. That concise statement embodies another principle that has consistently shaped Schlereth's work. For him, truth is complex as are the ways to it. Small revelations may come easily but grasping the whole picture is extraordinarily difficult. Schlereth's view of reality always incorporates conflict and change, winners and losers, contradictions and uncertainties.

Tom Schlereth was trained in the Enlightenment. That training has never left him. Like Diderot, he is a true encyclopedic. The range of materials, references, connections, and questions in his work is always impressive, and often dazzling. His commitment to education—"The aim of education is to enable individuals to continue their education"—even if expressed in the words of John Dewey, keeps Enlightenment values alive. If Schlereth's purpose had to be expressed in a single word, I think that word would be enlightenment.

It is wonderful to have this collection of Tom Schlereth's shorter pieces together in one book. Every essay provides rewarding reading. Taken together the cumulative effect is impressive and, to me at least, inspirational.

Kenneth L. Ames
Winterthur Museum
1 May 1989

Preface to the Paperback Edition

This is a book with many beginnings. I hope not too many. In addition to a foreword, acknowledgments, introduction, and prologue, the reader finds this preface. Fortunately, the book has no coda, afterword, or conclusion—only an epilogue.

Why so many starts? There are several reasons. First, and most important, this is the first issuing of a new, paperback, edition by the University Press of Virginia. That fact deserves to be announced; acquiring a new publisher is something akin to taking a new spouse. Public notice should be given.

A preface also affords, in a more visible way, an opportunity to single out special "friends of the work." I will do so momentarily. A final rationale for this preface is didactic. Although authors may publicly intone a quip of William Allen Neilson ("Prefaces are like speeches before the curtain; they make even the most self-forgetful performers self-conscious"), most of us privately covet the chance to say one more thing. I cannot resist saying *three*—perhaps because of reasons explained far below (p. 425). In any event, and in a moment, I wish to comment more fully than elsewhere in the book on three of its aspects: evidential materials, middle-class orientation, and methodological perspectives.

First, however, let me say that if prefaces had titles, I would call this preface "The Historical Archaeology of a Book." As will be evident in many of this book's chapters, I have learned from the writings of historical archaeologists such as James Deetz, Mark Leone, Robert Schuyler, and Bert Salwen regarding archaeology's special contribution to material culture studies (in addition to coining the term "material culture"). This book's introduction and epilogue chronicle the details of how the volume can be thought of as something of an archaeological site—one possessing two of archaeology's basic explanatory principles: stratigraphy and chronology.

This volume is the composite of at least three strata of publishing history. The earliest layer includes an assortment of work first published all over North America; the middle tier is located in Ann Arbor, Michigan, where the book assumed much of its present form, enjoying two successful printings. The most immediate stratum is what you hold in your hand, a product of a major university press with a long-standing reputation for publishing regional and American history. This most recent edition, besides this preface, also has a new cover—always important for the identity of any book but especially important when the book's content concerns itself with visual research and analysis.

Unlike the historical archaeology of most artifact assemblages, where relative chronology is usually the only feasible dating procedure, this book has a single absolute chronology. I will be the first to admit it is a short chronology. A few of the essays date from the 1970s, the majority were written in the 1980s, and a small number appeared in the early 1990s. What this bell curve of scholarship means in terms of the historiography of a lifelong career remains to be seen, but I do hope for future progeny. An author's greatest worry, of course, to invoke the archaeological metaphor a last time, is to learn that his or her work has been ditched in a recent midden site.

Hence a final reason for this preface. It affords a place to offer three ideas for "how-to-use-this-book" in historical research and teaching. I hope the volume contains helpful ideas and images for a diverse audience—American Studies scholars, historically minded folklorists, cultural geographers, museum professionals, material culture researchers, and an eclectic brood of American historians. I also think the book will be useful as reading in undergraduate and graduate courses dealing with material culture studies, museum education, American studies and American civilization courses, museum studies programs, and specialized American cultural history courses with an emphasis on late nineteenth- and early twentieth-century American cultural geography and urban and environmental history.

Scholars and students working in fields along this wide spectrum of research and study usually need appropriate visual evidence in order to do their tasks. I am pleased (as I explain in detail on p. 11) that this volume contains a substantial portfolio of graphic evidence—some 163 visual representations of the past. I consider such evidence to be as vital to the book's argument as its citations.

In addition to my use of such data to document and demonstrate my historical interpretations, others can put the graphics to other teaching and research purposes. For example, anyone interested in American art history, particularly paintings of the established canon, will find a score of images to review, ranging from (fig. 20) Benjamin West's *William Penn's Treaty with the Indians* (1771) to (fig. 71) Charles Sheeler's *American Landscape* (1930). For students of the landscape, there are numerous perspectives. In addition to examples of American landscape paintings, we have graphics dealing with urban parks, world's fairs, and city planning—many of which can be studied through comparative analysis. Art forms such as the collage (realistic and surrealist), the trompe l'oeil, and any self-conscious collection or construction of assorted material culture have fascinated me for a long time (fig. 35). Such imagery begins and ends this book. We find it in artistic photography, (fig. 2) Wright Morris, *Dresser Drawer, Ed's Place, near Norfolk, Nebraska* (1947); commercial photography (figs. 28–30), Sears Roebuck Illinois State Fair Pavilion Display (1912); in lithography, (fig. 8) a rebus, "A Good Cheer" (1852) and (fig. 15) "Wonders of Barnum's Museum" (ca. 1860); and in textiles, (fig. 153) a printed toile, New York City Hall, Surrounded by Fourteen Street Cries (ca. 1814).

Marshall McLuhan's forecast in his 1964 *Understanding Media* ("The historians and archaeologists will one day discover that the ads of our times are the richest and most faithful daily reflections that any society ever made of its entire range of activities") informs my selection of numerous nineteenth- and twentieth-century advertisements. I would argue that data also give us insights into changing American concepts of material wealth, economic abundance, and personal success. Examples of ads that present such cultural themes include (fig. 13) "Arrow Collars and Shirts"; (fig. 14) L. L. Bean Specialty Catalogs; (fig. 24) Montgomery Ward, "A Busy Bee-Hive"; (fig. 38) National Biscuit Co., "Slicker Boy"; (fig. 60) International Time Recording System; and (fig. 105) Abendroth Brothers, "The Uncle Sam Range."

Since the world of history museums (unlike most of our history classrooms) is a highly visual world (often like a three-dimensional rebus you can walk around in), I include as much pictorial documentation of these learning environments as possible. Here, as in the other visual topologies that I already suggested (i.e., paintings, landscapes, collages, ads), and others that might be proposed (e.g., costume, gender, technology, architecture), I encourage a comparative eye. Counterpoint, juxtaposition, and the contrast of ideas, behaviors, and artifacts are important in material culture studies; they are also vital in history museum analysis. Compare below, for example, the history presented in two different times, as in (fig. 118) the Plummer Hall gallery of the Essex Institute with that in (fig. 119) the Chicago History Galleries (1979) of the Chicago History Society or the history presented in a same time, as in (fig. 120) the University of Notre Dame Archives (1989) and (fig. 121) the King's Landing Historical Settlement (1989). Similar exercises are possible by viewing deliberate juxtapositions (as in each graphic set that precedes each of the book's parts), and in figs. 126–27, figs. 146–47, figs. 155–56, plus some not so obvious comparisons: figs. 145 and 152; figs. 148 and 152.

As with the two views (figs. 155–56) of the Noah Webster house study, this book surveys many of the arts, artifacts, and activities of the nineteenth- and twentieth-century North American middle class. This emphasis begins as early as figure 7 and is explained in detail on pages 9–11. Some of the many visual representations of middle-classness include its reform movements (e.g., fig. 12); its landscapes (e.g., figs. 88 and 91), and its institutions (e.g., fig. 102).

The visual layouts that I experimented with in this book assumed expanded forms in my cultural history, *Victorian America: Transformations of Everyday Life, 1876–1915* (1991), a volume that also monitors the middle class during one of its influential periods in American social and cultural history. That class contributed enormously to the proliferation of modern material culture, especially its mass-manufactured, mass-advertised, mass-distributed visual forms. No single historical study or even blockbuster history museum exhibition can convey the staggering visual impact of the expanded pictorial and polychromatic culture that flooded everyday life from the advent of photography in the 1840s to the beginning of talking pictures in 1920s. By 1915 Vachel Lindsay, writing in *The Motion Picture as Art,* realized that America had become a world of visual images, of signs and symbols—in his words, a "hieroglyphic civilization." The creation, manipulation, and consumption of images is an important premise of this book, as it is of *Victorian America*. In the latter book, however, I should note that despite my best efforts to find a convincing reason for including this book's final graphic (fig. 163) in that book, I did not. Nevertheless, I and my publishers past (UMT Research Press) and present (University Press of Virginia) hope that readers will, with regard to both books, follow the injunction of John Haberle's 1895 painting *The Slate.*

Cultural History anticipates *Victorian America* in other ways. Researching and writing the essays in this book helped me research and write many of the chapters in the book that followed. I think of this volume as a published (and republished) collection of theoretical, historiographical, and critical essays on the historical methodologies of material culture studies. Thus if *Cultural History* is theory, *Victorian America* is an attempt at practice. The first is method(s); the second, implementation of method(s); the first is exhortation, the second is example. Readers of both will realize these interconnections in various ways, but a single example will demonstrate the point.

For many years I have been urging historians to write history attentive to the visual as well as the verbal, to artifact as well as act (chap. 12 highlights five pioneers of material culture teaching and writing who have done so in the past). In doing so, I have been critical of many forms—history textbooks, curricula, exhibitions, museums—of presenting the past (chaps. 11–15 are particularly full of my critique). But criticism is not enough; one must practice what one preaches. In this sense, *Victorian America* is one direct application of the homilies found in *Cultural History*; I hope there will be others in the future.

In publishing *Cultural History* I have had generous colleagues. They have been true "friends of the work." Marilyn Meeker, my copyeditor, and Brad Taylor, my managing editor, at UMI Research Press, where the book was first published in 1990, believed in the volume from the beginning. They devoted enormous time and effort to its editorial and visual production. I thank them deeply for their creativity and collaboration. John McGuigan, then an acquisitions editor at the University Press of Virginia, deserves my thanks for championing the book's cause and for bringing about, with expedition and encouragement, the book's new status in this paperback edition.

Benjamin Disraeli, who wrote much and deservedly had good reasons to talk of his writings, once remarked: "An author who speaks about his own books is almost as bad as a mother who talks about her own children." But, just as few mothers (or fathers) can resist talking of their progeny—when for good or ill—neither have I been able. Books, as many authors have often commented, are like our children. As parent and author, one watches and wonders as one's offspring makes their way in the world; one does so with pride and anxiety; with self-satisfaction and self-consciousness; and a sense of loss. So, too with this new edition.

Acknowledgments

Numerous individuals and several institutions helped me craft this book. They are so numerous and their contributions so multiple, that I resort to the simple democracy of an alphabetical listing. One exception to this rule is to thank publicly several typists—Margaret Jasiewicz, Cheryl Reed, Nancy Kolb, Nina Gerhold, Nancy McMahon, who helped with various chapters, and particularly Sherry Reichold who assisted me repeatedly by re-typing the entire manuscript several times. I also wish to thank Alice Benjamin, Martha Fokey, Jane Fries, and Sylvia Phillips who aided me in various photoduplication tasks.

I am also grateful to Barbara Allen, Greg Baeker, Manny Banayo, Lee Baxandall, Rick Beard, James Bellis, Lynn Bettman, Patti Carr Black, Jo Blatti, Alberta Brandt, Christopher Buchanan, Robert Burke, Robert Burns, Stan Caine, Margie Callahan, John Carter, Barbara Fah Charles, Emily Clark, Grady Clay, Deborah Cooper, Wanda Corn, Pete Daniels, Betty Doak Elder, Anne Farnum, Stacy Flaherty, Alida Francis, Gary Gore, Steven Hamp, Nathan Hatch, John Herbst, Brooke Hindle, Toris Ilg Isselhardt, J. B. Jackson, Louis C. Jones, Polly Jontz, Kevin Knepp, Thomas Krasean, Gary Kulik, Charles Lamb, Warren Leon, Peirce Lewis, Margery S. Long, David Lowenthal, Steven Lubar, James Maroney, Charles Martin, Lorene Mayo, Lillian B. Miller, Cammie Naylor, Robert Nespo, Susan Nichols, Susan Otto, John Patterson, Gale Petersen, William Pretzler, Carroll Pursell, Hillary Ray, Barbara Riley, Howard Rock, Bart Roselli, Roy Rosenzweig, Charles L. Sacks, Jack Salzman, Nicholas B. Scheetz, Wendy Clauson Schlereth, Bob Staples, Carol Stapp, Carlene Stephens, John Stilgoe, Martha Strayhorn, Martin Sullivan, Lenore Swoiskin, Ellen Synder, Dell Upton, and Wilbur Zelinsky.

During the time spent researching and writing these essays, many institutions generously supported my scholarship. In preparing this volume, I am especially indebted to the Office of Fellowships and Grants, Smithsonian Institution, the University of Notre Dame College of Arts and Letters, the Lilly Library, the Jesse H. Jones Faculty Research Fund, the National Endowment for the Humanities, and the Institute for the Advancement of Scholarship in the Liberal Arts at the University of Notre Dame.

The Prologue, "Material Culture or Material Life? Discipline or Field? Theory or Method?" appeared in *Living in a Material World: Canadian and American Approaches to Material Culture,* ed. Gerald L. Pocius (St. John's, Newfoundland: Social and Economic Papers no. 19, Institute of Social and Economic Research, 1991).

Chapter 1, "Plants Past: The Natural Material Culture of the American Land," appeared in *Environmental Review,* 1980, under the title "Plants Past: An Historian's Use of Vegetation as Material Culture Evidence."

Chapter 2, "Mail-Order Catalogs as Resources in Material Culture Studies," appeared in *Prospects: The Annual of American Cultural Studies,* ed. Jack Salzman (New York: Burt Franklin & Co., Inc., 1982), reprinted by permission of Cambridge University Press.

Chapter 3, "The Material Culture of Childhood: Research Problems and Possibilities," appeared in *Material History Bulletin / Bulletin d'histoire de la culture matérielle,* 1985, under the title "The Material Culture of Childhood: Problems and Potential in Historical Explanation."

Chapter 4, "Artisans in the New Republic: A Portrait from Visual Evidence," appeared in *Material Culture,* 1989, under the title "The New York Artisan in the Early Republic: A Portrait from Graphic Evidence, 1787–1853."

Chapter 6, "The City as Artifact," appeared in the *AHA Newsletter,* 1977.

Chapter 7, "The New England Presence on the Midwest Landscape," appeared in *The Old Northwest,* 1983.

Chapter 8, "Chautauqua: A Middle Landscape of the Middle Class," appeared in the *Henry Ford Museum & Greenfield Village Herald,* 1984.

Chapter 9, "City Planning as Progressive Reform: Burnham's Plan and Moody's Manual," appeared in *Journal of the American Planning Association,* 1981, under the title "Burnham's *Plan* and Moody's *Manual*: City Planning as Progressive Reform."

Chapter 11, "The History behind, within, and outside the History Museum," appeared in *Curator,* 1980, reprinted with permission from *Curator,* copyright © The American Museum of Natural History, 1980.

Chapter 12, "Pioneers of Material Culture: Teaching History with American Things," appeared in *History News,* 1982, under the title "Pioneers of Material Culture: Using American Things to Teach American History."

Chapter 13, "It Wasn't That Simple," appeared in *Museum News,* January/February 1978. Copyright 1978, the American Association of Museums. All rights reserved.

Chapter 14, "Causing Conflict, Doing Violence," appeared in *Museum News,* October 1984. Copyright 1984, the American Association of Museums. All rights reserved.

Chapter 15, "History Museums and Material Culture," appeared in *History Museums in the United States,* ed. Warren Leon and Roy Rosenzweig (Champaign: Univ. of Illinois Press, 1989).

Cultural History and Material Culture

Introduction

Cultural History and Material Culture

To the cultural historian there are no banal things. . . . Modest things of daily life, they accumulate into forces acting upon whoever moves with the orbits of our civilization.

—Siegfried Giedion

I have had considerable difficulty deciding what to name this volume. The title I decided upon, while not trendy, is truthful. I am a cultural historian whose intellectual heroes include Giovanni Vico and Johan Huizinga. I am, thanks to the writings of scholars such as James Deetz, Siegfried Giedion, J. B. Jackson, Peirce Lewis, and Jules Prown, intrigued with the various ways men and women create, use, or discard material culture to mediate their relations with one another and with the physical environment.

My subtitle identifies several directions of my past research and writing. The time span of the work collected in this volume is relatively short. Compared to that of other authors in the Masters series, mine is brief. Yet I have been fortunate in that span to have my previous volumes on material culture prove useful in history courses, artifact research, and museum exhibitions. This volume touches on some of the subjects of those

---

(Opposite page)
Figure 1 *(above)*.
William Harnett, *Job Lot, Cheap*, 1878
Oil on canvas.
(Courtesy of Reynolda House Collection of American Art, Winston-Salem, North Carolina)

Figure 2 *(below)*.
Wright Morris, *Dresser Drawer, Ed's Place, near Norfolk, Nebraska*, 1947
Photograph.
(Copyright Wright Morris. Courtesy The Center for Creative Photography, University of Arizona, Tucson)

other books, but it is different. It consists of what I would call "working" papers. They are so in two ways. Several were reworked from courses or seminars, public lectures, or research colloquia that I gave. Others resulted from my rethinking their argument, evidence, or method (see, for example, chap. 12 where I include an article from 1978 which was updated in 1984).

This volume offers a place for other researchers to gain wider access to my essays, several of which first appeared in difficult-to-find journals, museum conference papers, and symposium reports. This book permits me to expand and improve several studies that I first published with editorial restraints as to length and documentation. It also offers readers an opportunity to see significant visual evidence that could not be incorporated in the original essays.

I saw this book as a self-conscious act of synthesis. It seemed useful to me to chart the contours of my historical research, to question what my contribution has been all about. Who influenced me the most? When and how? Had my ideas changed about history, material culture, or cultural history? Could one point to any particular themes in the type of material culture research I had tried over the past decades? Preparing and thinking about this volume yielded the three current leitmotifs—everyday life, public landscapes, museums as artifacts—that structure this self-assessment.

While pursuing a master's degree at the University of Wisconsin (1964) and writing a thesis ("The Progressive-Democrat Alliance in the Presidential Election of 1928") in political history, I began work in American intellectual history with the encouragement of William R. Hutchinson, then a visiting professor at Wisconsin and now Charles Warren Professor of the History of Religion in America at Harvard. Thanks to the urging of another graduate student, I occasionally sat in on the lectures of Andrew Hill Clark, unaware of his stature as one of the country's outstanding geographers. After completing my master's degree, I taught American history on the undergraduate level for a year, and decided to begin a history doctoral program at the University of Iowa in 1965. At Iowa, I prepared fields in European and American political thought; European intellectual history; American religious history, and American intellectual history for my doctoral program. I wrote a dissertation (1969) that became a book, *The Cosmopolitan Ideal in Enlightenment Thought* (1977).

While none of my graduate training specifically encouraged me to think about objects as historical evidence, a pivotal experience did. In 1968–69 I received Kent and Newberry Library Fellowships enabling me to research and write my dissertation over a two-year period in Chicago.

The Newberry experience changed my life in major ways. There I met my wife, Wendy Clauson, another historian. At the Newberry, I acquired firsthand knowledge of the excitement of working in one of the country's greatest research centers.

In Chicago, I also first experienced museums as learning environments. I occasionally ventured from the Newberry north to the Chicago Historical Society (fig. 3) and then south to the Art Institute of Chicago (fig. 4). At the CHS, Harold Skramstad was then reinterpreting the city's history through a series of new exhibitions; at the AIC, John Zukowsky was establishing a new department of architecture and mounting innovative shows on various aspects of Chicago's built environment. Both introduced me to the world of things; both took me behind the scenes and let me roam through their storerooms of artifacts; both encouraged me to think about how the physical remains of the past might be used to expand and enhance historical interpretation. Other historians working in museums—Kenneth Ames at Winterthur, Brooke Hindle at the National Museum of American History, Barnes Riznik at Old Sturbridge Village, Cary Carson at Colonial Williamsburg—have continued my education as to the possibilities and pitfalls of using material culture in my teaching and research.

My initial exposure to the museums of Chicago points up a parallel with my lack of academic training in object study. I never went to museums as a child or adolescent; libraries, yes, often fortnightly; but museums, no, neither in school groups nor while on a family vacation. As a latecomer and a newcomer to museums, I became intrigued by what I, as a historian, could learn from them. I was especially anxious to know how I could use their collections and exhibitions in my teaching of American history.

While in my first teaching appointment in the departments of history and American studies at Grinnell College, I used semester breaks and summer vacations to see places such as Colonial Williamsburg, Living History Farms, Old Sturbridge Village, and Plimoth Plantation. Invited back to teach as a faculty fellow at the Newberry, I explored the CHS and AIC more thoroughly. I tramped Chicago and its suburbs trying to learn how a historian would investigate such an artifact assemblage. During this amateur fieldwork, I concocted the idea of teaching an urban history course, covering 1870 to 1930, with the extant Chicago built environment as its evidential base.

I came to the department of American studies at the University of Notre Dame in 1972 as an assistant professor. There Ron Weber, a scholar of American literature, chaired the department. I told him about my idea for the Chicago course; he said, "Try it." A year later, I proposed a course

Figure 3.
"Chicago: Creating New Traditions," 1976
Exhibition, Chicago Historical Society.
(Courtesy Staples and Charles, Washington, D.C.)

called American Material Culture. He said, "Try it." It is not without reason, and with much appreciation, that my *Material Culture: A Research Guide* (Lawrence: University Press of Kansas, 1984) is dedicated to Ronald Weber, professor of American studies—a distinguished literary scholar and craftsman with words who has generously encouraged me as a cultural historian increasingly intrigued with the historicity of things.

Similarly, I thought it only appropriate to dedicate my *Artifacts and the American Past* (Nashville: American Association for State and Local History, 1980) to the "Students in American Studies 484 American Material Culture, Past, Present, and Future." To those venturesome undergraduates I owe a great deal. With them I tried to find out what world's fairs, mail-order catalogs, and photographs could tell us about American cultural history. To answer such questions, we read what we could find. We traveled to places like the Henry Ford Museum and Greenfield Village where curators Peter Cousins and Larry Lankton graciously gave us two-day seminars in object research. Bill Moore at Conner Prairie Settlement in Noblesville and Larry Viskochil at the Chicago Historical Society provided similar help as did Marsha Mullin at Discovery Hall Museum and David Bainbridge at Northern Indiana Historical Society, both located in South Bend, Indiana.

Figure 4.
"Chicago Architecture, 1872–1922," 1988
Exhibition, Art Institute of Chicago; John Zukowsky, chief curator; Stanley Tigerman, designer.
(Courtesy John Zukowsky and Van Inwegen Photography)

All this coming and going to history museums began to turn my head. I started thinking about the development of history museums in the history of American museums. Could such institutions have public and private histories? Was it possible they could have a historiography, even a philosophy of history? Could the ways they presented, exhibited, or demonstrated the material culture of the past be analyzed and differentiated for scholarly study? Deep speculation by an assistant professor; but, once an intellectual historian, always an intellectual historian. Such conjecturing led to my saying aloud what I thought about these issues, first, at a meeting of the Society of American Architectural Historians and, later, in the columns of *Museum News*. (For complete details, see chap. 12.)

I interrupt this personal odyssey here because I want to underline two concerns that initiated and have maintained my interest in material culture studies. One has obviously been pedagogical (fig. 5): I turned to artifact research because I felt it would expand and enrich my teaching of American history in my university classroom. A second, perhaps less obvious, reason for my intrigue with material culture has been epistemological: I examined research methodologies involving artifacts to see what such approaches could add to my research repertoire as a historian.

These two starting premises led in varied directions, three of which orient the structure of this book. Working backward, in "Museums as Artifacts" (Part Three), I have collected two essays that survey the multiple roles played by historians in museums and that summarize the careers of five material culture pioneers; two essays that critique history exhibitions, and one that assesses current trends in the use of material culture theory in history museums. The epistemological concerns of this section also turn up elsewhere, notably in chapters 3 and 8.

In "Public Landscapes" (Part Two), readers will find some of my earliest attempts at writing cultural history with an eye on physical sources as well as documentary and statistical evidence. One of these is a brief manifesto, with a few bibliographical suggestions, for teaching the city as an artifact. Three focus on Midwest topics, revealing a geographical substratum that surfaces in other essays. (As with F. Scott Fitzgerald, I write often of "my Middle West.") I also offer an overview of the material universe of three American world's fairs, one of which, understandably, is Chicago's Columbian Exposition of 1893.

While I have explored the White City in other writings and in my Chicago seminars, here I place the fair in the comparative context of two other artifact assemblages: Philadelphia's 1876 Centennial and San Francisco's 1915 Panama-Pacific Exposition. I use these three fairs to summarize changes and continuities in the American experience as manifested

Figure 5.
"The Schoolmaster"
Woodcut. From Edward Hazen, *The Panorama of Professions and Trades* (Philadelphia, 1832), p. 142.

in occupational trends, housing preferences, consumer choices, recreational developments, demographic and social patterns. I am also using the three fairs to provide an introductory, a midpoint, and concluding perspective for a forthcoming book dealing with the cultural history of Victorian America.

This brings us to this volume's Part One, "Everyday Life," a section with some things old and some things new. Plants and catalogs are old interests of mine, traceable to childhood and antedating any interest in their history or material form. Artisans and children are new preoccupations: the former because I, in imitation of French historian Marc Bloch appropriate (see the epilogue) the metaphor of craft for my work as a historian (fig. 6); the latter because (see fig. 41) I am the father of a six-year-old whose intellectual curiosity "about things" usually exhausts my own.

So what's new? In Part One only the essay on "The World and Workers of the Paper Empire." It will appear, in much briefer form and documentation, in my forthcoming cultural history tentatively titled *Transformations in American Everyday Life, 1876–1915.* This survey

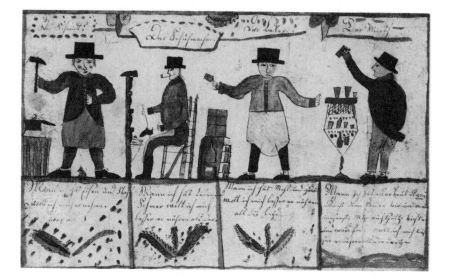

Figure 6.
Fraktur, *The Four Tradesmen,* ca. 1815
Watercolor on paper, southeastern Pennsylvania.
(Courtesy Sotheby Parke Bernet Inc., New York)

of how and where Americans worked, what they ate and wore, how they selected and furnished their homes, what they consumed, how they lived and died will be my most ambitious attempt to integrate, where appropriate, material research into cultural history.

In this work, and the essays to follow, I follow the lead of James Axtell's definition of culture, which I believe affords us a useful amalgam for including material culture in American cultural history: "Culture is an idealized pattern of meanings, values, and norms differentially shared by the members of a society, which can be inferred by the non-instinctive behavior of the group and from the symbolic products of their actions including material artifacts, language, and social institutions." The historian who works from these premises, Axtell argues, should attempt to determine "just what the patterns are in a particular society over time and how the individual parts—whether actions, beliefs, or artifacts—together constitute the functional whole."*

My limited forays into the artifacts of daily life (see fig. 2) have had no specific focus prior to the *Transformations* volume. One might consider some of the essays (for example, those on children, artisans, office

* James Axtell, *The European and the Indian: Essays in the Ethnohistory of Colonial North America* (New York: Oxford University Press, 1981), p. 6.

workers, in Part One) as on groups that scholars now realize were historically invisible in many previous assessments of the past. Another thematic spool on which to wind some of my everyday-life studies would be the nineteenth-century expansion of the American middle class and its preoccupation with consumer goods, child nurture, and white-collar status. Middle-classness manifests elsewhere in the present book in chapter 8 on Chautauqua, chapter 9 on city planning, chapter 10 on world's fairs, and chapter 15 on history museums.

I pay particular attention to the Victorian *middle class* because it increasingly controlled the country's political, social, and cultural agenda. Who made up this middle class? In part, those who always had—doctors, lawyers, ministers, skilled craftsman, small businessmen, bankers, newspaper editors, and settled farmers. By 1915 white-collar workers, technicians, civil servants, foremen, morticians, sales and service people, factory supervisors, merchants, and bureaucrats swelled the ranks of this "new" middle class. Plant managers or movie producers insisted their income level merited them entry. Interior decorators and advertising executives got in by their occupational novelty, while mechanical engineers, certified public accountants, and personnel directors made their case based on their claims to being new "professions."** This middle-class constituency, sprawled across a broad range of modest to substantial incomes, had its dissenters and deserters. Not everyone wanted or got into its ranks. People on the periphery—rural renters; most African, Hispanic, and Asian Americans; the urban proletariat—having no middle place, were kept in their place. But middle-class attitudes and aspirations so monopolized Victorian America that the term *embourgeoisement,* as Walter Nugent has used it, serves as an insightful concept in interpreting class as a facet of daily life (fig. 7; see also figs. 90 and 92). The idea applies not only in its literal meaning (a movement to towns, cities, and suburbs) but also in its more abstract connotation (a gradual assimilation of segments of the worker class into the expanding middle class). The increasing middle-classness of American everyday life took place only gropingly and incompletely. Severe depressions in 1873–77 and 1893–97 slowed its development. The decade 1879–89 was probably the most violent in American history. Socialism made its greatest advances as a viable political alternative in American politics. Yet new economic opportunities appeared after 1900, when increases in more nonfarm jobs, real incomes, and consumer goods began to insure more promising futures for large numbers of people, particularly urban dwellers. As a broad (sometimes contradictory) coalition, the middle class underwent a shift

---

** Burton Bledstein, *The Culture of Professionalism: The Middle-class and the Development of Higher Education in America* (New York: W. W. Norton, 1976).

Figure 7.
"Central Park: Music on the Mall"
Engraving. From *Harper's Weekly* (October 9, 1869).

in aspirations, a transformation, in Nugent's terms, from "land hunger to home-ownership hunger, money-hunger, or durable-goods hunger." This meant Americans became consumers rather than producers; they aspired more to material goods than to land acreages. In the process, many were either further entrenched within or assimilated into a reshaped and expanded urban and suburban middle class.* * *

Historians have usually paid most attention to the coalition's leadership—academics, engineers, managers, new and old professionals, reformers. But these were not enough. Followers had to come from the white-collar world of office, bureau, and business to forge a new middle-class perspective—a tentative consensus that admitted newcomers while simultaneously testing their ethnic, economic, and educational qualifications. Collectively the Victorian middle-class coalition imposed its will, not always without repressive methods nor class confrontations. While its attitudes exerted a pervasive influence in certain areas (for example, consumerism) of working-class everyday life, in other cultural sectors (for

---

* * * Walter Nugent, *The Structures of American Social History* (Bloomington: Indiana University Press, 1981).

example, new forms of recreation) working-class culture changed middle-class habits.

A word about the graphic evidence that I have included in this book's chapters. I have selected my visual data with several objectives in mind. First, I have chosen my material culture graphics in order to illustrate the range of artifactual evidence available to a researcher. While presented in an abbreviated photographic form, confined to a 6 × 9, black-and-white page, the images represent an introduction (but only that) to the spectrum of artifact forms common to American material culture research. Hence, in the book the reader will find measured drawings, trade catalogs, architectural elevations, paintings, lithographs, and, of course, numerous photographs. I also use visual evidence to introduce each section or chapter of the book. Here images serve as a visual metaphor for the interpretation that follows. Within each chapter one will also find visual evidence that documents my argument on that particular topic. Finally, I have also occasionally cross-referenced my graphic material in order to suggest to the reader how it can be compared or contrasted with the artifacts and arguments found elsewhere in the book.

Although I will provide a detailed provenance for each essay in its accompanying headnote, a quick word about the essays in general is in order. While the order of three sections is *not* meant to suggest a historical sequence, there is a relative chronology within each of the sections. The overall time span of the collected essays runs from the mid-1970s to the late 1980s, by no means a significant Baudelairian *longue durée*.

Following through on my posture (see the epilogue) of the historian as craftsman, I would inventory my wares (see fig. 1) as follows: *work commissioned by other scholars* (for Howard Rock, "Artisans in the New Republic"; for Susan Nichols, "The History Behind, Within, and Outside the History Museum"; for John Zukowsky, "City Planning as Progressive Reform"; *work commissioned by institutional clients* (for Canada's National Museum of Man, "The Material Culture of Childhood"; for the American Historical Association, "The City as Artifact"; for the American Association of Museums, "Causing Conflict, Doing Violence"); *work for hire* (for the Edison Institute, "Chautauqua: A Middle Landscape of the Middle Class"; for Warren Leon and Roy Rosenzweig, "Material Culture and History Museums"); *work expanded from earlier work* ("The World and Workers of the Paper Empire"; "The Material Universe of American World Expositions, 1876–1915"); *work submitted to the open market* ("Mail-Order Catalogs as Resources in Material Culture Studies"; "The New England Presence on the Landscape"; "It Wasn't That Simple"; "Pioneers of Material Culture"; and *work of personal whim* ("Plants Past"; "One Historian's Craft").

As I noted earlier and as I will repeat in several headnotes, I wish many of these essays to be read as works-in-progress. They were written in a spirit of invocation rather than benediction. I flinch slightly at the rhetorical quality of some of my manifestoes, but I have let the occasional hyperbole stand, remembering that many of these pieces were acts of persuasion as well as arguments of scholarship.

All the essays tend to come with excessive detail, perhaps reminiscent of the nineteenth-century German academic pedantry you might expect from someone named Schlereth. I use footnotes, endnotes, and bibliographical essays as does everyone else: to pay intellectual debts; to present contrary or dissenting interpretations; and to suggest other scholarship a reader might find valuable on the topic. Perhaps I am a bit compulsive about it; once, after presenting a paper at a meeting, a member of the audience came up afterwards, complimented me on my argument, and asked if I could send him just the citations, not the text: "I only buy your books for the references," he told me candidly.

In the references to this volume, he and anyone who consults them will often find the names of Simon Bronner, the editor of the UMI Research Press American Material Culture and Folklife Series, and Kenneth Ames, the gracious author of the foreword to this volume. Earlier in this introduction, I listed several individuals who have greatly influenced my work. I deliberately deferred mentioning Simon and Ken because I wanted to acknowledge my special indebtedness to each.

I met them at about the same time, the mid-1970s, but at two different places. One Indiana spring, Simon came to Notre Dame to converse on material culture theory and practice; one Delaware summer I showed up at Winterthur to listen to Ken spiel on the same topic. The conversations with both are now well into a second decade.

Simon first introduced me to the idea that one might devise a rough typology to sort the theories and theorists of American material culture research; his 1979 essay in *Folklore Forum* (1979) expanding Richard Dorson's categories of artifact research in *Folklore and Folklife* (Chicago: University of Chicago Press, 1972) inspired my own attempt in *Material Culture Studies in America* (1982). Our mutual interest in the history of material culture scholarship (he in folklore, I in cultural history) meant we planned American studies conference sessions together, collaborated on editorial boards, and wrote chapters for each other's books. His confidence in this project gratifies and honors me immensely.

The kind endorsement and thoughtful words of Ken Ames in his foreword do likewise. To Ken I also owe what I know of art and decorative arts history and of the theories for analyzing artifacts for their nonverbal meanings and messages as well as for their social and ideological influences. He has continually provided me with insights into the Victorian American *mentalité*. I am in his debt for many invitations to present my own work at Winterthur summer institutes, biennial conferences, and special seminars. We have worked together in various American Studies Association projects as well as on the Common Agenda for History. His imprimatur here is deeply appreciated.

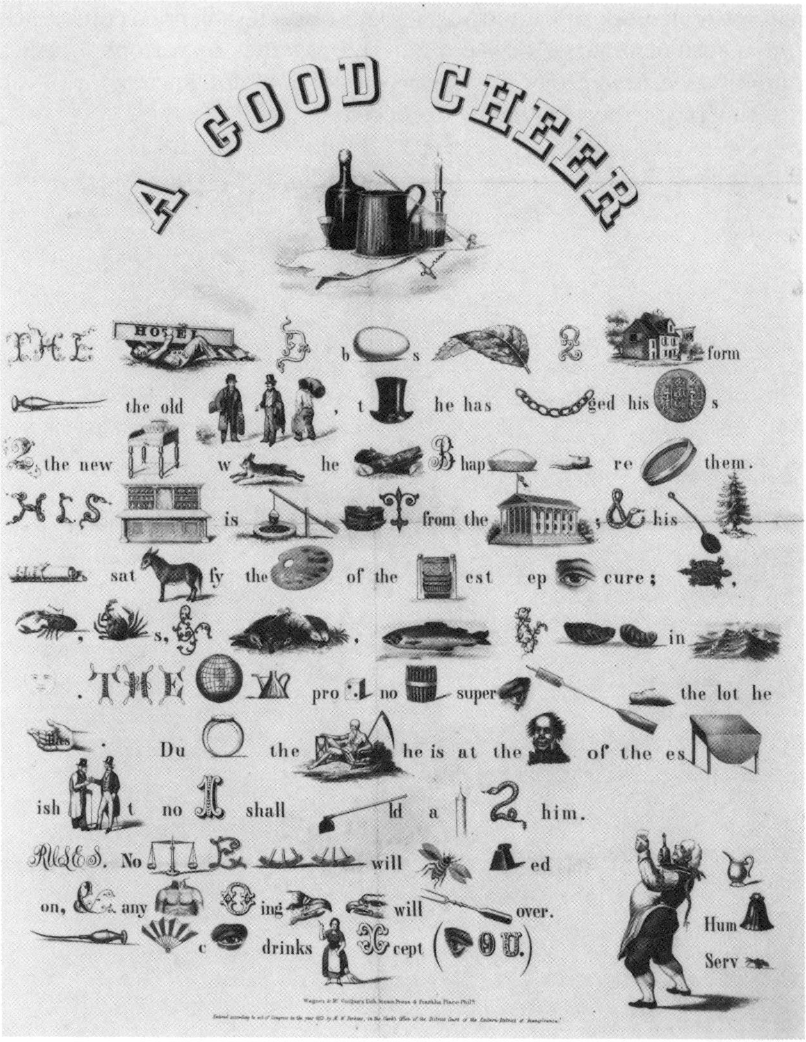

Figure 8.
"A Good Cheer," 1852
Rebus. Lithograph by Wagner and McGuigan, Philadelphia, Pennsylvania.
(Courtesy The Library of Congress, Division of Prints and Photographs)

Prologue

There are no Ideas but in Things.
—William Carlos Williams

Figure 9.
The University of Notre Dame Library and Museum, ca. 1895
(Courtesy University of Notre Dame Archives)

Material Culture or Material Life?
Discipline or Field? Theory or Method?

I place this brief position paper as an opening essay for several reasons. First, I think it raises several points presently under debate by serious students of material culture. Second, it indicates one of my perennial epistemological interests; that is, what are the most precise words to be used when talking or writing about things? Third, the original locale of this essay represents for me, personally, an important historical geography in my thinking about material culture theory and practice—more about which in a moment.

While I presently have nothing more to contribute to the nomenclature issue (what shall we call what we do?), and have not changed my preference for the best generic term to describe physical remains of the human past (material culture), I have noticed a change in the language by which I describe those who investigate material culture for its cultural meaning. In essays a decade ago, I often dubbed such scholars (myself included) with the infelicitous label of "material culturists," a phrase I have let stand, as a linguistic vestige, in a few of the pieces that follow. My original motive was simply to coin an appropriate covering term that would encompass the diverse cadre of researchers working with material culture evidence: historical archaeologists, cultural anthropologists, historians of technology, cultural geographers, art, architectural, and decorative arts scholars, folklife researchers, and cultural historians to name but the tribe's leading clans. Presently, I use "students of material culture" or "material culture scholars" when referring to this collective. In more imperialistic moments, however, I sometimes use "cultural history" as a general rubric for material culture; and some confreres in historical archeology, anthropology, and geography occasionally nod assent. Since my definition of cultural history, noted above in the introduction, demands appropriate attention to material artifacts, it follows that cultural historians should also be students of material culture. Might not the converse also be true? If those remaining material culture scholars can be persuaded to recognize the explanatory powers they would gain by approaching material artifacts from a historical perspective, might we not think of ourselves as cultural historians all? I'm not holding my breath but perhaps our Canadian colleagues, as I summarize below their interest in "material history," could be enlisted in such a campaign.

I write here, of course, with tongue well in cheek. Canadian scholars of material culture—historians all—have been enormously generous to me for the past decade.

In 1979 Barbara Riley and her associates at the National Museum of Man invited me to Ottawa to represent the United States in the continent's first International Conference on Material History. I gave a paper titled "American Scholarship on Material Culture, 1878–1978" which, after its publication in the *Material History Bulletin* (1979) as part of the conference proceedings, grew to be the lengthy first chapter of my *Material Culture Studies in America* (1982). Ten years later an abridged version of the following position paper was commissioned by Gerald Pocius who coordinated a joint conference sponsored by his academic home, the Memorial University at St. John's, Newfoundland, and the Winterthur Museum in Delaware. At the last moment, I was unable to travel to St. John's, but Ken Ames read my paper in my place. Jerry will include the essay in a forthcoming book he is editing, to be titled, *North American Material Culture* and published by the Institute for Social and Economic Research at the Memorial University, St. John's, Newfoundland.

This essay's footnotes also reveal my debts to other Canadian scholars such as Ann Gordon Condon, Gregg Finley, and John Mannion. Many colleagues— Kenneth McLaughlin, Bruce Snowden, Bob Clarke, Jack Hyatt, and others—at several universities—Toronto, Western Ontario, Waterloo, New Brunswick, Calgary, Edmonton—afforded me a platform and a public to discuss the intersections of cultural history and material culture. Particularly formative to my thinking on this relation were the graduate seminars I was invited to give by Gregg Finley at the University of New Brunswick at Fredericton and Saint John and by Walter Jamieson in the School of Environmental Design at the University of Calgary at Edmonton and Calgary.

Three issues deserve attention for the future of material culture research. Questions of nomenclature (what shall we call what we do?); questions of methodology (do the research strategies that we have developed constitute a field or a discipline?); and questions of theory (what hypotheses do we wish to answer?).

Nomenclature

The eclectic enterprise that now encompasses the varied work of those who see artifacts as significant cultural data has been called by diverse labels. The lexicon ranges from "pots-and-pans history" to "physical folklife," from "hardware history" to "artifact studies," from "concrete clio" to "above-ground archaeology."[1]

Three labels—material culture, material history, and material life— now contend for acceptance as the most appropriate rubric for describing North American object research. The first, material culture, has the oldest lineage, used in English-speaking research circles for over a century; the latter two are relatively new to our scholarly parlance, coming into vogue only in the past decade or so.

Nineteenth-century anthropologists first defined material culture. For example, as early as 1875, A. Lane-Fox Pitt-Rivers, in a paper, "On the Evolution of Culture," urged fellow researchers in the emerging social sciences to consider material culture as "the outward signs and symbols of particular ideas in the mind."[2] Since then, the term has undergone redefinition and reformulation. Out of favor among anthropologists in certain decades of the twentieth century, it is presently enjoying an interesting resurgence among some of them.[3] More important, perhaps, it has gained currency among researchers in the arts and humanities such as Jules Prown, Henry Glassie, Ken Ames, and James Deetz. In Deetz's estimate, material culture can be defined as "that segment of man's physical environment which is purposely shaped by him according to culturally dictated plans."[4]

In Canada, however, another term, "material history," has its supporters. They are institutional and individual. In the former instance, one would cite the *Material History Bulletin (MHB),* published at the National Museum of Man in Ottawa and the new Diploma in Material History Programme at the University of New Brunswick in Saint John. The work of Ann Gordon Condon, Robert D. Turner, and A. Gregg Finley can represent the latter.[5]

There have been different definitions of material history during its brief history. A definition first proposed by Barbara Riley and Robert Watt in the initial issue of the *MHB* ("material history is the study of artifacts produced or used throughout history") compared with one later advocated by Hardy and Wardrop in a 1981 special issue of the journal ("material history is the application of artifact-related evidence to the interpretation of the past"), suggests the two different emphases.[6] In a 1985 essay, Finley attempted to amalgamate both in an extended definition:

> material history refers to both the artifacts under investigation and the disciplinary basis of the investigation. The word "material" encompasses the broad range of historical objects which exist as concrete evidence of the human mind in operation at the time of construction and/or use, and as the three-dimensional, nonverbal record containing to a greater or lesser degree, the ideas, concepts, opinions, beliefs, intentions, and values held by people in the past. The word "history" refers to the scholarly preoccupation with the human past and with historical change that is implicit in the practice of history.[7]

Material history appears to be completely of Canadian origin (fig. 10). The term was coined by Canadians (first public usage is usually dated from the inauguration of the *Material History Bulletin* in 1972) and identifies many (but not all) of the country's monographs, articles, serials, courses of study, and conferences dealing with artifact research.

To complicate things a bit more, a third term, "material life" (or its

Figure 10.
Cargo Being Unloaded from *Brunswick Lion* Wood Boat, 1989
King's Landing Historical Settlement, St. John River,
New Brunswick, Canada.
(Courtesy A. Gregg Finley, King's Landing Historical Settlement)

sometime synonym, "material civilization") has entered the terminology debate. Fernand Braudel's confessed attempt to fabricate a label that would be an alternative to "technology," yet would "maintain a bridge to the material culture of anthropology and archaeology," and still convey an overview of "an economic culture of everyday life" is one source of this term. Others will be found among the French economic historians of the *Annales* School.[8]

While French historians first used the phrase to describe an elementary economic culture more basic and pervasive even than the market economy that took root in it, the term's vogue on the North American continent thus far has been among social historians of the American colonial period. We have, for example, the recent work by Robert St. George and Cary Carson.[9]

Carson, in a position paper, "Chesapeake Themes in the History of Early American Material Life," suggests some of the parameters and possibilities of the term. Postulating that "artifacts serve on one level as the devices men and women have always used to mediate their relationships with one another and with the physical world" and that "social history is preeminently a history of relationships," he argues that the study of material life would entail artifact research into both social institutions and social relations, viewed particularly "as the consequence of complex choices among alternative standards and styles of living and the equipment needed to sustain them."[10]

To give specificity to his definition, Carson concludes his proposal with thematic episodes from colonial Chesapeake history that would be included in a sample synthesis of its material life. They focus on issues like settlements as economic units of production (fig. 11), investment in homesteading, assimilation and acculturation of European and African folk traditions, improved living standards, the consumer revolution, and the spread of genteel manners.

Does what we call what we do—whether it be material culture, material history, or material life—make any difference for the future of what we do? Perhaps not, yet encapsulated in our choice of labels (see fig. 8) are decisions about method and theory. In our future debate over the merits of these terms we need to recognize that each is problematic in certain ways, each has assets and liabilities, and each betrays our scholarly predilections, institutional affiliations, and intellectual temperaments.

For example, arguments for adopting "material culture" as our covering term include common use in several disciplines, embodiment of the culture concept, historical lineage, and evocation of human behavior and belief, whereas critics could charge it with unmanageable comprehensiveness, a synchronic proclivity, and being a contradiction in terms.

Advocates of "material history" champion it principally because, in their view, "there is a distinct advantage to anchoring artifact studies to a clear disciplinary foundation, such as history."[11] Objections to such usage, however, might include its limitation to a single disciplinary method, a perspective that excludes the object research of many social scientists, and restricts artifact inquiry solely to the activities of the past.

"Material life," of course, has some of the drawbacks of material culture: indeterminateness, ambiguity, overgenerality. It may also prove excessively beholden to economics and demography. Yet its merits include attention to the ideology and politics of objects as well as to a large stratum of human experience heretofore largely ignored by researchers in many fields: the habitual, routine, ordinary structures of everyday life.

Methodology

Definitional differences will probably continue since many material culture (my preference showing) researchers do not agree as to the professional status of their craft. Is it a discipline? A field? Or a method?

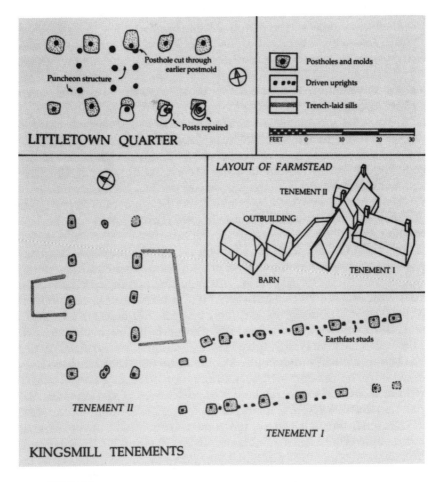

Figure 11.
"Early Structures at Kingsmill, James City County, Virginia, 1625–1650"
Drawing by Shearon Vaughn and Cary Carson (1981).

Each of these positions has champions. They range from those who propose, as has James Deetz, the eventual establishment of departments of material culture studies to others who consider the undertaking as simply another technique in the general tool kit of cultural investigation.[12]

If surveys are to be believed,[13] few practitioners envision material culture studies as a separate, established discipline in the traditional definition of a unique branch of knowledge with distinctive empirical data and special explanatory paradigms. While we have scholarly journals and academic conferences and occasionally talk of plans for a professional association, I do not think the present state of material culture research constitutes an academic discipline as usually defined.

As the late Richard Dorson was wont to remind us, for an activity to be considered as a scholarly discipline, it must be established in both a pragmatic and a philosophical way. Pragmatically, a discipline exists if it can reach an intellectual audience with scholarly works, earn a place in the accepted fields of learning of its day, preserve and enlarge its area of knowledge, attract converts and young disciples, and perpetuate itself for another generation. Philosophically, a discipline exists if it can lay claim to a distinctive methodology, empirical data, or explanatory theory important for humankind's knowledge of self and society.[14] At this state of its historical development, material culture performs several but not all of these requirements.

Jules Prown argues, however, we can claim material culture to be a type of discipline if we define both terms in a specific way. He suggests we constrict the definition of a discipline (consider Dorson's definition, for instance) to but one of its parts; that is, we should define a discipline principally as a methodology or, in Prown's words, "a mode of investigation" in order to differentiate it from a field of knowledge which Prown calls a "subject of investigation." In this, material culture differs from art history, for example, which is both a discipline (a mode of investigation), in its study of history through art, and a field (a subject of investigation), in its study of the history of art itself.

As a discipline, claims Prown, material culture must be content to be "a means rather than an end" in cultural study. It is disqualified from being a subject of investigation because the material evidence of its study (all manmade or modified things including art, diversions, adornments (figs. 12, 13), modifications of the landscape, applied arts, and technological devices) is simply too vast and diverse to be manageable as a single field of analysis.[15]

Dell Upton, on the other hand, suggests it is appropriate to think of material culture as "a subject matter" comparable, in his judgment, to fields such as "traditional tales or the French Revolution." In proposing "a landscape approach" to the study of objects, he is not daunted

Figure 12.
"Ladies' Dress-Reform Meeting at Freeman Place Chapel, Boston, Mass., 1874"
Woodcut. From *Harper's Weekly* (March 1874).

Figure 13.
Cluett, Peabody & Company, "Arrow Collars and Shirts"
Advertisement (1912).
(Courtesy The Warshaw Collection of Business Americana, National Museum of American History, Smithsonian Institution, Washington, D.C.)

by the immensity of material culture as a field. Rather this multiplicity could be an opportunity, a research hallmark that would require "taking all classes of artifacts into our purview." Upton urges us, therefore, to reclaim the initial catholicity of the first material culturists, those nineteenth-century antiquarians who were interested in numerous kinds of artifacts, from the smallest household utensils up to complete houses, and to set about developing material culture as a field of study that "would treat as many kinds and scales of objects as possible."[16]

Other scholars in various disciplines also seek to focus artifact research under the metaphor of "a field of study" or "a field of inquiry." Peter Rider would have it as "a field of history." The developers of the Diploma in Material History Programme at New Brunswick consider it a field of history with a particular institutional and vocational orientation, to wit:

> the field of material history brings a necessary concern with how the objects of that study are preserved and interpreted to the general public. This necessitates for the prospective student of material history at the very least an introduction to the practical aspects of archival and museum work and of restoration techniques, all skills not traditionally a part of normal historical training.[17]

Those who tend to emphasize the content, the subject matter, or the field of material culture study are not, it should be noted, averse to developing its methodological possibilities. Upton, for instance, recognizes that "material culture studies might have the potential, as a method of analysis, like statistics or textual criticism, to expand the possibilities for inquiry in a number of established disciplines."[18]

Does it make any difference, particularly for the future of material culture research, to think of the craft as a discipline or a field? Perhaps not, and yet it might orient our future efforts in certain directions, depending upon which perspective is emphasized. It could be argued, for instance, that to opt for the disciplinary definition might mean increased concentration on material culture as novel methodology (rather than as special evidence), on only the "means" of material culture research, and on material culture as but a branch of cultural history or cultural anthropology. To press for the subject matter approach might mean more attention to material culture as novel evidence (rather than as unique method), to the "ends" of material culture study, and to its status as a research movement (possibly analogous to American or Canadian Studies) within a cross-disciplinary context.

My own preference in the discipline-field discussion is to see the enterprise, at least for the present, as a mode of inquiry primarily (but not exclusively) focused upon a type of evidence. Material culture thus becomes an investigation that (see fig. 9) uses artifacts (along with relevant documentary, statistical, and oral data) to explore cultural questions both in certain established disciplines (such as history or anthropology) and in certain research fields (such as the history of technology or the applied arts).

To use the term discipline conjures up too much confusion given the many meanings the term connotes in the varied institutional contexts (museum, academy, historical society, governmental agency) in which students of material culture work. I am also not convinced that we are, other than in a limited bibliographical sense, yet a clearly articulated field of study. We have yet to reach a working consensus on how to fence the field. Should it encompass only traditional material culture as Warren Roberts would have it, or should it include the most modern objects of contemporary life (fig. 14), as William Rathje would wish? Are its boundaries to be limited only to the extant, three-dimensional artifact or should they also include public performance (fig. 15), behavioral gesture, and extemporaneous utterance?[19]

Theory

No matter what we eventually become—a specialized methodology, a unique subject matter, or a departmental discipline—we will still need to concern ourselves with a third issue: What role will theory play in our efforts?

With a few exceptions, most material culture research has been largely derivative. We have been consumers, rather than producers, of research techniques and interpretive models developed by others.

This is slightly less true if we distinguish methodological theory from explanatory theory. In the past decade there have been several attempts to develop techniques of analysis that could be claimed as indigenous to material culture research. Here the goal (whether successful or not is another matter) has been to establish a plan of work that could be pointed to as something by students of material culture for students of material culture. E. McClung Fleming's artifact primer of four operations (identification, evaluation, cultural analysis, interpretation), Jules Prown's three-state model (description, deduction, speculation), and Robert Elliot's five-step scheme (material, construction, function, provenance, and value) are examples of this quest.[20]

These models of artifact study were designed principally for heuristic purposes in classroom and seminar situations. They borrow much of their language and format from art history and archaeology. And while these how-to-do-it proposals can be critiqued on other grounds—overly in-

Figure 14.
L. L. Bean Specialty Catalogs Advertisement, Summer 1989
(Courtesy L. L. Bean, Inc., Freeport, Maine)

Figure 15.
"Wonders of Barnum's Museum," ca. 1860
Lithograph. Barnum's American Museum.
(Courtesy The New-York Historical Society, New York City)

tellectualist in their prescriptions for how a researcher's mind actually does work, limited in their application usually to single artifacts (a press cupboard or a Bricklin automobile) rather than to large aggregates of material culture—they are, nevertheless, a start in the search for a more rigorous, more systematic, more verifiable theory of methodology that may eventually prove novel to material culture studies in the future. Perhaps from these beginnings will develop a set of methodological procedures that will become standard in our own ranks, and eventually scholars in other disciplines may assimilate them into their work.

On the other hand, in terms of what might be called explanatory theory in material culture, we cannot even claim such a beginning. To be sure there are a few daring tour-de-force works that we all cite, but most of these draw much of their theoretical inspiration from other disciplines, particularly linguistics. They also remain largely untested by other scholars in other research contexts. To put it bluntly, when it comes to the generation of new explanatory theories about human experience or persuasive grand syntheses that chart wide panoramas of human history, material culture students are debtors.

Some years ago I attempted an assessment of how widespread and diverse this borrowing has been in American material culture scholarship.

I came up with nine conceptual positions (see table 15.2, pp. 393–95) on which we modeled most of our research. Peter Rider applied the topology to Canadian material culture, particularly as published in the *MHB*, and drew similar conclusions, although his analysis suggests that past Canadian work has been dependent on a more limited theoretical spectrum.[21]

We need not be embarrassed by this current imbalance of payments in the scholarly world of explanatory theory. In fact, such a borrowing can be looked upon as an asset rather than a liability. As John Mannion and George Kubler recognize, it has assuredly nurtured our interdisciplinarity—a characteristic that may prove to be an emblem of our future identity, whether as a discipline, a field, or a coalition of varied individuals simply intrigued with the (possibly novel) explanatory power of physical objects as cultural meaning.[22]

Interdisciplinarity in material culture research, I hope, will expand in the future. If it does, it would have at least two implications in our search for useful theory. One would be the possibility of a still richer lode of explanatory concepts to adopt or adapt to our purposes. One area of current research that may prove profitable could be the behavioral sciences, particularly social psychology, psycho-history, proxemics, and kinesics.

A second ramification of staying in the interdisciplinary crossfires would be to have the opportunity to play the role of revisionist of previously argued theories. Some have already ventured into this arena. James Deetz's *In Small Things Forgotten* and Merrit Roe Smith's *Harper's Ferry Armory and the New Technology* are examples on a macro and micro level of interpretation.[23] Modernization, urbanization, or *embourgeoisement,* to name but three examples, are explanatory concepts erected principally upon documentary and statistical data and yet largely unproved on the basis of artifactual evidence.

Of course, the more ambitious of our cadre will want to do more than test (or contest) the theories of others. There is an understandable eagerness to prove what we can do on our own. In addition to taking methods and theories from others, we need to frame our own questions, to formulate our own hypotheses.

I am persuaded that material culture researchers might show a noticeable advance in their search for distinctive methods and theories if we were to direct a large portion of our time and talent to probing the explanatory power of the artifact. As Upton has argued,

> whatever else they might be, artifacts are at the deepest level expressive forms. The manufacture of an artifact is an act of creation equal to, rather than reflective of, the manufacture of a social system or an intellectual concept. All are part of the symbolic process that continuously recreates the world by imposing meaning and order on it. As a primary phenomenon equal to social structure and intellectual reasoning, the artifact must be questioned on its own terms.[24]

If we were to take up the challenge of considering material culture as truly a "primary phenomenon" of human experience, what corollary hypotheses might follow from such a position? Perhaps several, at varying levels of theoretical discourse.

First, as a low level theory, we could systematically probe the assumption that all things are not created equal in evidential promise, that there is a scale of explanatory power within the categories of material culture. For instance, do arts reveal more than technics?

Second, we could press to their limits the claims that some of us have made (and not sufficiently proved) for an epistemological novelty within objects that differs from, complements, supplements, or contradicts what can be learned from other sources. Does, for example, an artifact have a unique veracity because it is a nontranslated, sensory, three-dimensional, affective, historical event?[25]

Third, answers to questions such as these could enable us to move onto larger issues such as the relations between behavior and belief or the origins and operations of creativity. In venturing into such mega-theory, we already have some provocative leads to follow.

In the first case, there is Braudel's parameter of the "limits of the possible" in material life, Carson's argument for a scale of "the state of furnishedness" in consumer behavior, and Prown's concept of "intentionality in ethical and esthetic belief decisions." These may grow into models illustrative of broad cultural patterns.[26] In the second instance, Henry Glassie's formulation of "artifactual grammars," Cyril Stanley Smith's "esthetic origins of manufacture," and Brooke Hindle's "emulation and invention" inventory may provide new explanatory theories about the creative process, still one of the most complex (and mysterious) of human acts.[27]

To be sure, this proposal for an extended analysis of what Hindle, almost a decade ago, referred to as the unexamined "inner processes of material culture," is not a wish for additional taxonomy or topology.[28] It is not a demand for expanded archives of artifactual evidence. Nor is it a clarion for concentration on the object for the object's own sake.

Rather it is a proposal to subject the spatial and analytical understanding offered by artifacts to new questions about human behavior. It is a claim to view material culture as a process whereby we attempt to see through objects (not just the objects themselves) to the cultural meaning to which they relate or that they might mediate. It is a suggestion to take our beginning forays into methodologies indigenous to material culture studies and apply them to exploring the subject matter of "thingness" to see just what discoveries such an inquiry might elucidate.

In short, it is a request for material culture students to engage in the careful scrutiny of artifacts in appropriately large aggregates or samples, within verifiable research controls. This would have a dual objective: first, to uncover new information for their own (or others') announced hypotheses about culture; and, second, to explore various serendipitous, random, insights that may be generated by systematic object research (particularly in its basic etymological meaning of "looking again and again") and that may ultimately prove to be enlightening ways of explaining a portion of human experience that heretofore has received little notice or understanding.

Notes

1. Richard Dorson, *Folklore and Folklife, An Introduction* (Chicago: University of Chicago Press, 1972), 2–3; E. McClung Fleming, "History 803: The Artifact in American History," unpublished course outline, Winterthur Program in Early American Culture (1969); Larry Lankton, "Reading History from the Hardware," *The Edison Institute Herald* 10.3 (1981): 23–29; Elizabeth B. Wood, "Pots and Pans History: Relating Manuscripts and Printed Sources to the Study of Domestic Art Objects," *The American Archivist* 30 (July 1967): 431–42; John Cotter, "Above-ground Archaelogy," *American Quarterly* 26.3 (August 1974): 266–80.

2. A. Lane-Fox Pitt-Rivers, "On the Evolution of Culture," in *The Evolution of Culture and Other Essays,* ed. J. L. Myers (Oxford: Clarendon Press, 1906), 23.

3. William L. Rathje, "A Manifesto for Modern Material Culture Studies," in *Modern Material Culture: The Archaeology of Us,* ed. Richard A. Gould and Michael B. Schiffer (New York: Academic Press, 1981), 51–66; Jane Powell Dwyer, *Studies in Anthropology and Material Culture,* vol. 1 of the Haffenreffer Museum Studies in Anthropology and Material Culture (Providence: Brown University, 1975), 5.

4. James Deetz, *In Small Things Forgotten: The Archeology of Early American Life* (Garden City, N.Y.: Anchor Doubleday, 1977), 24–25.

5. Ann Gordon Condon, "What the Object Knew: Material History Studies in Canada," *Acadiensis* 13 (1984) 136–46; A. Gregg Finley, "Material History and Museums: A Curatorial Perspective in Doctoral Research," *Material History Bulletin* 20 (Fall 1984): 2–4; Robert D. Turner, "The Limitations of Material History: A Museological Perspective," *Material History Bulletin* 20 (Fall 1984): 87–92.

6. Compare "Introduction," *Material History Bulletin* 3 (1976): 3, and "Editor's Note," *Material Culture Bulletin* 13 (Fall 1981): 2.

7. A. Gregg Finley, "Material History and Curatorship: Problems and Prospects," *Muse* 111.3 (Autumn 1985): 34.

8. Fernand Braudel, *The Structures of Everyday Life* (New York: Harper & Row, 1981); *Afterthoughts on Material Civilization and Capitalism* (Baltimore: The Johns Hopkins University Press, 1977); A. Hunter Dupree, "Does the History of Technology Exist?" *Journal of Interdisciplinary History* 11.4 (Spring 1981): 585.

9. Robert Blair St. George, ed., *Material Life in America, 1600–1800* (Boston: Northeastern University Press, 1988) and Cary Carson, "Chesapeake Themes in the History of Early American Material Life," paper presented at "Maryland, A Product of Two Worlds" conference, St. Mary's City, Maryland (19 May 1985), 1–11.

10. Carson, "Chesapeake Themes," 6, 9.

11. *Diploma in Material History, A Programme Proposal* (Department of History, University of New Brunswick, 1983).

12. James Deetz, "Material Culture and Archaeology—What's the Difference?" in *Historical Archaeology and the Importance of Material Things,* ed. Leland Ferguson (Columbia, S.C.: Society for Historical Archaeology, 1977), 10–12.

13. Simon Bronner, ed., "Material Culture Studies, A Symposium," special issue, *Material Culture* 17.2/3 (Summer–Fall 1985); Thomas J. Schlereth, *Material Culture Studies in America* (Nashville: American Association for State and Local History, 1982), 1–23.

14. Richard Dorson, "Is Folklore a Discipline?" *Folklore and Fakelore: Essays toward a Discipline of Folk Studies* (Cambridge: Harvard University Press, 1976), 101.

15. Jules D. Prown, "Mind in Matter: An Introduction to Material Culture Theory and Method," *Winterthur Portfolio* 17.1 (Spring 1982): 1.

16. Dell Upton, "Material Culture Studies, A Symposium," *Material Culture* 17.2/3 (Summer–Fall 1985): 85.

17. Peter Rider, "The Concrete Clio: Definition of a Field of History," *Material History Bulletin* 20 (Fall 1984): 92–96; *Diploma in Material History,* 1–2.

18. Upton, "Material Culture Studies," 85.

19. Warren Roberts, "Material Culture Studies, A Symposium," *Material Culture* 17.2/3 (Summer–Fall 1985): 89–93; Rathje, "A Manifesto," 51–66.

20. E. McClung Fleming, "Artifact Study: A Proposed Model," *Winterthur Portfolio* 9 (June 1974): 153–61; Prown, "Mind in Matter," 7–16; Robert S. Elliot, "Toward a Material Culture Methodology," *Material History Bulletin,* 22 (Fall 1985): 31–40.

21. Rider, "The Concrete Clio," 92–96; Schlereth, *Material Culture Studies in America,* 38–72.

22. John Mannion, "Multidisciplinary Dimensions in Material History," *Material History Bulletin* 8 (1979): 21; George Kubler, "Time's Perfection and Colonial Art," in *Winterthur Conference Report; Spanish, French, and English Traditions in the Colonial Silver of North America* (Winterthur: Henry Francis du Pont Winterthur Museum, 1969), 9.

23. Deetz, *In Small Things Forgotten* (Garden City, N.Y.: Anchor/Doubleday Press, 1977); Merrit Roe Smith, *Harper's Ferry Armory and the New Technology* (Ithaca: Cornell University Press, 1977).

24. Upton, "Material Culture Studies," 87.

25. Thomas J. Schlereth, "Material Culture Research and Historical Explanation," *The Public Historian* 7.4 (Fall 1985): 21–30.

26. Braudel, *Structures,* 27–29; Carson, "Chesapeake Themes," 6–9; Prown, "Material Culture Studies," *Material Culture* 17.2/3 (Summer–Fall 1985): 79.

27. Henry Glassie, *Folk Housing in Middle Virginia: A Structural Analysis of Historic Artifacts* (Knoxville: University of Tennessee Press, 1975), 17; Cyril S. Smith, *From Art to Science: Seventy-Two Objects Illustrating the Nature of Discovery* (Cambridge: Harvard University Press, 1980). Brooke Hindle, "A Retrospective View of Science, Technology, and Material Culture in Early American History," *William and Mary Quarterly,* 3rd ser., 41 (July 1984): 430–34.

28. Ibid., p. 433.

Part One

Everyday Life

I embrace the common, I explore and sit at the feet of the familiar, the low. What would we really know the meaning of? The meal in the firkin; the milk in the pan; the ballad in the street; the news of the boat; the glance of the eye; the form and gait of the body;—show me the ultimate reason of these matters . . . .

—Ralph Waldo Emerson

Figure 18.
Grant Wood, *Arbor Day*, 1932
Oil on masonite panel.
(Private collection. Courtesy James Maroney, New York)

Plants Past: The Natural Material Culture of the American Land

If I had not become a historian, I would have been a horticulturist. As a youngster, I grew up in the hills and hollows of western Pennsylvania, working spring and summer days on the region's truck farms and autumn and winter afternoons in the area's greenhouses. As a high school student, I took extension courses in forestry and floriculture from The Pennsylvania State University at University Park. As a college student, I cajoled my dean to allow me to substitute botany for physics as my freshman science requirement. In the midst of all this, however, several historians showed me the challenges and comforts of another life and livelihood: William P. Garvey, now president of Mercyhurst College; Robert E. Burns at the University of Notre Dame; William R. Hutchinson of Harvard University; and Stow Persons of the University of Iowa did their best to make me a historian.

I, however, never lost my love of plants. My wife and son and I deliberately settled on our northern Indiana farmstead (appropriately located between Birch and Current Roads) so that I could restore the nineteenth-century arboretum and orchard that once flanked our 1846, Italianate farmhouse. In the past our farmstead took its identity from the trees its inhabitants planted. Its builders and first owners, the Schmidts from Cambria County, Pennsylvania, liked conifers such as *Pinus strobus* and *Pinus resinosa,* planted them everywhere, and called their abode "The Pines" (fig. 19). A branch of the Studebaker clan, known for carriage and wagon manufacture, preferred hardwoods, reforested the site with *Acer baccharum* and *Acer rubrum,* and renamed it "The Maples" at the turn of the century. What the Schlereths will call their plantings has yet to be decided, but we are assuredly shaping our "environment according to culturally dictated plans"—one of James Deetz's definitions of material culture in *In Small Things Forgotten: The Archaeology of Early American Life* (Garden City, N.Y.: Anchor/Doubleday, 1977), 24. Trees mark wedding anniversaries and a child's coming of age as well as changes in property boundaries and our present interest in Oriental ornamentals that will survive in the USDA hardiness zone five. New trees now announce a part of the family's genealogy in the clusters of *Schlerehenzeu,* the sixteenth-century vernacular name for the wild plum trees native to Northern Europe that Linneaus in the eighteenth century so appropriately labeled *Prunus spinoza.*

This article originally appeared in *Environmental Review* 4.1 (November 1980): 20–29.

Figure 19.
"Farm Residence of Michael Smith, Harris Township"
From *An Illustrated Atlas of St. Joseph County, Indiana* (Chicago:
Higgins Belden Co., 1875).

It could be argued, depending on how you interpret the world's creation narratives, that in the beginning there was not the word, nor the thing, but the plant. Humankind were first gardeners, then toolmakers. This essay, avoiding such evolutionary speculation, surveys assorted topics that students of material culture might consider when assessing how past natural environment might be important in their research. While this overview might be placed in Part Two, "Public Landscapes," I locate it here because I think starting with land and its natural features is a fundamental strategy for material cultural analysis.

Despite its fixation on trees, the essay has been a durable cultivar for me. In addition to the species reprinted here, other varieties (with other examples) appeared in my *Artifacts and the American Past* (chap. 7), *The Orion Nature Review* (1984), and *The Morton Arboretum Quarterly* (1978). Another offshoot is "The Lawn and the Garden" section in my *Transformations* volume.

In the decade since "Plants Past" first appeared, other more systematic research has been published. I recommend *Discovering the Vernacular Landscape* (New Haven: Yale University Press, 1984) by J. B. Jackson, the dean of American landscape historians, and a brilliant survey of *Common Landscapes of America, 1580–1840* (New Haven: Yale University Press, 1982) by John Stilgoe. Equally valuable are William H. Tishler, *American Landscape Architecture: Designers and Places* (Washington: Preservation Press, 1988), Patricia Tice, *Gardening in America, 1830–1910* (Rochester: The Strong Museum, 1984), and Ann Leighton, *American*

Gardens of the Seventeenth, Eighteenth, and *Nineteenth Centuries,* 3 vols. (Amherst: University of Massachusetts Press, 1984–87). Pertinent research journals unknown to me in 1979 are *The Journal of Forest History, Garden History, Journal of Garden History,* and *A Bulletin of American Garden History.*

Historians have been tardy in recognizing that the environment, natural and man-made, is an unusually useful historical document. In our teaching we have not adequately explored how a landscape reveals, when rightly seen, as much of a society's culture as does a novel, a newspaper, or a Fourth of July oration. In our research, we have not sufficiently probed how urban, suburban, and rural terrains are palimpsests of linguistic, economic, technological, and social history. How do place-names reveal inter- and intra-urban migration and forgotten resources? How do road systems hint at military policies and former religious alliances? What boundaries and courthouse styles recall former political antagonisms? How do tree plantings document former landownership patterns, or how can the vegetation in public parks reveal nineteenth-century attitudes toward aesthestics, sanitation, or recreation?

A historical interest in landscapes and the plants found on them has been nurtured by scholars in other countries and in other disciplines. The importance of plants in historical research has long been acknowledged by the German *Volksbotanik* tradition of scholarship.[1] British local historians, preservationists, and antiquarians have also investigated their countryside from Land's End to John O'Groats as the "history on the ground." Community historians like Penelope Lively, medievalists such as Maurice Beresford, and W. G. Hoskins, the dean of English landscape observers, have developed excellent models and techniques for historical analysis of the environment.[2]

The use of plants as historical evidence has been heavily influenced by a number of American scholars. Ecologists and forest historians have dramatized the importance of previous forest covers, vanished natural resources, and climatic conditions.[3] Agricultural historians and folklorists have deciphered the enormous significance of plants and soils in the situation of houses and farms.[4] Cultural and historical geographers such as Carl Sauer, John Fraser Hart, and Fred Kniffen have explored the multiple ways that Americans have arranged their landscapes and the vegetation upon them.[5] Maverick investigators like J. B. Jackson and Grady Clay have also provided insights into the history that survives on the land.[6]

As a cultural historian within the field of American Studies I call what I currently do "above-ground archaeology, a series of techniques for identifying, interrogating and interpreting the natural and built environment in order to gain an increased sensitivity to an understanding of life as lived in the past.''[7] Taking a lead from the traditional archaeologist, who usually works ''below ground,'' the historian can also concentrate on: a) using material objects and physical sites as primary evidence; b) employing extensive fieldwork as a research technique: c) adapting anthropological explanatory concepts such as typology or diffusion to the approach where feasible; and d) having historical knowledge about humankind as the principal learning objective.[8] This is digging into the past ''above ground.''

Naturally such an investigator encounters an extensive array of vegetation on whatever landscape he or she traverses. More often than not, if the researcher knows what to look for and how to interpret it, he can gain significant historical insight from such data. For example, one type of plant life—trees—can tell the cultural historian a great deal. Trees are a highly visible natural shard, easily identifiable to the average traveler along a back road or to a walker in the city. Trees, for the most part, are also rather permanently located and they have long been a tool of climatologists and archaeologists concerned with dendrochronology.[9] Finally, they possess a durability to survive (barring natural and man-made wrath) as historical markers of various sorts. Indeed, in Texas state parks, they even have something of a ''life-after-death'' where the acclaimed ''first,'' although now quite dead, tree of the Texas high plains is memorialized in the smallest state park in the country.

Trees have played an intriguing role in American history. Among the first products sought from this continent were ship masts for the Royal Navy. In fact, shipmast locusts planted in the nineteenth century still survive in Branch, Smithtown, Long Island. One of the first ordinances of the Plymouth colony regulated the cutting of timber and the Broad Arrow policy of reserving trees was initiated even when over two-thirds of the continent was tree-covered. Consequently, the above-ground archaeologist must establish the status of any stand of trees. Is it virgin? Or, more likely, is it second, third, or fourth growth? If the tree cover is virgin, as is a twelve-acre tract that still survives on the University of Notre Dame campus, he naturally raises questions such as: How extensive was it? How might it have conditioned settlement patterns or farming practices? What influence might it have had on house building types or even industrial development? The hardwood forests of neighboring Michigan, for example, sustained the cabinet-making component of the Singer Sewing Machine Works in South Bend as well as the carriage and wagon manufacturing plants of the Studebaker Brothers. In northern Illinois, where a prairie-and-grove vegetation pattern prevailed, nineteenth-century cartography reveals how settlers resorted to tract timber lots in order to conserve their wood supplies and insure an allotment for all landowners.

Early immigrants to North America used plants as signs of good land. Settlers often selected their land according to the kinds of trees which grew upon it. Differences in the natural drainage of two glacial tills in Rush County, Indiana, produced differences in vegetation that were well known and clearly understood by early immigrants.[10] The better drained areas, dominated by sugar maple and oak, were known as "sugar-tree land," whereas the wet swampy ground was referred to as "beech land." "We cannot be certain that every purchaser used forest cover as an index of land quality," concludes Wayne Kiefer, "but there is good reason to believe that many of them did so and even better reason to believe that they were justified in doing so."[11]

Trees survive as ample documentation of rural history in their delineation of earlier boundaries, borders, and benchmarks. The careful observer can still locate metes and bounds markers by the black and white oaks used in 1850 to orient Newbold Road in McHenry County, Illinois or the huge catalpa at the corner of North and West Streets in Blooming Grove, Indiana. On the University of Notre Dame campus, a string of osage orange, paralleling Douglas Road, is all that remains of a long hedgerow that once divided one of the many fields of the 2400-acre University Farms. Throughout the nineteenth century such vegetation (e.g., benchmark beeches, county-line cottonwoods) were used to mark range boundaries and cadastral surveys as well as individual farmers' fields.[12]

Routes of explorers or immigrants can be retraced by following remaining trail trees along the "49er Road" in El Dorado County, California. "Summit trees" still beckon the observant traveler as he crosses nineteenth-century mountain passes and "snub-trees" signal a previous transportation technology to the highway driver.[13] Indian "trail trees" abound in northern Illinois where the Pottawatomi bent or buried young tree sprouts or saplings to indicate the direction of their travel routes east and west, to designate sources of fresh water, as well as to mark the path to the Chicago portage. To the above-ground archaeologist, identifying a trail tree is not difficult. These man-formed, natural road signs are inevitably found on ridges along glacial tills. In the upper Midwest, they are usually white oak and generally smaller than other trees of similar age due to early burying as in the case of the tree at 630 Lincoln Street in Wilmette, Illinois.[14] Examples of bent or tied trail trees survive in Missouri's Clark National Forest and in Southport, North Carolina.

Political, diplomatic, and military historians should note that important conferences have taken place beneath the branches of oaks, elms, or sycamores. Pennsylvania's Treaty Elm of 1681 is depicted by painters Benjamin West (*William Penn's Treaty with the Indians,* 1771) and Edward Hicks (*Penn's Treaty,* 1830–35) (figs. 20, 21). In 1844 George Harvey painted *The Apostle's Oak,* to depict the nineteenth-century everyday life that took place at the site where John Elliot (1604–1690), the Puritan "Apostle to the Indians," was reputed to have preached frequently

Figure 20.
Benjamin West, *William Penn's Treaty with the Indians,* 1771
Oil on canvas.
(Courtesy of the Pennsylvania Academy of the Fine Arts, Philadelphia. Gift of Mrs. Sarah Harrison, The Joseph Harrison, Jr. Collection)

to the Native Americans of New England (fig. 22). The Miami Indians met in council among themselves as well as with Robert Sieur de La Salle in 1681 at the famous Council Oak in St. Joseph County, Indiana. Similar council sites exist throughout the United States recalling parallel deliberations from the sixteenth to the end of the nineteenth centuries. More recently, there is a ''Council Elm'' in front of Eckhart Hall at the University of Chicago where, in April 1942, the world's leading atomic scientists held a highly secret discussion (outdoors for fear of being bugged). Moreover, it should not be forgotten that the tentative charter for the United Nations was drawn up at Bretton Woods and Dumbarton Oaks.

Plans for war were made during the Revolutionary War under Daniel Byrnes's sycamore (Stanton, Delaware); in the War of 1812 under the St. Michael's box elder (Talbot County, Maryland); and in the Civil War among the Union beeches (Holly Springs, Mississippi). In fact, if the evidence is to be believed, the strategy for practically every military campaign that Andrew Jackson ever fought in the southeastern United States seemed to have been first outlined at the base of a live oak or a loblolly pine.[15] American battlefields like those of Fallen Timbers or The Wilderness were fought with tactics imposed, in part, by the landscape's

Figure 21.
Edward Hicks, *Penn's Treaty*, 1830–35
Oil on canvas.
(Courtesy Abby Aldrich Rockefeller Folk Art Center)

vegetation. Finally, peace treaties are symbolized by natural artifacts such as the 1854 Medicine Creek Treaty Fir in the Nisqually Valley of Washington or the 1785 Cherokee Indian Treaty Oak at Lake Hartwell, South Carolina. And, of course, we cannot forget the fictive but famous cherry tree of Parson Weems's imagination to which young George Washington supposedly took an axe and that Grant Wood used for a visual parody (fig. 23).

Most of these tree sites are now historical monuments, with the same status as public sanctuary and other civic memorials. These take on the character of sacred groves or communal totems. The above-ground archaeologist identifies, documents, and interprets such artifacts for insights into a community's sense of history. W. Lloyd Warner's interrogation of the "ritualization of the past" in a New England town's monuments (including its historical vegetation) provides a useful technique to apply to any environment's communal symbols and shrines. Warner's analysis[16] recommends that the landscape analyst of "historic" vegetation take careful note of: a) where and when historical markers were placed;[17] b) what historical events or personalities are consistently noticed or neglected in a town's monuments; c) who in the community designated

Figure 22.
George Harvey, *The Apostle's Oak*, 1844
Oil on canvas.
(Courtesy The New-York Historical Society, New York City)

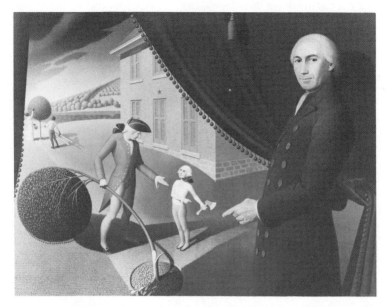

Figure 23.
Grant Wood, *Parson Weems' Fable*, 1939
Oil on canvas.
(Courtesy Amon Carter Museum, Fort Worth)

and funded such landmarks; d) if the events memorialized are spread evenly across a town's history or if they tend to cluster at one or more historical periods such as the Revolutionary or Civil Wars.

Cultural historians and geographers have already begun raising such questions about the placement of Bicentennial parks and plantings that have sprouted all over the American landscape since 1976.[18] The historian knows this to be a tradition that goes back to colonial "Liberty Trees" (symbolic artifacts that the British promptly chopped down whenever they captured an American town) as well as to the commemorative plantings that mark every major anniversary in U.S. history. The careful observer of any American urban environment can also find extant plantings by famous people memorializing what they and their age judged posterity would deem historic: John Kinzie's four Lombardy poplars in front of his Chicago River homestead; the Cassius Clay Kentucky coffee-trees; Andrew Jackson ("Old Hickory") and his shagbark hickories in Tennessee; the John Hancock elms on the Boston Commons; Brigham Young's walnuts in Utah; and the ornamental Japanese cherry trees planted in 1909 and in 1912 in Washington, D.C.

The landscape historian can also use the relict vegetation left by previous, but usually anonymous, generations. Consequently he or she is ever on the lookout for "wedding" or "bride and groom" conifers (usually in pairs of two or four trees) that nineteenth-century Midwestern rural folk planted religiously to mark major turning points in their own lives—a new home and a new spouse.[19] In southern Illinois, some extant tree plantings in front of farm houses reveal the demographic patterns of the population since parents planted a conifer or a hardwood for every child that lived past infancy. An excellent illustration of this folk custom also survives on the lawn of the Israel and Martha Washburn homestead in Livermore, Maine; here seven sugar maples were planted in the 1800s, one for each of the seven Washburn sons. Changes in the rural countryside can also be ascertained when one sees the persistence of the "wedding" or "children" conifers still towering, much like natural porticos to the Greek Revival houses they often fronted, even though the homesteads are now gone or have been replaced by twentieth-century building types such as mobile homes.

Vestiges of early settlement patterns also survive in double rows of sixty-foot Balm of Gilead trees that still line both sides of the ghost mining town of Vicksburg, Colorado. Former land use can be discovered by the parallel rows of Red Rome apple trees (the fragments of a nineteenth-century orchard) that now grace the backyards of the fashionable suburb of Bloomfield Hills, Michigan; and May T. Watts, in her noteworthy book, *Reading the Landscape of America,* has shown us how to recognize clumps of arborvitae, daffodils, and daylilies as natural fossils of former homesteads.[20] Watts also dates and interprets a typical American house and garden as of 1856, 1906, and 1963.

The vegetation of cemeteries, parks, forest preserves, town commons, market squares, and public and private gardens all tell the explorer of the landscape about the history of a place and its people. At Notre Dame, for example, the University Arboretum (see fig. 93), laid out by Philip Kunze in the late nineteenth century, survives as a testament to the German professor's aspiration to plant the campus with every tree species indigenous to the United States that would grow in the northern Indiana climate.[21]

There is an important physical record of personal, local, state, and federal involvement in the preservation and reestablishment of the natural environment, including the afforestation attempts of Father Ioann Veriaminov in the Alaskan Aleutian Islands as early as 1803, the conservation and forestry work of Gifford Pinchot and John Muir in the 1880s and 1900s, and the shelterbelt and reforestation of Franklin D. Roosevelt's Civilian Conservation Corps in the 1930s.[22] Following the lead of Phoebe Cutter, the above-ground archaeologist becomes adroit at "recognizing a WPA rose garden or CC privy."[23] In every American city there is abundant material culture evidence of the impact of the New Deal on the landscape.

In many highly urbanized areas of the United States, however, the vegetation of the past and its influence on the local history survive only in the region's place-names. George Stewart, the dean of American toponymists, correctly insists that "the history of any region can be read in terms of its nomenclature."[24] O'Hare Field in Chicago has a baggage tag labeled "ORD." That abbreviation recalls not the name of the person for whom the airport is named, but its former land use as a productive fruit-growing region known as Old Orchard—a place-name remaining as a nearby shopping center and a suburb.

Plant place-names are usually categorized by onomastic scholars as "objectively descriptive names." Inevitably, such names encapsulate a bit of local history. When Chicago real estate promoter S. E. Warner decided to name the main street of his development in honor of his political hero, Henry Clay, he called it "Ashland" in reminiscence of the Whig party leader's home, "The Ashland," in Kentucky. Warner left still another marking on the land when he planted both sides of his residential avenue with rows of white ash.

In Indiana place-names, the local flora has been extremely influential: Beechwood, Cloverdale, Maple Valley, Hemlock, Burr Oak, Pine, Quercus Grove, Plum Tree, and Sycamore are towns scattered throughout the state.[25] The sixteenth-century French presence in northern Indiana survives in *La Porte,* "the door," which recalls a natural opening in the primeval forest cover that served as a portal through which trade passed between southern and northern Indiana.

In addition to being fossils of past vegetation patterns, the plant place-names that now grace our cities and suburbs are often the result of political, religious, economic or aesthetic decisions made centuries ago. Take the example of Philadelphia. William Penn, with typical Quaker humility and love of equality, decided that his model town plan would have no streets named after special persons. Hence, beginning at the eastern boundary of his plat, he simply called the first street by that name. To distinguish the cross streets, however, he succumbed to the Quaker love of botany and applied "the names of the things that spontaneously grow in the country." Some of these names were later changed but enough of them still exist to make the famous rhyme for remembering the order:

Market, Arch, Race and Vine;
Chestnut, Walnut, Spruce and Pine.

If one drives west along the Indiana Toll Road one cannot help but be struck by the botanical logic of the nineteenth-century St. Joseph County surveyor who identified the sectional division roads, east to west, in alphabetical sequence, as Ash, Bittersweet, Currant, Dogwood, Elder, Fir, Gumwood, Hickory, Ironwood, Juniper on to Oak, Pine, and Quince. San Diego, California, has a similar pattern of tree place-names for a section of its streets, using "Upas" as a quiet joke on the unsuspecting residents of that particular street. This "most far-reaching and typical habit of American naming" consistently reappears in cities and towns across the country, even in the street patterns of arid Western communities where such tree species have never grown.[26]

Twentieth-century real estate developers all over the United States are equally enamored of flora place-names. They use them to elicit in prospective buyers' minds the image of English country estates, British and American history, as well as the social pretentions and economic status of living in a feudal deer park or imperial forest preserve.[27] Such Anglophilia, historical associationism, and reverie for the pastoral, intrigue the above-ground archaeologist. He or she finds, with almost monotonous regularity, the same binomial place-names formed by a collective noun (e.g., Forest, Green, Hurst, Wood) and often a deliberately horticultural modifying adjective (e.g., Locust, Pine, Oak, Poplar).

In addition to my fieldguide to decipher the history scattered about on the landscape, there are at least four other groups of historians that use vegetation in their work. For instance, historical preservationists have become more extensively involved in the restoration or reconstruction of botanical and pleasure gardens, parks, and the preservation of natural forest preserves, wilderness areas, and landscapes that are of outstanding historical and ecological significance.[28] A "Historic Gardens and Landscapes" conference discussed the importance of historical landscape architecture and preservation.[29] John T. Stewart and others have developed techniques of "landscape archaeology" in their research into existing plant material on historic sites as evidence of buried features and as survivors of historic species.[30]

In the area of historical ethnobotany, John R. Stilgoe has students do research using plants, particularly herbs and herbals, in his investigations of American folk medicine and folklore.[31] Folklorists with geographical interests and geographers with folklore proclivities are also studying the social and communicative functions of the visual folk art of private gardens, suburban front-lawn plantings, and the personal landscape habits of residential neighborhoods of varying economic, ethnic, and social backgrounds.[32]

Art historians likewise are turning to the American landscape and its vegetation not only to reanalyze the familiar American school of landscape painters such as Thomas Cole, Asher Durand, and Thomas Moran but also to explore the historical information depicted in other pictorial forms (engravings, lithographs, photographs) in order to discover what such sources can tell the field biologist, the agricultural historian, and the cultural historian. Two intriguing studies, both of which were originally museum exhibitions, reflect this trend: William C. Lipke and Philip Grime, eds. *Vermont Landscape Images, 1776–1976* (1976) and Jay E. Cantor, *The Landscape of Change: Views of Rural New England, 1790–1865* (1976).

Old Sturbridge Village in Massachusetts, where *The Landscape of Change* catalog is published, also includes the Pliny Freeman living history farm, an outdoor museum that seeks to recreate southern Massachusetts farming methods around the year 1840. This farm site is but one of over sixty living historical farms now in existence throughout North America. This form of historical museum interpretation, by definition, requires extensive research into the historical relationship between humans and plants. The curators and historians within the Association for Living Historical Farms and Agricultural Museums are presently investigating topics in current material culture research: the recreation of genetic diversity in seed banks and the documentation of all aspects of the American farm's cultural ecology, particularly its transformation and use of a region's natural resources. While the primary aim of such museums is to communicate a sense of reality and farm life in the past, they also have become involved in contemporary political and economic goals. Several curators envision their living history farms as bases for what Jay Anderson calls "experimental archaeology." In their exploration of the historical relationship between man, plants, and the environment, these historians see the potential of their museums as experimental stations preserving and rediscovering traditional foodways that may be drawn upon in the future if a need for alternative means of food procurement and processing is forced upon us by a breakdown in our present technological systems.[33] In attempting to reproduce for the people of today how individuals once lived and farmed at some specific time and place in the past, this innovative cadre of historians and curators is also grappling with many of the major interpretive challenges of modern museology.[34]

Despite initial neglect, some American historians have realized the immense potential of plants as a resource in their teaching and research. Historians interested in what John Stilgoe calls "the ghostly interface of inter-mingled landscapes," the natural and man-made shards that still exist in space past as well as in time past, are hopeful about the new directions of what some have called "environmental history." Like Francis Parkman, who tramped over every inch of a battlefield, a village, or a town site while writing his eleven-volume series on *France and England in America,* we are anxious to connect what we learn in archives and libraries with what material culture evidence we discover on rural countryside or still extant in the urban cityscape. Vegetation, as Eugene Kinkead and Neil Jorgensen show, is assuredly a vital element of this abundant artifactual record.[35]

Notes

1. See, for example, Heinrich Marzell's *Volksbotanik Die Pflauze im deutschen Brauchtum* (1935) and *Die Planzen im deutschen Volksleben* (1925) as well as Carl Baager *Wald und Bauertum* (1940).

2. Penelope Lively, *The Presence of the Past: An Introduction to Landscape History* (London: William Collins Sons, 1976); Maurice Beresford, *History on the Ground, Six Studies in Maps and Landscapes*, rev. ed. (London: Methuen, 1971); W. G. Hoskins, *The Making of the English Landscape* (London: Hodder and Stroughton, 1955, 1963)

3. Two journals, *Forest History* and *Environmental Review,* regularly explore these topics. Also consult James Tretethen, *The American Landscape: 1776–1976, Two Centuries of Change* (Washington, D.C.: Wildlife Management Institute, 1976).

4. Archer B. Hulbert, *Soil: Its Influence on the History of the United States* (New Haven: Yale University Press, 1930); K. S. Quisenberry and I. P. Reitz, "Turkey Wheat: The Cornerstone of an Empire," *Agricultural History* 48.1 (January 1974): 98–110; and Raymond Baker, "Indian Corn and Its Culture," *Agricultural History* 48.1 (January 1974): 94–97; James T. Lemon, *The Best Poor Man's Country: A Geographical Study of Early Southeastern Pennsylvania* (Baltimore: Johns Hopkins University Press, 1972).

5. John Leighly, ed., *Land and Life: A Selection from the Writings of Carl Ortwin Sauer* (Berkeley and Los Angeles: University of California Press, 1963); Carl Sauer, "American Agricultural Origins: A Consideration of Nature and Culture," in *Essays in Anthropology Presented to A. L. Kroeber* (Berkeley: University of California Press, 1936), 279–97; John Fraser Hart, *The Look of the Land* (Englewood Cliffs, N.J.: Prentice Hall, 1975); Fred Kniffen, "The Physiognomy of Rural Louisiana," *Louisiana History* 4.4 (Fall 1963): 29–99.

6. J. B. Jackson edited *Landscape* magazine from 1952 until 1967 and the back issues of this influential journal are a rich lode of insight for the above-ground archaeologist. Several of Jackson's famous essays have been republished by MIT Press in an anthology (*Landscapes: Selected Writings of J. B. Jackson,* edited by Erwin Zube (1970). Grady Clay, also an editor (*Landscape Architecture*), has done an important primer, *Close-Up: How to Read the American City* (New York: Praeger, 1972).

7. Thomas J. Schlereth, "The Town as Artifact: Discovering a Community's History through Above-Ground Archaeology," unpublished paper presented at Indiana Historical Society 1978 Spring Conference, Madison, Indiana, 12 May 1978. For a bibliography on the approach see chapter 6 of this volume.

8. In formulating this approach I have borrowed extensively, if ecclectically, from two books by James Deetz: *Invitation to Archaeology* (Garden City, N.Y.: The Natural History Press, 1967) and *In Small Things Forgotten: The Archaeology of Early American Life* (Garden City, N.Y.: Anchor/Doubleday, 1977) and various colleagues, particularly James O. Bellis (Department of Anthropology, University of Notre Dame), in the Society for Historical Archaeology. The Society's most recent publication,

Historical Archaeology and the Importance of Material Things, ed. Leland Ferguson, Special Publications Series, 2 (Columbia, S.C.: Society for Historical Archaeology, 1977) has also been useful.

9. John G. Evans, *An Introduction to Environmental Archaeology* (Princeton: Princeton University Press, 1978); G. W. Dimbleby, *Plants and Archaeology* (London: John Baker, 1967); Audrey Noel Hume, *Archaeology and the Colonial Gardener* (Williamsburg, Va.: Colonial Williamsburg Foundation, 1974).

10. Friedrich Ratzel, *Politische und Wirtschafts-Geographie der Vereinigten Staaten von Amerika* (Munich: R. Oldenbourg, 1893), 413. Most handbooks written for European immigrants to the United States in the nineteenth century contained at least one full chapter explaining the significance of the different hardwood tree species as indicators of soil quality, and no less than fifty extensively illustrated pages are devoted to this topic in C. I. Fleischmann, *Der Nordamerikanische Landwirt: Ein Handbuch fur Ansiedler in den Vereinigten Staaten* (Frankfurt: C. F. Heyer Verlag, 1853), 21–71.

11. Wayne E. Kiefer, *Rush County, Indiana: A Study in Rural Settlement Geography,* Geographic Monograph Series, vol. 2 (Bloomington: Indiana University Department of Geography, 1969), n. 8, pp. 47–48.

12. Eric Sloane, *Our Vanishing America* (New York: Ballantine Books, 1974), 29.

13. A natural feature of the terrain along Barlow Pass in the Mt. Hood National Forest in Oregon are the tall firs on the top of Little Laurel Hill. These trees were used to control the descent of the covered wagons down a 300-foot incline or chute. In practice, a rawhide rope was wrapped around a fir trunk with the wagon snubbed to the other end of the rope, thus providing a drag to brake or slow the wagon down the steep slope. Some of the rope-burned snub-trees still stand on Laurel Hill. They are about five miles east of the community of Rhododendron, on the south side of the Mount Hood Loop Highway (U.S. 26).

14. Leslie D. Bruning, "Early Road Signs," *Americana* (July–August 1977): 64.

15. Charles E. Randall and Henry Clepper, *Famous and Historic Trees* (Washington, D.C.: American Forestry Association, 1976) lists six tree sites associated with Jackson.

16. W. Lloyd Warner, *The Living and the Dead, A Study of The Symbolic Life of Americans* (New Haven: Yale University Press, 1959), chapter 4.

17. Since 1865 a tree, usually an aspen, has been growing out of the roof of the courthouse of Decatur County in southern Indiana. The current local landmark, the eleventh such tree since the 1860s, is considered a major historical monument and duly recorded as such on most Indiana state roadway maps.

18. David Lowenthal, "The Bicentennial Landscape: A Mirror Held up to the Past," *The Geographical Review* 67.3 (July 1977): 253–67.

19. Trees have also always been important to pioneer Americans at time of death. When southern Illinois was first settled in the early nineteenth century, many of the inhabitants came from the Carolinas. In their new homes, they noticed that the forests of the area were mainly of oak, hickory and maple—woods not easily worked. One of their concerns was to have fine coffins in which to be buried when death came. Hence they got relatives and friends who were to come later to bring some pine trees from their native Carolinas. These trees they planted in their front yards, usually two white pines, one for each spouse. Many of the "white coffin pines" have outlived their planters and can be found throughout southern Illinois, a number in Union County. Randall and Clepper, *Historic Trees,* 70.

20. May T. Watts, *Reading the Landscape of America* (New York: Collier/Macmillan, 1975), 15–16, first published as *Reading the Landscape: An Adventure in Ecology* (New York: Macmillan, 1957); especially useful for historical landscape and garden analysis is her playful essay, "The Stylish House, Or, Fashions as an Ecological Factor," 320–46.

21. Thomas J. Schlereth, *The University of Notre Dame: A Portrait of Its History and Campus* (Notre Dame: University of Notre Dame Press, 1976), 111–12.

22. See, for example, Roderick Nash, *The American Environment: Readings in the History of Conservation,* 2d ed. (Reading, Mass.: Addison-Wesley, 1976) and Douglas H. Strong, *The Conservationists* (Reading, Mass.: Addison-Wesley, 1971).

23. Phoebe Cutler, "On Recognizing a WPA Rose Garden or a CCC Privy," *Landscape* (Winter 1976): 3–9.

24. George R. Stewart, *U.S. 40: Cross Section of the United States of America* (Boston: Houghton Mifflin, 1953), 303.

25. Ronald L. Baker and Marvin Carmony, *Indiana Place-names* (Bloomington: Indiana University Press: 1975). Also see Ronald L. Baker, "Locational and Descriptive Settlement Names in Indiana Flora." *Newsletter of the Indiana Place-Name Survey* 5 (1975): 6–7.

26. George R. Stewart, *Names on the Land: A Historical Account of Place-Naming in the United States* (Boston: Houghton Mifflin, 1958), 104–5.

27. Robert Venturi, *Signs of Life: Symbols in the American City* (Philadelphia: Venturi & Rausch, 1978), 56.

28. Meredith Sylles and John Stewart, "Historic Landscape Restoration in the United States and Canada: An Annotated Source Guide, *A.P.T. Bulletin* 4.3–4 (1972): 114–58; John Stewart and Susan Bugger, "The Case for Commemoration of Historic Landscapes and Gardens," *A.P.T. Bulletin* 7.2 (1975): 99–123; David Streatfield, "Standards for Historic Garden Preservation and Restoration," *Landscape Architecture* 59.3 (April 1969): 198–200.

29. Dumbarton Oaks Research Library and Collection, ed., *Preservation and Restoration of Historic Gardens and Landscapes* (Washington, D.C.: Dumbarton Oaks, 1976).

30. John T. Stewart, "Landscape Archaeology: Existing Plant Material on Historic Sites as Evidence of Buried Features and as Survivors of Historic Species," *A.P.T. Bulletin* 9.3 (1977): 65–72; John Stewart, *Historic Landscapes and Gardens* (Nashville: American Association for State and Local History, 1974); Donald H. Parker, "What You Can Learn from the Gardens of Colonial Williamsburg," *Horticulture* 44.28 (1975). Stewart's use of "landscape archaeology" should not be confused with Michael Aston and Trevor Rowley, *Landscape Archaeology: An Introduction to Field Work Techniques on Post-Roman Landscapes* (London: David and Charles, 1974).

31. John R. Stilgoe, "Jack-o-lanterns to Surveyors: The Secularization of Landscape Boundaries," *Environmental Review* (1976):14–32; "Documents in Landscape History," *Journal of Architectural Education* 30 (September 1976):15–17; "The Puritan Townscape: Ideal and Reality," *Landscape* 20 (Spring 1976): 3–7; and "Colonial Space: Landscape as Artifact," paper presented at American Studies Association National Meeting, Boston, Massachusetts, 28 October 1977.

32. E. N. Anderson, Jr., "On the Folk Art of Landscaping," *Western Folklore* 31 (1972): 179–88; James P. Duncan, Jr., "Landscape Taste as a Symbol of Group Identity: A Westchester County Village," *The Geographical Review* 63 (July 1973): 334–55; David Lowenthal and Hugh C. Prince, "English Landscape Traits," *The Geographical Review* 55 (1965): 186–222.

33. Jay A. Anderson, "Foodways Programs at Living Historical Farms," *ALHFAM Annual Proceedings* 1 (1975): 21–23; Roger L. Welseh, "Sowbelly and Seedbanks: The Living History Museum as a Process Repository," *ALHFAM Annual Proceedings* 1 (1975): 23–26; Edward Hawes, "Historic Seed Sources and the Future," *ALHFAM Annual Proceedings* 1 (1975): 28–32.

34. Darwin P. Kelsey, "Historical Farms as Models of the Past," *ALHFAM Annual Proceedings* 1 (1975): 33–38; Edward Hawes, "The Living Historical Farm in North America: New Directions in Research and Interpretation," *ALHFAM Annual Proceedings* 2 (1976): 41–60; Daryl Chase, "Keeping Living Historical Farms Alive and Their Methods of Teaching Innovative and Creative," *ALHFAM Annual Proceedings* 3 (1977): 43–47.

35. Eugene Kinkead, *Wilderness Is All around Us, Notes of an Urban Naturalist* (New York: Dutton, 1978); Neil Jorgensen, *A Sierra Club Naturalist's Guide to Southern New England* (San Francisco: Sierra Club Books, 1978).

Figure 24.
"A Busy Bee-Hive," ca. 1900
Chromolithograph. Montgomery Ward & Co.
(Courtesy The Chicago Historical Society)

2

Mail-Order Catalogs as Resources in Material Culture Studies

"Without that [mail-order] catalog," recalls writer Harry Crews who grew up in southeast Georgia, "our childhood would have been radically different." While I cannot make that sweeping a claim, I remember as a young boy memorizing the Sears Christmas catalog's page numbers of my wished-for gifts. Then I had no idea that I would research and write of the catalog's import in artifact research.

A museum exhibition prompted that work and the following essay. In 1979, Joan Siedl and Nicholas Westbrook at the Minnesota Historical Society mounted a temporary exhibition titled, "The Wishbook: Mail Order in Minnesota." The American Studies Association met that fall in Minneapolis–St. Paul. The ASA program committee arranged a convention session around the MHS exhibition, and I was asked to prepare a short paper discussing how the exhibition might be useful to American Studies scholars.

As with much of my work, this essay is nothing more than one teacher passing on to other teachers some things that might and might not work in the undergraduate classroom. My teaching in American Studies departments (Grinnell College and the University of Notre Dame) since 1969 accounts for why this detailed lesson plan on mail-order catalogs connects with American literature and the social sciences. It also helps explain my suggestions for using mail-order catalogs in decorative arts and architectural history as well as in advertising and consumerism research. With all that going for catalogs, it was not difficult for me to come up with five ways in which they serve as resources in material culture studies.

Mail-order catalog research also quickly taught me what veteran students of the artifact knew well: physical evidence, like statistical data and documentary sources, has flaws. When I first saw the year-after-year sequences of Sears Roebuck's annual, semiannual, seasonal, and special mail-order catalogs amassed in Lenore Swoishin's company archive in Chicago's Sears Tower, I thought here it is! A data base in which to research late nineteenth-century consumerism. Here was an almost complete record of goods for sale beginning in 1886. All a historian would have to do would be to investigate systematically this comprehensive, albeit two-dimensional record, material culture emporium. It offered a guide to price range, a rough estimate

This article originally appeared in *Prospects: An Annual Journal of American Cultural Studies* 7 (1980): 141–61.

of object size and scale, plus advertising. If it was coupled with the company's yearly sales records, we could have empirical answers to questions like: Who bought what, when, where, how often, and in what quantity? Were customers rural, small-town, or even urban? Did they come principally from the Midwest, South, East, or West? What necessities or luxuries, household goods or personal items did they purchase most frequently? Was this not a chance to combine documentary, statistical, and artifactual data in attacking a research problem? Yes and no.

I soon learned, to my discouragement, that purchase-order forms before computerization did not exist in any statistically significant way. Mail-order houses usually returned order forms to customers along with the merchandise purchased. While the wishbooks did not fulfill my macroeconomic visions, they yielded other possibilities. Chapter 2 outlines them.

Reading mail-order catalogs led me to other trade catalogs, particularly those in the collections at the Winterthur Museum. Studying trade catalogs led me to consider other types of advertising, especially those directed at a rural market. This expanded probe looked at the consumerism of the country store and the county fair. My tentative conclusions on the complementary and at times contradictory functions of these three "agencies of modernization" will appear in Simon J. Bronner's *Consuming Visions* (New York: W. W. Norton, 1989), a volume containing several analyses of late nineteenth- and early twentieth-century material culture.

Other helpful scholarship from which I have learned since first drafting this mail-order essay include Kenneth Ames, et al., *Accumulation and Display: Mass Marketing Household Goods in America, 1880–1920* (Winterthur: Winterthur Museum, 1986); Susan Atherton Hanson, "Home Sweet Home: Industrialization's Impact on Rural Households, 1865–1925" (Ph.D. dissertation, University of Maryland, 1986); David Jaffe, "A Correct Likeness: Culture and Commerce in Nineteenth-Century Rural America," in *Folk Art and Art Worlds*, ed. John M. Vlach and Simon J. Bronner (Ann Arbor: UMI Research Press, 1986), 58–84; and Katherine Cole Stevenson and H. Ward Jandl, *Houses by Mail: A Guide to Houses from Sears, Roebuck Company* (Washington: The Preservation Press, 1986).

A Wisconsin woman in *Fanny Herself,* Edna Ferber's 1917 novel depicting the Chicago mail-order industry, remarks: "There's a Haynes-Cooper catalog in every farmer's kitchen. The Bible's in the parlor, but they keep the H.C. book in the room where they live."[1] Harry Crews, in his 1978 autobiography of his boyhood in Bacon County, Georgia, recalls a similar centrality accorded the secular "Big Book" or "Farmer's Bible" in his family's tenant-farmer shanty. The highest form of entertainment for him was to thumb through the Sears Roebuck catalog with his friend Willalee and make up fantasies about the models on the book's pages. Writes Crews, "The federal government ought to strike a medal for Sears, Roebuck Company for sending all those catalogs to farming families, for bringing all that color and all that mystery and all that beauty into the lives of country people."[2]

Many other interpreters of the American experience have recognized what Ferber and Crews claim: Mail-order catalogs have had an enormous impact on American life. Maintaining that the mail-order business is "very nearly indigenous to America," one of its historians insists that "nowhere else in the world has the catalog house assumed the unique status it enjoys in the United States."[3] Daniel Boorstin has argued that the mail-order catalog is a "characteristically American kind of book" like the almanac or the how-to-do-it manual,[4] and that we are something of a catalog civilization. To wit: Today you can send away for *The Dance Catalog, The Whole Sewing Catalog, The New England Catalog,* and *The Whole Sex Catalog.* Of course, there exist both a finding aid to such modern "wishbooks" (*The Catalog of American Catalogs*) and a self-help manual (*Mail Order Moonlighting*), "satisfaction guaranteed or your money back," to bring out the Richard W. Sears in every one of us.[5]

Boorstin contends that nineteenth-century rural and small-town Americans viewed the mail-order catalog as a "Farmer's Bible," the secular gospel of what he calls the "new rural consumption communities." For many Americans, urban as well as rural, the catalogs of the Chicago giants—Montgomery Ward and Sears—probably did express some of their hopes for salvation. There is, for example, the oft-quoted folktale of the little boy who, on being asked by his Sunday school teacher where the Ten Commandments came from, unhesitantly replied, "From Sears, Roebuck, where else?"[6]

Let us define the mail-order–catalog industry as "a system of merchandising which distributes goods to consumers upon receipt of orders, placed not in person but by mail after the inspection of a catalog listing the products for sale, and which delivers the goods to the customers by utilizing some transportation device such as express, freight or post."[7] The origins of this business practice can be traced (the claims of Montgomery Ward notwithstanding)[8] to D. H. Lawrence's "sharp, little snuff-colored" Ben Franklin, the only one of the Founding Fathers to have a chain store named after him. Although relatively few eighteenth-century mail-order catalogs have been recorded in Charles Evans's twelve-volume *American Bibliography* (1903–34), Lawrence Romaine is persuaded that hundreds were printed and that Franklin's 1744 mail-order promotion of his Pennsylvania fireplaces and other items was the first American example of this genre.[9] Appropriately enough, both Sears's and Ward's catalogs still list Franklin stoves as available for purchase by mail.

Franklin stoves are not the only historical reproductions sold in post-Bicentennial America. Reprint publishers and remainder houses currently sell any number of replicas of an 1897 Sears, Roebuck catalog or an 1895 Montgomery Ward catalog, advertised, more often than not, by modern mail-order catalogs.[10] This nostalgia craze, besides being a significant cultural phenomenon to scholars who study present-day American popular culture, can also be a boon for those of us in American Studies who wish to introduce our students to the uses of material culture evidence to study the past. Today there are at least eight different reproduction editions of the Sears, Roebuck catalog, extending from the 1890s to the 1930s.[11] To date, only one reprint of a Ward catalog (the 1895 Spring–Summer edition) has appeared, but that reproduction (fig. 25) is a valuable unabridged facsimile.[12] No one has yet marketed reprints of the vintage catalogs of Alden, Spiegel, or J. C. Penney, the three other giants of the U.S. industry. But there have been reprints of the major Canadian mail-order houses (Woodward's, Eaton's, Hudson Bay), providing researchers with the opportunity to attempt cross-cultural analyses.[13] Finally, Sears has deposited complete microfilm-reproduction sets of its semiannual catalogs in 130 public libraries, colleges, and universities around the country. These microfilmed editions begin with the 1896 Sears catalog and are updated each year.[14] Hence, besides the proliferation of reprint mail-order catalogs now available, most teachers also have easy access to an expansive yet heretofore largely unexploited primary source, rich in word and image, detailing numerous facets of late-nineteenth- and twentieth-century American experience.

To date, only a few teaching historians have used the "Big Book" as a casebook, sourcebook, textbook, or "question book" on American history. One of these instances, appropriately enough in the state where Richard Sears (a native of Stewartville, Minnesota) got his start, is an exercise developed by the Education Division of the Minnesota Historical Society. A second is a learning activity developed by the Education Department staff at the Chicago Historical Society. A third and fourth include William R. Smith's work with mail-order catalogs in secondary-school social-studies courses and James Kavanaugh's efforts at Hobart and William Smith colleges.[15] A fifth is what is proposed here.

In this essay two teaching and research strategies are suggested. The first deals with mail-order catalogs as "Resources in American Studies"; the second, in some ways a subset of the first but in other ways an independent field of inquiry, evaluates mail-order catalogs as "Resources in American Material Culture Studies." Before I offer several illustrative research and teaching techniques for using catalogs in each of these categories, it should be noted that I will also be considering the mail-order catalog itself as an artifact. Although it is a verbal document, it is also a physical object, a form of American material culture. As such, the mail-order catalog is a historical artifact that, like all artifacts, both answers and raises questions about the past. Hence the American mail-order catalog, in addition to being the "wishbook" that Nicholas Westbrook and others have so thoroughly analyzed,[16] is also a most provocative

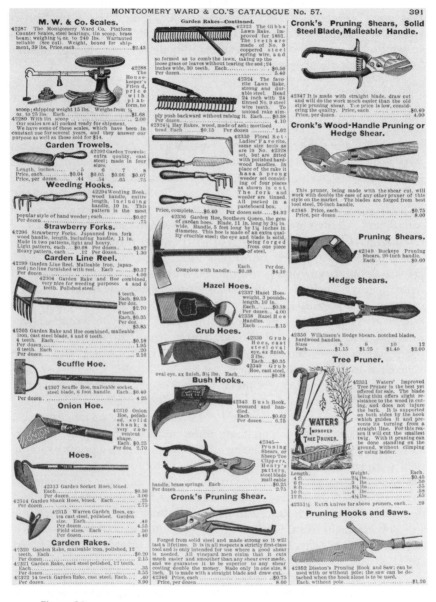

Figure 25.
"Garden Implements"
From *Montgomery Ward & Co.'s Catalogue and Buyer's Guide* (Spring and Summer 1895). Reprinted from unabridged facsimile (New York: Dover Publications, 1969).

"question book," extremely useful in the inquiry approach to history teaching.[17] Nonetheless, despite this principal emphasis on mail-order *catalogs* as such, I recognize that they cannot be studied apart from at least two other contexts: the products they describe (mail-order *goods*) and the processes that create them (mail-order *merchandising*).[18]

Under the broad umbrella of the American Studies movement, several disciplines and their subfields can make ample use of the mail-order catalog. On the level of popular literature, for example, mail-order catalogs deserve serious attention inasmuch as they have inspired at least two novels—Ferber's earlier-mentioned *Fanny Herself* and George Milburn's *Catalogue: A Novel* (1936). The mail-order catalog was critically reviewed by Lovell Thompson in *The Saturday Reivew of Literature* and in 1946 was selected by the Grolier Society as one of the hundred American books having the most impact on American life and culture.[19] Catalogs have also been the subject of satire and parody, such as the *Rears and Robust Mail Order Catalogue for Spring/Summer/Fall/Winter* (1940)—a 600-page volume interlarded with lessons about sex gleaned from pages advertising underclothing and pharmaceuticals in actual catalogs, many spoofs on WPA workers and FDR's New Deal, plus numerous samples of every type of toilet tissue that you would expect a complete mail-order supply house to offer, from cellophane ("For People Who Like to See What They are Doing") to ditto sheets ("For People Who Like to Make an Impression").[20]

All written literature—popular, folk, or classic—is simultaneously a commodity, a physical art object, a cultural window, an example of communications theory and practice, and a medium for imaginative and abstracted expression. Recognizing these multiple dimensions of literature, Fred Schroeder evaluates the mail-order catalog as a prime example of a popular literary document. Catalog terminology, grammar, and syntax, he argues, served to standardize the American language inasmuch as the dialect of the Chicago-based mail-order houses homogenized the nomenclature of much American material culture. For example, what is still known in the rural South as a "sling-blade" or "slam-bang" must be ordered from Sears by recognizing a catalog picture labeled "weed cutter."[21]

Much like the New England primer of the seventeenth century, the Sears catalog of the nineteenth doubled as a reader, text, and encyclopedia in many one-room schoolhouses. With it, children were drilled in reading and spelling; they practiced arithmetic by filling out orders and adding sums; they studied geography using its postal-zone maps; they tried drawing by tracing the catalog models. Novelist Harry Crews credits the Sears catalogs of his youth with being a primary catalyst for his literary career. He claims that throughout his childhood he made up outlandish stories about the people he found on the catalog's pages.[22]

Researchers might consider mail-order catalogs another form of the American almanac because the "Big Books" often contained inspirational readings, bits of verse, cracker-barrel wisdom, epigrams, and farming and household tips—all interlaced with pictorial materials and adverisements. Sayings from Franklin's *Poor Richard*—"A good workman requires good tools" or "He who hesitates is lost"—abound throughout the catalogs. Montgomery Ward, on realizing this characteristic of his catalogs, began issuing a separate publication, calling one issue the *Almanac for 1897: A Book of Practical Information for the Farmer and the Stock Raiser.*[23]

First and foremost, mail-order catalogs were (and still are) vehicles to sell things. Consequently, they are textbooks of American economic history that demonstrate several important trends in late-nineteenth- and early-twentieth-century macro- and microeconomics. Because few corporate records from before World War II of either Sears or Montgomery Ward survive, scholars have had to depend primarily on their catalogs as a key source for documenting the history of these firms and their founders.[24]

Exposing students to the catalogs invariably leads them to investigate the business history that has been written about the companies. Such a perspective enables them to grasp what an enormous "economic transformation," to use Robert Heilbroner's phrase,[25] took place in America between the Civil War and World War I—an overwhelming change involving mass production, mass marketing, mass advertising, mass transportation, mass communication, and mass consumption.

Moreover, the catalogs indirectly hint at other economic forces at work during the period: the decline of the small town, cyclical national depressions and recessions, the nationwide debate over rural free delivery (RFD) (fig. 26) and parcel-post mail service, plus the prolonged and vitriolic anti–mail-order campaigns waged by local merchants and country storekeepers.[26] In the last instance, general-store merchants (fig. 27) and newspaper editors such as R. E. Ledbetter in Milburn's novel invited townspeople and farmers to bring their catalogs to a "Home Town Industry Jubilee and Bonfire," whereupon local merchants paid a bounty of one dollar in trade for every new catalog turned in to fuel the grand auto-da-fé staged in the town square.[27] This bitter, but as yet largely unresearched, example of economic conflict prompted, among other things, the epithets surrounding mail-order merchandising that have become part of the American language: "Monkey Wards," "Rears and Robust," "Shears and Sawbuck," "Shears and Rears."[28]

Figure 26.
"Where the Mail Goes, Cream of Wheat Goes"
Advertisement (ca. 1900).
(Courtesy The National Biscuit Company)

Figure 27.
Gibson's General Store, Main Street, Bennington, Vermont, 1895
*(Photograph by Madison E. Watson. Courtesy The Weichert-Isselhardt
Collection, Bennington, Vermont)*

If examined carefully, the mail-order catalog (particularly the book's order instructions and explanation of business policies) provides evidence of what two revisionist historians, one writing at the peak of mail-order merchandising (Ida Tarbell, *The Nationalizing of Business, 1878–1898*) and one our contemporary (Robert Wiebe, *The Search for Order, 1877–1920*), have recognized as a central tendency of modern American corporate enterprise.[29] The search for order, efficiency, rational planning, automation, and high productivity is nowhere more graphically or unashamedly portrayed than in successive catalogs containing detailed descriptions and illustrations of these Chicago firms' growth in national business. Sears even marketed fifty stereographic views of its "mail-order army," thousands of men and women shown working at their desks, receiving orders, processing orders, mailing orders. These "Views of Sears, Roebuck and Company" were first sold complete with a leatherette case and a stereoscope for fifty cents.[30] Extant in many local historical-society collections this set of stereographs provides an excellent pictorial source for illustrating the internal operations of a national corporation (at least as projected by company management) and a graphic example of Frederick Taylor's principles of Scientific Management.[31]

Unfortunately, we know little about those people who purchased Sears stereographs or any of the thousands of other items for sale in the catalogs. Without a doubt, the most important questions raised by the

"Big Book" for the economic historian are: Who were its customers? Who bought what, when, where, how often, and in what quantity? Were customers as rural, as Midwestern, as agrarian as our conventional wisdom and history textbooks suggest? In brief, is it possible, besides gaining insight into entrepreneurial history and mercantile history, to achieve some understanding of consumer history? Can the self-proclaimed, semiannual "Consumers' Guide" (as the Sears catalog began to be labeled with the 1894 edition) provide us with new historical information about past American consumers?

In the almost total absence of completed purchase-order forms for any period before computerization, the catalogs are the only available resource for reconstructing a tentative social, economic, or cultural profile of the past mail-order consumer. Neither Sears nor Montgomery Ward has retained a significant number of past purchase orders, primarily because it was their policy to return the order form to the customer along with the merchandise purchased. If purchase orders had survived, such data would be invaluable for the social historian interested in demography and quantification. Random orders do exist in private papers and manuscript collections in historical societies and museums, as well as in mail-order–company archives. Even if they could be examined collectively, such orders would probably not yield an adequate sample for creating a statistical portrait of the material needs and wants of late-nineteenth-century lower-middle-class American consumers. They lack the comprehensiveness of, for instance, the household inventories and probate records that are being used by social historians to research consumers of the late seventeenth century.[32]

Nonetheless, the mail-order catalog can be a heuristic tool in teaching social history in an American Studies context. Deborah and William Andrews, Susan May Strasser, Elizabeth Baker, and Ruth Schwartz Cowan offer us scholarly approaches to domestic material-culture evidence (fig. 28) equally applicable to mail-order research.[33] Cowan's study "The 'Industrial Revolution' in the Home: Household Technology and Social Change in the Twentieth Century," for example, investigates assorted domestic artifacts—washtubs and washing machines, vacuum cleaners, and electric irons—asking, is it primarily technology that influences how we live, or is it principally our changing social values that prompt innovations in our technology? Cowan's research objective is to explore this relationship between technology and social change, particularly as those forces have affected the history of the family and the history of women.

Mail-order catalogs can also be used to investigate such questions. Moreover, the catalogs are a data base wherein one can research several corollaries of the Cowan thesis, that is, the various interconnections of

Figure 28.
Stove and Kitchen Equipment Display
Sears, Roebuck Company model home exhibition, Illinois State Fair,
Springfield, Illinois, 1912.
(Courtesy Sears, Roebuck Company Archives)

factors such as the decline of domestic service, a proliferation of child-care requirements for mothers, the unprecedented expansion of the cosmetics industry after World War I, an increase in (rather than a liberation from) domestic activities in the home, and the mechanization, electrification, and specialization of American household technology.[34] To cite a single example: When one discovers, by a systematic examination of the catalogs from 1890 to 1930, that there was rapid decline in the availability of such an item as sewing pattern books (particularly in the 1920s), coupled with a marked increase in ladies' machine-made clothing (advertised by repeated injunctions to "buy ready-made"), a significant question is raised regarding what such a shift in material-culture history means in social history.[35]

Social historians should also consider mail-order catalogs as etiquette books, advice manuals, and self-improvement primers. We have studied the influence of *Godey's Lady's Book* (1830–98) and other forms of late-nineteenth-century normative literature but have neglected mail-order catalogs as another type of guide to social conduct, proper fashion, and acceptable personal behavior befitting either the status a person had achieved or that to which he aspired.[36] For some recently arrived immigrants, catalogs also served as guides in their assimilation and Americanization. In short, the catalog as a conduct book offered its semiannual readers a series of mobility patterns, role models, and even heroes to emulate. For instance, some of the most persuasive examples of evidence to substantiate John William Ward's claims for the spontaneous, highly symbolic, public fascination with Charles Lindbergh's 1927 trans-Atlantic solo flight can be found by tracing through the pages of the mail-order catalogs artifacts such as "Lucky Lindy" aviator caps and "Spirit of St. Louis" model-airplane kits, which appeared almost immediately after the historic event.[37] Fred Schroeder proposes that the catalogs lend themselves to this American Studies "fact-and-symbol" approach, or as his essay title suggests, that they can be read as a "popular icon."[38]

Mail-order catalogs, whether analyzed individually, researched sequentially, or studied comparatively, afford scholars many approaches for an interdisciplinary study of the past. Catalogs also rank as an important resource in American material culture studies, a field of research and teaching that since the 1950s in the United States has found its most hospitable academic home within American Studies programs and departments.[39] The mail-order catalog can be used as a resource in material-culture studies in at least five ways: (1) as a reference work, (2) as a graphics and advertising library, (3) as a primer for artifact exercises, (4) as a paperback museum, and (5) as a resource for various case studies.

Mail-order catalogs contain immense quantities of information for the researcher seeking to identify and date extant late-nineteenth- and early-twentieth-century artifacts. What Kenneth Ames has written of trade catalogs can also be said of mail-order catalogs: "They can provide a scholar with more images of thoroughly documented artifacts than he could hope to gather in years of scouring museums, historical societies and private collections."[40] Like the analogous trade catalog (a genre of evidence that Lawrence Romaine has collected and classified and the Pyne Press has reprinted in its American Historical Catalog Collection),[41] the mail-order catalog provides accurate evidence of objects actually in production or available on order. As Emilie Tari, curator of collections at Old World Wisconsin, suggests, "the range of material handled by these [mail-order] companies is almost all-inclusive and covers a complete range of domestic as well as farm ware. Objects in these categories are by and large rarely illustrated elsewhere. . . . Descriptions also frequently provide valuable tidbits such as material, type of construction, color choices, and price range."[42] Consulted as reference works, mail-order catalogs therefore can yield answers to such questions as (1) How long were certain articles manufactured? (2) How did design and cost change over time? and (3) How and to what extent were certain styles reflected in given classes of objects?

In the past, the "Big Book" has answered these and other questions common to material culture studies for a diverse lot of researchers: set designers at Warner Brothers studios (where a complete run of Sears catalogs is maintained), scholars writing books on toys as indices of American social history, antique collectors, university drama departments,[43] historic preservationists, exhibit designers at the Louvre, directors of research at living-history farms and their collection curators such as those responsible for restoring the German Rankinen House (ca. 1898) and the Finnish Ketola farmstead (ca. 1918) at Old World Wisconsin.[44]

In many historical museum exhibitions the catalog has been an essential reference tool, as it was for two Smithsonian Institution exhibits: "Suiting Everyone: The Democratization of Clothing in America" and the "Hall of Everyday Life in the American Past." Claudia Kidwell, curator of the "Suiting Everyone" exhibit, found mail-order catalogs of immense value in determining what ready-made clothing was being offered and when (fig. 29).[45] In the historical reconstruction and refurnishing of a tenant-farmer's house from Prince Georges County, Maryland, for exhibition in the Smithsonian's Hall of Everyday Life, George McDaniel and Rodris Roth also used mail-order catalogs. McDaniel tracked down some of the former occupants of the house, as well as neighbors. Armed with catalogs, he asked his informants to select from the books the various domestic artifacts they recalled using in the house.[46] Understandably, in several of Chicago's historical museums depicting that city's urban history, the mail-order catalog has been used as both artifice and artifact.[47]

Ofttimes the mail-order catalog is the only comprehensive source by which a student can establish an accurate, detailed design chronology, particularly for more mundane objects still unresearched in the modern period. Take the instance of the stove: We know a great deal about the stove's design history in the nineteenth century but less of its development in the twentieth. A design chronology reconstructed from Sears catalogs would show that Sears offered the first gas-burning stoves to the public in 1895. Enameled porcelain gas ranges made their first appearance in 1915; tabletop ranges were brought out in 1931, and the Kenmore line of built-ins (gas and electric) was introduced in the 1966 fall line. The 1972 spring book was the first to advertise the Kenmore range with a ceramic cooking top by Corning. Any number of valuable methodological exercises can be developed by the imaginative teacher with access to a substantial chronological run of catalogs. An excellent model for developing such exercises can be adapted from Craig Gilborn's essay "Pop Pedagogy: Looking at the Coke Bottle," where techniques are found for analyzing a commonplace object's diagnostic attributes, temporal sequence and duration, and stylistic evolution.[48]

Figure 29.
Ready-Made Clothing Display
Sears, Roebuck Company model home exhibition, Illinois State Fair,
Springfield, Illinois, 1912.
(Courtesy Sears, Roebuck Company Archives)

As Nicholas Westbrook and Joan Siedl have shown on a panel in the "Mail Order in Minnesota" exhibition, the catalog can be an aid in the analysis of historical photographs.[49] Photographs of domestic interiors (fig. 30) can become fascinating exercises in material-culture research when their contents are identified and interpreted with the aid of the catalog's pictorial images and descriptive text. Local historical societies and family albums abound with such photographs. But should these sources be unavailable, there are now many pictorial anthologies that teachers can use, such as William Seale's *The Tasteful Interlude: American Interiors Through the Camera's Eye, 1850–1917* or George Talbot's *At Home: Domestic Life in the Post-Centennial Era, 1876–1920.*[50]

Finally, mail-order catalogs can sometimes provide us with a method of establishing a relative chronology by which to classify unidentified late-nineteenth- and early-twentieth-century photography. A photograph of a Nebraska farm family, posed in front of their sod house, for example, can be dated to the 1880s, because that was the decade when Montgomery Ward introduced the particular type of "Montgomery Ward's calico" from which the mother in the picture made her dress and the shirts of her three boys.[51]

Figure 30.
Living-Dining Room Furniture Display
Sears, Roebuck Company model home exhibition, Illinois State Fair,
Springfield, Illinois, 1912.
(Courtesy Sears, Roebuck Company Archives)

In addition to being pictorial sources for basic artifact research, catalogs are comprehensive collections of graphic art, advertising techniques, and examples of the changing technology of printing. Under the pressure of competition, the catalog developed rapidly not only in size but also in techniques of presentation. In point of fact, the mail-order catalog can be cited as the vehicle for introducing several new developments in the graphic arts.[52] For instance, the first commercial use of the patent binding process was for the Montgomery Ward catalog of 1896, an edition that also included four pages of halftone photographs showing baby bonnets and corsets worn by "live models." Curtains, shoes, and carpets were shown in color photographs in 1889, the year when the Montgomery Ward catalog also represented an early commercial use of the rotary printing press.[53] By 1903 Sears had set up its own printing plant and had turned to four-color printing, which required an improved ink to dry rapidly without smearing. The firm then had to produce a new paper that would take color printing and still be lightweight enough for cheap mailing even when bound into a 600-page catalog. Despite the many changes in mail-order printing technology, as late as 1905 more than half the illustrations were still woodcuts, leading art historians to suggest that it was the mail-order catalog that kept alive the art form of wood engraving.[54]

"Advertisements of artifacts" could easily serve as a shorthand description of mail-order catalogs that were, simultaneously, automatic marketing-research devices, laboratories of salesmanship, and vivid pictorial archives of advertising graphic art. Only a few historians (such as David Potter and Daniel Boorstin) have explored the interrelationship between artifacts and advertising; most have ignored Marshall McLuhan's forecast that "historians and archaeologists will one day discover that the ads of our times are the richest and most faithful daily reflections that any society ever made of its entire range of activities."[55] In the catalogs, however, students can explore the often symbiotic relationship between artifacts and their advertisements in a number of ways.

With the methodology provided by Erving Goffman in his book *Gender Advertisements,* material culture students can evaluate mail-order catalogs as a resource in an aspect of women's history.[56] They can investigate "Advertising and Material Civilization," as American Studies scholar Donald McQuade and his associates do in the book *Edsels, Luckies, and Frigidaires: Advertising and the American Way.*[57] Or they can compare mail-order depiction of objects with illustrations of similar items advertised in other contemporary media, such as those collected in sourcebooks like Edgar Jones's *Those Were the Good Old Days* or by Victor Margolin and his associates in *The Promise and the Product* (for example, illustrated newspapers, magazines, posters, handbills).[58] Students can do sequential and comparative studies of catalog covers (see fig. 24) just as other researchers have used sheet-music covers and long-playing–record jackets as material culture evidence.[59] Or they can take David Potter's thesis (claiming advertising to be "the institution of abundance and democracy") and test it against the visual and verbal data of mail-order merchandising.[60]

As catalogs once served multiple educational purposes in nineteenth-century rural schoolhouses, they can now be similarly employed as textbooks for launching twentieth-century students into material culture studies without material objects. I fully recognize, however, that the catalogs can only provide us with images that are but reminders of objects. To appreciate scale, volume, color, and surface, one must eventually turn to the objects themselves, which is where all artifact research must ultimately focus. Yet as a primer, as a basic text that raises many of the perennial questions of material culture studies, mail-order catalogs prove extremely useful in introducing the beginning student to the field.

For example, with the catalogs at hand one can have students test the various material culture classification systems that have been devised by E. McClung Fleming, Charles Montgomery, and Sidney Brower.[61]

Researchers can use catalogs to chart the year-by-year impact of a new energy source, such as electricity, and its expanding influence on, say, the material culture of the American home or farm with the advent of the Rural Electrification Administration. Instances of innovation and invention likewise surface on the catalog's pages, where, if the new product is truly a breakthrough, subsequent "Big Books" will chronicle its refinements. The famous 1905 Sears, Roebuck cream separator, for example, is not only a major landmark in catalog and mail-order merchandising history but also a significant turning point in the technological history of the American dairy industry.[62] Moreover, preliminary research on other nineteenth-century inventions—the lawn mower, the flush toilet, the phonograph, the stereoscope, the typewriter, the electric iron—can be done in the mail-order catalogs.[63] The "wishbooks" also contain items that do not sell when they are first introduced but then reappear, sometimes several decades later, and become highly marketable items. The Montgomery Ward catalog featured aluminum kitchen utensils as early as 1895, yet such artifacts only began to be used in significant quantities in American households in the 1940s. The catalog as a question book prompts the student to ask: Why was this so? Why did Sears begin selling automobiles in 1909 only to discontinue them in 1912? Why didn't the catalogs ever sell liquor? Why tombstones but never coffins? When did they begin selling birth-control devices? Why did they stop selling patent medicines after 1906, or pistols after 1924?

The dissemination and diffusion of high style, particularly in the decorative arts, are other aspects of material culture research that can be monitored in the catalogs. Consider the popularization of the arts-and-crafts movement. On one hand, this aesthetic trend symbolized a refutation of the mass-produced, ornate, machine-made goods that the mail-order houses sold by the millions; on the other hand, the mail-order catalogs helped advertise the movement of William Morris and Gustav Stickley (fig. 31). Sears, Roebuck featured three-piece "Arts and Crafts Library Suites" made of solid oak, as well as "Mission Art Glass Lamps" that burned kerosine. As early as 1902 a version of Morris's famous reclining chair appeared in a Ward catalog, and six years later the catalog carried a complete line of Mission furniture.[64]

If mail-order catalogs are considered to be two-dimensional paperback museums, it follows that they might prove useful in another aspect of material culture work: museum studies. With a series of reprint catalogs at hand or, better still, an entire run of Sears or Montgomery Ward books, students can be assigned the task of simulating the type and arrangement of artifacts in assorted period rooms of residents with various economic, social, religious, and cultural backgrounds in, say, 1887, 1904, 1929, and 1941. Besides exposing students to many aspects of social, women's,

Figure 31.
Mission Furniture Advertisement
Spiegel, May Stern Company mail-order catalog, Chicago, Illinois, 1900.

family, architectural, and technological history, such an exercise will dramatize for them both the possibilities and the problems of using period room settings as means for historical interpretation.[65] Now that several museums (such as the Minnesota Historical Society and the Chicago Historical Society) have used catalogs as artifacts in exhibitions, students can be commissioned to write critical reviews of such curatorial publications; their critiques can serve as an excellent basis for seminar discussion of the theory and practice of museology.[66]

Another project might be to have students explore the similarities and differences between the mail-order catalogs as gigantic emporiums of what Lewis Mumford has called the "goods life"[67] and other nineteenth-century institutions indicative of the Victorian fascination with the material world: institutions such as world's fairs and trade expositions, art and historical museums, as well as department stores.[68] Still another comparative analysis might be attempted between the material culture of the general or country store and its reputed nemesis, the mail-order catalog.[69] Research exercises might compare country-store inventories before and after mail-order catalogs began bringing goods into local communities; before and after the beginning of rural free delivery in 1893; and before and after 1913, with the coming of parcel post.[70]

Such case studies emerge easily once one begins to ask various questions of the mail-order catalog. Two final examples of the catalog as a resource in material culture studies can be cited in this context: one from an American Studies course in regional studies, concentrating on Chicago's role in Midwestern cultural history, 1871–1933; another in conjunction with an American material culture research seminar with a particular focus on the post-Civil War built environment.[71]

For more than a quarter of a century, mail-order houses sold thousands of precut, mass-produced, balloon-frame houses—a domestic structural innovation perfected in Chicago in the 1840s. Such prefabricated buildings left a permanent mark on rural and small-town America (figs. 32, 33). Much of this housing stock, especially that built early in the twentieth century, survives throughout the Midwest and deserves careful study as a part of American architectural history.[72] Some of this research can be done in the mail-order catalogs, beginning with the spring 1908 Sears catalog where a Modern Homes Department was introduced, selling complete homes and offering mortgages on them anywhere east of the Mississippi and north of the Ohio rivers. Sears had to reacquire a number of these properties during the Depression, and in 1934 the Modern Homes Department was liquidated. But for more than twenty-five years anyone could buy a complete new house of a standard style from the "Big Book." Letters such as "Dear Sir, For the enclosed check please send me one house number 476" were not uncommon in the Modern Homes Department. In different parts of the country, various corporations bought enough mail-order houses to create entire model company-towns or instant subdivisions, as at Carlinville and Wood River in Illinois, at Chester and Plymouth Meeting in Pennsylvania, and at Akron, Ohio.[73]

As the mail-order architecture business expanded, companies such as Ward and Sears published specialized catalogs, for instance, the *Wardway Home Catalog* of 1925 or the *Sears, Roebuck Modern Homes Catalog* of 1926. Such pattern books, complete with floor plans, building specifications, and building elevations, were in many ways the twentieth-century counterparts of such volumes as George Palliser's *Model Homes for the People* (1876) or A. J. Bickell's *Specimen Book of One Hundred Architectural Designs* (1880). Local contractors planned homes for their customers by resorting to mail-order building books, borrowing from them verbatim or adapting parts of them to fit a particular client's preferences.[74]

The 1926 *Sears, Roebuck Modern Homes Catalog*, a book of 144 pages, provides the researcher with a sample of mail-order architecture promotion at its height. Printed almost entirely in color, the text of the

Figure 32.
Bungalow at Illinois State Fair, 1912
Color postcard. Bungalow was built and furnished by Sears, Roebuck
Company, Springfield, Illinois.
(Courtesy Sears, Roebuck Company Archives)

catalog promises the reader an easy installment-payment plan and cites
every possible advantage of home ownership. Seventy-three "Honor
Modern Homes" are listed by their several names, from the "Albany"
to the "Woodland." Also listed are eight "Standard Built" low-priced
homes (from the "Estes" to the "Selby"), as well as plans for sun parlors,
garages, summer cottages, and outhouses. Homes sold by mail-order companies came complete with hardware, various interior items such as
closets, and three coats of exterior paint. Prices ranged from $474 for
the "Hanson" (two bedrooms, living room, kitchen, bath, and porch)
to $4,319 for the "Lexington" (an elaborate two-story Colonial Revival).
Garages started at $82.50; apartment buildings, at $2,099; and commercial structures, at $2,240.[75]

In Edna Ferber's 1917 novel about mail-order merchandising, the pro-
prietor of a general store in Winnebago, Wisconsin, reflects on the
mesmerizing effect the catalog has on many Midwestern folk who buy
from its pages rather than from her shelves. "I honestly think it's just
the craving for excitement that makes them do it," concluded Molly
Brandeis, "they want the thrill they get when they receive a box from
Chicago."[76] For many Americans mail-order catalogs symbolized Chicago,
and conversely, Chicago meant mail-order catalogs. Mail-order houses

Figure 33.
Bungalow Porch Furnishings
Sears, Roebuck Company model home exhibition, Illinois State Fair,
Springfield, Illinois, 1912.
(Courtesy Sears, Roebuck Company Archives)

aspired to make that city the country's emporium of the "goods life" and, on occasion, the font of Midwest sophistication. Such commercial and cultural imperialism pervades the "Big Books," thereby providing us with semiannual editions of Chicago's famous booster press.

For example, the catalogs offer ample documentation of the railroad's role in Chicago's history. Chicago's position at the center of the nation's railroad network influenced Richard Sears to abandon his first head-quarters, in Minneapolis. Through panoramic maps, alluring illustrations, and enticing prose, mail-order writers continually expounded the economic significance of the Chicago rail nexus. For today's American Studies students, this represents a quick lesson in the geography of a major American break-in-bulk depot and its role in the interrelation of nineteenth-century transportation patterns. "Chicago is the commercial center of America," boasts the Ward catalog of 1895, "and is now recognized as the largest and closest market for manufactured goods."[77] Felix Fay, the hero of Floyd Dell's autobiographical novel *Moon-Calf*, recognizes it too. He recalls a small-town railroad depot and its "map with a picture of iron roads from all of the Middle West centered in a dark blotch in the corner . . . CHICAGO!'' It was a place that many a mail-order reader could imagine, via a mental map often stimulated by actual catalog cartography, showing an urban landscape containing a panoply of material things.[78]

Mail-order catalogs thus invited their readers to visit Chicago as either armchair travelers or actual tourists. For those content to stay down on the farm, the catalogs shaped an image of Chicago for several generations. This was done largely through pictorial depictions of the city's mercantile environment. The catalogs featured several sets of stereographs of Chicago's points of interest, the fifty stereographic views that Sears sold of its own plant operations along with such illustrated pamphlets as *A Visit to Sears, Roebuck and Company* (Chicago, 1923).

The semiannual catalogs, bulky but engaging travel brochures that they were, enticed readers to travel to the big city, especially to the mail-order merchandising plants, where visitors were given guided tours and assorted souvenirs. When Americans were abroad, the Chicago catalogs sometimes followed them. Julius Rosenwald, then president of Sears, Roebuck, even toured the battle lines of the American Expeditionary Forces during World War I, distributing thousands of copies of what the doughboys had requested most often as a memento of home: the current mail-order catalog from Chicago.

Like the Chicago it so well embodies, and like so many of that city's other symbols (such as the Water Tower, the Loop, and State Street), the Chicago mail-order catalog is a curious mixture of crudeness and culture, provincialism and cosmopolitanism, vulgarity and aggressiveness, and, of course, abundant Chicago bravado: "World's Cheapest Store!" "World's Largest Supply House!" "The Greatest Price Maker," "Largest Mail-Order Business in the United States," "Cheapest Cash House in America!" When Sears, "The World's Largest Store," secured its own radio station in 1924, it naturally enough adopted WLS as its call letters.[79] Such fanfaronade, trumpeted from every nineteenth-century catalog's front and back cover, reiterated on page after page within the "Big Book," is but another example of the postbellum American delight in braggadocio, boldness, and bigness—especially bigness, a cultural and physical trait that David Burg argues pervaded much of fin-de-siècle American material culture, be it in monument, landscape plan, furniture, or architecture.[80]

Mail-order catalogs are multifaceted artifacts of late-nineteenth- and early-twentieth-century America. In Fred Schroeder's estimate, they are laden with such American values as material well-being, middle class equality, universal literacy, and democratic mutual respect.[81] I agree, and I think they can be viewed as texts with inordinate versatility, helpful in many types of American Studies courses that seek to explore the American experience from many different angles of vision.

For the student of American material culture, mail-order catalogs are equally salutary. From them we learn not only of the garments of men, women, and children but of their undergarments as well; not only of the vernacular architecture of a people but also of the tools and building materials used to construct their homes. We can extract specific data about parlors and privies, toys and turbines. We come to know not only how things were measured and made but also how they were maintained and repaired—the latter activities being a dimension of artifact study often neglected in material culture research.

If anyone doubts that mail-order catalogs are authentic American material culture, he should remember that the archivists of the major mail-order firms still receive orders, with payments enclosed, from customers who want products offered in the original catalogs or their recent reprints. If that's not wishful thinking generated by a "wishbook," I don't know what is. Moreover, in addition to serving as resources for material culture studies (for instance, as reference works, graphics libraries, artifact-studies primers, paperback museums, and data bases for research case studies), the catalogs have now assumed a second life as material culture evidence of our own time's fascination with the collectible and the antique. Vintage mail-order catalogs are becoming increasingly costly and respectable objects of material culture, eagerly sought out by collectors at flea markets and garage sales and in the antique-book market. In 1980 a 1924 Montgomery Ward catalog sold for $24 and a 1918 edition was considered a bargain at $35, while a 1916 Sears catalog, describing the company that issued it as the "Cheapest Supply House on Earth," sold for $65.[82] Not bad prices for artifacts that after 1905 were usually mailed out free to more than 15 million Americans each year.

Notes

1. Edna Ferber, *Fanny Herself* (New York: Frederick A. Stokes, 1917), 115.

2. Harry Crews, *A Childhood: The Biography of Place* (New York: Harper & Row, 1978), 54.

3. Boris Emmet and John E. Jeuck, *Catalogues and Counters: A History of Sears, Roebuck and Company* (Chicago: University of Chicago Press, 1950), 9. A basic mail-order–industry bibliography would also include: Frank B. Latham, *A Century of Serving Customers: The Story of Montgomery Ward* (Chicago: Montgomery Ward, 1972); Nina Baker, *Big Catalogue: The Life of Aaron Montgomery* (New York: Harcourt Brace, 1956); and *Our Silver Anniversary: Being a Brief and Concise History of the Mail Order or Catalog Business Which Was Invented by Us a Quarter of a Century Ago* (Chicago: Montgomery Ward, 1897); on Sears, consult David L. Cohn, *The Good Old Days: A History of American Morals and Manners as Seen through the Sears, Roebuck Catalogs, 1905 to the Present* (New York: Simon & Schuster, 1940); Louis Asher and Edith Neal, *Send No Money* (Chicago: Argus Books, 1942); and Gordon L. Weil, *Sears, Roebuck, U.S.A.: The Great American Catalog Store and How It Grew* (New York: Stein & Day, 1977).

4. Daniel Boorstin, *The Americans: The Democratic Experience* (New York: Random House, 1973), 128–29.

5. See Maria Elena De La Iglesia's *The Catalog of American Catalogs* (New York: Random House, 1973) and her *The Complete Guide to World Wide Shopping by Mail* (New York: Random House, 1972); Cecil C. Hoge, *Mail Order Moonlighting* (New York: E. P. Dutton, 1975).

6. Viola I. Paradise, "By Mail," *Scribner's Monthly* (April 1921): 480.

7. Rae Elizabeth Rips, "An Introductory Study of the Role of the Mail-Order Business in American History, 1872–1914," master's thesis, University of Chicago, 1938, 2–3.

8. For the cover of the *1926 Spring/Summer Catalog,* Montgomery Ward reproduced John Trumbull's painting of Franklin, John Adams, and Thomas Jefferson drafting the Declaration of Independence, as the store's tribute to the American sesquicentennial. Inside the catalog (p. 3), the company claimed its own founder, not Franklin, as the mail-order catalog's originator: "Selling goods by mail was unknown in 1872. A. Montgomery Ward, the pioneer, was the young man with vision who foresaw a new merchandising method—who laid down his principles, and so won a niche in the 'World's Hall of Business Fame.' "

9. Lawrence B. Romaine, "Benjamin Franklin: The Father of the Mail Order Catalog and Not Montgomery Ward," *The American Book Collector* 11.4 (December 1960): 25–28. For a still earlier claim for a mail-order prototype, see Gerald L. Alexander, "Widlldey's Enterprising Map of North America," *Antiques* (July 1962): 76–77.

10. *Publishers Central Catalog* (Summer 1979), 26; *Marlboro Books Catalog* (Spring 1979), 14.

11. For ordering and pricing information on Sears catalog reproductions, write to Book Digest, Inc., 540 Frontage Road, Northfield, Ill. 60093, for the 1897, 1900, 1908, and 1923 editions; Castle Books, 100 Enterprise Avenue, Secaucus, N.J. 07094, for the 1906 edition; and Crown Publishers, 34 Engelhard Avenue, Avenel, N.J. 07001, for the 1902 and 1927 editions and the anthology *Sears Catalogs of the 1930s.*

12. *Montgomery Ward and Company Catalogue and Buyers Guide No. 57* (Spring and Summer 1895), with an introduction by Boris Emmet (New York: Dover Publications, 1969).

13. See, for example, Robert D. Watt, ed., *The Shopping Guide of the West: Woodward's Catalogue, 1883–1953* (North Vancouver, Canada: Douglas and McIntyre, 1978).

14. For the location of Sears catalogs on microfilm in the libraries and research centers in any state, write to Lenore Swioskin, Archivist, Sears, Roebuck and Co., Fortieth Floor, Sears Tower, Chicago, Ill. 60606.

15. Published accounts of this pedagogy include Minnesota Historical Society Education Division, *The Wishbook: Mail Order in Minnesota—A Study Guide for Teachers* (St. Paul: Minnesota Historical Society, 1979); William R. Smith, "Social Studies: Making Comparisons with Mail Order Catalogs," *The Instructor: A Journal of the New York State Educational Association* (September 1976): 71–72; and James Kavanaugh, "The Artifact in American Culture: The Development of an Undergraduate Program in American Studies," in *Material Culture and the Study of American Life,* ed. Ian M. G. Quimby (New York: W. W. Norton, 1978), 69–71.

16. Nicholas Westbrook, "The Wishbook as History Book," unpublished paper delivered at the seventh biennial national meeting of the American Studies Association, Minneapolis, 28 September 1979 ; Fred E. H. Schroeder, "Semi-annual Installment on the American Dream: The Wishbook as Popular Icon," in *Icons of Popular Culture* ed. M. Fishwick and R. B. Browne, (Bowling Green, Ohio: Bowling Green University Popular Press, 1970), 73–86; Fred E. H. Schroeder, "The Wishbook as Popular Icon," in *Outlaw Aesthetics: Arts and the Public Mind* (Bowling Green, Ohio: Bowling Green University Popular Press, 1977), 50–61; Joan Siedl and Nicholas Westbrook, "The Wishbook: Mail Order in Minnesota," exhibition at the Minnesota Historical Society, St. Paul, Minn., 1979–80.

17. For an application of the inquiry approach to another historical topic, see my "A Question Is an Answer: An Experimental Inquiry in American Cultural History," *The History Teacher* 6.1 (November 1972): 97–106.

18. To date no scholar has done a systematic, definitive study of either mail-order catalogs or mail-order goods. The best work on catalogs has already been cited in n.3; mail-order goods, as a type of material culture evidence, however, still await their cultural historian. Mail-order merchandising, although discussed in several individual corporate histories (cited in n.3 above), still suffers from a lack of a broad, interpretative historical overview of the entire industry.

19. Lovell Thompson, "Eden in Easy Payments," *The Saturday Review of Literature* (3 April 1937):15–16; Ralph Andrist, *American Century: One Hundred Years of Changing Life Styles in America* (New York: American Heritage Press, 1972), 8.

20. *Rears and Robust Mail Order Catalog for Spring/Summer/Fall/Winter* (Wheeling, W.Va.:*The Morning Call,* 1940). Copy available in the research library of the Chicago Historical Society. In his 1970 article, "Semi-annual Installments on the American Dream," Fred Schroeder suggests (p. 76) that little folklore about mail-order catalogs has been collected or indexed in standard sources such as the *Journal of American Folklore* or B. A. Botkin's *Treasury of American Anecdotes.* I am persuaded that the *Rears and Robust* compendium would qualify as an excellent example of catalog folklore and fantasy.

21. Schroeder, "The Wishbook as Popular Icon," 56; *Sears, Roebuck Catalog* (Spring–Summer 1969):1079.

22. Crews, *A Childhood,* 54–55, 57. In similar fashion, nine-year-old R. Waldo Ledbetter, Jr., a character in George Milburn's novel about the impact of the mail-order catalog on an Oklahoma town in the 1920s, kept both a Ward and a Sears catalog "in a big pasteboard box in his room under his bed." "His father [who later organizes the town's anticatalog campaign] didn't understand about catalogs. His father never would know how much fun a person could have with mail-order catalogs, making believe he is a rancher fitting himself out with everything from branding irons to angora chaps; or a farmer equipping a model farm; or simply a father ordering toys for his son. The toy list was the most fun of all" (George Milburn, *Catalogue: A Novel* [New York: Harcourt, Brace, 1936], 83–84).

23. In 1918, Sears offered, via its mail-order catalogs, a series of "useful knowledge" almanacs on farm life. These volumes are superb documents for studying the agrarian material culture of this particular period. The books were titled *Farm Knowledge: A Manual of Successful Farming, Written by Recognized Authorities in All Parts*

of the Country . . . The Farmers' Own Cyclopedia, ed. E. H. D. Seymour (New York: Doubleday and Sears, Roebuck, 1918). The four volumes were: *Farm Animals* (I); *Soils, Crops, Fertilizers and Methods* (II); *Farm Implements, Vehicles, and Buildings* (III); and *Business Management and the Farm Home* (IV).

24.   See, for example, Rips, "Role of the Mail-Order Business in American History," 17–34; Emmet and Jeuck, *Catalogues and Counters,* 718.

25.   Robert Heilbroner, *The Economic Transformation of America* (New York: Harcourt Brace Jovanovich, 1977). Also useful on this point is Herbert Casson's "Marvelous Development of the Mail-Order Business," *Munsey's Magazine* 38 (January 1908): 513–15.

26.   For a good contemporary summary of the various positions in the anti–mail-order campaign see the December 1908 issue of *The Outlook,* which provides an overview of the conflict; likewise, see Lewis Atherton, *Main Street on the Middle Border* (New York: Quadrangle Books, 1966), 231–33.

27.   Milburn, *Catalogue,* chap. 18; see also Cohn, chap. 28, "The Burning of the Books," *Good Old Days,* 510–17.

28.   Harold Wentworth and Stuart Berg, *The Dictionary of American Slang* (New York: Simon & Schuster, 1967), 221.

29.   Ida M. Tarbell, *The Nationalizing of Business, 1878–1898* (New York: Macmillan, 1936), and Robert Wiebe, *The Search for Order, 1877–1920* (New York: Hill & Wang, 1967). The view of corporate growth as an economic system that demanded disciplined patterns of rational objective order is also the theme of two books by Samuel P. Hays, *The Response to Industrialism* (Chicago: University of Chicago Press, 1957) and *Conservation and the Gospel of Efficiency* (Cambridge, Mass.: Harvard University Press, 1959).

30.   *Sears, Roebuck Catalog* (Spring–Summer 1908): 309. The stereo views were later called "Trip through Sears, Roebuck Company."

31.   On Taylorism, see Samuel Haber, *Efficiency and Uplift: Scientific Management in the Progressive Era, 1890–1920* (Chicago: University of Chicago Press, 1964), and David Noble, "Harmony through Technological Order: Taylor, Ford and Veblen," in his *The Progressive Mind, 1890–1917* (Chicago: Rand McNally, 1969), 37–52.

32.   See, for instance, Bruce Daniels, "Probate Inventories as a Source for Economic History," *Connecticut Historical Society Bulletin* 37.3 (January 1972): 1–9; Abbott Cummings, *Rural Household Inventories* (Boston: Society for the Preservation of New England Antiquities, 1964); and Monroe Fabian, "An Immigrant's Inventory," *Pennsylvania Folklife* 25.4 (Summer 1976): 47–48.

33.   Deborah C. and William D. Andrews, "Technology and the Housewife in Nineteenth-Century America," *Women Studies* 2.3 (1974): 309–28; Susan May Strasser, "Never Done: The Ideology and Technology of Household Work, 1850–1930," Ph.D. dissertation, State University of New York at Stony Brook, 1977; Elizabeth Faulkner Baker, *Technology and Woman's Work* (New York: Columbia University Press, 1964); Gwendolyn Wright, "Sweet and Clean: The Domestic Landscape in the Progressive Era," *Landscape* 20.1 (October 1975): 38–43; and Ruth Schwartz Cowan, "The 'Industrial Revolution' in the Home: Household Technology and Social Change in the Twentieth Century," *Technology and Culture* 17.1 (January 1976): 1–23.

34. See Siegfried Giedion, *Mechanization Takes Command: A Contribution to Anonymous History* (New York: Oxford University Press, 1975); Anthony Garvan, "Effects of Technology on Modern Life, 1830–1880," and Melvin Rotsch, "The Home Environment," both in *Technology in Western Civilization,* ed. Carroll Pursell and Melvin Kranzberg (New York: Oxford University Press, 1967), 1:546–62, and 2: 217–36; Joann Vanek, "Time Spent in Housework," *Scientific American* 231 (November 1974): 116–20; and Joann Vanek, "Household Technology and Social Status: Residence Differences in Housework," *Technology and Culture* 19 (July 1978): 361–75.

35. Cohn, *Good Old Days,* 285–316.

36. See Arthur M. Schlesinger, *Learning How to Behave: A Historical Study of American Etiquette Books* (New York: Macmillan, 1946); R. Gordon Kelly, *Mother Was a Lady: Strategy and Order in Selected American Children's Periodicals, 1865–1890* (Westport, Conn.: Greenwood Press, 1974); Gerald Carson, *The Polite Americans: A Wide-Angle View of Our More or Less Good Manners over 300 Years* (New York: William Morrow, 1966); and Stow Persons, *The Decline of American Gentility* (New York: Columbia University Press, 1973).

37. Ward's assessment of "The Meaning of Lindbergh's Flight" can be found in *American Quarterly* 10 (1958): 3–16.

38. Schroeder, "The Wishbook as Popular Icon," 51–53, 60.

39. Thomas J. Schlereth, "Material Culture Studies in America: Notes toward a Historical Perspective," in *Proceedings of the First International Conference on Material History* (Ottawa, Canada: National Museum of Man, 1979).

40. Kenneth Ames, "Meaning in Artifacts: Hall Furnishings in Victorian America," *The Journal of Interdisciplinary History* 9.1 (Summer 1978): 26.

41. Lawrence B. Romaine, *A Guide to American Trade Catalogs, 1744–1900* (New York: Arno Press, 1976). The Pyne Press American Historical Catalog Collection includes seventeen reprint catalogs that are extremely useful in comparative material culture exercises. The subjects of the catalogs range from glassware to ornamental ironwork, architectural elements to sporting goods, carriages to cameras. For a catalog of the reprint catalogs available, write to the Pyne Press, 92 Nassau Street, Princeton, N.J. 08540.

42. Correspondence with Emilie Tari, Curator of Collections, Old World Wisconsin, 27 August 1979; likewise, Robert G. Chenhall's *Nomenclature for Museum Cataloging: A System for Classifying Man-made Objects* (Nashville: American Association for State and Local History, 1978) uses several Sears and Ward catalogs as key reference texts; see pp. 501, 504.

43. Interview with Lenore Swioskin, Archivist, Sears, Roebuck and Co., Chicago, 1 June 1979.

44. Curator Emilie Tari, describing her work at Old World Wisconsin, notes in a letter to the author, "The catalogs are without question a basic research tool in any fully conceived interior restoration that dates after approximately 1890. . . . Taken in combination with photographic evidence and oral history material, it [is] possible to pull together quite a broad and comprehensive picture of the material culture of a social/economic group that has rarely been methodically studied or researched."

45. Claudia Kidwell, *Suiting Everyone: The Democratization of Clothing in America* (Washington, D.C.: Smithsonian Institution Press, 1977), 160–64; author's correspondence with Claudia Kidwell, Curator of Costume, Smithsonian Institution, 20 August 1979.

46. Correspondence with Rodris Roth, Curator, Division of Domestic Life, Smithsonian Institution, 10 September 1979.

47. See "Chicago History Galleries," Chicago Historical Society, and "The History of Chicago Exhibit," Chicago Museum of Science and Industry. A temporary Bicentennial exhibition, "Creating New Traditions," at the Chicago Historical Society also paid considerable attention to mail-order catalogs, as did its accompanying publication: Perry Duis, *Creating New Traditions* (Chicago: Chicago Historical Society, 1976), particularly chap. 5—"Merchandising."

48. Craig Gilborn, "Pop Pedagogy: Looking at the Coke Bottle," *Museum News* (December 1966): 12–18.

49. Exhibit Panel, "The Wishbook: Direct from the Factory To You," in "The Wishbook: Mail Order in Minnesota," temporary exhibition at the Minnesota Historical Society, St. Paul, 1979–80.

50. William Seale, *The Tasteful Interlude: American Interiors through the Camera's Eye, 1850–1917* (New York: Praeger, 1975); George Talbot, *At Home: Domestic Life in the Post-Centennial Era, 1876–1920* (Madison: State Historical Society of Wisconsin, 1976); and Clay Lancaster, *New York Interiors at the Turn of the Century* (New York: Dover Publications, 1977).

51. See this photograph, reproduced from the collections of the Nebraska Historical Society in Andrist, *American Century,* 3; for parallel uses of historical photographs in American Studies, see Barnard Mergen and Marsha Peters, "Doing The Rest: The Uses of Photographs in American Studies," *American Quarterly* 29.3 (Summer 1977): 280–303.

52. Milburn, *Catalogue,* 167.

53. Andrist, *American Century,* 7; also see Daniel Boorstin, "A. Montgomery Ward's Mail Order Business," *Chicago History* n.s. 2 (Spring–Summer 1973): 147.

54. Boorstin, *The Americans,* 128.

55. David Potter, *People of Plenty: Economic Abundance and the American Character* (Chicago: University of Chicago Press, 1954); Daniel Boorstin, *The Image: A Guide to Pseudo-Events in America* (New York: Atheneum, 1961); Marshall McLuhan, *Understanding Media: The Extensions of Man* (New York: McGraw-Hill, 1964).

56. Erving Goffman, *Gender Advertisements* (New York: Harper & Row, 1979). This monograph first appeared as vol. 3, no. 2 of *Studies in the Anthropology of Visual Communication* (Fall 1976); also see Betty Friedan's analysis of the "sexual sell" in *The Feminine Mystique* (New York: Dell, 1970).

57. Robert Atwan, Donald McQuade, and John W. Wright, *Edsels, Luckies, and Frigidaires: Advertising the American Way* (New York: Dell, 1979), 111–246.

58. Edgar R. Jones, *Those Were the Good Old Days* (New York: Simon & Schuster, 1979), and Victor Margolin, Ira Brichta, and Vivan Brichta, *The Promise and the Product: 200 Years of American Advertising Posters* (New York: Macmillan 1979); also useful

in this context is Clarence P. Hornung's *Handbook of Early Advertising Art,* 3d ed. (New York: Dover Publications, 1956), particularly the introduction (pp. ix–xiv) and the bibliography.

59. Lester S. Levy, *Picture the Songs: Lithographs from the Sheet Music of the Nineteenth Century* (Baltimore: Johns Hopkins University Press, 1976).

60. Potter, *People of Plenty,* 166–208; likewise consult Ivan L. Preston, *The Great American Blow-up: Puffery in Advertising and Selling* (Madison: University of Wisconsin Press, 1975).

61. E. McClung Fleming, "Artifact Study: A Proposed Model," *Winterthur Portfolio* 9 (June 1974): 161–73; Charles Montgomery, "Some Remarks on the Practice and Science of Connoisseurship," *American Walpole Society Notebook* (1961):7–20; and Sidney Brower, "Tools, Toys, Masterpieces, Mediums," *Landscape* 19.2 (January 1975): 28–32.

62. Kenan Heise, "Mail Order Democracy," *Chicago Magazine* 25.11 (November 1976): 106–7, and Eric M. Lampard, *Rise of the Dairy Industry in Wisconsin 1820–1920* (Madison: University of Wisconsin Press, 1963).

63. Cohn, *Good Old Days,* xi–xix.

64. Russell Lynes, *The Tastemakers* (New York: Harper & Bros., 1949), 190, and Perry Duis, *Chicago: Creating New Traditions* (Chicago: Chicago Historical Society, 1976), 116.

65. Edward P. Alexander, "Artistic and Historical Period Rooms," *Curator* 7.4 (1964): 263–81, and E. McClung Fleming, "The Period Room as a Curatorial Publication," *Museum News* 50.10 (June 1972): 39–42.

66. Thomas W. Leavitt, "Toward a Standard of Excellence: The Nature and Purpose of Exhibit Reviews," *Technology and Culture* 9 (1968): 70–75.

67. Lewis Mumford, *Technics and Civilization* (New York: Harcourt, Brace, 1934), 105.

68. On the relationship between world's fairs, department stores and museums, see Neil Harris, "Museums, Merchandising, and Popular Taste: The Struggle for Influence," in *Material Culture and the Study of American Life,* ed. Quimby, 140–74. A case study of this relationship in Chicago can be done by comparing either the Sears or the Ward catalogs with the information found in Helen Lefkowitz Horowitz, *Culture and the City: Cultural Philanthropy from the 1880s to 1917* (Lexington: University of Kentucky Press, 1976); David F. Burg, *Chicago's White City of 1893* (Lexington: University of Kentucky Press, 1976); and Lloyd Wendt and Herman Kogan, *Give the Lady What She Wants* (Chicago: Rand McNally, 1952). For additional department-store history, consult Boorstin, *The Americans,* 101–9, and his bibliographic notes (pp. 629–30), along with Robert Hendrickson, *The Grand Emporiums: The Illustrated History of America's Great Department Stores* (New York: Stein & Day, 1978).

69. The country store has been studied by Lewis Atherton (for example, in his *Pioneer Merchant in Mid-America* [Columbia: University of Missouri Press, 1939] and *The Southern Country Store, 1800–1860* [Baton Rouge: Louisiana State University Press, 1949]), as well as by Gerald Carson (*The Old Country Store* [New York: Oxford University Press, 1954]) and Thomas D. Clark (*Pills, Petticoats and Plows: the Southern Country Store* [Indianapolis: Bobbs-Merrill, 1944]).

70. For additional information on rural free delivery and parcel post, see Wayne E. Fuller, *RFD: The Changing Face of Rural America* (Chicago: University of Chicago Press, 1964), as well as his *The American Mail: Enlarger of the Common Life* (Chicago: University of Chicago Press, 1972).

71. American Studies 486: *Chicago: Studies in a Regional Culture, 1871–1933,* Spring 1979; American Studies 484: *American Material Culture: The History on the Land,* Fall, 1979—Department of American Studies, University of Notre Dame, filed with, and copies available from, National American Studies Faculty, American Studies Association.

72. Arthur A. Hart, "M. A. Disbrow and Company: Catalog Architecture," *Palimpsest* 56.4 (1975): 98–119.

73. John F. Hart, *The Look of the Land* (Englewood Cliffs, N.J.: Prentice-Hall, 1975), 155–56; *Sears Midwest* (June 1969): 8.

74. In its book department, Sears also published its own builders' manuals, such as William A. Radford's two-volume *Practical Carpentry* (Chicago: Radford Architectural Company and Sears, Roebuck and Company, 1907), which purported to contain "a complete, up-to-date explanation of modern carpentry and an encyclopedia on the modern methods used in the erection of buildings from the laying out of the foundation to the delivery of the building to the painter." This pattern book of twentieth-century vernacular architecture contained fifty perspective views and floor plans of low- and medium-priced houses. A local builder could buy all fifty plans and illustrated views for only $5. Sears also sold another book of plans (*Twentieth-Century Practical Barn Plans*), likewise edited by Radford (who also published the journal *The American Carpenter and Builder*), and containing fifty building-plans of farm structures.

75. *Sears, Roebuck Modern Homes Catalog* (Chicago: Sears, Roebuck, 1926); also see Emmet and Jeuck, *Catalogues and Counters,* 522–24.

76. Ferber, *Fanny Herself,* 115.

77. *Montgomery Ward and Company Catalog and Buyers Guide* (Spring–Summer 1895): 108.

78. Floyd Dell, *Moon-Calf: A Novel* (New York: Alfred A. Knopf, 1920), 2.

79. Gary Deeb, "Radio: What It Was, What It is, and What It Is Most Likely to Become," and Clifford Terry, "The Glory Days of Radio," *Chicago Tribune Magazine* (4 March 1979): 22–24, 28–33.

80. David F. Burg, "The Aesthetics of Bigness in Late-Nineteenth-Century American Architecture," in *Popular Architecture,* ed. Marshall Fishwick and J. Meredith Neil (Bowling Green, Ohio: Bowling Green University Press, 1976), 106–14.

81. Schroeder, "Semi-annual Installment on the American Dream," 82–83.

82. C. W. Fishbaugh, "Collectible Catalogues," in *Collector Editions Quarterly* 4(1979): 6.

Figure 34.
"Jemy" French Schultze, 1892
Unattributed photograph.
(Courtesy The Library of Congress, Division of Prints and Photographs)

The Material Culture of Childhood: Research Problems and Possibilities

A museum symposium prompted this essay's first draft on the history of childhood and childhood history. Mary Lynn Stevens Heininger, the historian who orchestrated the Strong Museum's exhibition, "A Century of Childhood, 1840–1940" and edited the book of essays of the same name published by the Strong in 1984, invited me to open the scholarly conference she coordinated in conjunction with the museum exhibition. I found the Strong's three-stage model of promoting and presenting material culture research admirable. Bill Alderson, then director, and Harvey Green, vice president for research and interpretation, had decided as early as the museum's first major exhibition to include a research publication and a scholarly symposium with every new exhibition.

My part in the childhood conference took me into children's museums. Research at the Children's Museum in Indianapolis and at the Please Touch Museum in Philadelphia made me realize how extensive the artifactual world of the modern child had become. I also became intrigued with how much the material culture of children past revealed about the adult society of the same era. Heininger's introductory analysis of the use of children in advertising in late Victorian America prompted me to pursue this topic in the National Museum of American History's Warshaw Collection for my *Transformations* study.

Finally, in preparing the Strong Museum lecture, I read everything I could turn up on the artifacts of childhood. With the exception of writing on toys, it was not an extensive corpus. Hence, I decided to use the conference's forum to think about why this was so.

This musing continued in other contexts, first at a conference cosponsored by the National Museum of Man and the Canadian Museums Association and later at material culture colloquia at the University of Southern Illinois, and, coming full circle, at a meeting at the Indianapolis Children's Museum. After each of these talks, I received helpful comment and critique. Many unanswered questions still remain on the research agenda I propose in its argument. I still wanted to know what the material culture of old institutions (like the Children's Building at Chicago's 1893 World's Fair) and new ones (such as the interior design and furnishings of modern child-care

This article originally appeared in *Material History Bulletin* 21 (September 1985): 1–14.

centers) could tell us. There are two larger hypotheses I also hoped to test (or see someone test). The first would entail a systematic investigation of the photography of children from 1840 to 1940. As I speculate below, could it be that the new technology of the camera and its increasingly widespread use contributed to the "discovery" of childhood and adolescence in the late nineteenth century? My second unresolved question concerns rural childhood, a historic topic largely ignored except by historians of education. Simply put, I ask whether there were quite different childhoods for the rural, agrarian young in comparison with their urban, middle-class counterparts in the period from 1870 to 1920?

In this essay, I complain about other issues. One was the lack of attention to true "kids' toys," that is, material culture made or modified by children themselves rather than toys given them to accomplish a set task, a specific educational objective, or a toy manufacturer's advertised goal. Steven Zeitlin and his folklore colleagues on New York's City Lore project mounted in 1988 an engaging exhibition at the Museum of the City of New York entitled "City Play." It contains excellent examples of artifacts made, remade, remodeled, or renamed by children (and adults) in their urban play. A catalog of essays, also named *City Play* (New York: Museum of the City of New York, 1989), accompanied the exhibit. Also see Simon Bronner's fine chapter, "We Made It Ourselves: Toys and Constructions" in his *American Children's Folklore* (Little Rock: August House, 1988), 199–236.

As a new, first-time (1983), middle-aged father, I surveyed the historiography of childhood from a perspective different from that I would have had had I been examining the literature as a young, unmarried graduate student. I could find very little research on the history of fatherhood in relationship to childhood. (Middle-age, while not directly germane to our topic here, is also another largely unexplored phase of life course history.) As it turned out, others were at work on these issues of gender and family history. I would recommend John Demos, *Past, Present, and Personal: The Family and Life Course in American History* (New York: Oxford University Press, 1986); Peter Filene, *Him/Her/Self: Sex Roles in Modern America* (Baltimore: The Johns Hopkins University Press, 1974, 1986); and Steven Mintz and Susan Kellogg, *Domestic Revolutions: A Social History of American Family Life* (New York: Free Press, 1988).

The easiest way of becoming acquainted with the mode of thinking, the rules of conduct, and the prevailing manners of any people is to examine what sort of education they give their children, how they treat them at home, and what they are taught in their places of public worship.
—Hector St. John Crèvecour,
Letters from an American Farmer (1782)

Hector St. John Crèvecour's insight—that understanding how a culture views its children provides a viewpoint from which to evaluate the culture—serves as a basic assumption for many contemporary historical studies of North American childhood. Knowing the child is, in part, a way of knowing the parent, the family, and the society.[1]

The discovery of childhood over the past two centuries, initially by educators, clergy, merchandisers, and sociologists throughout the nineteenth century, and then by child psychologists, antique dealers, writers, and social historians in the twentieth century, has meant an ever-expanding interest in the role of children and the concept of childhood.[2] Part of this interest has focused on the things of children, on the surviving artifacts of past infancy, childhood, and adolescence.

In this essay, two questions are posed about this interest in extant childhood artifacts: How and why has the material culture of childhood intrigued so many collectors, curators, and scholars? What are the problems and possibilities of using such physical evidence in historical explanation? These questions are explored by reviewing how the objects of the child have been collected, exhibited, and interpreted over the past century. The essay's argument and supporting data, while largely drawn from the American historical experience, aim at providing a tentative overview of the topic. It is hoped that this perspective will be useful in comparison with parallel social history research in other countries.

Collecting Childhood

What motivates collectors of childhood artifacts? To begin with, all the basic impulses of general collecting: acquisitiveness, an attraction to the past, investment potential, innate curiosity, historical associationism. Can we, however, point to any particular reasons why the artifacts of childhood might be of any special interest to collectors? No one really can say for sure since no one has yet systematically explored the ethnography of the collecting of childhood material culture. In the United States, we know something about why individuals such as Margaret Woodbury Strong, Louis Hentz, or Electra Havermeyer Webb were attracted to childhood artifacts, but we know very little about the personal motivations behind collections in thousands of North American local museums and county historical societies.[3]

Perhaps, in addition to the motivations of the general collecting tendency, we are also attracted to the objects of the child for specific reasons. These may be partially gender-related, partially scale-related, and partially time-related.

For example, it is statistically true that until our own time the vast majority of childhood collectors have been women. The female functions of bearing and (until the recent past) of raising children is one obvious reason for this. The injunction to be a "madonna-in-the-nursery" as

Harvey Green has characterized this demanding task was but another of the nineteenth-century American woman's many roles as the "light of the home." The Victorian cult of domesticity underlies, in part, the feminine inclination to collect the domestic.[4]

The human delight in miniaturization may also account for why many individuals, men as well as women, collect the things of the child. A child and a child's things permit one to invert the average adult's proportion of scale. Childhood material culture enables us to re-examine life at a Lilliputian level (fig. 35). For modern adults who live so much of their lives in physical environments of gargantuan and grotesque proportions—the world of the skyscraper and the freeway—the opposite world of the diminutive and the dwarf is both cognitively relaxing and aesthetically pleasing.

Adults are drawn to the doll house or the model train, perhaps for some of the same reasons they are taken by material culture exhibitions featuring patent models or dioramas. A child's world, as the Indiana poet James Whitcomb Riley reflected in his evocation of "A Boy's World," is a deliberately small world, a manageable world, a world that we adults can hold in our hands or in our arms.

The child's world is also a world we have lost. We try to regain it, in part, as parents and grandparents, as collectors and curators, but try as we may, it is gone as is all the past. And yet its artifacts remain, some in memory and some in museums. In collecting such material culture, adults may be trying to recollect a universal human experience, childhood. As adults, endowed with all the knowledge gained during our own childhood, we cannot help but often view the childhood of others as a metaphor for our own previous experience. Childhood is our own first historical era, an era we know first-hand, not vicariously, as we know so much of the past. To be sure, our remembrance of that childhood is extremely fragmentary and even fearsome, but it is also one of fantasy and fun.

Twentieth-century children's literature, progressive education theory, and much child psychology foster the cultural belief that childhood was, or should be, fun. This is another way of saying childhood means games and toys—the largest category of all extant childhood material culture. Fun is also simply another reason for collecting the things of the child. The old adage, "The only difference between men and boys is the size of their toys," has a corollary that would suggest that many adults, still boys and girls, take great delight in playing with children's toys. William Blake put it this way: "The child's toys and the old man's reasons are [but] the fruit of two seasons."

Toys are, without doubt, adults' favorite form of childhood material culture. Entire private collections are devoted only to them; whole

Figure 35.
"A Boy's Wartime Easter," 1942
(Photograph by John Schlereth. Courtesy the photographer)

museums house their special genres.[5] This is not surprising since most manufactured toys are objects made by adults to appeal and to sell to other adults, ostensibly, of course, for children. Toys are the artifacts of two cultures. They can reveal as much about a society's adults as its children. Perhaps more. Moreover, what individual collectors amass of an earlier childhood era may reveal as much about the collectors themselves as about the historical period from which they collect.

Since toys are probably the most exhibited and most written about of all childhood artifacts, only two observations, one obvious and one usually ignored, will be made here about them.[6] The obvious is, that in the selection of toys, children have often been encouraged to follow the role models, the occupations, and the technological fads of their elders. Such toys have usually been advertised as being more appropriate for one sex than the other. Adult collectors, male and female, have been similarly attracted to such toys.[7]

They have not, however, been as thorough in saving what Sidney Brower labels "makeshift toys"; George Basalla calls "transformed objects"; Mac Barrick labels "folk toys"; or what might simply be called "kids' toys."[38] Such homemade or modified toys can be any object that a child continually delights in and uses as a means for deriving amusement or entertainment rather than as a means for accomplishing a set task, a specific educational objective (fig. 36), or a toy manufacturer's advertised goal. "Kids' toys" are often concrete proof of the material

Figure 36.
The Kindergarten Interior, The Women's Building, Philadelphia Centennial
Exhibition, 1876
Stereograph.
(Courtesy The Library of Congress, Division of Prints and Photographs)

culturist's dictum: "One man's trash is another's treasure." Of course, anyone who has ever watched a child (or been one) knows "kids' toys." Such artifacts may be among the few distinct authentic artifacts of childhood in that they are made, remade, remodelled, or renamed by children themselves.

Take, for example, a typical two- or three-pronged pitchfork commonly found on many nineteenth-century North American farmsteads. In a child's imagination, this agricultural tool can be not only a device for pitching hay, but also a horse to ride, a writing or drawing tool for marking on the ground, a boat to float down a rivulet, a javelin or spear to throw, or even another person ("a stick man") to befriend. In the past, as in the present, a plaything could be and was anything the mind imagined—for a moment, an hour, for months or years. To the bounty of nature, the nineteenth-century consumer and industrial revolutions added a vast material world from which children might craft their own toys or play objects: pie plates (probable prototype for the first Frisbee), key rings, tires, clothespins, coat hangers, tin cans, ball-point pens, bottle tops, rubber bands, and paper clips, paper cups made into rattles, metal washers used in tossing games, coins used for tabletop football, clotheslines cut down for jump ropes, broomsticks modified for bats in stickball games.

Some of these items have been modified by children in the course of play, others have not. Some of them researchers will be able to decipher and interpret; others will remain known and understood only by their original creators. We need to collect and study more of this childhood material culture. While some of it may prove highly idiosyncratic, enough of it may reveal patterns that will tell us as much about creativity, imagination and aesthetics as any of the manufactured or educational toys that predominate in most museum collections.[9]

Costume, after toys, is probably the second largest category of childhood material culture. The collectors of children's costume have gathered data that help us understand gender, age, class differentiation, rites of passage, and concern for healthy physical development in child rearing.[10]

Yet many childhood costume collections share the same evidential biases that costume historians and curators bemoan for adult clothing: far fewer male costumes than female ones; far more examples of formal clothing than work or play clothing; greater instances of specialty dress (for example, school uniforms, debutante dresses, and sailor suits) than everyday knock-about hand-me-downs. In material culture research, this illustrates the fecklessness of data survival.[11]

Private collections of childhood artifacts are also lacking in the material culture of nurture. Nursing bottles, feeding trays, eating utensils, processed baby foods, diapers, chamber pots, potty chairs, sanitary and toilet artifacts, and medical aids are not often found in such collections. Underrepresented as well are the artifacts of child discipline: rulers, whips, belts, rods, birches, or the infamous paddling "sticks" are found in few museum collections and fewer museum exhibitions.[12]

A third popular medium in the museum collecting of childhood is graphics, particularly photographs (see fig. 34). Postmortem daguerreotypes as well as Kodak Brownie snapshots are part of this extensive visual record. So, too, are the innumerable photographs of rites of passage, kinship patterns, parent-child relations, and school functions.[13]

While child photography will be analyzed again in the next section, "Exhibiting Childhood," two observations about this type of material culture are pertinent here. First, no child has lived long enough to comprehend fully the dangers and delights of recorded life. No child's experience has provided him or her with the time and the space that give one a true sense of the past, of moments lost forever or, antithetically, a developed sense of the future, of the inevitable process of aging and death. Therefore, unlike adults, children (until a certain age) face the camera largely innocent of all but the present moment and often with a startling purity of motive. This characteristic can be very useful in cultural explanation and historians might explore it more systematically than they have to date.[14] The photographer (usually an adult) behind the camera, however, is another case entirely. He or she invariably brings a fixed set of beliefs about the nature of childhood to the task of photographing children.

A second point that might be made concerning the relationship of photography and children is that the century of our expanded awareness of the latter (roughly 1840–1940) coincided with the century of the former's democratization in our culture. Perhaps this coincidence is causal. Could it be that the invention of the camera and its widespread use over the past hundred years has helped make us much more sensitive to the various stages of infancy, childhood, youth, and adolescence? As soon as the family photograph album encouraged us to marvel how much a young boy had grown between the ages of six and eight or how much a young girl had matured between thirteen and sixteen, did we not find the idea of childhood reinforced so strongly that we began to divide up and also chronologically expand this pre-adult stage of the life cycle?

Exhibiting Childhood

Photography has figured extensively in many past museum exhibitions of childhood. For example, a selection of artifacts and images of American children were displayed at the Women's Building at the 1876

Centennial Exposition in Philadelphia. Less than twenty years later, a separate Children's Building was designed for the Columbian Exposition in Chicago in 1893. At such international trade fairs, of course, children were also on display as advertising icons (figs. 37, 38), as potential consumers for the numerous child-specific objects (such as miniature tablewares, children's furniture, or ready-made clothing) and as culture totems in a highly sentimental age. For instance, Bertha L. Corbett's "Sunbonnet Babies" were but one of the numerous generic, turn-of-the-century stylized icons that became popular decorative elements of many domestic goods such as napkin rings, trivets, platters, and postcards.[15] Perhaps no one exploited this use of children-as-objects like Currier and Ives did in their two hundred lithograph images of children, depicting them on one hand as symbols of lost innocence in a Gilded Age and on the other, as James Russell Lowell expressed it in *The Changeling,* as an active force for godliness and reform.

Photographic firms and photographers also often exhibited children in these two ways. The George Eastman Company, for example, claimed that their cameras were so simple, even a child could "Push the Button" and they would do the rest. Brownie Cameras, capitalizing on the popularity of Palmer Coxe's amusing elves as well as suggesting the name of the camera's designer Frank Brownell, were developed largely for a pre-adolescent market. As a consequence of the enormous expansion of photography in the twentieth century, the modern child may be the target of the camera more than anyone. Almost every life moment can be captured; thus we have photos of children before birth, during birth, at birth, in the hospital, at home, in school, at play, at work.

American photographers such as Jacob Riis and Lewis Hine worked diligently that we would one day no longer see children at work in factories, mills, and mines (fig. 39); at "home" or "piece" work in tenements; or in selling goods and services in saloons, shops, and city streets. This child labor photography formed the core of various exhibitions during the Progressive era. In recent times, institutions such as the Brooklyn Museum, the New York Historical Society, and the Chicago Historical Society have mounted exhibitions, particularly of Hine's work, usually with special emphasis on his laboring children.[16]

In these exhibitions of the child-as-innocent-victim, early documentary photographers have resorted to an old documentary ploy: using the child as an instrument to stimulate adult indignation over a particular social evil and attempt to change it. No one used this reform technique better than the U.S. Government's Farm Security Administration (FSA) photographers of the Great Depression. This visual material culture has been used repeatedly since the 1930s to characterize our visions of that decade. Father may be out of work, out of town, and out of hope, but

Figure 37.
"Allen's Root Beer Extract for Making Home-Made Beer"
Trade card (ca. 1880). Charles E. Carter, pharmacist, Lowell,
Massachusetts.

Figure 38.
"Slicker Boy"
National Biscuit Company advertisement for Uneeda Biscuit (1888).
(Courtesy The National Biscuit Company)

Figure 39.
Lewis Hine (photographer), Workers at Singer Manufacturing Company
Entrance, South Bend, Indiana, ca. 1920
(Courtesy The Library of Congress, Division of Prints and Photographs)

mother and child are always together. This mother and child conceit, an ancient one in iconography, pervades this enormous corpus of childhood visual data as well as the museum exhibitions, catalogs, and other publications that have interpreted the FSA data.

Such imagery can be found in many American museum exhibitions. *Images of Childhood,* a 1977 show of popular daguerreotypes, prints, and photographs prepared by the Museum of Our National Heritage (Lexington, Massachusetts) documented the now familiar nineteenth-century transition of the child from a miniature adult to an innocent child at play. Susan Kismaric's *American Children,* mounted at the Museum of Modern Art (New York City, New York) in 1980, was a more ambitious use of photographs in childhood research and a more successful one. The photographs included in the catalog were presented in reversed chronological sequence. One sees them, therefore, as a pictorial record, viewed backward through time, enabling one to understand both children and photographers, especially how the latter reveal their own personal and cultural perspectives in various eras. At the same time the movement from past to present, an act comparable to looking at one's family album from the back to the front, evokes the memories of one's own childhood history and proves doubly revealing.

American Children emphasizes, as most museum exhibitions on American childhood do not, the life and times of twentieth-century children. The modern photography of Diane Arbus, Edward Weston, and Helen Levitt also provides us with valuable counterparts to the nineteenth-century work of Francis Benjamin Johnson, John Bullock, and Timothy O'Sullivan. Finally, this photographic exhibition displays an awareness of adolescent sexuality that is almost always completely ignored by most museums interested in childhood. In both Diane Arbus's and Emmet Gowing's photographs of adolescent couples, we are shown the beginnings of the male/female bond that presages their future and reveals the photographer's acknowledgment of burgeoning sexuality; in work by these two photographers the young boys attempt the postures of grown men, wrapping their arms around the girls in possession and protection. To make a further point, Godwin posed one couple before an automobile, the American symbol of social liberty and, on occasion, teenage sexual opportunity.[17]

In addition to temporary and permanent museum exhibitions devoted to children, numerous children's and youth museums presently exist in the United States. From the A.M. Chisholm Children's Museum in Minnesota to the Zigler Museum for Children in Louisiana, there exists a particularly American museological phenomenon worthy of attention in the study of American childhood. Yet few museum exhibitions or museum historians recognize the role that museums in general, and children's museums in particular, have played in the social, educational, and cultural history of the American child.[18]

The Brooklyn Children's Museum, often acclaimed as the first in the world, opened its doors in December 1899. Other American cities followed this innovation in museum theory and practice: Boston in 1913, Detroit in 1917, Indianapolis in 1925. Canada's first children's museum was the London Regional Museum opening in 1975. The real children's museum boom in America, however, can be closely correlated with the post–World War II baby boom. When Eleanor M. Moore wrote *Youth in Museums,* an early, classic, 1941 study in the otherwise barren terrain of children's museum history, only eight children's museums were housed in their own buildings—those in Boston, Brooklyn, Cambridge, Detroit, Duluth, Hartford, Indianapolis, and San Francisco. Now that number is well over fifty.[19]

The first four American children's museums, particularly their early history, philosophy, and exhibition techniques, reveal much about their use of childhood material culture and what it suggests about the museum interpretation of American children in the first quarter of the twentieth century. Although most American children's museums began without professional leadership or sizeable collections, behind each of these institutions was an aggressive, talented, often affluent, woman or cadre of women. Such women had visions of a children's museum as a necessary intermediary institution (like the school or the family) to improve the life of American young people who lived in a society that was increasingly becoming industrialized, commercialized, and urbanized. Not surprisingly, most of the early children's museums were (and still are) in urban settings. Among the first four, at least two—the Adams House in Brooklyn and the Cary Mansion in Indianapolis—were established first in old family homes, quaint domiciles with local history associations then thought appropriate for childhood nurture.

An interest in child psychology and progressive education theory can also be detected among American children's museum founders, especially among their directors and curators. For instance, Louise Condit, supervisor of education at the Brooklyn Children's Museum, was an ardent disciple of John Dewey. The first name of the Indianapolis Children's Museum was the Progressive Education Association and a "learning by doing" philosophy guided its early efforts. Close liaison in many children's museums was often maintained with many city school systems, with some children's museum curators seeing themselves as public school faculty and part of departments of public instruction.[20]

Most of the early collections of children's museums were the proverbial "cabinets of curiosities," mixtures of natural history, technological, and historical objects. However, early curators appear to have been more permissive in their tolerance of children handling the collections, a pioneering inquiry approach that we now call "hands-on" or "interactive learning" and an educational philosophy that one museum (the *Please Touch Museum* in Philadelphia) incorporates in its name. Unfortunately, to date, we have only one major institutional history of an American children's museum, The Children's Museum of Indianapolis, that explores the role of these early children's museums and their cultural aspirations.[21] What were their relationships with each other? What were their relationships with other contemporary institutions that also occasionally had museums and organizations such as settlement houses, boys and girls clubs, historical societies? In what areas, science, art, history, did they develop first and best? How did they relate to traditional museums? In what ways were they influenced, for example, in formulating their own organization, the American Association of Young Museums, by the larger museum community? In what way did they influence (for instance, with "hands-on exhibitions"?) mainstream museum practice? In short, the history of North American childhood would profit from a systematic examination of the history of childhood museums in their institutional and cultural context.

Researching Childhood

In addition to collecting and exhibiting the artifacts of childhood, a small group of scholars have been at work researching the history of childhood, particularly in the nineteenth century, as a subfield of their wider interests in literary, or psycho-, or social history. This cadre, largely based in North American universities and, in one sense, the last to take up the topic of childhood after private collectors and museum curators, has been principally concerned with the meaning of the extant documentary and statistical evidence in the interpretation of past childhood.[22] Only recently have a number of such historians turned to probing the explanatory potential of the things of the child.

The relationship of literature and childhood was among the first to be pursued both by literary scholars interested in what is written by, for, and about children as well as by social scientists and historians fascinated by the enormous outpouring of normative children's literature that the United States has produced from John Cotton's *Spiritual Milk for Boston Babies in Either England* (1656) to the latest edition of Benjamin Spock's *The Common Sense Book of Baby and Child Care* (1985).[23] The research of Ann McLeod, Margaret Maloney, Mary Rubio, and Barbara Harrison has greatly expanded our understanding of the special literary interest group that Virginia Haviland calls "the open-hearted audience."[24] Scholarship on children's literature now has achieved such an academic visibility in the United States that at Simmons College in Boston there is even a Center for the Study of Children's Literature leading to an M.A. degree in the speciality.

Research on children's playthings and playing has been organized for the last decade by The Association for the Anthropological Study of Play (TAASP). Published proceedings of these international meetings suggest that much hard work (or, is it just scholarly play?) is being done on play in a wide range of disciplines. The TAASP lists the research interests of its members as anthropology, physical education, psychology, recreation, history, pediatrics, folklore, dance, the arts, competitive athletics, ritual, kinesiology, learning research and development, film, political action, urbanization, archaeology, human kinetics, games, dramaturgy, fantasy, humor, symbolic play.

Bernard Mergen's *Play and Playthings* (1982), Helen Schwartzman's *Transformations: The Anthropology of Play* (1978), Brian Sutton-Smith's *Folk-Games of Children* (1972), and Alice Cheska's *Play as Context* (1981) typify current American research in the field of children's play, perhaps the most widely studied area of childhood research.[25] Mergen's book has a particularly useful chapter on the material culture of public play, especially on urban playgrounds and playground equipment.

Parallel with the social scientific studies of American childhood, an enterprise whose history extends back into the late nineteenth century in the United States, is the more recent work of the past two decades in the social history of childhood, particularly as it is manifested in family history and to a lesser extent, in women's history. Child rearing, for example, as studied by Philip Greven, John Demos, Alice Ryerson, and others, has been a major concern of historians monitoring the American family.[26] Those using material culture evidence explored various forms of child control (toys, chairs, playpens, harnesses, playgrounds), child foodways, and child educational toys.[27] In this context, however, still more research is needed on child toilet training, on non-parental child care (nannies, wet nurses, governesses, baby sitters), and the role of children's pets in child life.

Social historians interested in childhood also need to research motherhood and fatherhood in more systematic ways than they have. Motherhood has received attention, but American fatherhood has only begun to be given historical evaluation. J. Jill Suitor's study, "Husbands' Participation in Childbirth: A Nineteenth-Century Phenomenon," and Charles Strikeland's "The Child-Rearing Practices of Bronson Alcott" are examples of this type of research.[28] On the topic of fathers, we might ask what types of artifacts and activities do they choose for their daughters as opposed to sons? Has this pattern been true throughout North American history? Do rural fathers relate differently to sons and daughters than urban fathers?

Scholars have largely neglected the material culture history of rural childhood. Differences as to education, recreation, and work between rural and urban child life prompt us to recognize that during the period 1820–1920 there were various childhoods in North America—various as to ethnic background, economic class, religious persuasion, and geographic region. Such comparative study also suggests that historians might explore, with a special research effort devoted to the rural young, whether or not the currently held hypothesis that sees the adult perception of North American children as something of a triple-stage metamorphosis (a miniature adult in the eighteenth century, an innocent child needing nurture in the nineteenth century, and a special and separate youngster in the twentieth century)[29] needs revision for certain segments of the rural adult and child populations during certain historical periods. Could it be that rural children, at least prior to the early twentieth century, were less likely to be viewed in this way? Might their involvement in fewer formal educational activities and more "play" times relating closely to work (4-H; Future Farmers), their recognized status as a responsible part of their farm family's economy, and their earlier (compared to urban middle-class children) full-time entry into the adult world of work and worry have meant that many American rural parents regarded their offspring at the end of the nineteenth century in a fashion not all that different from American parents at the end of the seventeenth century?

Another way of asking this question would be, to use sociologist David Reisman's terms, have there been both "inner-directed" and "outer-directed children" as there have been adults? If so, how can the historian probe this inner life, this psychohistory of his or her subjects? What can we ever know of children's personal or private history other than what we see when we hold them up to us and usually see but ourselves writ small?

The psychohistory of the North American child has yet to be, and may never be, written. Historians such as David Potter, Peter Gay, and Michael Kammen, given their interest in social psychology, child training, sexual initiation, and the life cycle, urge us, however, to attempt such history if we are to approximate a more comprehensive understanding of past childhood experience.[30]

Admittedly one of the major drawbacks in researching the private, as opposed to the public, history of childhood is the paucity of child-generated sources. Most historical data on childhood is either adult-generated or adult-controlled evidence. As such, it is prone to exaggerate human efficacy in the past, a common liability of material culture evidence.[31] Yet certain material culture may help us partially explore a child's inner worlds (fig. 40). Perhaps research investigations of their personal environments (such as private rooms, basement or attic domains, or special closet enclaves) that the child can modify may prove revealing. There are also artifacts in addition to folk or "kid's toys" mentioned earlier that children personally manufacture—clubhouses, hideaways, tree-houses, and other special places off limits to adults. In a new study of California vernacular architecture, *Home Sweet Home,* several architectural historians examine such data, much of it highly transient and ephemeral, but also informative and insightful in a way that offers clues as to how we might better understand past and present children's sense of space and self.[32]

In addition to the neglect of the private past of childhood, historians have not adequately researched its deviant underside. Middle-class reform crusades to control rowdiness, tobacco and alcohol use, truancy, and other misdemeanors among children are being documented.[33] But the nineteenth-century history of the urban street gang, the unwed teenage mother, the physically disabled, or the hardened juvenile criminal remains to be written. Nor should we forget adult deviancy with regard to children. What do we know of the forms of child abuse, sexual harass-

Figure 40.
George Washington Marks, *Young Girl at Door,* ca. 1845
Oil on canvas.
(Courtesy The Collections of the Henry Ford Museum and Greenfield Village)

Figure 41.
"Miss Sherry's (Keesler) Kindergarten Class," 1988
Red Barn Learning Center, Granger, Indiana.
(Photograph by Stacy Seggerman. Courtesy the photographer)

ment, and commercial exploitation to which nineteenth-century children were subjected? Although grisly and unsavory subjects, they are nevertheless part of the historical record. Some work has been done—Sharon Burston's plotting of infanticide rates and Myra Glenn's survey of the form and extent of corporal punishment—but numerous facets of past domestic violence are still ignored, even by many social historians.[34]

Finally, social historians are only beginning to study the separation, segmentation, and segregation of childhood—a trend that begins in the nineteenth century in institutions such as children's aid societies, the YMCA and the YWCA, the Boy Scouts and the Girl Scouts and a social phenomenon that has accelerated throughout the twentieth century.[35] The material culture record of this historical trend is abundant: children's kindergartens, children's museums, children's prisons, asylums, and hospitals, children's chautauquas, children's beauty pageants, children's athletic leagues and sports clubs, children's courts, children's radio, television, and film, and of course, children's playgrounds, soap-box derbies, photo studios, day-care centers (fig. 41), and camps.[36]

In addition to this brief review of the material culture collection, exhibition, and interpretation of childhood that has been done and might be done, can we point to any other reasons in attempting to explain why an increasing number of researchers are presently intrigued with the history of North American childhood?

Perhaps part of the answer is personal in that many scholars recognized the insight of the Dutch historian Johan Huizinga who wrote so eloquently of the human species as *Homo Ludens*—man, the player. Huizinga thought much of human creativity, society, and history could be viewed as play, and to many at times, childhood seems to be a time of almost pure play.[37]

Another part of the answer is professional in that many of us have either been trained in or been seriously influenced by social history and its interest in the history of powerless groups. Children have often been such a group, not only in their physical, economic, and legal dependency but also in their historical invisibility, that is, their inability to write or tell their own history. Many scholars seek to rectify this oversight. They wish to make a research contribution to the history of childhood and to integrate that story into the larger epic of the history of society.

Finally, the artifacts of childhood are an especially problematic type of evidence in general material culture studies.[38] The physical evidence of past childhood, flawed as it is by the fecklessness in collection, romanticism in exhibition, and gender and age bias in generation, offers material culture researchers a special methodological challenge in their quest for possibilities and liabilities of artifacts as resources for culture inquiry.

Notes

1. For Crèvecour's discussion of the interrelation of the study of childhood and the study of culture, see *Letters from an American Farmer and Sketches from 18th-Century America: More Letters from an American Farmer,* ed. H. L. Bourding, R. H. Gabriel, and S. T. Williams (New Haven, Conn.: Yale University Press, 1963), 121. Surveys of the subject based, in part, on this methodological premise include: Philippe Aries, *Centuries of Childhood: A Social History of Family Life* (New York: Vintage Books, 1962); Anita Schorsch, *Images of Childhood: An Illustrated Social History* (New York: Mayflower Books, 1979); Bernard Wishy, *The Child and the Republic: The Dawn of Modern American Child Nurture* (Philadelphia: University of Pennsylvania Press, 1968); Sandra Brant and Elissa Cullman, *Small Folk: A Celebration of Childhood in America* (New York: E. D. Dutton, 1980); John Sommerville, *The Rise and Fall of Childhood* (Beverly Hills, Calif.: Sage Publications, 1982).

2. A distinction is often made between the *child* (pl. children), a biological person who has always been part of the human experience, and *childhood,* a comparatively recent cultural invention marked by an increasing preoccupation of adults with special needs of children, by a growing belief that children were appreciably different in personality from adults, and by a gradual separation, temporally and spatially, of the activities and artifacts of childhood from those of adults. For refinement of the distinction, consult Michael Kammen, "Changing Perceptions of the Life Cycle in American Thought and Culture," *Massachusetts Historical Society Proceedings* 91 (1979): 35–66.

3. William T. Alderson, "Right from the Start: The Strong Museum Opens Its Doors," *Museum News* G1:2 (November/December 1982): 49–53; William C. Ketchum, ed., *The Collections of the Margaret Woodbury Strong Museum* (Rochester, N.Y.: The Margaret Woodbury Strong Museum, 1982), 48–53; Louis Hertz, *The Toy Collector* (New York: Funk and Wagnalls, 1969).

4. Harvey Green, *The Light of the Home: An Intimate View of Women in Victorian America* (New York: Pantheon, 1983); also see Ann Douglas, *The Feminization of American Culture* (New York: A. A. Knopf, 1978).

5. Pauline Flick, *Discovering Toys and Toy Museums* (Tring, England: Shire Publications, 1971); William S. Ayres, *The Warner Collector's Guide to American Toys* (New York: Warner Books, 1981); Inez and Marshall McClintock, *Toys in America* (Washington, D.C.: Public Affairs Press, 1961); Karen Hewitt and Louise Roomet, eds., *Educational Toys in America: 1800 to Present* (Burlington, Vt.: Robert Hall Fleming Museum, 1979).

6. Useful bibliographies of the enormous literature on toys are Bernard Mergen, "Games and Toys," in *Handbook of American Popular Culture,* ed. Thomas Inge (Westport, Conn.: Greenwood Press, 1980), 163–90. Two other studies by Mergen are valuable in this context: "The Discovery of Children's Play," *American Quarterly* 27 (October 1975): 399–420; and "Toys and American Culture: Objects as Hypotheses," *Journal of American Culture* 3.4 (Winter 1980): 743–51.

7. Carroll Pursell, Jr., "Toys, Technology, and Sex Roles in America, 1920–40," in *Dynamos and Virgins Revisited: Women and Technological Change in History,* ed. Martha Trescott (Metuchen, N.J.: Scarecrow Press, 1979), 252–67; Donald W. Ball, "Toward a Sociology of Toys: Inanimate Objects, Socialization, and the Demography of the Doll World," *Sociological Quarterly* 8 (1967): 447–58. For a discussion of the historical development of the "Barbie Doll" and its role in socializing children to certain sex roles, see Ronald Marchese, "Material Culture and Artifact Classification," *Journal of American Culture* 3.4 (Winter 1980): 605–19.

8. Sidney Brower, "Tools, Toys, Masterpieces, Mediums," *Landscape* 19.2 (January 1975): 28–32; George Basalla, "Transformed Utilitarian Objects," *Winterthur Portfolio* 17.4 (Winter 1982): 183–202; Mac E. Barrick, "Folk Toys," *Pennsylvania Folklife* 29.1 (Autumn 1979): 27–34; Janet Holmes and Loet Vos, "Children's Toys in the Nineteenth Century," joint session at Ontario Museum Association's "Children and Changing Perspectives of Childhood in the Nineteenth Century" Conference, Toronto, Canada, 30 January–2 February 1985.

9. Examples of beginning research in the topic include: Mary and Herbert Knapp, *One Potato, Two Potato . . . The Secret Education of American Children* (New York: Norton, 1976), 225–31; Fred Ferretti, *The Great American Book of Sidewalk, Stoop, Dirt, Curb, and Alley Games* (New York: Workmann, 1975); Robert Cochran, "The Interlude of Game: A Study of Washers," *Western Folklore* 38.7 (April 1979): 71–82, and Jerome L. Singer, *The Child's World of Make-Believe: Experimental Studies of Imaginative Play* (New York: Academic Press, 1973).

10. Elizabeth Ewing, *History of Children's Costume* (New York: Charles Scribners & Sons, 1977); Linda Martin, *The Way We Wore: Fashion Illustrations of Children's Wear, 1870–1970* (New York: Charles Scribners & Sons, 1978); Karin Calvert, "Children in American Family Portraiture, 1670 to 1810," *William and Mary Quarterly* 39.1 (January 1982): 87–113.

11. On the ramifications of this problem in general material culture research, see Thomas J. Schlereth, "Material Culture and Cultural Research" in *Material Culture, A Research Guide* (Lawrence: University Press of Kansas, 1985), 14–15.

12. Scholars interested in these usually neglected artifacts include Karin Calvert, "Cradle to Crib: The Revolution in Nineteenth-Century Children's Furniture," in *A Century of Childhood, 1820–1920* (Rochester, N.Y.: The Margaret Woodbury Strong Museum, 1984), 33–64; Felicity Nowell-Smith, "Feeding the Nineteenth-Century Baby: Implications for Museum Collections," *Material History Bulletin* 21 (Spring 1985): 15–24; and Hilary Russell, "Training, Restraining, and Sustaining: Infant and Child Care in the Late Nineteenth Century," *Material History Bulletin* 21 (Spring 1985): 35–50.

13. On representative studies of child photography, see Alison Mager, ed., *Children of the Past in Photographic Portraits: An Album with 165 Prints* (New York: Dover, 1982); Old Dartmouth Historical Society, *Images of Childhood: An Exhibition of Pictures and Objects from Nineteenth-Century New Bedford* (New Bedford, Mass.: Old Dartmouth Historical Society, 1977); Rosamond O. Humm, *Children in America: A Study of Images and Attitudes* (Atlanta: High Museum of Art, 1978).

14. The interrelation of children and photography is tentatively explored in Josephine Gear, *The Preserve of Childhood, Adult Artifice and Construction: Images of Late-Nineteenth Century American Childhood* (Binghamton, N.Y.: University Art Gallery–SUNY, 1982), and Susan Kismaric, *American Children* (New York and Boston: New York Graphic Society, 1980), 5–11.

15. On the nineteenth-century commercial use of child imagery, see Mary Lynn Stevens Heininger, "Children, Childhood, and Change in America, 1820–1920" (Rochester, N.Y.: The Margaret Woodbury Strong Museum, 1984), 23–28.

16. Naomi and Walter Rosenblum, *America and Lewis Hine: Photographs, 1904–1940* (New York: Aperture, 1977); Naomi Rosenblum, *The Lewis W. Hine Document* (Brooklyn: The Brooklyn Museum, 1977); Mara Gutman, *Lewis W. Hine, 1876–1940: Two Perspectives* (New York: Grossman Publishers, 1974). Dover Publications has reprinted the documentary work of Riis and Hine as well as other reform photography collections such as *New York Street Kids: Photographs Selected by the Children's Aid Society.*

17. Susan Kismaric, *American Children* (New York and Boston: New York Graphic Society, 1980), 24, 34.

18. Gregory G. Baeker, "The Emergence of Children's Museums in the United States, 1899–1970," Master of Museum Studies Thesis (Department of Museum Studies, University of Toronto, 1981) could serve as a research model to rectify this neglect.

19. Eleanor M. Moore, *Youth in Museums* (Philadelphia: University of Pennsylvania Press, 1941). For a helpful finding aid on the topic, see Office of Museum Programs, *Children in Museums, A Bibliography* (Washington, D.C.: The Smithsonian Institution, 1979); for an interpretation of the contemporary growth in children's museums, see Eliane Gurian, "Children's Museums: An Overview," unpublished paper, Washington, D.C., 1984, 9–12.

20. On the interconnection between developments in child psychology, progressive education, and children's museums, see R. S. Peter, ed., *John Dewey Reconsidered* (London: Routledge and Kegan Paul, 1977) and A. E. Parr, "Why Children's Museums?" *Curator* 3.3 (1960): 217–36.

21. Nancy Kriplen, *Keep an Eye on That Mummy* (Indianapolis: The Children's Museum, 1982).

22. Examples of this orientation are found in Robert H. Brenner, ed., *Children and Youth in America, A Documentary History,* 3 vols. (Cambridge: Harvard University Press, 1970–72) and David Rothman, "Documents in Search of a Historian: Toward a History of Childhood and Youth in America," in *The Family in History,* ed. Theodore Raab and Theodore Rotberg (New York: Harper & Row, 1978), 179–89.

23. R. Gordon Kelly has done the most comprehensive finding aids to both approaches to American children's literature; see his chapter, "Children's Literature," in *Handbook of American Popular Culture,* ed. Thomas Inge (Westport, Conn.: Greenwood Press, 1982), 49–76, and his reference work, *Children's Periodicals of the United States* (Westport, Conn.: Greenwood Press, 1985).

24. Anne Scott McLeod, *A Moral Tale: Children's Fiction and American Culture, 1820–1860* (Hamden, Conn.: Anchor Books, 1975); Barbara Harrison, "Why Study Children's Literature?" *Quarterly Journal of the Library of Congress* 38.4 (1981): 243–53; Margaret Maloney, "Save All Your Rags: Children's Literature in the Nineteenth Century," and Mary Rubio, "The Child in Literature: *Anne of Green Gables* as a Case Study" (Papers delivered at the Ontario Museum Association Heritage Conference '85 "Children and Changing Perspectives of Childhood in the Nineteenth Century," Toronto, Ontario, 30 January–2 February 1985).

25. Bernard Mergen, *Play and Playthings* (Westport, Conn.: Greenwood Press, 1982); Helen Schwartzman, *Transformations: The Anthropology of Play* (New York: Plenum Press, 1977); Brian Sutton-Smith, *The Folk-Games of Children* (Austin: University of Texas Press, 1972); Alice Cheska's *Play as Context* (West Point, N.Y.: Leisure Press, 1981).

26. Philip Greven, *The Protestant Temperament: Patterns of Child-Rearing, Religious Experience, and the Self in Early America* (New York: Oxford University Press, 1977); John Demos, *A Little Commonwealth: Family Life in Plymouth Colony* (New York: Oxford University Press, 1976); Alice J. Ryerson, "Medical Advice on Child Rearing, 1550–1900," *Harvard Educational Review* 31 (1961): 302–23. A popular treatment of the topic is Mary Cable, *The Little Darlins: A History of Child Rearing in America* (New York: Charles Scribners & Sons, 1975).

27. Calvert, "Cradle to Crib," 33–64; Mergen, *Play and Playthings,* 103–24; Roy Rosenzweig, "Middle-Class Parks and Working-Class Play: The Struggle over Recreational Space in Worcester, Massachusetts, 1870–1910," *Radical History Review* 21 (Winter 1979–80): 31–46; Hewitt and Roomet, *Educational Toys in America,* 40–60.

28. J. Jill Suitor, "Husbands' Participation in Childbirth: A Nineteenth-Century Phenomenon," *Journal of Family History* 6.3 (1981): 278–93; Charles Strickland, "A Transcendentalist Father: The Child-Rearing Practices of Bronson Alcott," *History of Childhood Quarterly* 1 (Summer 1973): 4–51.

29. A popular summary of this interpretive model is found in J. H. Plumb's overview, "The Great Change in Children," *Horizon* 13.1 (Winter 1971): 6–12.

30. David Potter, *People of Plenty: Economic Abundance and the American Character* (Chicago: University of Chicago Press, 1954); Peter Gay, *The Bourgeois Experience: Victoria to Freud: Education of the Senses* (New York: Oxford University Press, 1984); Kammen, "Changing Perceptions of the Cycle," 40–42. Also of use on the historical

life cycle in the New England context are: Peter Gregg Slater, *Children in the New England Mind in Death and in Life* (Hamden, Conn.: Archon Books, 1977) and Ross W. Beales, Jr., "In Search of the Historical Child: Miniature Adulthood and Youth in Colonial New England," *American Quarterly* 27 (1975): 378–98.

31.   Schlereth, "Material Culture and Cultural Explanation," in *Material Culture, A Research Guide* (Lawrence: University Press of Kansas, 1985), 16–17.

32.   Barbara and Arlan Coffman, "Building by the 'Little Folks': Early Architectural Construction Toys in America" and James Volkert, et al., "Rough Housing" in *Home Sweet Home: American Vernacular Architecture,* ed. Charles W. Moore, Kathryn Smith, and Peter Becker (New York: Rizzoli, 1983), 54–62, 63–69. M. Lynne Struthers Swanich, *Children and Architecture: Play Needs—A Checklist of Sources,* Vance Bibliographies, Architecture Series A 278 (Monticello, Ill.: Vance Bibliographies, n.d.) is a valuable finding aid for literature on children's uses of space. Also see Mergen, *Play and Playthings,* 81–102.

33.   Pioneering works on childhood deviancy include: Joseph M. Hawes, *Children in Urban Society: Juvenile Delinquency in 19th-Century America* (New York: Oxford University Press, 1971); David Rothman, *The Discovery of the Asylum: Social Order and Disorder in the New Republic* (Boston: Little, Brown, 1971); Stanley M. Schultz, *The Culture Factory: Boston Public Schools, 1789–1860* (New York: Oxford University Press, 1973); Steven L. Schlossman, *Love and the American Delinquent: The Theory and Practice of Progressive Juvenile Justice, 1825–1920* (Chicago: University of Chicago Press, 1977).

34.   Sharon Ann Burston, "Babies in the Well: An Underground Insight into Deviant Behavior in Eighteenth-Century Philadelphia," *Pennsylvania Magazine of History and Biography* 106.2 (1982): 151–86; Myra C. Glenn, *Campaigns against Corporal Punishment: Prisoners, Sailors, Women, and Children in Antebellum America* (Albany: State University of New York Press, 1984); Barbara Finkelstein, "In Fear of Childhood: Relationships between Parents and Teachers in Nineteenth-Century America," *History of Childhood Quarterly* 3.3 (Winter 1976): 321–27; Howard Tolley, *Children and War: Political Socialization to International Conflict* (New York: Teachers College Press, 1973); Neil Postman, *The Disappearance of Childhood* (New York: Dell, 1984).

35.   A sampling of research on the organization of childhood would include: David I. Macleod, *Building Character in the American Boy: The Boy Scouts, YMCA, and Their Forerunners, 1870–1920* (Madison: University of Wisconsin, 1984); Martha Saxton, "The Best Girl Scout of Them All," *American Heritage* 33.4 (June/July 1982): 38–46; Dominick Cavallo, *Muscles and Morals: Organized and Urban Reforms, 1800–1920* (Philadelphia: University of Pennsylvania Press, 1981).

36.   Mergen, *Play and Playthings,* 81–138; Patricia Schaelchin, " 'Working for the Good of the Community': Rest Haven Preventorium for Children," *Journal of San Diego History* 29 (Spring 1983): 96–114; Barbara Finkelstein, "Uncle Sam and the Children: A History of Government Involvement in Child-Rearing," *Review of Journal of Philosophy and the Social Sciences* 3.2 (1978–79): 139–53; Daniel T. Rodgers, "Socializing Middle-Class Children: Institutions, Fables, and Work Values in Nineteenth-Century America," *Journal of Social History* 13: 354–67; David J. Rothman, *The Discovery of the Asylum;* Joseph F. Rett, *Rites of Passage: Adolescence in America, 1790 to the Present* (New York: Basic Books, 1977); Carol T. Williams, *The Dream*

beside Me: The Movies and Children of the Forties (Rutherford, N.J.: Fairleigh Dickinson University Press, 1980).

37.   Johan Huizinga, *Homo Ludens: A Study of the Play-Element in Culture* (Boston: Beacon Press, 1955).

38.   For a review of the general methodological problems in material culture research see Thomas J. Schlereth, "Errors in Material Culture Explanation," *Material Culture* 17.1 (Spring 1985): 107–14.

Figure 42.
John Neagle (1796–1860), *Pat Lyon at the Forge*, 1826–27
Oil on canvas.
(Henry M. And Zoë Oliver Sherman Fund, courtesy Museum of Fine Arts, Boston)

4

Artisans in the New Republic:
A Portrait from Visual Evidence

In an oblique way this modest overview harkens back to my doctoral training and dissertation topic. In the 1960s, I thought I would always be a student of the eighteenth century, particularly the trans-Atlantic Enlightenment centered in the Philadelphia of Benjamin Franklin, the artisan printer, in the Edinburgh of David Hume, the cosmopolitan *philosophe,* and in the Paris of Denis Diderot, the impresario of the *Encyclopédie.*

Because of this background work in colonial America and because of my new interest in artifactual evidence, Stephanie Wolf, then coordinator of the Winterthur Program in Early American Culture and now in the department of history at the University of Pennsylvania, asked me to give the opening lecture at a Winterthur Museum conference on "The Craftsman in Early America" in 1979. My lecture, titled "Artisans and Craftsmen: A Historical Perspective," was published in the conference proceedings, *The Craftsman in Early America,* ed. Ian M. G. Quimby (New York: W. W. Norton, 1984), 34–61.

Another colonial historian, Howard Rock, whose *Artisans of the New Republic: The Tradesmen of New York City in the Age of Jefferson* (New York: New York University Press, 1979) I cited in my lecture, attended the Winterthur conference. He later invited me to join him in a related research project, a documentary history of the New York artisan. I was asked to prepare a final chapter for a book assessing appropriate visual resources that would parallel the verbal data Howard was assembling. As the book moved through the slow process of editorial review and revision, the word proved mightier than the image. The publishers purged the artifact chapter and Howard had to cut the number of his documents in half. Howard's study appeared as *The New York City Artisan, 1790–1825: A Documentary History* (Albany: SUNY Press, 1989). My essay found another life in the journal *Material Culture.* A slightly expanded version appears here.

Assorted birthmarks betray this essay's genesis. Its strict geographical concentration on the New York City craftsman circumscribes focus; two New York urban celebrations—the 1787 constitutional festivities and America's first world's fair in 1853—frame its chronology. At first I hoped to include over fifty graphics to give

This article originally appeared in *Material Culture* 20.1 (Spring 1989): 1–32.

my iconographical survey a greater empirical basis, but other editorial decisions reduced the number to the fourteen reproduced here.

Learning more about graphic forms and conventions in the eighteenth century meant I returned to Diderot's *Encyclopédie* with a more skeptical perspective than when I first used it in my dissertation and my book on *The Cosmopolitan Ideal.* Of course, in that earlier research I only had eyes for the verbal, not the visual; a re-looking showed me several evidential flaws in these otherwise superb examples of the engraver's art and printer's skill.

The lesson has not been lost in related projects. In my forthcoming *Transformations* volume, I play close attention to what Sean Wilentz calls "the theatrics of craft" as manifested in the first (1883) celebration of Labor Day. Howard Rubenstein's National Museum of American History exhibition, *Symbols of American Labor,* later a traveling SITES (Smithsonian Institution Traveling Exhibition Service) show, taught me much. Workers' dress also required investigation, and here I profited from Claudia Kidwell's *Suiting Everybody: The Democratization of Clothing in America*: (Washington, D.C.: Smithsonian Institution Press, 1981); Ricki Dru, *The First Blue Jeans* (New York: 1978), and Jonathan Prude's "The Uniform of Labor: Some Thoughts on the Changing Meaning of Occupational Costume in Nineteenth-Century America," presented to the Delaware Seminar in Material Culture Studies (Newark: University of Delaware Department of American Civilization) in the fall of 1984. My preliminary research on white-collar worker dress is found in the next chapter.

This working paper, while concentrated on the artifacts of artisans' personal, working, and communal life, raises two other questions important in material culture research. Often in the fetish we make of finished things or the hero worship we accord individual artisans, we forget that in pre-industrial times craftsmen often spent as much (or more) time repairing objects for clients as in making them. This may be less so in our present age of planned obsolescence, but perhaps students of contemporary material culture should also investigate the work of a service corps of uniformed men and women who repair our appliances and automobiles, computers and cameras.

In studying times past and present we also need to examine not only the acquisition and use of goods, but their storage and disposal. Here mention is made of artisan venues and auctions (which sold new as well as used goods), but we need to know more about warehousing and advertising. We also should investigate attic and basement storage, recyclers of charity goods like the Salvation Army, and Goodwill Industries, and the Society of St. Vincent De Paul, and purveyors of profitable goods in consignment businesses and pawn shops.

Artisans assumed important roles in the New York City festivities celebrating the adoption of the U.S. Constitution in 1788. In one parade, the city's shipwrights constructed floats mounted on wheels and outfitted to look like full-rigged vessels. Blacksmith shops atop wagons carried working smiths toiling at their anvils and forge fires. Carpenters, instrument-makers, and printers demonstrated to all who lined the parade route the manual and muscular dimensions of their crafts. The Society

Figure 43.
Pewterers' Flag
Silk banner carried by the Society of Pewterers of New York City in Federal
procession (July 23, 1788).
(Courtesy The New-York Historical Society, New York City)

of Pewterers proudly carried aloft an ornately painted silk banner on which they depicted their society's heraldry, its motto ("Solid and Pure"), and an illustration of pewterers at work (fig. 43).[1] The moving, three-dimensional panorama suggested what today we would call outdoor living history.

Three score years later another artifact extravaganza took place in New York City. In 1853 the New York Crystal Palace Exhibition of Arts, Sciences, and Manufactures, America's first world's fair, opened just south of the Croton Reservoir. The building itself, a product of the vastly expanded foundry, forge, and glass-making industries contained an enormous array of machines—machines that now did much of the work that artisans had previously done by hand. The Corliss steam engines, Colt pistols, Thomas brass clocks, and Singer sewing machines on display in 1853 signaled a new way of making things. Machines now played a significant role in each of these manufactures. President Franklin Pierce opened the fair, but the many artisans who had constructed the fair site and crafted the objects on display were not, as Horace Greeley observed, invited to share in any appropriate or official way in the inaugural ceremonies.[2] Their products and processes were celebrated, but not their persons. By the 1850s, industrialization had begun its impact, with mechanization to extend its influence and capitalism to expand its domain. Despite initial attempts at union organization, political activity, and craft solidarity, American laborers in 1853 did not exert the collective identity they had exerted in 1787. It would be another thirty years before such consciousness would reassert itself and then in a still different economic environment.

To learn more about the person, place, and politics of New York artisans in antebellum America, I seek in this essay—deliberately subtitled "a portrait"—to examine their role in American history as depicted in the material culture evidence they left behind.[3] One can say "they" in a double sense because the visual data that support this analysis were made by and for eighteenth- and nineteenth-century artisans. The portrait drawn here of the artisan in the early republic is something of a triptych. In the first frame, we are most interested in the artisan as an individual *artiste,* a person associated with a certain skill which, in turn, contributes to his special identity and personality. In the middle view, it is how he practices his *artisanry* by means of his mental and manual acumen that concerns us. The third perspective focuses on the artisan as a historical *actor* within his society, principally as a citizen. In sum, the following thus might be seen as moving from the analysis of individual personality ("The Artifacts of Personal Life"), to that of craft identity ("The Artifacts of Work Life"), to that of collective identity ("The Artifacts of Communal Life").

Artifacts of Personal Life

In colonial sources as well as in much contemporary scholarship, the terms "artisan" and "craftsman" are often used synonymously. To complicate the issue still further, one finds the designations "mechanic" and "tradesman" in both eighteenth- and nineteenth-century parlance and twentieth-century book titles. It has been suggested that there is a progression of usage: that "artisan" was accorded more popularity in the early eighteenth century, that "craftsman" was continually in vogue from the eighteenth century onward, and that "mechanic" gained ascendancy in the late eighteenth and early nineteenth centuries.[4]

Nineteenth-century mechanics in northern cities, suggests Alfred Young, drew a distinction between themselves and those below them by using the terms "mechanics" and "laborers." Outside the skilled system there were, argues Young, large numbers of semiskilled wage workers: merchant seamen, the largest single group; stevedores; and common laborers. There was also a large cadre of truckmen and cartmen, licensed movers who owned their own carts and horses. Lower still on the hierarchy were indentured servants, fewer in number by the 1780s. At the very bottom of this economic grouping were black slaves, some skilled, most household servants.[5]

Since no consensus presently exists among modern scholars regarding the four terms artisan, craftsman, tradesman, and mechanic, I will refer to each of the four in this essay. I will, however, most frequently say "artisan" since I wish to emphasize the use of artifacts in my historical interpretation of this group.[6]

Personal portraits are one resource for ascertaining some understanding of artisan life. More painted likenesses of colonial and early national period artisans survive than one might suspect, but they are still quite rare when compared to portraits of upper-class individuals. Commissioning a personal portrait was usually considered a prerogative reserved for merchants, professionals, and government officials.

Paul Revere is probably the most famous colonial artisan, and his likeness has been rendered by several of his fellow artists including Gilbert Stuart and John S. Copley. Perhaps most well known of these formal portraits is Copley's *Paul Revere* (fig. 44). Here we look in on Revere, the master craftsman, holding a silver teapot that he has made, seemingly pondering the final artistic design before taking up an engraving tool to finish the masterpiece. Copley has included in the painting several of the tools commonly used by the engraver. We can also partially envision both Revere as an artisan at work (that is, with his leather, sand-filled engraving cushion, and his burin and needle) and the artisan as worker (that is, Revere in a simple body shirt and unpowdered hair).

Unsigned formal portraits are the exception rather than the rule among those that survive of artisans. Most are of the well known by the well known. Portraiture evidence, understandably, also tends to favor certain types of artisans: goldsmiths as illustrated by John Singleton Copley's *Nathaniel Hurd;* printers as represented in the innumerable portraits of Benjamin Franklin; and architects and artists as illustrated by John Neagle's *William Strickland* and Charles Willson Peale's *Gilbert Stuart.* Thomas McCary, a New York City painter and glazier, achieved both a self-portrait and a self-advertisement in designing his trade card, which displayed him at his easel with palette in hand and ready for hire.[7]

Portraits are also primarily of master craftsmen and not of journeymen, much less of apprentices. Hence, formal artisan portraiture tells us little of the interrelations among different strata of craftsmen, the complex processes of craft production, or even the nature of the final products of the craftman's work. The portraits do, however, hint at when the artisan has arrived in early American society in terms of economic

Figure 44.
John Singleton Copley, *Paul Revere*, 1768–70
Oil on canvas.
*(Gift of Joseph W., William B., and Edward H. R. Revere,
courtesy Museum of Fine Arts, Boston)*

status. They are artifacts of acceptance and a degree of affluence. For example, Patrick (Pat) Lyon commissioned John Neagle to paint his portrait (see fig. 42) in 1826–27 in order to symbolize Lyon's rise from being a typical blacksmith, who had once been incarcerated on charges of false accusation in the city's Walnut Street Prison (which Lyon had Neagle include in the top left of the portrait) to the position of successful businessman by the end of his career.[8]

When one adds the crafts of lithography and photography—two visual media introduced in the early nineteenth century—to the visual evidence of paintings, woodcuts, and engravings, the number of individual artisans expands considerably. For example, we learn much about the dress and deportment of butcher Charles Brown (fig. 45) from an image done by water-colorist Nicolino V. Calyo about 1840. The careful observer can ascertain something of the spatial dimensions of Brown's market stall, his carving tools, and even the types of meat cuts favored by consumers in antebellum New York.

With the introduction of the daguerreotype process into America by New York artist and inventor Samuel F. B. Morse in 1839, a new democratic art form suddenly existed for documenting American life. Often thought of as a craft, this photographic process made image making more widely available to more ranks of society. Bakers in New Orleans, tolemakers in New England, miners in California, and cabinetmakers in New York had their pictures "taken," and consequently we have their mirror images to scrutinize for information and insight.[9]

For example, the glass-plate ambrotype of a young apprentice carpenter (see fig. 158) provides just such an opportunity. In addition to his armful of several basic wood-working tools—claw hammer, flat-edge chisel, crank-handled wood bit brace, and cross-cut saw—we acquire a vivid picture of the artisan's working attire. Dressed in a tam-o'-shanter hat, work blouse with tie, and corduroy coveralls with leather leg protectors, the craftsman has even converted two tools of his trade (note the three-inch wood screws) to act as substitute buttons or buckles for his bib overalls.

Symbols of craft identity are also evident in the variety of markings that artisans left directly on products in the form of maker's marks or maker's labels. While these self-markings are rare, when they do appear they remind us of the person behind the product. A stamped or branded mark has something of a personal signature about it. A printed label, while usually entailing the collaboration of other craftsmen such as an engraver and a printer, may also often betray a personal touch. For example, Samuel Prince, "a New York joyner," used a label that also identified his shop, appropriately, as "At the Sign of the Chest of Drawers," located in Cart and Horse Street.

Figure 45.
Nicolino V. Calyo, *The Butcher,* ca. 1840
Watercolor drawing.
(Courtesy Museum of the City of New York)

With advances in the printer's technology came another medium, the trade card, by which an artisan could proclaim his identity and promote his wares. Trade cards were used in various ways. Often they doubled as maker's labels and were pasted inside a bombe chest, a clock case, or a traveler's trunk. They also served as handouts for product promotion or as formats for newspaper advertisements. Students of American trade cards claim that the majority of such cards (until they went out of fashion in the 1870s, being replaced by larger advertising cards) advertised the crafts, skills, or trades of specific individuals rather than companies. Unlike the artisan's trade card, the larger advertising card of the post–Civil War era promoted products manufactured more and more by corporations.[10]

Tools contributed to craftsman individuality since they were physical extensions of their users. Often artisans engraved their tools with their personal mark and kept them in specially made cases such as Duncan Phyfe's massive tool chest now on display at the New York Historical Society.[11] The individuality of the early American artisan's tools, however, should not be given excessive emphasis. For one, during the period when handicraft was the major production unit, the basic design and function of most hand tools changed very slowly. For instance, the wood-working tools described in Joseph Moxon's *Mechanick Exercises, Or The Doctrine of Handy-Works* (London, 1679) were largely the same as those found in the early nineteenth-century shops of the Dominy family and Phyfe. Second, it should be remembered that many tools and parts of tools (most often metal components like plane blades or drill bits) were imported into this country well into the early republic period.[12]

The Artifacts of Working Life

Production of goods and services, of course, oriented craftsman life; artisans existed to produce artifacts. Few craftsmen neglected this obvious axiom of business, a fact attested to by their invoices and billheads, advertising broadsides (fig. 46), promotional handbills, newspaper advertisements, and trade catalogs. Such iconographic data are often extremely useful to scholars principally interested in the craft object. A number of these artifacts of the early republic artisan survived in various museums, historical agencies, and private collections.

The latter evidence comes to us, however, often seriously flawed by the fecklessness of historical survival and the penchant of most collectors to save only those objects (such as silverware, glassware, furniture, paintings, ceramics, and the like) that once had the highest monetary value and now do likewise as antiques. Frequently only the best or the most expensive of past craftwork has survived to be enshrined in museums

Figure 46.
"The Hoe Printing Press, Machine and Saw Manufactory"
Advertisement lithograph (ca. 1840).
(Courtesy Museum of the City of New York)

and ensconced in private antique collections. Such artifacts have been
the dominant material culture evidence historians have used to study the
New York artisan, particularly in two geographical areas: the cultural
hearth of metropolitan New York City and the cultural corridors of the
Hudson and Mohawk valleys. Two strata of objects have been most
studied: the elite decorative arts of New York City and the regional folk
art of the northern half of the state.[13]

What do these detailed, object-centered analyses tell us about the
New York artisan? For one, they suggest that the work of Duncan Phyfe
and his shop enjoyed a spectacular vogue in the early republic. With a
large shop in which many men were employed and a following of emi-
nent New Yorkers who relied upon him for their furniture, Duncan Phyfe
quickly assumed leadership in the introduction of what some decorative
arts historians regard as America's first neoclassical style that had national
appeal. The Phyfe forms, ornament, and design idioms were diffused in
at least two ways. First, Phyfe's journeymen craftsmen, like many early
nineteenth-century artisans, were an itinerant lot and periodically moved
on to work for others or to set up shops for themselves. A second factor
in spreading Phyfe's style was his aesthetic influence in New York City

where other cabinetmakers sought to imitate his work in their work. When *The New York Book of Prices for Manufacturing Cabinet and Chair Work* was published in 1817, Phyfe's designs were institutionalized in a pattern book that amply demonstrates how the cross (or lattice) back, the ogee scroll back, and the lyre and harp, combined with Grecian front and rear legs, had become standard for New York chair designs.[14]

To date, however, we really have no systematic correlation, even in the case of Phyfe, between artisan values and ideals and the form and style of the objects they crafted. There are, of course, romantic explanations that claim to account for unique regional products and producers as somehow "expressions" of the spirit of a place. In the case of New York artisan history, a more plausible explanation takes into account factors such as: 1) the geographical context, that is, New York as a major seaport and cosmopolitan urban environment; 2) the availability of raw materials for sustained production; 3) the available network of product marketing and distribution of craft products; and 4) the history of the trades in the city and the degree of craft organization and labor specialization within the trades producing the goods. A fifth factor that must also be included is the artisan-client relation, particularly the economic circumstances and personal taste of potential clients. While pictorial evidence only tangentially affords information into artisan-client relations, visual data do provide us with some insight into several of these factors, particularly if we examine graphic materials that portray the artisan engaged in his work process and at his work place.

Unfortunately, early American artisans working at their crafts have all too often been illustrated from the plates of Denis Diderot's famous *Encyclopédie* and its twelve-volume *Receuil des planches* (Paris: 1762–77). This practice began with Carl Bridenbaugh's widespread use of Diderot's engravings as surrogates for American examples and has continued as other scholars accepted and followed Bridenbaugh's rationale for his use.[15]

While the *Encyclopédie* plates of working artisans are superb examples of the engraver's and printer's art, they, like so many illustrations of the craftsman at work, also contain certain liabilities as material culture evidence. For example, although *Encyclopédie* editors aspired to catalog and publish all the aspects of the contemporary French craftsman at work, their final engravings are flawed in at least two ways. First, it cannot be assumed that the artisan depicted at his work table has the full complement of tools he will need to craft an artifact. Second, and more important, eighteenth- and early nineteenth-century illustrators of artisanry often resorted to a contemporary graphic device that represented, in a single view, several craft operations occurring at one time. Since different sequential steps in the assembly process are pictured in a single image, it appears as if they occur simultaneously in the fabrication of a product.[16] Finally, it should also be remembered that single-frame illustrations of the work process, in addition to condensing the duration and sequence of certain operations, also usually altered the physical scale of the entire work process.

As Charles Hummel points out, most artisan shop interiors were quite small by modern standards, at least until 1800. For example, three generations of craftsmen in the Dominy family worked between 1750 and 1850 in slightly less than 345 square feet of space (see fig. 157). At any given time no more than four workmen performed their duties in this area. Examinations of other surviving artisan work spaces suggest this would have been typical.[17]

To be sure, some craft processes demanded greater work areas and storage facilities. The grimy operations of enterprises like soap boiling, tanning, or iron foundrying consumed larger parts of the landscape as well as despoiling the surrounding terrain. Here too the interpreter must beware, since the visual evidence of the working conditions of such craft processes often depicts them as much cleaner, tidier, and more pleasant than they actually were.

Despite these qualifications, there is much to learn from the woodcuts, prints, engravings, and other visual media that attempt to capture the artisan at his artisanry. Sequential work processes are evident, for example, in visual data such as those describing bricklayers in the woodcut, "Brickmasons at Work" (fig. 47), suggesting all the major elements of laying brick in a common course.

Many other examples of New York artisans at work can be found in the iconography of extant bank notes, trade manuals, billheads, newspaper advertisements, invoices, and trade cards. The membership certificate (fig. 48) of the New York Cooper's Society, for instance, shows the various steps of making a barrel, from the beginning use of the draw knife to the final crafting of the finished product. A Shearman and Hart Lithographers advertisement, itself a lithographic product, shows fourteen different types of work involved in this communication craft.[18]

In attempting to reconstruct the artisan's world, Dean Failey has demonstrated in his study of Long Island craftsmen a fact that we (and the visual evidence as well) tend to forget: a very large part of the typical artisan's day was devoted to tasks other than those finished objects we revere in museums. Two such tasks—the production of miscellaneous items and repair work—were part of a craftsman's business. For instance, a rural cabinetmaker might make, in addition to furniture, numerous small household items such as bread trays, saltboxes, brooms, picture frames, and dry sinks. Such woodworkers also repaired furniture, farm equip-

Figure 47.
"Brickmasons at Work, New York City," ca. 1830
Woodcut.
(Courtesy Museum of the City of New York)

ment, and household articles. Entries for "mending" occur so frequently in craftsmen's account books that one is led to believe that few pieces of furniture were ever discarded.[19]

The diversity of craftwork raises up another point to remember about the surviving visual material culture of early American craftsmen. Artisans working outside metropolitan areas such as New York tended to be multi-skilled individuals. The rural Dominys, for instance, worked as cabinet-makers, carpenters (both house and mill), clock makers, watch repairers, wheelwrights, gun repairers, and metal workers. On the other hand, artisans employed in a shop like Phyfe's in the center of New York City engaged in a greater degree of division of labor and specialization of product. Phyfe's business organization between 1803 and 1847 reflected this urban trend. Journeymen, cabinetmakers, chair makers, turners, upholsterers, inlay makers, carvers, and gilders worked under his roof, and he may have employed at times more than one hundred men.[20]

Artisan-shop trade signs served as both signs and symbols of crafts-man culture. As self-images of their proprietors, they suggested an individual craftsman's advertising pitch, feel for aesthetics, and even sense of humor. Trade signs, in addition to surviving intact, also sometimes

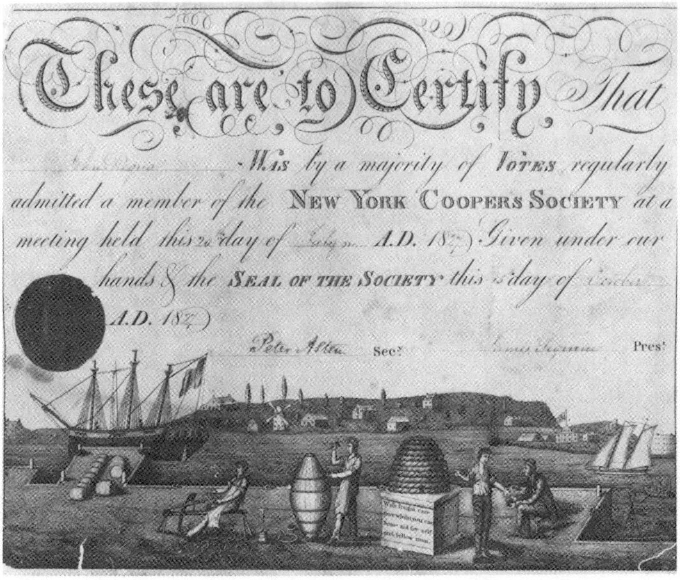

Figure 48.
Membership Certificate for the New York Coopers Society, July 1827
Unattributed engraving.
(Courtesy The New-York Historical Society, New York City)

reappear on billheads, in newspaper advertising, and even on trade cards.[21] Trade signage is most valuable to the material culture researcher when found in the context of an outdoor view or streetscape, wherein we often find a complete visual representation of an artisan's work place. For example, an early photograph (fig. 49) of a ship joiner's shop of Daniel Coger and his son John J. Coger, conveys some of the ambience of a work place at mid-nineteenth century. We see a ship's wheel used as an advertising logo atop the firm's roof, signage of all types, storage sheds, carts and wagons, building materials, ship parts in various stages of fabrication, assorted tools, and, most important of all, the firm's workers and their supervisors. The new craft of photography has captured all of these details (and many others), bringing a realism to the visual documentation of artisan life often unparalleled prior to 1839.

By contrast, the tidy, formal façades of Duncan Phyfe's shop and warehouse (fig. 50) on Fulton Street immediately demonstrate the social and economic stratification that existed among artisans. Phyfe, one of New York's most successful craftsmen both artistically and financially, lived in (and with) high style. His workshop and salesroom, a symmetrical assortment of pilasters, balustrades, and fanlight windows, paralleled the

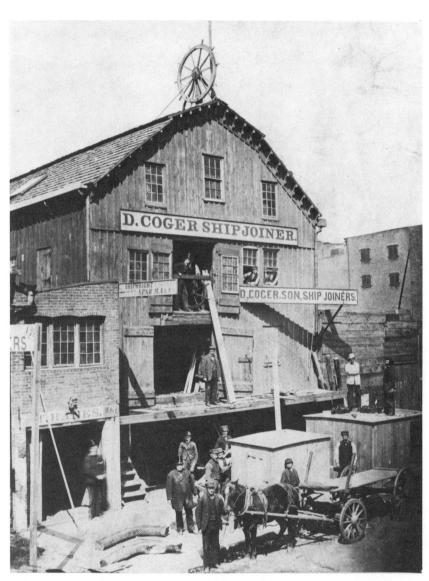

Figure 49.
Ship Joiner Shop of Daniel Coger and His Son, 480 Water Street, New York
City, ca. 1865
(Courtesy The New-York Historical Society, New York City)

Figure 50.
Artist Unknown, *The Shop and Warehouse of Duncan Phyfe, 168–172 Fulton Street, New York City*, ca. 1815
Pencil, ink and watercolor.
(Courtesy The Metropolitan Museum of Art, New York City, Rogers Fund, 1922 [22.28.1])

classical idiom that he made the hallmark of his furniture style. An American eagle in the shop building's pediment suggests the nationalism of the period.

The work places of other artisans catering to wealthy customers also tended to reflect their class status and that of their clients. Often visual representations of their establishments reveal additional information about the more elite commercial districts.[22] To be sure, many of these artisans continued the traditional practice of having their living quarters either behind or above their shops. Most also housed their apprentices and servants in these multipurpose residences. Nonetheless, the work places of these master artisans of "bespoken work" are often built in the most current architectural styles, located in the more fashionable neighborhoods, and suggest an aspiration for social respectability.

The close proximity of the residence of the master craftsman or owner to the work place continues up to the middle of the nineteenth century. Billheads, lithographs, engravings, trade cards, photographs, trade catalogs, even bank notes[23] repeatedly demonstrate the close geographical relationship that the craftsman-entrepreneur maintained with his home, office, and work place. For example, despite the abundant land that a Staten Island candler apparently possessed, he chose to locate right next to his invariably dirty and foul-smelling work site.[24] Other material culture evidence suggests this was typical. Many master artisans considered daily surveillance of their craft shops or factories necessary to maintaining production levels. Once various mechanized methods of large-scale production entered the work place, makers of goods indulged in the luxury of offices and residences more removed from their work sites.

Advanced mechanization, of course, came at different times to different crafts. While this shift from craft enterprise to automated industry was only beginning in the late 1840s, its origins should be recognized. The American artisan's work place was changing in the early nineteenth century because of several factors: expanded technology, new energy resources, and changes in worker mentality and work habits. The surviving visual material culture of this era (1780–1850), a period that Brooke Hindle calls "the great technological divide," confirms that the changes were not necessarily all linear or all progressive as many written histories of the period would suggest. Hence it should be remembered that millers had been largely mechanized by the 1850s, but potters, coopers, and smiths continued to do the majority of their work by hand. Steam power was used as early as 1750 in some crafts, but as late as 1860 water power still dominated much industrial production and was even advancing in technological efficiency.[25]

The Artifacts of Communal Life

The artisan population of a large city such as New York formed a community, a social group with a common heritage as well as mutual interests and characteristics. As suggested by the visual evidence surveyed thus far, that identity was often personal and occupational. In their work dress of leather apron, trousers, and cap, and especially in their professional skills and the products that those skills created, the artisans knew they were different both from the unskilled laborers below them and the mercantile classes above them.

Three other characteristics reinforced this special identity of early American artisan culture: first, housing and location of residence; second, increasing participation in craft fraternities and mechanic societies; and third, political activity as a voting bloc and lobbying interest.

In the case of craftsman housing, unfortunately, the visual sources are sparse. While numerous lithographs and engravings survive of fashionable places like the Fraunces Tavern, Trinity Church, the Tontine Coffee House, the Bank of New York, and the lower wards (first through third) of Manhattan, we have only a few views of less fashionable places. Throughout the history of most nineteenth-century American cities, this imbalance of visual sources continued as artists (and then photographers) concentrated, usually for commercial reasons, more on the "public" rather than the "private" city. Main streets and civic buildings are recorded while worker's neighborhoods and lower-class residences go unnoticed. The record of photography for the rural artisan sites is equally scarce. A lithograph of Provost and Chapel Streets in winter does, however, afford us a perspective on artisan housing conditions. The artist, J. Milbert, a Frenchman who came to New York in 1816, considered this view "the most typical of the city," a conclusion similarly reached by the Baronness de Neuville a decade earlier in her depiction of the same scene.[26] Milbert accurately recognized how densely packed most artisan neighborhoods were in the early nineteenth century. Most of these dwellings were rental properties, and frequently a number of extended families, plus boarders lived in four- and five-room tenements. Young, unmarried journeymen usually lived in boarding houses scattered through such artisan districts, especially on the streets close to the city's docks. As is also evident from Milbert's winter scene, streets were not paved in most neighborhoods, and no public lighting, sewerage, or waste removal is in evidence. Backyards acted as barnyards where tenants kept livestock, pigs, and chickens.

This neighborhood milieu does not drastically change if we compare the work of another artist, Francis Guy, who during his residence in Brooklyn from 1817 until his death in 1820, painted several summer and winter scenes (fig. 51) of craftsmen's Brooklyn. His favorite subject was the view from his second-floor window at No. 11 Front Street where he could look down (into the left background of the painting) to Main Street, up James Street, and to the right along the curve of Front Street to Fulton Street. Brooklyn's rapid growth in the early nineteenth-century resulted in a visual time collage when, in 1820, Guy recorded the interesting juxtapositions of the eighteenth-century Dutch farmhouses with the new Federal-style houses so much in vogue with the Manhattan upper middle class then migrating into Brooklyn. In both the summer and winter scenes, we have an excellent visual description of the residence and shop of Benjamin Meeker, a house carpenter and joiner, who lived at the corner of Front and James Streets.

Curiously, in the two Guy views the Brooklyn neighborhood's city streets are deserted in summer but alive with numerous activities in winter. Seeing artisans, their spouses, and their children out and about,

Figure 51.
Francis Guy, *Winter Scene in Brooklyn,* 1817–20
Oil painting.
(Courtesy Museum of the City of New York)

however, prompts us to recall how much of the craftsman's communal life was street life—a street culture that entailed shopping, visiting, selling, gossiping, advertising, playing, and celebrating.

Vendues or public auctions of a craft shop's products periodically took place (especially to dispose of excess or outdated stock) in the streets and sidewalks in front of the shops.[27] E. Didier's *Auction in Chatham Square,* a painting (fig. 52) the artist entered in the National Academy of Design's 1843 exhibition, captures this aspect of street life. Shop signs (W. N. Seymour's Hardware Store, H. Kipp's Furniture Warehouse) as well as the products up for auction (unpretentious chairs, baskets, crockery) show Chatham to be a neighborhood where journeymen and laborers' families resided.

Although they worked long hours (craftsmen usually did not return home until sundown) every day but the Sabbath, there still was communal recreation. Neighborhood taverns were a vital component of artisan life. National holidays such as the Fourth of July and local celebrations were occasions for parading and declaring artisan identity. Windsor and rush chair makers in the New York Federal Procession of 1788 carried a banner depicting a river view with ships and the motto "Free Trade. The Federal States in Union bound, O'er all the world our chairs are found."[28]

In a perceptive analysis of "Artisan Republican Festivals and the Rise of Class Conflict in New York City, 1787–1837," Sean Wilentz has demonstrated how much a historical reading of public ceremonies—trade

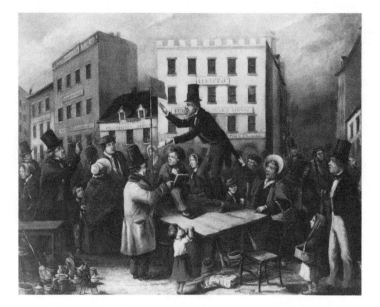

Figure 52.
E. Didier, *Auction in Chatham Square,* 1843
Oil painting.
(Courtesy Museum of the City of New York)

parades, fairs, and other "theatrics of craft"—can reveal about popular *mentalité.* Mechanics marched by trades arranged either alphabetically from bakers to wheelwrights or by "branch" (the leather trades, the building trades, and others in separate units). Masters marched at the head of journeymen and apprentices. Each trade displayed either a finished product of its making dubbed with an appropriate name—the bakers with "a giant Federal loaf" of bread—or a float on which men plied their trade—the coopers making a barrel, hooping thirteen staves together, or the printers casting off copies of the Constitution. Often a small ship built by the ship carpenters was mounted on wheels, drawn by a team of horses, and called "The Ship of State," "Constitution," or in New York, sometimes, "The Hamilton."[29] Artisans also staged parades with elaborate regalia to celebrate the opening of the Erie Canal and the July Revolution in France in 1830. Annual displays of the artifacts of crafts consciousness took place on Evacuation Day (November 15) and Independence Day.

By the 1830s, new artifacts of the mechanic mentality appeared, signaling a bifurcation of New York artisan traditions at least as manifested in public ritual. On one hand, there was the annual trade fair of the American Institute (founded in 1928) that became one of New York's most renowned public spectacles of craft production. By the end of the Jacksonian period, the institute had set a standard for industrial and trade fairs unmatched in the United States until the opening of the New York Crystal Palace exposition in 1853.[30] The exhibits of artifacts were monuments to enterprise and innovation, containing what Philip Hone deemed "every object which the versatility of invention and the ingenuity of our artisans and manufacturers could produce."[31]

On the other hand, quite different festivities began in 1833, argues Wilentz, under the aegis of the General Trades Union and its constituent unions. Almost as soon as the GTU elected its officers and adopted a constitution, it decided to celebrate itself with a public procession. New emblems of unity, like the GTU banner of Archimedes lifting a mountain with a lever, announced to all that the union was an entirely new type of organization, one composed solely of journeymen wage earners from various crafts.[32] Yet while the unionists' parades brought numerous innovations in ritual and meaning, they also retained many of the themes and forms of earlier artisan proceedings. Although they marched separately, the journeymen in the different crafts repeated earlier pageant practices in what one reporter called a "highly pleasing spectacle" of craft iconography.[33] Despite their new brotherhood, the journeymen continued to march trade by trade, evincing a strong consciousness of the special ties within each individual craft. In the GTU anniversary march of 1834, the Union Society of House Carpenters carried the carpenters' arms with a picture of two workmen at their jobs and the motto "We Shelter the Homeless"; in the same parade, women cordwainers carried the crest of their trade, followed by two tradeswomen (one holding a slipper, the other holding a boot), declaring "Protective Industry, a Nation's Wealth."

New York artisans also turned out at times of mourning of one of their own such as the famous James O'Connell funeral procession of 22 September 1847. Mechanics' societies with their respective flags and insignia led the hearse. Many artisans wore their ceremonial aprons over mourning dress clothes. Political rallies also spawned artisan parades like the one elaborately described, engraved, and published by Thomas Strong in his *Pictorial and Descriptive Sheet of the Whig Procession in New York, 1844.* This broadside depicts carriage and wagon makers, lithographers at their presses, leather dressers working hides, printers publishing and distributing an ode, ship and steamboat joiners at work, as well as tin-plate makers, wheelwrights, stonecutters, whip and cane makers, and glass blowers all demonstrating their skills in a parade lasting several hours before an estimated 10,000 people.[34]

Individual craft fraternities also displayed their identity in membership certificates. In part indebted to the heraldry of the medieval guilds, in part imbued with the optimistic nationalism of the early nineteenth century, and in part helping to fulfill a need for craft solidarity, these membership certificates rank among the most visually interesting and culturally significant of all the surviving material culture evidence of the early artisan. Their iconographic detail could be as simple as the insignia of the Journeymen Stone-Cutters Society or as elaborate as the New York Bakers Benefit Society. On the surface, the membership certificates proclaimed an alliance between master craftsmen and journeymen but, after the 1820s, masters and journeymen increasingly had acute differences of opinion particularly over economic issues. The growing conflict between masters and journeymen is documented by the increase in a distinctive, separate consciousness among journeymen that is reflected in their own membership certificates, banners, and other artifacts of group identity. Wilentz and Young have begun the analysis of this artifactual evidence, and it may prove a valuable resource in probing the dimensions of the levels of political culture of urban mechanics other than the masters. The disagreements between journeymen and masters prompted a nascent, if not long-lasting, trade union movement among some urban artisans, particularly those in the quantity production crafts such as leather making, construction, and shoe making.

To validate their status and to articulate their cause, craft organizations printed various visual documents that promoted artisan identity. From a member's ticket of the Union Society of Journeymen House Carpenters one learns, for example, that this local organization is a branch of the General Trades Union and that the local society's motto is "combined to protect but not to injure." Enshrined in a classical Greek portico of simple Doric columns and unpretentious pediment and entablature, an allegorical figure atop a stone pedestal holds a Phrygian cap of liberty in one hand and points to the society motto with the other. If this classical muse represents the inspiration and continuity of the past, the American eagle (overhead looking down from the pediment) stands as the ruling icon for the present and future.[35]

The contrast between past and present appeared frequently as a convention of artisan society membership certificates. Nowhere is this better illustrated than by comparing, in some detail, a certificate of 1786 (fig. 53) with one in use by the late eighteenth century and throughout the nineteenth (fig. 54). The General Society of Mechanics and Tradesmen was a benevolent and fraternal organization begun in 1786 and chartered by the New York state legislature in 1792. As an umbrella organization aspiring to represent all artisan interests, it assisted members in sickness, and in the case of death helped provide for the deceased's widow and children. Amendments to the charter established in 1821 a school for the children of poor or deceased members and an apprentice library.[36]

A focal point of the 1786 General Society membership certificate (see fig. 53) is, of course, an artisan's muscular right arm, exposed to the bicep with a smith's hammer in hand, in the process of performing craftwork. Above this powerful and perennial image of artisanry flies the banner of the society's motto: "By hammer and hand, all arts do stand." Below this component of the certificate is the largest element of the document, the center portion where the artisan's name and date of election to the craft fraternity are entered and validated by the signatures of the president and secretary of the society and where the organization's official seal is affixed.[37]

Framing the society's motto and symbol (a mark of collective identity), the artisan's name (an individual identity), and the society's seal (another mark of collective identity) are two sets of panels, one to the left and the other to the right, that reveal the ambitions and aspirations of the early American artisan. For example, on the left we have three tableaux that suggest the state of North America in its era of initial discovery and early settlement. The overall impression given on this side of the certificate is one of a primitive New World. In the top left panel, a male Indian hunter-and-gatherer dressed in animal skin sits in an Arcadian bower with bow and quiver in hand. The Native American is confronted with civilization's benefits in the form of two muses: Classical Liberty with her staff (symbol of authority) and her Phyrgian cap (symbol of liberty), and Classical Industry with her beehive (a symbol of cooperative enterprise) and her spade (a symbol of agriculture enterprise).

If we take this top left panel to represent Antiquity, the middle panel beneath it appears to represent the Middle Ages. In this section we get a view of two ancient crafts: in the foreground a turner works on his lathe, while in back of the shop, a smith is busy at his forge fire and bellows. Although the convention of locating the shop window close to the working area of artisans is employed, the window does not appear to yield sufficient light. In contrast to the bright shop (with open window) of the modern turner depicted directly across the page on the right, the left scene suggests a stereotype of dark ages. The final left panel, however, moves us outdoors again in close contact with the primitive New World wilderness. Here, nature dominates the panel by means of its watercourses and land forms as well as its extensive new flora and fauna. Nonetheless, nature has begun to yield, if grudgingly, to humankind's domestication in the form of early husbandry (a single ox is used to plow) and milling (upstream a mill site can be seen).

The certificate panels on the right are everything those on the left

Figure 53.
Certificate of Membership in New York Mechanick Society,
New York City, June 3, 1791
Etching by Abraham Godwin. Laid paper, wax, wood.
(Courtesy Winterthur Museum)

are not. The top right section champions the importance of mutual assistance and social welfare. A representative from the mechanic's society comes to comfort a mourning widow who receives him in the context of a family burial plot (wherein her husband now lies) and two grieving children. The fellow artisan representing the society arrives with the promised burse as dictated by the society's constitution, a document so forthright that any child can understand and recognize its veracity and its value for all artisans. When in dire straits, the hunter-gatherer (of the certificate's top left panel) has no one to turn to other than himself and his wits; by contrast, the artisan who bands together with his fellows has the assurance of both cooperative enterprise and communal assistance in times of personal hardship.

If the rhetoric of their society constitutions and the iconography of their fraternities are to be believed, early American artisans considered such mutual aid a sign of a progressive civilization. Such a motif also dominates the middle right panel of the Mechanics and Tradesmen's certificate. Although still powered by apprentice labor, the shop depicted is considered modern in comparison with its counterpart to the left; that

Figure 54.
Membership Certificate, General Society of Mechanics and Tradesmen,
New York City, ca. 1810
Engraving by B. Tanner.
*(Courtesy The Winterthur Library: Printed Book and Periodical
Collection)*

craftsmen are responsible for this progress is certainly suggested by the
lower panel on the right. Shipwrights construct vessels to navigate watercourses, while lumbermen clear forests. With the timbers resulting from
forest clearance, housewrights construct new homes, some of which are
being designed by architects working in the latest classical mode. The
primitive natural surroundings of the past are now being mastered by the
collective ingenuity and mutual cooperation of artisans at work in the
present.

By the early nineteenth century, artisans in New York's General
Society of Mechanics and Tradesmen had made collective ingenuity and
mutual cooperation an even more dominant theme (see fig. 54) of their
membership certificates. The identity of the individual artisan has now
been relegated to the lower margins of the document. The print centers
spatially and visually on the insurance benefits that accrue to an artisan's
family upon his death. What was only a single theme (top right panel)
in figure 53 has become the principal image in this later membership certificate. The master artisan is evolving into a businessman-employer.[38]

Before examining this major shift it might be useful to note other changes. To begin, the moral tag, "By Hammer and Hand, All Arts Do Stand" has been replaced by a lengthy, nineteenth-century motto: "To Dry the Tear from Misery's Eye, to Succour the Afflicted, and to Save the Sinking Is Our Aim." The muscular arm and hammer have assumed a more ethereal quality; the image is inserted in a distant heavenly cloud, radiating out inspiration like the All-Seeing Masonic Eye later to appear on American paper currency. Finally, the six side panels of the 1786 certificate have been replaced by four cherubs representing Agriculture, History, the Arts, and Industries.

The didacticism of the main tableaux needs little explication. The scene, set along a stylized version of New York's harbor, shows a flourishing shipbuilding industry. Also illustrated is the progressive state of the art of water transport, with a steam vehicle looking faintly like Fulton's *Clermont* plying the harbor waters. (There is, however, no hint of what this new power source will mean for the work habits and working conditions of traditional artisanry.)

The principal dramatis personae in the nineteenth-century engraving are, with the exception of an added society member and a babe in arms, the same as in the eighteenth-century certificate. Two artisans attempt to comfort a forlorn mother seemingly more worried about her children than the burse that one of the artisans is attempting to give her. One of her sons implores her to recognize this representative from the society; the other youngster is held in hand by a second artisan who suggests that the son might attend the apprentice's school—an imposing Greek Revival structure that has some resemblance to the society's actual headquarters on Chambers Street.[39] Thus not only will the family crisis be averted in the immediate future by the society's pension fund, but economic stability can be insured as at least one of the sons follows in the craft of his father after attending the Mechanics School and Library.

Artisan societies such as the General Society of Mechanics and Trades also engaged in political activity. Howard Rock notes they

> lobbied effectively for goals that all craftsmen, Republican and Federalist, journeymen and master, shared. These included increased tariff protection, the defeat of New York Republican Mayor Edward Livingston's "Workshop" [a project proposed by Livingston in 1803 for the creation of public workshops cosponsored by the General Society of Mechanics and Tradesmen and the New York City government that would allow the poor and disadvantaged to learn trades such as shoemaking and hat making] and, as a culmination of many years' effort, the incorporation of the city's highest capitalized bank.[40]

The material culture evidence of these political activities by New York artisans is, like the assorted occupational constituencies that generated it, a diverse lot. Campaign memorabilia such as buttons, souvenirs, and banners were part of the American electoral process by the 1820s and, as several scholars of such artifacts have argued, quickly became important components of political life.[41] Artisan involvement in local and national politics is probably best charted by means of broadsides and political cartoons, two visual genres through which craftsmen expressed their views on economic, social, and political issues. In the presidential campaigns of the 1830s, for example we have political cartoons depicting Andrew Jackson as a wood worker, while others show then-President Martin Van Buren being battered by an artisan with hammer in hand. Other views, directed against Jackson and Van Buren's fiscal policies, suggest the widespread demoralizing effects of the 1837 depression on craftsmen.[42]

Many of these visual materials make extensive use of political symbols. One dominant symbol has been the American eagle. Others have included the U.S. shield, the allegorical figures of Liberty, Columbia, and eventually Uncle Sam. The craftsman himself likewise became a popular American symbol. In the early republic, he was personified by the most widely known of all American craftsmen, Benjamin Franklin, the master printer, after whom more American place-names, banks, and businesses have been designated than any other colonial hero. Franklin's image continually appeared on the artifacts of craft societies' mastheads and on transfer-printed ceramics, not to mention the numerous times his personae can be found in paintings, sculpture, and other facets of the fine arts. Although he was most closely associated with Philadelphia, even New York artisans recognized the authority that Franklin's name and image lent to their cause. Thus we find Samuel Maverick, a New York engraver and copperplate printer, including Franklin in a prominent place on his billhead. A. Dyott put Franklin to a similar use on the fifty-dollar bank notes issued by his ill-fated Manual Labor Bank. Christian Schussle provided us with one final example in his famous lithograph of *Men of Invention,* wherein Franklin favorably looks down upon an assembly of American geniuses (many of them artisans) of the early nineteenth century.[43]

Throughout the nineteenth century workers drew on the heritage of artisan symbolism of the new republic. For example, when their newspaper (*The Awl*) appeared, the shoemakers of Lynn, Massachusetts, reprinted the Declaration of Independence in the first issue and went on in the next to compare their bosses to King George III. The women factory workers in New England's Lowell mills wrote poems in *The Lowell Offering,* glorifying the Fourth of July and its soldier-artisans of the Revolution. Archibald Willard's 1876 painting of ''The Spirit of 76''—

three bloodstained soldiers of the Revolution marching, defiantly, one with a fife, one with a drum, one carrying the flag—was a tableau used by railroad workers in the great railroad upheaval of 1877. In the first (1882) Labor Day parade in New York City one of the leading banners was "Labor Is the Source of All Wealth." Young argues it might well have come from the New York Mechanics Society Certificate of 1786: "By Hammer and Hand All Arts Do Stand."[44]

As I hope is evident from this brief review of selected graphic representations of the New York artisan from 1787 to 1853, the extant visual sources of the craftsman in early America can be found in diverse formats: broadsides and billheads, trade cards and catalogs, dictionaries and directories, journals, newspapers, and other printed or engraved advertising materials. Such pictorial information, together with paintings, drawings, and photographs, better focus our present image of past artisanry. Although this material culture evidence is not without its explanatory limitations and evidential biases, its full research potential has only begun to be realized in widening our understanding of everyday life. As Jonathan Fairbanks rightly observes, such visual data serve as "mirrors to the past, sometimes distorted or imperfect, but nonetheless a means by which we may reflect upon and, in part, enter into a visual world now gone."[45]

Notes

1. Charles Montgomery, in his book *American Pewter,* suggests that the pewterer's shop depicted on the banner was not necessarily a New York shop, only a typical eighteenth-century one. Charles Hummel also thinks the visual precedent for the shop was one cribbed from an English or French source. Correspondence with the author, 2 November 1983. I am particularly indebted to Mr. Hummel, as well as to Professors Alfred Young and Howard Rock, for valuable critical readings of this essay in several earlier drafts.

2. Eugene S. Ferguson, "The Critical Period in the History of American Technology, 1788–1853," Unpublished paper, Iowa State University (December 1962), 1–3.

3. Briefer in focus and compass, it is indebted to I. N. Phelps Stokes, *The Iconography of Manhattan Island, 1498*–1909, 6 vols. (New York: Robert Dodd, 1915) and John A. Kouwenhoven, *The Columbia Historical Portrait of New York: An Essay in Graphic History* (New York: Harper & Row, 1953; Icon Editions Reprint, 1972).

4. Carl Bridenbaugh, *The Colonial Craftsman* (Chicago: University of Chicago Press, 1966), i; Herbert Gutman, "Work, Culture, and Society in Industrializing America, 1815–1919," *American Historical Review* 78.3 (June 1973): 558.

5. Alfred F. Young, "By Hammer and Hand All Arts Do Stand: Mechanics and the Shaping of the American Nation, 1760–1820," paper presented at the National Meeting of the Organization of American Historians, San Francisco, (April 1980), 10.

6. Of course, another name for artifacts is material culture, a phrase often used to describe all physical objects formed by humankind. Simply put, material culture can be de-

fined, as James Deetz does in *In Small Things Forgotten: The Archaeology of Early American Life* (Garden City, N.Y.: Anchor Doubleday, 1977, 24–25), as any way we shape the physical world according to culturally dictated plans. For purposes of this essay, such material culture evidence is principally the extant work of the eighteenth- and nineteenth-century artist, engraver, limner, paper maker, woodcut-maker, lithographer, printer, bookbinder, daguerreotypist, and type maker. From this visual data, a collective portrait is sketched of New York City artisan culture from 1787 until 1853.

7. Copley's *Nathaniel Hurd* (1765) is in the Cleveland Museum of Art and Neagle's *William Strickland* (1829) is in the Yale University Art Gallery.

8. The Lyon portrait is reproduced in Scott Williamson, *The American Craftsman* (New York: Crown Publishers, 1940).

9. Daguerreotypes of such artisans have been reproduced in Beaumont Newhall, *The Daguerreotype in America* (Boston: New York Graphic Society, 1976), pl. 15–18; Morris B. Schnappen, *American Labor: A Pictorial History* (Washington, D.C.: Public Affairs Press, 1972), 36; Floyd Rinehart and Marion Rinehart, *The American Daguerreotype* (Athens: University of Georgia Press, 1981).

10. Robert Jay, *The Trade Card in Nineteenth–Century America* (Columbia: University of Missouri Press, 1987); David Winslow, "Trade Cards, Catalogs, and Invoice Heads," *Pennsylvania Folklore* 19.3 (Spring 1970): 21–22; George Furness Dow, "Trade Cards," *Old-Time New England* 26.4 (April 1936): 116.

11. Daniel M. Semel, "A First Look at Duncan Phyfe's Tool Chest," *Chronicle of Early American Industries* 29.4 (December 1976): 56–60.

12. Charles F. Hummel, "English Tools in America: The Evidence of the Dominys," *Winterthur Portfolio* II (1965): 27–29. Hummel notes that both rural craftsmen like the Dominy family in East Hampton, Long Island and city artisans such as those employed in Phyfe's operation on Fulton Street in New York City worked with both imported and locally made tools.

13. V. Isabelle Miller, *Furniture by New York Cabinetmakers, 1650–1860* (New York: Museum of the City of New York, 1956); Dean Failey, *Long Island Is My Nation: The Decorative Arts and Craftsmen, 1640–1830* (Society for the Preservation of Long Island Antiquities, 1976); V. Isabelle Miller, *New York Silversmiths of the Seventeenth Century* (New York: Museum of the City of New York, 1962); Jean Lipman, *The Flowering of American Folk Art* (New York: Viking Press, 1974).

14. Twentieth-century scholarship on Phyfe extends from Charles O. Cornelius's catalogue, *The Furniture Masterpieces of Duncan Phyfe* (New York: Doubleday Page & Co., 1922), done for the 1922 Metropolitan Museum of Art exhibition to Michael K. Brown, "Duncan Phyfe, 1768–1854," unpublished master's thesis, University of Delaware (1978), Charles F. Montgomery, *American Furniture: The Federal Period* (New York: Bonanza Books, 1978), and Deborah Dependahl Waters, *An Elegant Assortment: The Furniture of Duncan Phyfe and His Contemporaries, 1800–1840* (New York: Museum of the City of New York, 1987).

15. Carl Bridenbaugh, *The Colonial Craftsman* (Chicago: University of Chicago Press, 1950), ix. Bridenbaugh explained his usage as follows: "Diderot's engravers drew heavily on English examples for illustrations of the several crafts, and thus they are much nearer to colonial practice, which closely imitated the English." Also, "they are, moreover, unusually faithful representations, for each piece was designed for the head of a plate explaining the nature of a given craft."

16. On the interpretation of Diderot's plates, I have been helped by two unpublished essays, Eugene S. Ferguson, "The Iconography of Technological Change in the Industrial Revolution," paper presented to University of Delaware faculty (23 May 1979) and Jonathan L. Fairbanks, "Craft Processes and Images: Visual Sources for the Study of the Craftsman," in *The Craftsman in Early America*, ed. Ian M. G. Quimby (New York: W. W. Norton, 1984), 299–300.

17. Charles F. Hummel, "The Business of Woodworking, 1700 to 1840," in *Tools and Technologies: America's Wooden Age*, ed. B. Kebabian and William C. Lipke (Burlington, Vt.: University of Vermont, 1979), 1–22. Hummel compares the Dominy shop to the size (540 square feet) of the Christopher Layman [Leamon] shop, originally (1795) located in Frederick County, Maryland, and now a part of Georgetown, D.C. As part of the Old Stone House, it is administered by the National Park Service. See Historic American Buildings Survey (HABS), 10–2 (1934) Original dimensions l. 30'5¾" × w. 18'8" × h. 7'.

18. For representative examples of such materials see illustration 158, "Money Issued by Dyott's Ill-Omened Bank," in *The American Craftsman*, ed. Scott G. Williamson (New York: Crown Publishers, 1940), 177.

19. Failey, *Long Island Is My Nation*, 196.

20. Hummel, *With Hammer in Hand*, 5.

21. Clarence Hornung, *A Treasury of American Design* (New York: Abrams, 1968) provides a useful sample of the changing graphic and iconographic components of the American trade sign from the eighteenth to the nineteenth century.

22. For example, see the view of Jonathan Gostelowe's cabinetmaking shop as depicted in the illustration, "High Street, With First Presbyterian Church, Philadelphia," Williamson, *American Craftsman*, pl. 75.

23. An 1814 bank note of Vermont Glass Factory (American Numismatic Society) as reproduced in Schnapper, *American Labor*, 19. Lithographed advertisement, Novelty Iron Works reproduced in John A. Kouwenhoven, *Columbia Historical Portrait of New York*, 205.

24. The Staten Island graphic is in The Special Collections of the Winterthur Museum.

25. Brooke Hindle, *Technology in Early American Culture* (Chapel Hill, N.C.: University of North Carolina Press, 1966), 3–29; Thomas J. Schlereth, "The Artisan in Early America: A Historical Perspective," in *The Early American Artisan*, ed. Ian M. G. Quimby (New York: W. W. Norton, 1983), 34–61.

26. John K. Kouwenhoven, *Columbia Historical Portrait*, 124.

27. A typical auction announcement by Robert Kelley, cabinetmaker, can be found in the *New York Evening Post* (5 November 1819).

28. As Alfred Young has documented in his essay, "By Hammer and Hand," one can see "craft and producer consciousness was carried out on the banners the trades carried." All seemed to have carried flags with the traditional symbols of their trade, the coats of arms of the London guilds. The pewterers of New York added to the English slogan, 'Solid and Pure,' a picture of four craftsmen at work in a pewterer's shop, a large American flag, and a verse in support of the Constitution. Others reached back into antiquity for the ancient allegorical symbolism of their craft. The tailors carried a banner of Adam and Eve, properly covered with fig leaves, and the motto, 'And they

did sew fig leaves together'; the painters and glaziers in Baltimore carried a painted figure of Michelangelo, while the coopers displayed a cask with Bacchus seated upon it" (Young, 9).

29. Sean Wilentz, "Artisan Republican Festivals and the Rise of Class Conflict in New York City, 1787–1837," in *Working-Class America: Essays on Labor, Community and American Society*, ed. Michael H. Frisch and Daniel J. Walkowitz (Urbana: University of Illinois Press, 1983), 45–48.

30. Thomas McElrath, "Sketch of the Rise and Progress of the American Institute," *Transactions of the American Institute* 1 (1860): 86–87.

31. Allan Nevins, ed., *The Diary of Philip Hone, 1828–1851* (New York: Arno Press, 1970), 28.

32. Wilentz, "Artisan Republican Festivals," 57.

33. Ibid., 58.

34. *Strong's Pictorial and Descriptive Sheet of the Whig Procession in New York, 1844* (New York: T. W. Strong, 1844), New-York Historical Society Prints and Graphics Collection.

35. This graphic is reproduced in *American Labor*, 31.

36. Thomas Earle and Charles T. Congdon, eds., *Annals of the General Society of Mechanics and Tradesmen of the City of New York, from 1785 to 1880* (New York: Francis Hart & Co., 1882), 40.

37. Alfred Young, "The Mechanics and the Jeffersonians, 1789–1801," *Labor History* 5.3 (Fall 1964): 225–46.

38. Young, "By Hammer and Hand," 41.

39. Earle and Congdon, *Annals*, 41–43.

40. Howard Rock, *Artisans of the New Republic: The Tradesmen of New York City in the Age of Jefferson* (New York: New York University Press, 1979), 130–31.

41. Roger A. Fischer, *Tippecanoe and Trinkets Too: The Material Culture of American Presidential Campaigns, 1828–1984* (Urbana: University of Illinois Press, 1987); also see Edith Mayo, "Campaign Appeals to Women," *Journal of American Culture* 3 (March 1980): 722–41.

42. For an illustration of this graphic and several other nineteenth-century political cartoons, see Schnapper, *American Labor*, 31–32.

43. Hampton L. Carson, *The Hampton L. Carson Collection of Engraved Portraits of Jefferson, Franklin and Lafayette* (Philadelphia: W. F. Fell, 1904); Charles C. Sellers, *Benjamin Franklin in Portraiture* (New Haven: Yale University Press, 1962); Daniel Boorstin, *American Civilization* (New York: McGraw-Hill, 1974).

44. Young, "By Hammer and Hand," 37; Wilentz, "Artisan Republican Festivals," 64–65.

45. Fairbanks, "Craft Processes and Images: Visual Sources for the Study of the Craftsman," in *The Craftsman in Early America*, 330.

Figure 55.
Women Clerical Workers Trimming Currency, Records of the Public Building
Service, 1907
(Courtesy The National Archives, Washington, D.C.)

5

The World and Workers of the Paper Empire

Historical scholarship on white-collar worker culture is presently something of a growth industry in academia. I first became intrigued by the topic after reading Alan Dundes's very original and very funny *Urban Folklore from the Paper Empire* (Austin, Tex.: American Folklore Society, 1976). Two other books, one a museum catalog, *Wooton Patent Desks: A Place for Everything and Everything in Its Place* (Indianapolis: Indiana State Museum; and Oakland: The Oakland Museum, 1983), on the Wooten Desk Company's famous line of gargantuan office furniture, and the other an insightful work on material culture by Adrian Forty with a marvelous title, *Objects of Desire* (New York: Pantheon, 1986). Forty surveys all types of objects—household goods, transportation vehicles, costume—and devotes a chapter to "Design of the Office."

As I researched various types of work for my late nineteenth-century cultural history survey, I found abundant secondary literature on agrarian toil and industrial labor. Office work and workers, however, attracted little notice from historians. Fortunately, early on in my research, Carlene Stephens, curator in the National Museum of American History's Division of Engineering and Industry, provided me with several seminal suggestions. She has also generously read and critiqued this article.

I anticipate that research on the material culture of the modern office will expand. For example, several museums have done computer exhibitions, and we now have a Computer Museum in Boston. Since many office artifacts are primarily vehicles of information handling—from steel pens to telephones to word processors—it is natural that scholars in various fields (sociologists, anthropologists, and historians) will enter the fray to decide how often the medium is the message.

Such research on the technics of white-collar work cannot, however, focus solely on objects alone, no matter how engaging the internal history of the calculator or the latest photoduplication model may prove to be. We need to combine such research with an understanding of the changing internal structures of business and government. As Carlene Stephens and Steve Lubar document in their essay, "A Place for Public Business: The Material Culture of the Nineteenth-Century Federal Office" (*Business and Economic History*, 2d ser., 15 [1986]), communication in most pre-industrial business took place face-to-face. The main form of record keeping was simple accounting. Even large-scale enterprises that relied upon written correspondence required little more than chronological letter files. Similarly most bureaus in the pre–Civil War federal government kept only three categories of records: incoming correspondence, outgoing correspondence, and miscellaneous papers.

By the last quarter of the nineteenth century, however, big government and big business were generating enormous piles of paperwork, both for internal use and for external purposes. Record keeping alone became highly specialized. Work formerly done by a clerk might be divided among typists, stenographers, secretaries, file clerks, mail handlers, bill clerks, and accountants. New divisions of labor resulted from specialized data collection, processing, and distribution in departments of market research, economic forecasting, and, of course, advertising. All of this activity generated new material culture.

The artifactual environment of the modern office interconnected with other work places such as the sales floor, the research and development laboratory, the factory floor, the insurance agency, the banking house, and the stock exchange. These also provide opportunities for future material culture research. To my knowledge only Deborah Gardner's study (*Marketplace: A Brief History of the New York Stock Exchange,* New York: NYSE, 1982) and exhibition (*Bulls and Bears: Fifty Years of Progress at [the New York] Exchange* [New York: NYSE, n.d.]) and Joanne Yates's scholarship have explored these physical contexts as an important aspect of American business as well as cultural history.

In the past several decades, American historians have discovered numerous minority groups, subcultures, or occupational cadres that previously had been almost invisible in their scholarship on the past. It is striking, therefore, that it has taken so long to recognize ourselves as, in Alan Dundes's phrase, a small cohort in a gigantic "paper empire."[1]

To be sure, we continually produce a type of historical self-assessment in the historiographies we generate about our work, but we are not prone, as a professional group, to write many biographies of each other much less autobiographies of ourselves.[2] Although many wear the uniform, most do not view themselves as white-collar workers.

Within the past decade, however, a few historians have begun looking at the world and work of a labor force that has enormously increased in size and specialty over the past century. Most of this scholarship assesses the evolution of bureaucratic structures and the expansion of managerial operations in big business and big government. Its sociological theory comes from C. Wright Mills's 1951 classic, *White Collar: The American Middle Classes,* and its historical paradigm from Alfred D. Chandler's 1977 work, *The Visible Hand: The Managerial Revolution in American Business.*[3] Recently, the woman office worker in the period between the Civil War and World War I has received attention by several women historians; less is known about the white-collar, rank-and-file male in the same era.[4]

The physical environments of the paper empire likewise merit historical analysis. Might it be possible to integrate the information and insight that economic, social, and business history has uncovered with the commercial architecture, the interior spatial organization, and the business technology of the office world? How have gender roles been historically related to changing office tools and tasks? Have such artifacts affected class and gender definitions? What might be the relationship between office work sites, interior design, furnishings, and decor? How has spatial organization reflected the attitudes of employers and supervisors toward employees? In what ways have status and authority been given spatial or material definition? Do we have physical evidence of how companies attempted to create an internal or external image through office layout and location, corporate dress codes, advertising, award programs, or office furnishings? How have workers manipulated objects, environments, and spaces either to resist or to counter the official material culture of the office? In what ways might the artifacts employees add to their work places reveal personal identities or ideologies?

No small agenda this material history of the American office. To manage it, I will delimit my survey of its contours to an early, but crucial, phase in its history, 1870–1920. First, I survey office work places as to site and structure; second, I profile the new worker types that populated the postbellum office; third, I sketch what certain innovations in business machinery (from typewriter to time clock) and growing specialization in office furniture and furnishings (who has what and where) might mean in a social history of white-collar work. I conclude with a brief assessment of the changing relationships between those who worked in the white-collar world of the front office and those who labored in the adjoining factories and plants of early twentieth-century, industrial America.

A final preliminary. Several statistics, gathered by one of the paper empire's most ancient outposts, help orient us to the subject's numerical dimensions. The Bureau of the Census in 1870 counted 82,000 clerical and kindred workers in the United States; by 1920 the number rose to 3,112,000. The census also enumerated the rise in professionals from 342,000 (1870) to 2,171,000 (1920). A final demographic fact concerns the changing gender ratio of selected categories of office employees as noted in table 5.1.

Skyscrapers and Front Offices

To maximize production and profits, corporate capitalism and industrial technology created a corresponding need for enlarged bureaucracies capable of administering massive flows of personnel, materials, and money. This need, largely documentary and statistical in nature, transformed every aspect of office work by 1915. Mechanized work replaced hand work as specialized machines sped up paper transactions; different

Table 5.1.   Clerical Workers in the United States, by Sex, 1870–1930

Job Category	1870	1880	1890	1900	1910	1920	1930
Bookkeepers, cashiers, and accountants							
Total	38,776	74,919	159,374	254,880	486,700	734,688	930,648
Male	37,892*	70,667†	131,602	180,727	299,545	375,564	447,937
Female	884˸	4,252†	27,772	74,153	187,155	359,124	482,711
% Female	2.0	5.7	17.4	29.1	38.5	48.8	51.9
Office Clerks							
Total	29,801	59,799	187,969	248,323	720,498	1,487,905	1,997,000
Male	28,878§	59,484†	163,686†	229,991†	597,833	1,015,742	1,290,447
Female	923¶	315†	24,283†	18,332†	122,665	472,163	706,553
% Female	3.1	.5	12.9	7.4	17.0	31.7	35.4
Messenger, errand, and office boys/girls							
Total	8,046	12,818	47,183	66,009	108,035	113,022	90,379
Male	7,967#	12,421	44,294	59,392	96,748	98,768	81,430
Female	79	397	2,889	6,617	11,287	14,254	8,949
% Female	.9	3.1	6.1	10.0	10.4	12.6	9.9
Stenographers and typists							
Total	154	5,000	33,418	112,364	316,693	615,154	811,190
Male	147	3,000†	12,148	26,246	53,378	50,410	36,050
Female	7	2,000†	21,270	86,118	263,315	564,744	755,140
% Female	4.5	40.0	63.6	76.6	83.1	91.8	95.4

SOURCE: Alba M. Edwards, *Comparative Occupation Statistics for the United States, 1870 to 1940.* Part of the Sixteenth Census of the United States: 1940 (Washington, D.C.: Government Printing Office, 1943), Tables 9 and 10.

* Census figures estimated, and 372 added because of undercount in thirteen Southern states. For an explanation of the undercount, see Edwards, *Comparative Occupation Statistics,* Appendix A, note 3.
† All figures estimated. For information about how estimates were arrived at see Edwards, *Comparative Occupation Statistics,* Appendix A, notes 32, 42, 43, and 44.
˸ Census figures estimated, and 2 added because of undercount in thirteen Southern states.
§ Census figures estimated, and 488 added because of undercount in thirteen Southern states.
¶ Census figures estimated, and 6 added because of undercount in thirteen Southern states.
# 70 added because of undercount in thirteen Southern states.

From: Cindy Sondik Aron, *Ladies and Gentlemen of the Civil Service: Middle Class Workers in Victorian America* (New York: Oxford University Press, 1987).

record containers for storing and retrieving information were invented. Expansion, specialization, and division of labor came to the office just as they had to the factory.[5]

In 1876 when John R. Asher and George H. Adams published their *Pictorial Album of American Industry,* a celebratory history of national business firms, only 35 of the 112 companies pictured (fig. 56) therein had separate office facilities. Most of these were attached to the manufacturing complex. By 1898, when William B. Birkmire wrote *The Planning and Construction of the High Office Building,* commercial offices dominated the downtown core of the nation's cities. Born in Chicago, the skyscraper became the building type of American corporate business.[6]

Skyscrapers reflected the nation's changing economy, an economy floated on mergers and capital transfers rather than mercantile trading. Corporation administrations requiring huge staffs to keep track of regional and national operations located in city centers because such ''downtowns'' were the loci of communications, legal and financial expertise, and prestige. Big buildings advertised big business. Skyscrapers provided firms with expanded interior space and corporate symbols. Beginning in 1886 with Chicago's Home Insurance Building, the country's first skyscraper, cities of towers arose to dwarf other activities of everyday urban life: in Chicago, the Monadnock in 1889, the Reliance in 1894, and the Marquette in 1895; in New York, the Flatiron in 1901, the Singer in 1907, and the Woolworth in 1913. Alfred Stieglitz's 1910 photograph, *Old and New York,* encapsulated this momentous change in a single image.

Skyscrapers were only the most obvious artifacts in the late nineteenth-century commercialization of American city centers. Banks, advertising firms, insurance companies, and service-oriented businesses expanded on another scale and at an even more prolific rate. Each often required central, regional, and local offices. Here again exterior façades were important as the commercial core became a capitalist collage, a panoply of competing images embodying the rivalry of the market place.[7] Interior office space also deserves close investigation. Did the smaller offices experience the same trends of mechanization and standardization as their larger counterparts? Did common floor plans evolve for different business office functions. Who worked where and why?

Women Typists and Men Monitors

Prior to the 1870s the typical business office was a small affair, staffed entirely by men. In insurance offices and banks, the clerks enjoyed higher status and better pay than their counterparts in railroad companies and

Figure 56.
"View of the Ludlow Valve Manufacturing Works, Troy, New York"
From John R. Asher and George H. Adams, *Picture Album of Industrial America* (1876).

lawyers' offices. Senior clerks, involved in most stages of a business transaction, controlled their work. Usually they began their careers as messengers or office boys, eventually becoming copyists or bookkeepers, hoping ultimately to run a company of their own. As an old boy–new boy network, it operated on a daily, face-to-face basis in offices of three or four rooms. Jay Cooke, J. D. Rockefeller, and Frank Cooperwood in Theodore Dreiser's 1912 novel, *The Financier,* all launched their business careers as apprentice bookkeepers. The office staff generally enjoyed high status through regular contact with their employers, by the responsibilities entrusted to them, and because their wages equaled those of most skilled craftsmen. Even a novice clerk in the mid-nineteenth century, like "Bartleby, The Scrivener" in Herman Melville's 1856 short story, was an aspiring businessman apprenticed to be a capitalist sometime in the future.[8]

Fifty years later office work had changed dramatically. Most evident was the feminization of its worker force, a trend in which the growing federal bureaucracy led the way. First hired by the Treasury Department in 1862, female clerks (see fig. 55) penetrated other Washington bureaus, setting a precedent for the influx of other women workers who entered business and government offices in the following decades. By 1900 women constituted a third of all federal employees.[9]

Clerks became clerical workers. In 1876, 97.5 percent of office labor was male; by 1920, women made up more than a half of such workers. The rapid expansion of businesses, especially their consolidation in the 1890s merger movement, coupled with the successful marketing of the typewriter as a particularly "feminine" machine, paved the way for women's quick entry into offices (fig. 57).[10] Because of the lack of job opportunities for women in the professions, with the exception of nursing and teaching, literate women turned to clerical work.

These workers tended to be native-born, white, young (18 to 24 years old), single women, many of whom increasingly tended to live away from home. Some learned their tasks directly on the job, but many took courses in arithmetic, typing, shorthand, penmanship, and bookkeeping in the rapidly growing commercial schools (fig. 58), at the YWCA, or in the commercial course in the new high schools.[11] In these courses they pounded out the 1872 Republican rallying slogan for U. S. Grant ("Now is the time for all good men to come to the aid of their party") and practiced William McKinley's 1901 Pan-American Exposition speech (a standard shorthand exercise). Clerical jobs paid better than many jobs open to women. A high school graduate of the classical course teaching in an urban public school earned $50 a month, or $450 per year. Her counterpart from the commercial course received $660. Most mill women averaged a $5 weekly wage whereas, in a 1910 Boston survey, copyists in personal service earned an average $6.78, cashiers $7.43, and bookkeepers $6.55.[12] Hence many worked in offices for the money. In Booth Tarkington's 1921 novel, *Alice Adams,* a middle-class daughter goes into clerical work because a family business fails. To many daughters of working-class parents, like Rachel Toomis in Dorothy Richardson's 1905 *The Long Day: The Story of a New York Working Girl,* office work offered economic and social mobility. Such families often regarded a clerical job as having higher status than factory work, domestic service, or clerking in stores.[13] Other women chose the office because they wanted a change in everyday life: independence, release from boredom at home, or the excitement of new experiences in the city.

Whatever her motivations for working, the office woman's place came to be largely restricted to the typewriter or some other business machine (fig. 59). A talented woman office worker might become a supervisor of a typing pool or a head of a bookkeeping department, but she could never expect to become a junior executive or a full partner. Viewed by male monitors to have no ambitions of their own, and hence unlikely

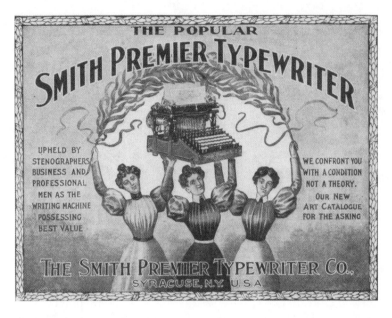

Figure 57.
"The Popular Smith Premier Typewriter"
Advertisement (1910) for the Smith Premier Typewriter Company, Syracuse,
New York.

to be dissatisfied if their jobs offered no prospect of advancement, office women became the equivalent of semiskilled workers in the mill or plant.

The gender hierarchy of pay and power that characterized the office by 1915 occurred largely because of specialization and technology. Managers divided companies into departments—accounting, purchasing, auditing, credit, personnel, marketing, filing—each carrying out part of the work process, with every clerk in a given department doing the same work. Departments might be arranged on a single floor or require separate floors or even buildings. With the departments connected by the flow of paperwork, the corporate office resembled a factory in organization. The clerical worker, instead of being an autonomous male clerk charged with the whole of a business transaction, acted primarily as a process worker. Perhaps the most potent sign of the parallel of clerical worker with plant worker was the appearance of the time clock (fig. 60) in business offices by 1910.

Scientific management manuals like Walter D. Scott's 1911 *Increasing Human Efficiency in Business* furthered the division of office labor. They urged reducing each office worker's task, such as opening the mail or answering complaint letters, to the most efficient motions.[14] Amazing

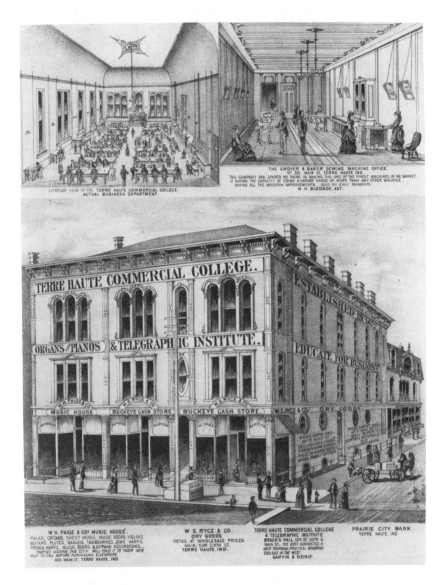

Figure 58.
Terre Haute Commercial College, Terre Haute, Indiana
Advertisement (1890).
(Courtesy The Library of Congress, Division of Prints and Photographs)

Figure 59.
"The Calculus"
Advertisement for the James J. Hinde Company, Cleveland, Ohio. From
System magazine (1912).

Figure 60.
International Time Recording System
Advertisement (1912) for the International Time Recording Company,
Endicott, New York.

results were promised: correspondents who had previously managed with difficulty to answer twenty letters per hour were shown how to do sixty; letter opening increased from 100 to 300 per hour. Managers often charted the statistical output of individual workers and recognized those who exceeded the weekly norms. They set up other intra- and inter-office competitions to see who could achieve the most in a work week.[15]

Successful typing contests often determined office status. Everyone knew everyone else's "words-per-minute" rate. Ironically, the typewriter—the invention of a man, Christopher L. Sholes, who first exhibited it at the 1876 Centennial—both eased the entry of women into the formerly masculine office and enslaved them to subservient status once there.[16] When first marketed, it had no historical ties to either sex, which meant that female typists did not have to counter (as women did in factories) the argument that they were operating "a man's machine." By the 1880s, advertisers and office managers, however, changed this, by calling it a "literary piano" and claiming the most efficient typing required the supposedly greater nimbleness of women's hands. Hence when Mark Twain, the typewriter's staunch publicist, bought his first machine, the salesman had a "type girl" to demonstrate it to him. In 1870, 4.5 percent of typists were female; by 1930, that figure was 91.8 percent.

In its early years of development and use, some women hoped to use the typewriter as a tool by which to achieve financial independence as an "amanuensis," "stenographer," or "secretary." G. Gissing's novel, *The Odd Women* (London: W. Heineman, 1893), describes women owning their own machines and operating typewriting salons or working freelance in their homes.[17] Eleanor Marx, Karl's daughter, trained herself in typewriting and shorthand and hired herself out as a public stenographer. This vision of personal ownership of the means of production was, however, rapidly eclipsed by the typist or secretary who operated a machine owned by her office.

Business initially resisted the typewriter as too impersonal an instrument for correspondence. Sears, for instance, continued to write customer letters by hand long after typewriters enjoyed widespread use. Signing (in ink) typed correspondence remains a vestigial ritual of this concern.

An irony of the typewriter (fig. 61) is its technological inefficiency. Sholes, its principal inventor, had a devil of a time keeping its keys from jamming. He originally arranged them alphabetically. Later he worked out the most frequent combinations of letters in English, then scattered them as widely as possible so they would be less likely to foul each other. Thus was born the Qwerty keyboard we use today.

Figure 61.
"Typewriters"
Advertisement section from *McClure's Magazine* (1896).

Although early typewriters resembled sewing machines (Remington) or had a semicircular keyboard (Hammond), most office models by 1900 were black, with white lettering on black keys, and a sturdy metal carriage—all suggesting industrial design attributes such as efficiency, rationality, and reliability.

What about the machine's operators who quickly became known as "typewriters"? How did working at the typewriter change women's office work? How did what they wore to work relate to how they worked?

To address the last question first, shirtwaists and skirts dominated women clerical workers' dress much as suits and ties did the dress of their male counterparts. Shirtwaists sold as separate items of apparel, a great boon to working women who, with a skirt or two and a half dozen shirtwaists, could appear daily at the office in different changes of clothing. Women wore shirtwaists on all occasions since the fashion came in numerous forms. There were mannish tailored waists, hand-embroidered waists, nursing waists, and very dressy silk taffeta waists. Advertised in department stores, women's magazines, and mail-order catalogs at prices ranging from fifty cents to seven dollars, shirtwaists fulfilled the expectations of everyone, ranging from the affluent to the girls who made them. When artist Charles Dana Gibson sought to capture "the typical American girl" of his time, he depicted her in the standard shirtwaist-and-skirt costume (see fig. 66). The "Gibson Girl," in turn, became one of the symbols of the era—a role model for the "new" woman; a steel-engraved lady who embodied a new aesthetic and femininity; and an advertising icon used to sell skirts, jackets, blouses, and waists.

Most office women emulated "the Gibson look" because it was fashionable and practical. Technical training manuals such as the Stenographic Efficiency Bureau's 1916 publication, *How to Become a Successful Stenographer: For the Young Woman Who Wants to Make Good,* likewise urged dressing for success, advocating a middle ground in clothing, one neither too feminine (avoid "fluffy, frilly furbelows") or too masculine (shun "tweeds and cheviots").[18] What was appropriate to the new business environment? A black skirt and a white shirtwaist, resembling in color and effect the sober, organized, clean look and lines of the secretary's typewriter.

Books, manuals, and magazines (fig. 62) written for women training to be typists taught women to be a typewriter in two senses of the word, that is, how to operate the machine and how to operate the self. As Joli Jensen demonstrates, this normative literature depicted the typist as an expert, an individual as efficient, reliable, and durable as the machine

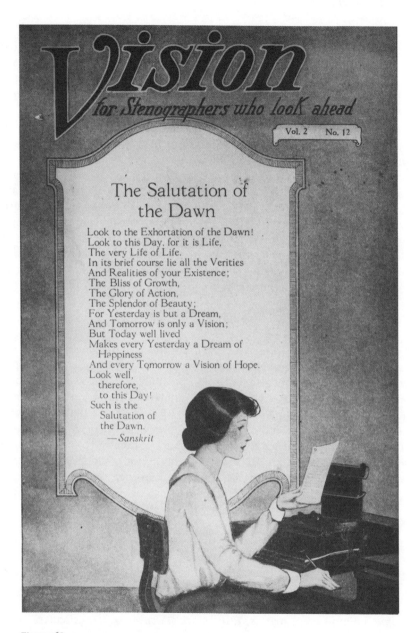

Figure 62.
Vision Magazine, 2.12 (1914)
(Courtesy The Warshaw Collection of Business Americana, National Museum of American History, Smithsonian Institution, Washington, D.C.)

itself. As early advertisements promoted the speed and efficiency of the new technology, the early manuals urged these as the qualities of the new office technicians. For example, another book published by the Stenographic Efficiency Bureau in 1916, entitled *Making the Body an Efficient Machine,* offers advice to typists about health rules, correct food (a sample menu is offered), an exercise routine, sensible hours, and outside interests.[19] Following such a regimen of physical culture, "you can tax your body with an enormous amount of work without affecting it injuriously."[20]

Touch typing, a technique developed in the 1890s, required typists to think of their bodies as artifacts, as machines. In order to achieve fast, neat, and accurate copy, touch typing demanded a rigid upright posture, with properly arched wrists, fingers hovering on the home keys, eyes on the text to be transcribed, not on the typewriter keyboard. Such "scientific" or "rational" typewriting, with its horror of any waste of motion or energy, was a form of Frederick W. Taylor's scientific management extended from the factory floor to the front office.[21]

Environment and Equipment

Typewriters were only one of several innovations in the postbellum office. Furniture was redesigned and new machines were installed to manage work and workers more efficiently and profitably. Desks, as Adrian Forty has traced, changed first. The standard nineteenth-century, senior clerk's desk such as the famous Wooton Desk (fig. 63) had a high back with pigeonholes and drawers in it, and sometimes a roll top. A clerk seated at such a desk "could see his work in front of him and a little to either side. He could not see ahead beyond his desk, nor could anyone else see what he was doing without coming to look over his shoulder." A clerk at such a desk was assumed responsible for its contents; it represented a small personal domain, "perhaps with a roll top that could be closed down at any time to secure its privacy. From his desk, the clerk collected and delivered office papers at his own pace; he filed papers as he chose in its drawers and pigeonholes."[22]

The "Modern Efficiency Desk" (fig. 64), designed in 1915, suggests a totally different view of everyday office work. Gone is any sense of a worker's private enclave. The new desk form is only a table with shallow drawers. Filing space matters little, since scientific office managers made that chore a separate task of filing clerks. A "sanitary," flat-top desk, arranged according to an officewide "desk system"—say, top left drawer for unfinished work, middle for stationery, top right for completed work, facilitated paper flow and employee supervision. Managers periodically

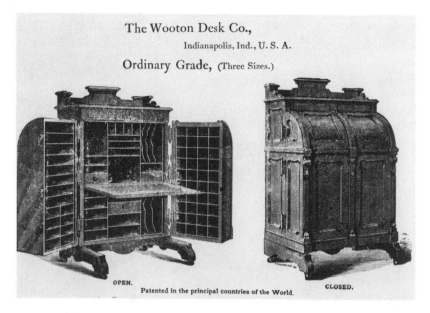

The Wooton Desk Co.,
Indianapolis, Ind., U. S. A.
Ordinary Grade, (Three Sizes.)

OPEN.
Patented in the principal countries of the World.
CLOSED.

Figure 63.
"Ordinary Grade Desk"
Trade catalog advertisement (1876) for the Wooton Desk Company,
Indianapolis, Indiana.

inspected desk drawers to compare a clerk's volume of "in" and "out" work.[23]

The standardization of desks, arranged in uniform order on the office floor, extended even to providing identical rulers, paper clips, erasers, and pens. Office managers argued that "instead of supplying different pens to suit the handwriting idiosyncrasies of individual clerks, one nib style would be more economical and would give the firm's paperwork more uniformity." The Spencerian Method of scripting, introduced in schools in 1874, further standardized the nation's penmanship. Thus, "even in handwriting, the most individual and personal characteristic left to the clerk, nonconformity meant inefficiency."[24]

Scientific management should have been applied with equal force to everyone in an office. Managers, it turned out, usually received different environments than clerks, although their basic activity in terms of time-and-motion study—sitting, reading, or writing at a desk—was exactly the same. While clerks had standardized dip pens, managers wrote with fountain pens first perfected by Benjamin Watermann in 1883 (fig. 65). Redesign of the clerk's desk failed to apply to an executive's

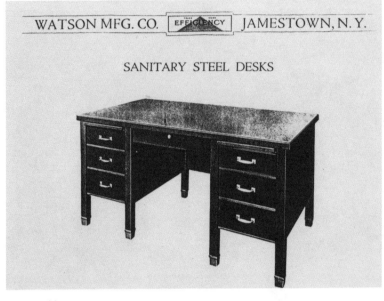

Figure 64.
"Sanitary Steel Desks"
Trade catalog advertisement (1910) for the Watson Manufacturing Company,
Jamestown, New York.

desk. Although centralized filing had eliminated storage need and efficiency required no more space than necessary for writing, executive desks
(usually situated in glass enclosures or separate rooms) continued as obvious status symbols. Their size and style immediately established who
was boss.

With the exception of the dictaphone—the one new (1885) business
machine personally used by the executive and hence disguised in a
wooden cabinet to make it more appropriate furniture for the manager's
suite—most other office technology—the mimeograph (1876), the adding
machine (1884), and other specialized equipment—was overtly mechanical and industrial in appearance. Painted black and supported on tubular
metal frames, these new mechanisms, run by the female office staff, speed-
ed up and further segregated traditional office tasks.[25] Duplicating
machines churned out thousands of copies an hour; addressographs could
mail hundreds of letters a minute; tabulators added a 30-digit column in
a second. Dictating machines separated the tasks of the typist-steno-
grapher, forcing her into full-time typing and contributing to the eventual demise of shorthand as a work technique. Bookkeeping machines

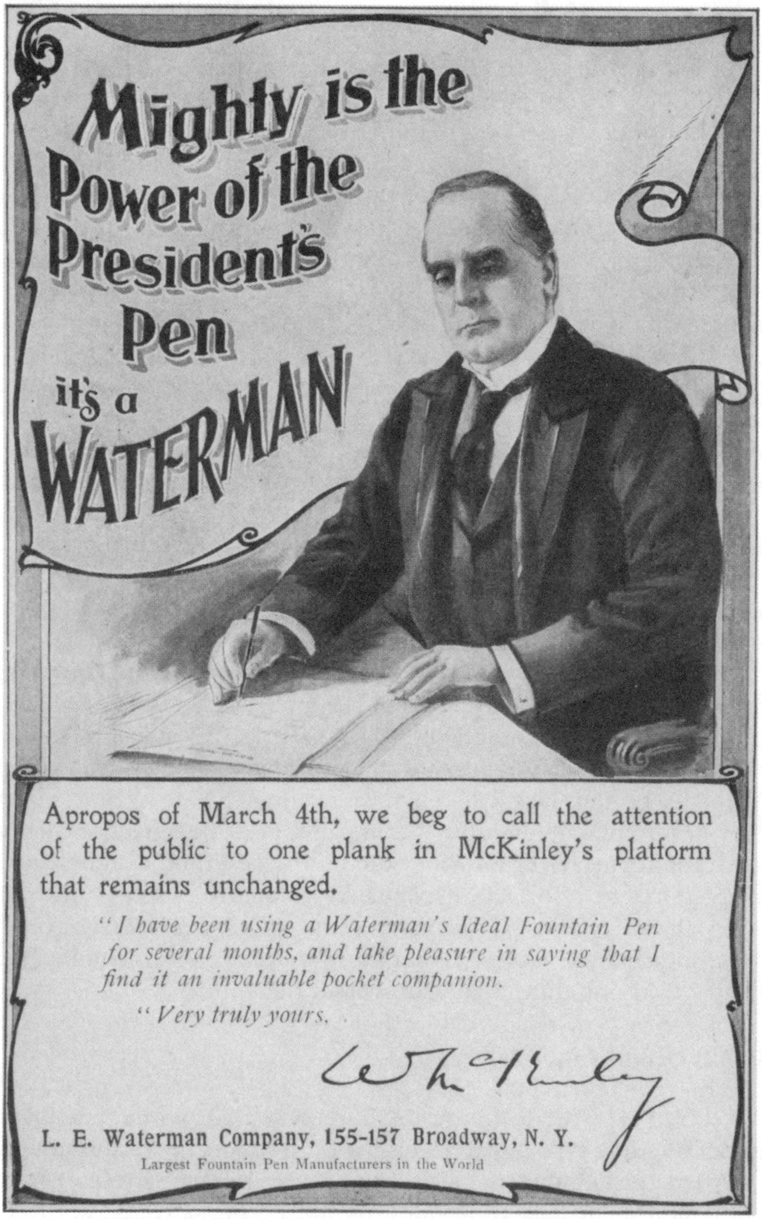

Figure 65.
Harper's Weekly, 1901
Advertisement for the L. E. Waterman Company, New York City.

of all types further divided clerical work into subspecialties of billing, crediting, and auditing.[26]

Even filing took on a revolutionary new format. Take, for example, the traditional record-management procedures of a federal government office. Consider a letter sent to the Treasury from one of its routine correspondents (a customs house official, or a taxpayer). First, a clerk registered it; that is, the name of the writer, the date of the letter, and the date of its receipt, its subject, the name of the clerk or division to which the letter was given for reply, and the number assigned to the letter were recorded in a central file. These files were ordered first by the initial letter of the writer's name or office, and then chronologically. Eventually, these incoming letters were bundled with white or red woven-cloth string (hence the expression, "bureaucratic red tape") and eventually bound into sets of volumes by year. The answer to that letter retraced the same route, more or less. The clerk, or whoever answered the letter, drafted a reply for the signature of the secretary or the assistant secretary. A clerk made a press copy of the letter. This copy was transcribed into one of a large set of bound volumes, arranged by subject or function of the addressee, and then chronologically. (The press copies, too, were later bound into similar volumes). Government files were, therefore, multiple, permanent, and unwieldy.[27]

Though no private firm approached a government department's paperwork, the traditional system of chronological press books, indexed alphabetically by correspondent, slowly gave way to other systems. Vertical files—first available in expandable modular box units like those made by Globe-Wernicke Elastic Cabinet, later refined by the Kraft Company's "Ever-Resortable, Re-Fileable" Company in 1900 changed the way Americans kept track of how they did business. With the humble manila folder—portable, resortable, expandable—and its four-drawer file cabinet (fig. 66) the chronological tyranny of the press-book archive was broken. All the information on an account, a transaction, or an employee was enveloped in one thin, easily accessible, file.[28]

Managers and Engineers

As skyscrapers arose to house the burgeoning corporate bureaucracy, another building type more celebrated for horizontality rather than verticality emerged on the American industrial landscape. Between 1840 and 1920, American manufacturing moved from a water-powered, small-scale, rural base to a steam- (later electric-) driven, immense urban one. Factory buildings evolved from wood frame to brick to brick-covered steel frame, and by 1910 exotic materials such as terra cotta, poured concrete,

Figure 66.
"Vertical Filing: Down-to-Date"
Advertisement (1915).
(Courtesy The Warshaw Collection of Business Americana, National Museum of American History, Smithsonian Institution, Washington, D.C.)

and wired glass were being accepted even by tradition-minded company owners.[29] Plant managers, instructed by systems engineers in the most productive means of channeling worker and material flow, considered the one-story, sprawling factory or works as vastly more productive than the multistory, elevator-serviced structures.

The scale and complexity of the industrial plant could be only adequately captured by aerial photography, another innovation of the period. For example, Armour's Chicago plant, the largest slaughtering and packing plant in the world, employed over 6,000 workers, and Swift's, the second largest, over 4,000. In 1915, the Ford Plant at Highland Park, Michigan, had a work force of over 16,000 workers and the United States Steel complex at Homestead, Pennsylvania, over 9,000.[30]

Plants became small cities, complete with their own railroad terminals, street systems, water supplies, energy sources, telephone networks, fire departments, canteens, restaurants, hospitals, and security forces. Requiring vast amounts of space, new plants reoriented the geography, transportation patterns, and housing markets of many cities. While some plants, such as the Disston Saw and Stetson Hat works in Philadelphia, were the result of steady expansion of nineteenth-century family mills, others like the U.S. Steel Plant in Gary were massive sites newly built in outlying areas. Plant management also assumed monumental proportions, creating a hierarchy of foremen, general foremen, superintendents, and managers who coordinated purchasing, manufacturing, and marketing on a grand scale. Paper flow and record-keeping escalated as every worker had to report what he did and how long it took him to a supervisor who did the same to his superior.[31]

In a way parallel to the postbellum division of the responsibilities and authority of a senior male clerk in a commercial office, a plant foreman's duties and status were reduced and delegated to new workers who wore white collars and who had desks in the plant's front office. That office housed the plant manager and his pyramidal chain of command.

New industrial managers revamped the manufacturing process and in so doing extended the boundaries of the paper empire. A line-and-staff structure organized this increase in bureaucracy and white-collar workers. The Remington typewriter factory at Illion, New York, reorganized in 1910, provides a good illustration of this managerial expansion. All units involved in the fabrication and assembling of parts were placed in the manufacturing department—the line department. Each subunit had its own foreman responsible for its output. The other departments—purchasing, stock order, shipping, inspection, time and cost, works, engineering, and labor—became staff departments, reporting directly to the plant manager and his assistants.[32]

White-collar workers increasingly managed activities formerly the domain of the blue-collar foreman. Accountants filled out and tabulated "cost sheets" detailing statistics about every aspect of production. Time keepers monitored a worker's job time. Industrial welfare secretaries kept track of workers' life away from the plant. Time-study engineers calculated the most efficient "system" for doing a particular job. Quality control inspectors reviewed finished work. Personnel departments, like the one instituted at the National Cash Register Company in 1902, did the hiring and firing.

As David Noble and Monte Calvert have shown, engineers invariably occupied these new managerial posts. While their names—Charles Sorensen at Ford, Frederick Taylor at Midvale Steel, William Dodge at Armour—are neglected even in general American business history, they changed how many Americans did everyday factory and office work. They introduced important technical innovations into mass production via their experiments with new materials, power sources, plant designs, and new machinery. Equally significant was their social engineering of managerial procedures required to synchronize the work place and to supervise the work force.[33] Their prowess in these and other tasks appears in the vogue of "engineer" novels such as Samuel Merwin's 1905 *The Road Builders* or Charles Barnard's 1881 *Knights of Today*.[34]

Managers also introduced inventory control plans to keep track of what work and materials cost. Using cards or tickets they conveyed instructions to foreman and workers, detailing the scheduling and sequence of work. Other forms, usually a type of "cost sheet," demanded detailed information on "prime costs," "indirect costs," and "overhead costs." Factory accounting, increasingly done by an enlarged clerical staff, meant additional management control. As James Bridge, a supervisor in Carnegie Steel works noted: "The minutest details of cost of materials and labor in every department appeared from day to day and week to week in the accounts; and soon every man about the place was made to realize it. The men felt and often remarked that the eyes of the company were always on them through the books."[35]

Plant managers and industrial engineers used three material forms of time—the synchronized clock system, the time clock, and the stopwatch—to extend and maintain front-office order over the vast reaches of the manufacturing plant floor.

The Self-Winding Clock Company, a shadow corporation of Western Union, provided electric synchronized clock systems and daily time signals to factories, schools, and offices. An exhibitor at Chicago's 1893 exposition, the firm demonstrated its product's accuracy by regulating over two hundred clocks from its central pavilion.[36] The "master clock" in such systems linked "slave" or "controlled" clocks; the master clock could be programmed to ring bells or trigger machines on or off. A company brochure claimed that the firm's best model, the "Autocrat," eliminated the caprice of a forgetful bell ringer or a supervisor's unreliable watch by providing an infallible time standard that disciplined tardiness, divided days into segments, and prevented early departures.[37]

Synchronized clock systems with time-stamping mechanisms added another control on industrial laboring. Prior to the 1890s, most factories stationed a man or woman at the mill gate. The timekeeper logged a handwritten record of employees' names as they came and went; other companies assigned each worker a numbered brass check to present to the timekeeper who recorded name and number in a ledger. In large firms, this meant waiting in long lines; arguments about whose watch—the timekeeper's or the worker's—had the "right" time; and the possibility of forged accounts to protect a tardy friend or to dock a punctual enemy. American patents for time-recording clocks followed quickly after the standardizing of time by the American Railway Association in 1883.[38] Some time clocks required a worker to insert a brass key into the machine, triggering a stamp that printed the employee's number and the time on a tape or card (fig. 67); others used an Autograph Recorder (fig. 68) where employees signed in and out of work; and still others presented each employee with a large dial with numbers on it. The worker swung a pointer around to his or her number, then pushed a small rod, which printed time on a prepared sheet. Employers sometimes housed time clocks in special "time offices." The timekeeper's building at H. J. Heinz's Pittsburgh plant featured stained-glass windows depicting the company's origins, the city's seal, portraits of Republican presidents, and mottos urging energy, thrift, temperance, and punctuality. Workers daily checked in and out of this office, which also served as an early personnel department.[39] Promising promptness, order, and discipline, time clocks became standard fixtures of many large plants and offices. By 1907 nearly all the leading manufacturers had been bought up by the International Time Recording Company, later known as IBM.[40]

"Time studies of work," claimed Frederick Winslow Taylor in 1911 in *Principles of Scientific Management,* "form the basis of modern management."[41] Taylor, a pattern maker, machinist, and industrial consultant, sought to standardize factory production with his stopwatch. At Pennsylvania's Midvale Steel in 1908, he first conducted time and motion studies of the most efficient way for men to load pig iron. He and his followers went on to time needless motions and unproductive distractions in bricklaying, arms manufacture, metal cutting, and steel making. With stopwatch in hand, Taylorites attempted to ascertain the minimum time in which any work might be done or, put another way, to establish an unvarying, uniform, and supremely efficient standard time for any job.[42]

Taylorism or "scientific management" struck many Victorians as a rational way for eliminating many economic and social evils. To a generation suckled on William McGuffey's readers and Catherine Beecher's home manuals, Taylor's determination to extract the maximum yield from a given effort with the least amount of time and money spent meant an appropriate way to use one's time.

Taylor's time imposed a machine logic on the workday of mill and plant. Combined with other material culture manifestations of the mass-production process—precision jig and gauge systems, conveyor materials handling, sheet metal stamping, electric resistance welding, and special- or single-purpose machinery—it choreographed the human motions of hands, arms, backs, and legs to perform with clocklike regularity. It influenced various work places—Lodge and Shipley's machine tool works

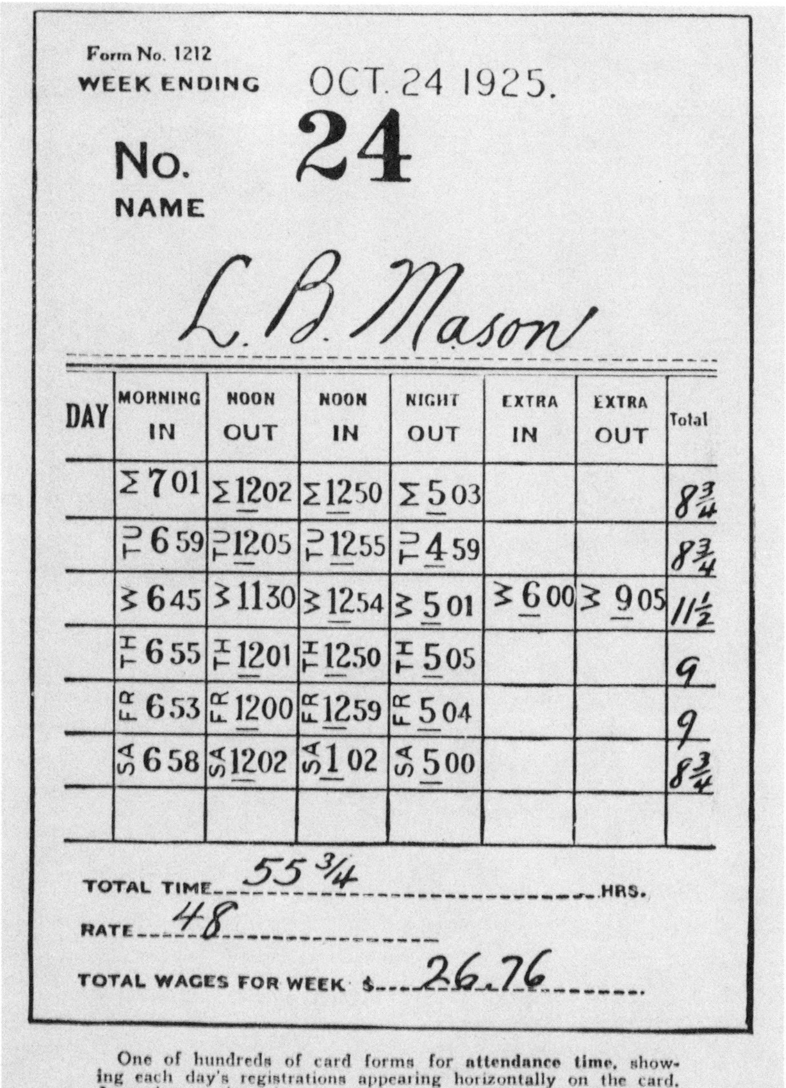

Form No. 1212

WEEK ENDING OCT. 24 1925.

No. 24

NAME

L. B. Mason

DAY	MORNING IN	NOON OUT	NOON IN	NIGHT OUT	EXTRA IN	EXTRA OUT	Total
	M 7 01	M 12 02	M 12 50	M 5 03			$8\frac{3}{4}$
	TU 6 59	TU 12 05	TU 12 55	TU 4 59			$8\frac{3}{4}$
	W 6 45	W 11 30	W 12 54	W 5 01	W 6 00	W 9 05	$11\frac{1}{2}$
	TH 6 55	TH 12 01	TH 12 50	TH 5 05			9
	FR 6 53	FR 12 00	FR 12 59	FR 5 04			9
	SA 6 58	SA 12 02	SA 1 02	SA 5 00			$8\frac{3}{4}$

TOTAL TIME $55\frac{3}{4}$ HRS.

RATE 48

TOTAL WAGES FOR WEEK $ 26.76

One of hundreds of card forms for **attendance time**, showing each day's registrations appearing horizontally on the card. Irregular registrations appear in red on original record. International Time Recorders in their various models print daily, weekly, two-weekly, semi-monthly, tri-monthly, quadri-monthly or monthly records.

NOTE—Card forms for use with International Time Recorders are furnished in accordance with the individual requirements of any business.

Figure 67.
Sample Employee Time Card, Dial Time Clock
International Business Machines trade catalog (1926).
(Courtesy The Warshaw Collection of Business Americana, National Museum of American History, Smithsonian Institution, Washington, D.C.)

Series 2000
**JOB TIME
RECORDER**
Clock Driven

Prints Starting and
Stopping Time on jobs
or operations

Job Time Recorders
furnished in thirty-
eight models

*See specimen record,
page 39*

Series 3000
**AUTOGRAPH RE-
CORDER**, in which
employees sign their
n a m e s alongside
printed time registra-
tions.

No. 9106
CARD RECORDER
Electrically Operated
Two Color Record
Semi-Automatic

Card Time Recorders
furnished in 166 models

*See specimen records,
pages 37 and 38*

Figure 68.
Job Time, Autograph, and Card Time Recorders
International Business Machines trade catalog (1926).
*(Courtesy The Warshaw Collection of Business Americana, National
Museum of American History, Smithsonian Institution, Washington, D.C.)*

in Cincinnati, International Harvester in Chicago, Westinghouse Electric in Pittsburgh—but reached its zenith in Ford's Highland Park plant in 1914.[43]

A phalanx of managers in large corporations like Ford, Armour, or General Electric controlled highly regulated work environments. No artifact summarizes the progress of the managerial revolution more graphically than a corporation's organization chart (fig. 69). Here, in a streamlined format much admired by the administrative mind, was depicted the expansion of general managers, managers, superintendents, and supervisors into everyday work. This white-collar empire formed a huge maze of central, branch, regional, and district offices, theoretically bridging the gap between the capital capabilities of the stockholders and the technical skills of factory workers. Here, in rational arrangement and sanitized precision, could be found new features of American big business: parallel product operations, foreign market expansion, research and development laboratories, by-product utilization. Here, in an administrative hierarchy where everyone knew his place but hoped to move to the one above, managers and supervisors were hired to know how to perform, and thereby control, work in which they did not participate.

While the new corporate ladder had many administrative rungs, by 1915 it had only one form of proper dress: the business suit. The suit, "the trusty blue serge" introduced in the 1890s, descended from several nineteenth-century forms of male dress including the frock, the cutaway or morning coat, the ditto suit (coat vest, trousers cut from same cloth), the clawhammer or tail coat, and, most important, the sack coat. The two- or three-piece business suit superceded these older modes of attire and became the standard uniform for executives and managers, professionals and clerks. Suits, if advertisements for them are to be believed, symbolized modern masculinity—the American male as thinker, expert, and manager. Whereas the "Perfect Gentleman" dressed in a Prince Albert long coat personified the male sartorial ideal of the 1870s, the "Coming Man" in business suit, tie, and Arrow white shirt embodied the ideal of the 1910s.[44]

Ready-to-wear suits diffused the monotony of male dress throughout the society. (Sears, for example sold 9,000 in a single day in 1896.) While middle-class men owned several suits for both work and play, most working men had only a single, "Sunday best" suit for the formal routines (church, wedding, funeral) of everyday life. The dark suit's simplicity

---

(*Overleaf*)
Figure 69.
Organization Chart of Armour and Company
From *System* magazine (September 1907).

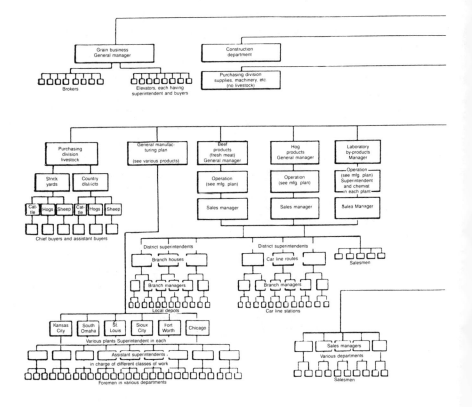

Grain business
General manager

Brokers

Elevators, each having
superintendent and buyers

Construction
department

Purchasing division
supplies, machinery. etc.
(no livestock)

Purchasing
division
livestock

Stock
yards

Country
districts

Cat-
tle

Hogs

Sheep

Cat-
tle

Hogs

Sheep

Chief buyers and assistant buyers

General manufac-
turing plan

(see various products)

District superintendents

Branch houses

Branch managers

Local depots

Kansas
City

South
Omaha

St.
Louis

Sioux
City

Fort
Worth

Chicago

Various plants Superintendent in each

Assistant superintendents
in charge of different classes of work

Foremen in various departments

Beef
products
(fresh meat)
General manager

Operation
(see mfg. plan)

Sales manager

Hog
products
General manager

Operation
(see mfg. plan)

Sales manager

District superintendents

Car line routes

Branch managers

Car line stations

Laboratory
by-products
Manager

Operation
(see mfg. plan)
Superintendent
and chemist
in each plant

Sales Manager

Salesmen

Sales managers

Various departments

Salesmen

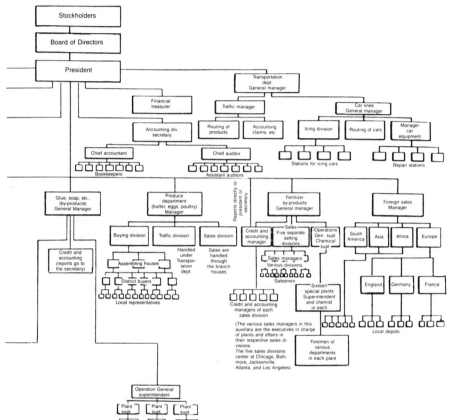

made it versatile—one could wear it at all times and places; it showed dirt and wear less; it was economical (a typical 1897 price range at Browning, King, and Co. went from $8 to $30); its inconspicuousness was manly but not showy; its somberness provided a contrasting, but not competing, setting for the usually more colorful costume of women.

Business suits demanded white shirts. Since colonial times gentlemen clothed themselves in "white" linen. Workers wore colored, soft-collared shirts because they showed dirt less easily. Once manufacturers began in the 1880s producing shirts with detachable collars and cuffs—which were made out of paper or celluloid—the starched, white, shirt façade theoretically meant any man could upgrade his status. In fact, however, the artificial shirt appendages tended to reinforce the increasingly rigid division between white-collar and blue-collar workers.

By World War I white-collared managers ran the day-to-day operations of most large industrial plants. For example, the number of supervisory employees in manufacturing, mining, and transportation grew by 66.3 percent compared to a 27.7 percent increase among wage earners.[45] This managerial concentration, succinctly diagrammed by dense stratifications of organization chart, had three important ramifications. Skilled craft workers almost ceased to be production workers. Instead they now did ancillary tasks—model making, trouble shooting, setup, toolmaking. Production work came to be done by specialized operatives whose routines, output, and status were controlled by an assortment of supervisory technicians.[46] Finally, as the functions of many skilled artisans shifted in mills and factories and the number of specialized operatives increased, the cadre of office workers and the number of their work places grew enormously in industrial America. Women of the white shirtwaist and men of the white collar in their hierarchical ranks (stenographer-typist to chief executive officer) stationed at many posts (factory front office to skyscraper penthouse suite) filed, budgeted, processed, audited, and managed the American paper empire.

Notes

1. Alan Dundes, *Urban Folklore from the Paper Empire* (Austin, Tex.: American Folklore Society, 1976); Dundes has updated this work with a new collection titled: *When You're Up to Your Ass in Alligators: More Urban Folklore from the Paperwork Empire* (Detroit: Wayne State University Press, 1987).

2. On biographies of historians by historians see Ray Allen Billington, *Frederick Jackson Turner* (New York: Oxford University Press, 1973); Gregory M. Tobin, *The Making of a History: Walter Prescott Webb and the Great Plains* (Austin: University of Texas Press, 1976); John Herbert Roper, *C. Vann Woodward, Southerner* (Athens: University of Georgia Press, 1987); Susan Stout Baker, *Radical Beginnings: Richard Hofstadter and the 1930s* (Westport, Conn.: Greenwood Press, 1985); Clyde N. Wilson, ed.,

American Historians 1866–1912 (Detroit: Gale Research Co., 1986); Clyde N. Wilson, ed., *Twentieth-Century American Historians* (Detroit: Gale Research Co., 1983). Historians' autobiographies include: Roy F. Nichols, *A Historian's Progress* (New York: A. A. Knopf, 1968); Arnold Toynbee, *Acquaintances* (London: Oxford University Press, 1967); Henry Farnham May, *Coming to Terms: A Study in Memory and History* (Berkeley: University of California Press, 1987); C. Vann Woodward, *Thinking Back: The Perils of Writing History* (Baton Rouge: Louisiana State University Press, 1986); Thomas Andrew Bailey, *The American Pageant Revisited: Recollections of a Stanford Historian* (Stanford, Calif.: Hoover Institution Press, 1982).

3. C. Wright Mills, *White Collar: The American Middle Classes* (New York: 1951); Alfred D. Chandler, *The Visible Hand: The Managerial Revolution in American Business* (Cambridge, Mass.: Harvard University Press, 1977).

4. Margery Davies, *Women's Place Is at the Typewriter: Office Work and Office Workers, 1870–1930* (Philadelphia: Temple University Press, 1982); Martha Vicinus, *Independent Women: Work and Community for Single Women, 1850–1920* (Chicago: University of Chicago Press, 1985); Carole Srole, "A Position That God Has Not Particularly Assigned to Men: The Feminization of Clerical Work, Boston, 1860–1915," Ph.D. dissertation, University of California, Los Angeles (1984); Elyce J. Rotella, *From Home to Office: U.S. Women at Work, 1870–1930* (Ann Arbor: UMI Research Press, 1981); Anita J. Rapone, "Clerical Labor Formation: The Office Woman in Albany, 1870–1930," Ph.D. dissertation, New York University (1981); Mark Stuart Sandler, "Clerical Proletarianization in Capitalist Development," Ph.D. dissertation, Michigan State University (1979).

5. Adrian Forty, *Objects of Desire: Design and Society from Wedgewood to IBM* (New York: Pantheon, 1986), esp. chap. 4, "Design of the Office." Specialized literature on office mechanization can be reviewed in contemporary sources such as: John William Schulze, *The American Office, Its Organization, Management, and Records* (New York: McGraw-Hill, 1913); H. J. Barrett, *Modern Methods in the Office* (New York, 1918); William Henry Leffingwell, *The Office Appliance Manual* (Chicago: National Association of Office Appliance Manufacturers, 1926); and many others.

6. Carl Condit, *The Chicago School of Architecture: A History of the Commercial Office Building, 1870–1920* (Chicago: University of Chicago Press, 1964); Paul Goldberger, *The Skyscraper* (New York: A. A. Knopf, 1981); John R. Asher and George H. Adams, *Pictorial Album of American Industry* (New York: Asher & Adams, 1876; reprint New York: Rutledge Books, 1976); William H. Birkmire, *The Planning and Construction of High Office Buildings* (New York: John Wiley and Sons, 1898).

7. Larry Ford, "The Diffusion of the Skyscraper as an Urban Symbol," *Association of Pacific Coast Geographers Yearbook* 34 (1973): 49–60; Robert A. M. Stern et al., *New York 1900: Metropolitan Architecture and Urbanism, 1890–1915* (New York: Rizzoli, 1983); Karen Luehrs and Timothy J. Crimmins, "In the Mind's Eye: The Downtown as Visual Metaphor for the Metropolis," *Atlanta Historical Journal* 26 (Summer–Fall 1982): 177–98.

For an exterior-form primer on commercial buildings see Richard Longstreth, *The Buildings of Main Street: A Guide to American Commercial Architecture* (Washington: Preservation Press, 1987). Also useful are Francis Duffy, "Office Buildings and Organizational Change," in *Buildings and Society,* ed. A. D. King (London: Routledge and Kegan Paul, 1983) and an older work, R. W. Sexton, *American Commercial Buildings of Today* (New York: Architectural Book Publishing, 1928).

8. A. St. Horlich, "Counting Houses and Clerks: The Social Control of Young Men in New York, 1840–1860," Ph.D. dissertation, University of Wisconsin (1960); Jurgen Kocka, *American White Collar Workers in America, 1890–1940* (Beverly Hills: Sage Publications, 1980). See also Theodore Dreiser, *The Financier* (New York: Harper and Brothers, 1912; reprint New York: Signet Books, 1967) and Herman Melville, "Bartleby the Scrivener" in *The Piazza Tales* (1856).

9. Cindy Sondik Aron, *Ladies and Gentlemen of the Civil Service: Middle-Class Workers in Victorian America* (New York: Oxford University Press, 1987), 40–61.

10. On business consolidations see *Historical Statistics of the United States,* pt. 2. (Washington, D.C.: U.S. Government Printing Office, 1975), 909, 911, 913–14; Alfred D. Chandler, Jr., *The Visible Hand: The Rise of Modern Business Enterprise in the United States* (Cambridge, Mass.: Harvard University Press, 1977); G. P. Porter and H. C. Livesay, "Oligopolists in American Manufacturing and their Products, 1909–1963," *Business History Review* 43 (1969): 282–98; A. D. Chandler, Jr., and L. Galambos, "The Development of Large-Scale Organizations in Modern America," *Journal of Economic History* 30 (1970); R. L. Nelson, *Merger Movements in American Industry* (Princeton: Princeton University Press, 1959); L. Neal, "Trust Companies and Financial Innovation, 1897–1914," *Business History Review* 45 (1971): 35–51; T. R. Navin, "Investment Banking since 1900," *Bulletin of the Business History Society* 27 (1953): 60–65. On the feminization of the typewriter, consult Davies, *A Woman's Place,* and also Joli Jensen, "Women as Typewriters," paper presented at the American Studies Association National Meeting (November 1987).

11. Benjamin R. Haynes and Harry P. Jackson, *A History of Business Education in the United States* (Cincinnati: Southwestern Publishing Co., 1935); Janice Weiss, "Educating for Clerical Work: The Nineteenth-Century Private Commercial School," *Journal of Social History* 14 (Spring 1981): 411–17.

12. C. D. Wright, *The Working Girls of Boston* (Boston, 1889), 87.

13. Booth Tarkington, *Alice Adams* (Garden City, N.Y.: Doubleday, Page and Company, 1921); Dorothy Richardson, *The Long Day: The Story of a New York Working Girl* (New York, 1905).

14. Walter D. Scott, *Increasing Human Efficiency in Business* (New York: Ronald Press, 1911).

15. Samples of the topic's normative literature include: R. P. SoRelle, *Office Training For Stenographers* (New York, Chicago: The Gregg Publishing Company, 1916); E. L. Spencer, *The Efficient Secretary* (New York: Frederick Stokes Co., 1916).

16. Early historians of the typewriter stressed the achievements of its masculine inventor; see, for example, Bruce Bliven, *The Wonderful Writing Machine* (New York: Random House, 1954) and Richard Current, *The Typewriter and the Men Who Made It* (Urbana: University of Illinois Press, 1954).

17. G. Gissing, *The Odd Women* (London: W. Heineman, 1893).

18. Stenographic Efficiency Bureau, *How to Become a Successful Stenographer: For the Young Woman Who Wants to Make Good* (New York: Remington Typewriter Co., 1916), 63.

19. Stenographic Efficiency Bureau, *Making the Body an Efficient Machine* (New York: Remington Typewriter Co., 1916), 27.

20. Jensen, "Women as Typewriters," 7.

21. Samuel Haber, *Efficiency and Uplift: Scientific Management in the Progressive Era, 1890–1920* (Chicago: Chicago University Press, 1964).

22. Forty, *Objects of Desire,* pp. 124–25; Page Talbot, "Office Furniture," in *Wooton Patent Furniture: A Place for Everything and Everything in Its Place* (Indianapolis: Indiana State Museum, 1983).

23. Examples of the new desk line can be seen in 1915 publications of the Watson Manufacturing Company, in the "Trade Mark Efficiency Steel Furniture" catalog (Jamestown, N. Y.), and in the "Y and E" Company's Vertical Filing catalog (Pittsburg, Penn.) in the National Museum of American History Warshaw Collection of Business Americana; also see Forty, *Objects of Desire,* pp. 124–25.

24. Forty, *Objects of Desire,* p. 128.

25. Compare office catalogs of A. B. Dick, 1900 and 1915 in the National Museum of American History Warshaw Collection. Also see Forty, *Objects of Desire,* pp. 133–34, and Vincent Giuliana, "The Mechanization of Office Work," *Scientific American* 247.3 (September 1982): 148–64.

26. The changing technology of office equipment can be monitored by examining two of the trade's journals, *The Office* and *Office Appliances.*

27. Stephens and Lubar, "A Place for Public Business," 166–71; also see Aron, *Ladies and Gentlemen,* 86–95.

28. Joanne Yates, "From Press Book and Pigeonhole to Vertical Filing: Revolution in Storage and Access Systems for Correspondence," *Journal of Business Communication* 19 (Summer 1982): 5–26.

29. John Stilgoe, *The Metropolitan Corridor: Railroads and The American Scene* (New Haven: Yale University Press, 1983), 81–88.

30. Grant Hildebrand, *Designing for Industry: The Architecture of Albert Kahn* (Cambridge, Mass.: The MIT Press, 1974) and Walter Licht, *Working Sites: The Industrial Buildings of Philadelphia* (Philadelphia: Temple University Press, 1986).

31. In addition to the work cited above by Chandler and Nelson on the expanding bureaucratic structures at plant and office, see James R. Beniger, *The Control Revolution: Technological and Economic Origins of the Information Society* (Cambridge, Mass.: The MIT Press, 1986) and Joanne Yates, *Control through Communication: The Rise of System in American Management* (Baltimore: The Johns Hopkins University Press, 1989).

32. Chandler, *Visible Hand,* 240–85.

33. David Noble, *America by Design* (New York: Oxford University Press, 1977); Monte Calvert, *The Mechanical Engineer in America* (Cambridge, Mass.: The MIT Press, 1967); David Hounshell, *From the American System to Mass Production, 1800–1932: The Development of Manufacturing in the United States* (Baltimore: The Johns Hopkins University Press, 1984).

34. Samuel Merwin, *The Road Builders* (New York: The Macmillan Co., 1905); Charles Barnard, *Knights of Today, or Love and Science* (New York: C. Scribner's Sons, 1881).

35. Chandler, *Visible Hand,* 268.

36. *Scientific American* 69 (29 July 1893): 69.

37. As quoted in Michael O'Malley, "The Idea of Time in American Culture," Ph.D. dissertation, University of California, Berkeley (1989), chaps. 4, 11.

38. Carlene Stephens, *Inventing Standard Time* (Washington, D.C.: Smithsonian Institution Press, 1983).

39. A. G. Bromley, "Charles Babbage and the Invention of Workmen's Time Recorders," *Antiquarian Horology* 13 (September 1982): 442–47; Robert C. Alberts, *The Good Provider: H. J. Heinz and His 57 Varieties* (Boston: Houghton, Mifflin, 1973).

40. See catalogs, International Time Recording Company, *Time: The Gateway to a Better Business* (1916) in National Museum of American History Division of Engineering and Industrial Files; *International Business Machines,* National Museum of American History Warshaw Collection, Office Equipment File, Box 2.

41. Frederick Winslow Taylor, *Principles of Scientific Management* (New York: Harper and Brothers, 1911).

42. Daniel Nelson, *Frederick W. Taylor and the Rise of Scientific Management* (Madison, Wisc.: University of Wisconsin Press, 1980); Hugh Aitken, *Taylorism at the Watertown Arsenal: Scientific Management in Action, 1908–1915* (Cambridge, Mass.: Harvard University Press, 1960) and Milton Nadworny, *Scientific Management and the Unions* (Cambridge, Mass.: Harvard University Press, 1955). See also Sudhir Kakar's hostile psycho-biography, *Frederick Taylor: A Study in Personality and Development* (Cambridge, Mass.: 1970) and the discussions of Taylor in Daniel T. Rodgers, *The Work Ethic in Industrial America, 1850–1920* (Chicago: University of Chicago Press, 1974).

43. David Montgomery, *The Fall of the House of American Labor: The Workplace, the State, and American Labor Activism, 1865–1925* (Cambridge: Cambridge University Press, 1987).

44. Claudia Kidwell, *Suiting Everyone: The Democratization of Clothing in America* (Washington, D. C.: Smithsonian Institution Press, 1974); Jonathan Prude, "The Uniform of Labor: Some Thoughts on the Changing Meaning of Occupational Costume in Nineteenth-Century America," paper presented at the Delaware Seminar on Material Culture Studies, University of Delaware, Fall 1984.

45. J. B. S. Hardman, ed. *American Labor Dynamics in Light of Post-War Developments* (New York: Harcourt, Brace and Company, 1928), 60.

46. Montgomery, *The Fall of The House of American Labor,* chap. 5, "White Shirts and Superior Intelligence," 216–56.

Part Two

Public Landscapes

We shall not cease from exploration
And the end of all our exploring will
be to arrive where we started
And know the place for the first time.
—T. S. Eliot

Figure 72.
Richard Haas, *Chicago Architecture*, 1983
Oil on linen mural, designed for the reception space of the Chicago offices of
Lohan Associates, 225 North Michigan Avenue.
(Courtesy Lohan Associates; photo by Barbara Karant, Karant + Associates)

6

The City as Artifact

"God made the country," wrote William Cowper, "and man made the town." The city is assuredly humankind's great collective work of art and artifice. Yet this essay about it presents a small irony. It is the briefest, thinnest (in a historiographical sense), and most dated work in the book. It is the shortest treatment I have ever given to the world's largest artifact assemblage. Not that what we have here is wrong, but I now recognize its incompleteness. It represents an artisan's sketch rather than a complete mural. I am glad I had the modesty to call it "a limited survey."

I include it because it reveals several things. It was one of the first things that a boy who grew up in the country ever wrote about life in the city. Here I first used the term "above-ground archaeologist," which I had appropriated from a real archaeologist, John Cotter, who first used it as a way of investigating public landscape in his article, "Above-Ground Archaeology," *American Quarterly* 26.3 (August 1974): 266–80. It, too, adumbrated my penchant for *big* landscapes: cities like Chicago (chaps. 7, 9); a 2,000-acre university campus (*The University of Notre Dame: A Portrait of Its History and Campus* [Notre Dame: University of Notre Dame Press, 1976]); a transcontinental road (*U.S. 40: A Roadscape of the American Experience* [Bloomington: Indiana University Press, 1984]).

Historical archaeologists, whom I neglected to recognize in this 1979 agenda for urban, above-ground archaeology, were then and certainly are now making significant contributions to the study of urban material culture. Here one thinks of the work of Barbara Ann Liggett (*Urban Archaeology in the Eastern United States* [Ann Arbor: University Microfilms International, 1975]), Bert Salwen ("Archeology in Megalopolis," in *Research and Theory in Current Archeology,* ed. Charles L. Redman [New York: John Wiley and Sons, 1973]), 151–63, Robert L. Schuyler ("Archaeology of the New York Metropolis," *Bulletin of the New York State Archeological Association* 69 [1977] 1–19), and Mark Leone ("Interpreting Ideology in Historical Archaeology: Using the Rules of Perspective in the William Paca Garden in Annapolis, Maryland," in *Ideology, Power and Prehistory,* ed. D. Miller and C. Tilley [New York: Cambridge University Press, 1984], 25–35).

Cultural geographers figure prominently in this short survey and here I would recommend some of their current work on the urban environment: John Jakle,

This article originally appeared in the *American Historians Association Newsletter* 15.2 (February 1977): 7–10.

American Small Town: Twentieth-Century Place Images (Hamden, Conn.: Anchor Books, 1982); J. B. Jackson, *Discovering the Vernacular Landscape* (New Haven, Conn.: Yale University Press, 1983); Peirce Lewis, et al., *The Philadelphia Region: Selected Essays & Field Trip Itineraries* (Ephrata, Penn.: Science Press, 1979); and John Stilgoe, *The Metropolitan Corridor* (New Haven: Yale University Press, 1983) and *Borderland: The Suburb in America* (New Haven: Yale University Press, 1989).

As with the physical city itself, the material culture study of it is heterogeneous. Thus we learn much from urban planners such as John Fondersmith who edits *The American Urban Guides Newsletter* (P.O. Box 186, Washington, D. C. 20044), updating readers on recently published work on city architecture, cartography, parks, cemeteries, and public art. Journalist Grady Clay continues the posture of critical city watching developed in *Close-Up: How to Read the American City* (New York: Praeger, 1973) and *Right Before Your Eyes: Penetrating the Urban Environment* (Chicago: American Planning Association, 1987). Also useful is Michael Middleton, *Man Made the Town* (New York: St. Martin's Press, 1987); Donald J. Olsen, *The City as a Work of Art* (New Haven: Yale University Press); and David Schuyler, *The New Urban Landscape: The Redefinition of City Form in Nineteenth-Century America* (Baltimore: The Johns Hopkins University Press, 1988).

In the past ten years, historians have also developed new tools, models, and techniques for using artifacts in research, teaching, and museum exhibitions. Three university presses—Columbia, Temple, and Ohio State—all based in American cities are publishing important monographs analyzing the physical environment on topics such as real estate companies, work place sites, and cemeteries. Studies such as those by David Goldfield and Blaine A. Brownell (*Urban America: From Downtown to No Town* [Boston: Houghton Mifflin, 1979]), Norval White (*New York: A Physical History*), and Kenneth Jackson (*Crabgrass Frontier: The Suburbanization of the United States* [New York: Columbia University Press, 1985]) are sensitive to material culture evidence. Several established city museums are revising their interpretations of their urban past through new, long-term museum installations: the Brooklyn Historical Society, the Fort Worth History Center, the Baltimore City Museum, the Valentine Museum in Richmond, the Cincinnati Historical Society, and the Western Pennsylvania Historical Society in Pittsburgh.

Many American cities grew with the parallel development of photography, an insight Peter B. Hales explores in *Silver Cities: The Photography of Americanization, 1839–1915* (Philadelphia: Temple University Press, 1984). Allen F. Davis, Fredric M. Miller, and Morris J. Vogel have done two fine studies, *Still Philadelphia: A Photographic History, 1890–1940* and *Philadelphia Stories: A Photographic History, 1920–1960* (Philadelphia: Temple University Press, 1983, 1988). We may also have new forms of urban rivalry to match the late nineteenth century's criteria for American urban greatness. At the turn of the century, who had the best fine arts museum or city park system or the tallest skyscraper claimed superiority; in our time high marks are given to who has the biggest theme park, largest domed stadium, and most comprehensive encyclopedia of urban history. While only one, *The Encyclopedia of Cleveland History,* edited by David van Tassel and John J. Grabowski (Bloomington: Indiana University Press, 1987), has been published, at least two others are projected by two long-time city rivals: Chicago (Paul Kleppner, editor) and New York

(Kenneth Jackson, editor). Can Los Angeles be far behind? Whatever the final page count or selling price, I anticipate material culture students will find such tomes useful reference works, for the history of the city is written in stone and steel, macadam and cast iron.

Reference works and specialized research guides (for example, the American Public Works Association's *History of Public Works in the United States, 1776–1976* [Chicago: APWA, 1976]) are essential to anyone doing above-ground archeology. I realized this repeatedly while in the field with students and during my own expeditions in North American cities such as Indianapolis, Toronto, South Bend, Edmonton, Wilmington, Calgary, and, of course, Chicago. My bibliographical knowledge and, I hope, my interpretive savvy expanded as I had the opportunity to give lectures, seminars, or courses on the "City as Artifact" at institutions such as the Indianapolis Museum of Art, the Faculty of Environmental Design at the University of Calgary, the Delaware Museum of Art, Chicago Historical Society, the Institute for Long Island Studies at Hofstra University, and the Art Institute of Chicago.

To document my own journey toward this goal, a reader can follow my halting steps in various "what-I-tried-and-how-it-worked" essays: "Above-Ground Archaeology" in *Artifacts and the American Past*, 184–203; "Above-Ground Archaeology: Discovering a Community's History through Local Artifacts," in *Local History Today*, ed. Thomas K. Krasean (Indianapolis: Indiana Historical Society, 1979), 53–83; and "Local History as Universal History," in *To Know the Place*, ed. Joan Krieg (Hempstead, N.Y.: Hofstra University Press, 1988), 19–27. In the final section in this book, chapter 11, "The History Behind, Within, and Outside the History Museum," provides additional references.

When future historians write the historiography of the past decade, surely it will be identified as a time when scholars rediscovered the city. Not since the Progressive Era has there been such a fascination with the history of urban life. Contemporary urban historians, however, have primarily studied and taught the American urban environment through documentary verbal sources and, only recently, by means of the statistical records of urban dwellers. Unlike the Progressives, who were extremely interested in the physical urban fabric (its city plans, its architectural forms, and its civic spaces), we have neglected the abundant material evidence of past urban life that lies extant all about us. For those historians who are willing to become "above-ground archaeologists," and thereby try to discover, identify, decipher, and interpret the surviving physical evidence of the urban past, the city can be examined as a mammoth artifact (fig. 73), an open-air classroom wherein urban history can be taught in a novel way.

Some historians, such as Sam Bass Warner, Gilbert Osofsky, Roy Lubove, Dana White, and Richard Wade, have investigated the physical city's settlement patterns, housing stock, and land uses in their studies of Boston, Harlem, New York, Atlanta, and Chicago. Nonetheless, the

Figure 73.
"A Glimpse of New York's Dry Goods District," 1872
Unattributed chromolithograph.
*(Courtesy The Library of Congress, Division of Prints
and Photographs)*

abundant artifacts that make every American city a living museum (see
fig. 72) continue to be largely overlooked by most urbanists. First of all,
few of us are trained to interpret material evidence as are anthropologists
or archaeologists; we do not know how to "read" the history contained
in artifacts. We must begin to look outside our discipline to the technical
literature of architectural historians, historical geographers, art historians,
landscape architects, and city planners for many of the tools, models,
and techniques for using physical evidence in our urban history research
and teaching.

Grady Clay's *Close-Up: How To Read The American City* (1973), Vincent Scully's *American Architecture and Urbanism* (1969) and Kevin
Lynch's *What Time Is This Place?* (1972) are three excellent primers that
show students how to begin to probe the built urban environment for
historical evidence. Clay, the editor of *Landscape Architecture Magazine*
(a journal that urbanists should read regularly), offers the novice city-
watcher numerous visual clues for uncovering signs of change in gridiron
patterns, commercial strips, city centers, and suburbs. Architectural historian Scully equips students to move beyond the memorization of

architectural styles by learning how vernacular urban structures (e.g., tenements, row houses, commercial blocks, factories) reflect the historical periods in which they were constructed. Urban planner Lynch walks his readers through downtown Boston and in the process provides them with techniques for ascertaining the historical evolution of any city by means of its extant material culture.

Architectural historians in the past concentrated primarily on high styles, unique residences or skyscrapers when discussing urban environments. With the recent expansion of the historical preservation movement, however, the historical diversity and import of American building types is finally being recognized and studied in a surfeit of monographs, walking tours and pictorial guides. Construction techniques, floor plans, interior designs, space allocations, and geographical settings of specialized urban structures can also yield important information for urban historians. Useful in this regard are: Carroll Meeks, *The Railroad Station, An Architectural History* (1956); the American Public Works Association's *History of Public Works in the United States, 1776–1976* (1976); John D. Johnson and Grace Goldin, *The Hospital: A Social and Architectural History* (1976); and Norman Johnson, *Human Cage, A Brief History of Prison Architecture* (1973).

Buildings are the most obvious element for probing the physical city as a historic site. Teachers of urban history, however, need not restrict their students' inquiry merely to these structural artifacts. The topographical and geographical features of the city (particularly its parks, public squares, recreation facilities, water fronts, and open spaces) provide indices for measuring urban change (fig. 74). In a thoughtful essay, "Living History: The Physical City as Artifact and Teaching Tool" (*The History Teacher,* August 1975), David Goldfield urges historians to seek out the historical function and context of every neighborhood or metropolitan park, mall, gap site, and public commons. For other ways of looking at these aspects of the city see also: Albert Fein, *Frederick Law Olmstead and the American Environmental Tradition* (1972); Paul Zucker, *Town and Square* (1970); Caroline Shillaber, *Landscape Architecture, A Bibliography* (1975); and particularly the innovative scholarship of John Brinckerhoff Jackson, former editor of *Landscape* (another prerequisite journal for the above-ground archaeologist). Jackson's insightful techniques for extracting history from the natural and man-made environment have been collected in an anthology, *Landscapes* (1970), by Ervin Zube. Historians will also profit from Jackson's compilation of a special issue, "Teaching the Landscape," in the *Journal of Architectural Education* (September 1976).

Historical geographers naturally have used material evidence in their

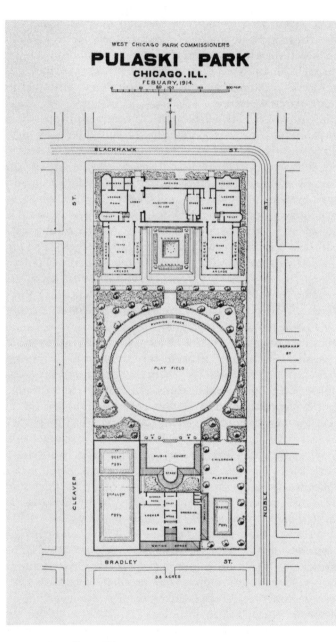

Figure 74.
Pulaski Park and Fieldhouse Site Plan, 1914
West Chicago Park District.
(Courtesy Chicago Historical Society)

scholarship, and urban historians should be aware of their growing interest in American cities. This trend among geographers is well summarized by John Jakle's thorough bibliographical essay on "Urban Environments" in his *Past Landscapes* (1974). Jakle's study is but one in a superb series published by the Council of Planning Librarians, a national organization that disseminates extremely useful bibliographies about all aspects of city planning and history. Interpretive insights from historical geographers can also be found in journals such as *The Geographical Review,* the *Annals of the Association of American Geographers* and the *Journal of the American Institute of Planners.* A few urban and architectural historians—Walter M. Whitehill, *Boston, A Topographical History* (1968); Reyner Banham, *Los Angeles, The Architecture of Four Ecologies* (1971); and Richard Wade and Harold Meyer, *Chicago: Growth of a Metropolis* (1969)—have taken geographical features seriously as historical evidence, but we do not yet have any analysis of an American city quite comparable to Pierre Couperie's *Paris through the Ages, An Illustrated Historical Atlas of Urbanism and Architecture* (1971).

As Thomas Hines (*Burnham of Chicago, Architect and Planner,* 1974) and William Wilson (*The City Beautiful Movement in Kansas City,* 1964) have demonstrated, the civic art of an urban environment can also tell the visually astute historian much about the political, economic, social, and cultural past of a city (fig. 75). James Goode in a definitive and innovative analysis of *The Outdoor Sculpture of Washington, D.C.* (1973) clearly shows why urban statues and sculpture groups "deserve equal attention for their historical messages" as for their stylistic designs. Similar public art has been interpreted in New York by Frederick Fried and Edmund Gillon (*New York Civic Sculpture,* 1976) and in Philadelphia by the Fairmont Park Association (*Sculpture of a City,* 1976). A handbook for such fieldwork is Wayne Craven's *Sculpture in America* (1968), and many other visual clues can be found in the journal *Classical America.*

Mural art, likewise, should not be neglected by the urban historian. From the New Deal's ubiquitous Federal Art Projects (see Francis V. Connor, *Art for the Millions,* 1973) to the contemporary street murals of Sante Fe (see Eva and James Cockcroft, *Towards a People's Art,* 1975) there survives a dramatic, socially oriented, historically significant public urban art form that reveals much about the twentieth-century history of local communities and neighborhoods.

Funerary art and sculpture and the cemeteries wherein they are found are still other material resources for urban history. To date, scholars such as Allan Ludwig and James Deetz have largely focused on the historical role of colonial graveyards, but their research techniques and iconographic analyses are adaptable to nineteenth- and twentieth-century city

Figure 75.
Frances Johnson (photographer), Court of Honor, Lagoon and Palace of
Mechanic Arts
World's Columbian Exposition, Chicago, Illinois, 1893.
(Courtesy The Library of Congress, Division of Prints and Photographs)

cemeteries. Geographical placement and design of cemeteries often reveal
past concerns for urban open spaces as well as sanitation and health practices. Useful guides for introducing students to field research in this area
are Leonard Huber's *New Orleans Architecture: The Cemeteries* (1974)
and David Stannard's *Death in America* (1975).

Urban historians need to pay more attention to street patterns and
remnants of urban plans. John Reps has done two surveys (*Town Planning in America,* 1965, and *The Making of Urban America,* 1965) that
can be supplemented by Ian Stewart, *Nineteenth Century Public Landscape Design* (1959) and Mellier Scott, *American City Planning Since
1890* (1969). Students can learn to extract historical information from
the size, direction, and usage of "Main Streets," alleys, commercial strips,
and freeways. Christopher Tunnard's *American Skyline* (1956), *Man-
Made America* (1963), and *City of Man* (1970) each suggest how city
streets provide examples of traffic and settlement patterns. Moreover,
urban streets usually contain fragments of previous transportation arteries
and artifacts: horsecar barns, trolley tracks, ferry slips, or interurban lines.
And as Robert Alotta has shown in his *Streets of Philadelphia* (1976),

place-names can encapsulate bits of urban history for the perceptive observer. Finally, city streets are filled with street fixtures that can yield pertinent historical information. For example, Sarah Noreen has cleverly demonstrated in a study of the *Public Illumination of Washington, D.C.* (1975) how extant street lights can tell us much about a city's changing economic, social, technological, and even racial history. Robert and Mimi Melnick have done a similar analysis, *Manhole Covers of Los Angeles* (1974).

The consumer-oriented, automobile-dependent society of post–World War I America spawned a plethora of artifacts that remain part of the urban and suburban landscape. Architects like Robert Venturi (*Learning from Las Vegas,* 1972) and cultural observers like Tom Wolfe (*The Kandy-Kolored Tangerine,* 1965) have begun to analyze this material culture. The omnipresence of gasoline stations, diners, motels, drive-ins, parking lots, billboards, and shopping centers has likewise fascinated Richard Gutman, Paul Ivory, and Peter H. Smith. Their studies of what they call "commercial archaeology" should be known and used by urban historians. Techniques for interpreting the cultural history embedded in commercial strips and roadside America can be found in a variety of prepared slide kits and handbooks that can be ordered from Environmental Communications (64 Windward Ave. Venice, Calif.) and also in the exhibition catalog of Venturi and Rauch, *Signs of Life: Symbols in the American City* (1976).

Teachers of urban history can also borrow ideas from another cadre of above-ground archaeologists who are primarily concerned with interpreting industrial and technological sites. Appropriately enough, industrial archaeology had its origin in the cities of Great Britain, but now the movement has spread to this country where the urban landscape is littered with artifacts of labor and business history, of energy and engineering development, and of the impact of industrialization and technology on urban life (fig. 76). Theodore A. Sande's *Industrial Archaeology: A New Look at the American Heritage* (1976) is the first thorough survey of American industrial sites and greatly expands upon the American Society of Civil Engineers' pamphlet, *ASCE Guide to History and Heritage Programs* (1974). R. A. S. Hennessey's essay, "Industrial Archaeology in Education" (*The History Teacher,* November 1975) suggests several possible approaches for use in the classroom. How-to-do-it field research techniques can be adapted from Kenneth Hudson's several publications, particularly the *Handbook for Industrial Archaeology* (1967). Urbanists should also consult the *Newsletter and Journal* of the Society for Industrial Archaeology, as well as the quarterly numbers of *Technology and Culture.*

Photographs, a result of nineteenth-century technology, are a final

Figure 76.
Water Tower and Power Plant, 1879
Pullman Palace Car Company, Pullman, Illinois; S. S. Beman, architect.

type of material evidence for the historian of cities. As early as the 1850s, amateur and professional photographers became fascinated with the changing profile of the American city, recording its many economic, social, and cultural faces (fig. 77). Their surviving photographs, now surfacing in numerous visual anthologies, pictorial histories, and photographic exhibitions, constitute a priceless archive that enables teachers to reconstruct the shifting physical shape of urban environments. A summary of how photographs can be used as historical documents is found in my methodological statement, "Discovering the Past in Print, Person and Photography," *The University of Notre Dame: A Portrait of Its History and Campus* (1976). Models for an investigation of urban life through photography include John Kouwenhoven's *The Columbia Historical Portrait of New York, An Essay in Graphic History* (1956); Meyer and Wade's already mentioned *Chicago, Growth of a Metropolis;* and Michael Lesy's *Real Life: Louisville in the Twenties* (1976).

Glen Holt has argued persuasively ("Chicago through a Camera Lens: An Essay on Photography as History," *Chicago History,* 1971) that photographic documentation is especially useful in describing urban expansion, internal settlement patterns, land usage, and transportation configurations. Photographs for such research are available from companies like

Figure 77.
"Photographing New York City"
Underwood and Underwood stereograph card (1905).
(Courtesy The Library of Congress, Division of Prints and Photographs)

Documentary Photo Aids (P.O. Box 956, Mount Dora, Fla.), the graphic collection of various WPA projects (e.g., see Bernice Abbott, *New York in the Thirties*, 1973), as well as from local photography firms and clubs, newspaper morgues, aerial photosurvey companies, historical societies, public libraries, and the scrapbooks of ordinary citizens. Kenneth Jackson at Columbia University is currently amassing a prodigious slide collection from various sources to form what may become the first slide bank of the physical city. Students in urban history courses can be enlisted to conduct similar photographic fieldwork in their own cities, thus expanding the type of visual census that we still need for many American urban areas.

As is hopefully apparent from this limited survey of the material evidence extant in any city, urban history can be read in stone and steel, macadam and cast iron, street sign and equestrian statue, road map and photograph, as well as in libraries and municipal records offices; the urban past is visual as well as verbal. By examining the city as artifact, students naturally acquire a visual historical literacy. Such a perspective permits them to recognize and interpret the past as it survives in the present with an intimacy that enables them to discover the delight of doing history themselves.

Figure 78.
Noah Webster House (built in 1822–23)
Moved in 1944 to Greenfield Village, Dearborn, Michigan.
*(Courtesy The Collections of the Henry Ford Museum and
Greenfield Village)*

7

The New England Presence
on the Midwest Landscape

The Henry Ford Museum and Greenfield Village in Dearborn initially prompted me to think about New England's influence on the extant environment of the Middle West. Henry Ford's cultural imperialism seemed omnipresent on my first visit to the Greenfield Village that he mass-assembled in the 1920s and 1930s (fig. 79). In one sense, Ford was imitating as well as competing with eastern museum czars, several of them New Englanders (such as Electra Havermeyer Webb and William Appleton), in the philanthropic control of the American past. One of Ford's acquisitions, the 1822 Noah Webster House from New Haven, has proved one of the village's most popular visitor attractions since its migration to Dearborn, Michigan, in 1936–37 (opposite and fig. 80). I included its interpretive focus in my first attempt at history museum criticism (see chap. 13). Thanks to museum historians Steven Hamp, Peter Cousins, and William Pretzler I was asked back (despite what I said in 1974 and wrote in 1975) to be one of the consultants assisting in reinterpreting the Webster structure and site in 1986–88. I laud the museum's intellectual courage in undertaking a revisionist approach to one of its revered icons, not only because I have greatly enjoyed being on the consulting team but, more important, because the research and analysis for the new interpretation have involved a comprehensive search, in New England and the Midwest, for the relevant documentary, literary, and material culture evidence on the Webster structure and its inhabitants.

Place-names figure more prominently in this essay than they do in the Webster house research, but we have not forgotten that Noah also pursued geography as an avocation. My own attention to toponymy grows out of an above-ground archaeology premise that every place-name encapsulates a historical decision about the place. I have also been influenced by scholars who devoted much of their landscape analysis to thinking of words as things: J. B. Jackson, John Stilgoe, and George Stewart, the man who wrote the book on American place-names: *Names on the Land* (Boston: Houghton Mifflin, 1958).

Toponymists often use cultural geography's concept of diffusion to monitor cultural transfer, a phenomenon that can also be investigated by tracing architec-

This article originally appeared in *The Old Northwest: A Journal of Regional Life and Letters* 9.2 (Summer 1983): 125–42.

Figure 79.
Henry Ford's Funeral, 1947
Aerial view of gatehouse *(foreground)* and Greenfield Village.
(Courtesy The Collections of the Henry Ford Museum and Greenfield Village)

tural styles, vernacular house forms, and special building types. In my reassessment of two classic studies written by Lois Matthews (*The Expansion of New England: The Spread of New England Settlement and Institutions to the Mississippi River, 1620–1825* [Boston: Houghton Mifflin, 1909]) and another by Stewart H. Holbrook (*The Yankee Exodus: An Account from New England* [New York: Macmillan, 1950]), I try to suggest what these histories, written primarily from documentary sources, leave out by not considering place-names, building styles, and urban plans. My purpose was to take an earlier interpretation and expand its explanatory range by testing it with material culture evidence.

In the course of reading and looking, I encountered research questions I did not solve. Was there a network of native-born New England builders and carpenter-architects who migrated to and within the Middle West? What influence did New England architectural pattern books exert in such occupational migrations? What material forms were changed, modified, or abandoned in the New England material world as they diffused from its cultural hearth into a transition zone such as New York State? How did New England landscape features other than residences and city plans—that is, cemeteries, field patterns, church architecture, inns, fencing types—influence the built environment of the Old Northwest?

While a Midwest landscape first interested me in its New England impress, my research on the topic had its initial public presentation in New Hampshire. I gave

Figure 80.
Noah Webster House (built in 1822–23)
Original site in New Haven, Connecticut (ca. 1900).
(Courtesy The Collections of the Henry Ford Museum and Greenfield Village)

the first version of this paper at the 1979 Dublin Seminar on New England Folklife ("New England Prospect: Maps, Place-names, and the Historical Landscape"), which was held within the long shadow of that state's Mount Monadnock, whose name Owen Aldis, a Boston financier, gave (1890) to the fourteen-story office building that Burnham and Root designed in Chicago and that currently stands as the tallest load-bearing building in the United States. The argument also received comment and critique at a Chicago Public Library Seminar.

In 1835 French observer Alexis de Tocqueville wrote: "The principles of New England spread at first to neighboring states; they then passed successively to more distant ones; they now extend their influence . . . over the whole American world."[1] This New England presence, particularly evident in landscape features such as place-names, building types, and town plans, left an especially strong imprint on one part of de Tocqueville's "whole American world", that is, on the first colony of the United States, officially known as "the Territory Northwest of the River Ohio." As ordained by Congress 13 July 1787, the territory was subsequently divided into five states (Ohio, Indiana, Michigan, Illinois, Wisconsin) and part of a sixth (Minnesota east of the Mississippi River). Originally known as "the Old Northwest," now "the Midwest," the opening of this multimillion-acre tract produced an entirely new chapter in United States land use history.

New Englanders played a significant role in the migration to the new lands. Once the Indian threat had been removed and Indian land title extinguished, the movement began (fig. 81). Spurred on by the availability of fresh farm lands, an increasingly liberal credit system of land purchase, and a desire to work land that did not "stand on its edge" (they were tired of farming in the steep hills), the New Englanders moved west. The expansion of slavery in the Southwest discouraged movement to that area even if there had been such an inclination. Nineteenth-century contemporaries, mostly New Englanders like Timothy Flint and Margaret Fuller, wrote of the epoch, as did twentieth-century historians like Lois Mathews and Stewart Holbrook, who plotted the "Yankee Exodus" into what many emigrants called "the second New England."[2] Since the two studies by Mathews and Holbrook are now, respectively, eighty and forty years old, reassessment seems in order. Moreover, lacking modern demographic techniques, both authors confined themselves to the numbers of New Englanders migrating westward and neglected the physical artifacts they left on the Midwest landscape. These artifacts survive as contemporary historical evidence of how men and women from Maine to Massachusetts, Rhode Island to New Hampshire used, planned, exploited, named, planted, divided, and built on the land.

The reappraisal of New England's influence upon the Midwest that follows is organized into three main topics: "Naming the Land," "Building on the Land," and "Planning the Land." This brief survey of the New England presence in the Midwest concludes by demonstrating its visibility in a short case study of Chicago, the city often considered archetypical of the region.[3]

Naming the Land

Francis Bacon once wrote that "a name, though it seem but a superficial and outward matter, yet it carrieth much impression and enchantment." Bacon, a historian of sorts, might also have added that a place-name (say, of a county, township, or any community) invariably encapsulates a bit of local, regional and, sometimes, even national history.

The transference of place-names westward in the settlement process of the United States beyond the original colonies has always been a familiar theme in the literature of American toponymics. As John Leighly and others have pointed out, colonial New England (itself one of the oldest

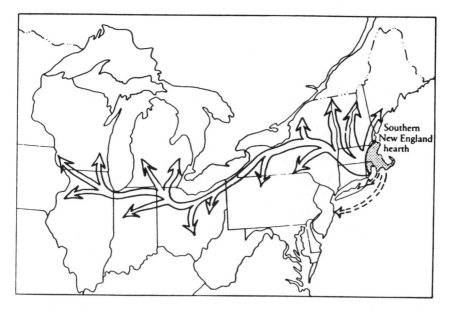

Figure 81.
Path of Migration from New England in the Nineteenth Century
Drawing by M. Margaret Geib. From Alan Noble, *Wood, Brick, and Stone*
(Amherst: University of Massachusetts Press, 1984).

place-names for a major American region in use today) contained the largest stock of names available for transfer; and this same region provided a significant fraction of westward-bound migrants when the Middle West was first being settled.[4] The distribution of these New England place-names on the twentieth-century Midwestern landscape provides a clue to the westward spread of cultural elements from the northeastern states, supplementing other evidence such as building types, social institutions, land subdivisions, and town plans. Of the twelve states of the Midwest, the first four in the adoption of New England place-names are states of the Old Northwest. Ohio leads with a 5.5 percent replication of colonial New England names, followed by Wisconsin (4.6 percent), Michigan (3.5 percent), and Illinois (3.1 percent). Indiana, however, is near the bottom of the Midwest states with only 1.9 percent, for the impact of the "Yankee Exodus" is not as pervasive in the Hoosier state. The names most favored by the settlers, in order of frequency of their occurrence, are Salem, Fairfield, Springfield, Concord, Newton (or Newtown), Chester, York, and Richmond, all being repeated at least twenty-six times in the Midwest. Geographers have also traced single recurrent names such as

Andover, Manchester, and Winchester as they were carried westward by New Englanders.[5]

The first stop for many was Ohio, some to homestead in the 1,500,000 acres of land that the Ohio Company (formed in the Bunch of Grapes tavern in Boston in 1786) sought to develop at the confluence of the Ohio and Muskingum Rivers; others trekked to a strip of territory in the northeastern corner of the state promoted by the Connecticut Land Company and known variously as "New Connecticut," "the Connecticut Reserve," or "the Western Reserve." The initial permanent settlement in the Northwest Territory was established at Adelphia (later renamed Marietta for Queen Marie Antoinette, who gave aid to the Americans in the War for Independence), a frontier town that replicated the New England villages from which its inhabitants came and, in turn, influenced settlement in other Ohio places such as Sharon and Athens. The early influx of settlers from the Northeast also assured a permanent linguistic settlement in the same part of southeastern Ohio. Termed the Marietta speech island, it became known as an area in which such Yankee words as teeterboard, swill, Dutch cheese, pail, boss, angelworm, clingstone, griddle cake, come-by-chance, and belly kechug survived well into the twentieth century.[6]

To the north in the Western Reserve and its later extensions, the "Firelands" and the "Sufferers land," New England place-names are even more predominant.[7] As Timothy Flint, writing in his *Geography and History of the Western States,* observed in 1828, a brief list of the chief towns in the Reserve reads like an atlas of Connecticut: New Haven, Collins(ville), Fairfield, Greenwich, Lyme, New London, Norwalk, Norwich, Bristol, Farmington, Hartford, Newton, Orange(ville), Southington, Bedford, Brimfield, Chester, Columbia, Goshen, Guilford, Litchfield, Milton, Montville, New Milford, Oxford, Suffield, Windham, Yale, Andover, Colebrook, New Lyme, Saybrook, and Windsor.[8]

New Englanders like General Moses Cleaveland, who led the first surveying party into the Reserve, found Indian names already attached to rivers and bodies of water. In some cases the newcomers tried to change these, as did Cleaveland when he reached the Ashtabula River and offered his companions two gallons of wine for the privilege of christening the stream with the name of his daughter Mary Esther. The name lasted until the wine was drunk, when the river again became the Ashtabula, meaning "the place of many fish." However Cleaveland's own name became the place-name of the region's largest area after a newspaper's error dropped the first "a."[9]

While other town founders besides Cleaveland bestowed their surnames or given names on Old Northwest communities (e.g., the four Collins brothers from Litchfield, Connecticut, established Collinsville,

Illinois; Herman Ely founded Elyria in Ohio), transfer names recalling the geographical origin of early settlers were more characteristic of the New England presence on the Midwest landscape. In Illinois, one could cite Bunker Hill, Springfield, Tremont, Rutland, and Bristol; in the state of "Michigania," to cite the popular name of an 1820s Yankee folk ballad,[10] New Englanders were responsible for Plymouth, Hudson, Schoolcraft, Troy, Battle Creek, Dundee, Dexter, and Vermontville.[11] In Wisconsin, the New England influence is almost as intense as in Ohio; and even Indiana—largely settled by upland Southerners in its early years—has its Bennington, Middlebury, Plymouth, Bristol, Concord, New Haven, and Boston—mostly located along transportation corridors in the northern third of the state.

While these place-name transfers are recognized by cultural geographers interested in demographic and settlement patterns, other geographers like Peirce Lewis, Fred Kniffen, Henry Glassie, and Wilbur Zelinsky note material evidence, in housing and institutional buildings, similarly transferred from New England.[12]

Building on the Land

"The predominance of the simpler methods of corner timbering square and saddle notching over v-notching and dovetailing in the northern tier of states," writes Kniffen, "tends to support the conclusion that the migrating New Englanders, like the English of Tidewater, regarded log construction as so temporary as to be unworthy of the skills they undoubtedly possessed as workers in wood."[13] In addition to certain log construction methods (e.g., that of the Goodrich log building at Milton, Rock County, Wisconsin), other New England influences in the built environment of the Midwest can also be noted in both the migration of vernacular building forms as well as the transplanting of academic architectural styles.

Scholars have only begun to classify and assess the dimensions of the New England vernacular building influence, but already several traditional forms appear to occur repeatedly as direct residuals of Northeastern settlement in the Northwest Territory (fig. 82).[14] These building forms include the gable-front, such as that of Connecticut emigrant Stephen Mack in Rockton, Illinois; the upright-and-wing that is sometimes named the "full Western Reserve house"; the saltbox, with its numerous subregional variants; and the story-and-a-half extended or classical cottage, so-called because of its predilection for the symmetrical front facade.[15] Other students of the New England vernacular house types argue that Yankees also carried both the gambrel-roof two-story and the bowed-roof cottage with them into the Midwest.[17]

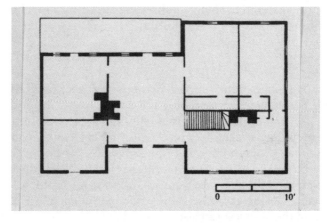

Figure 82.
New England Upright-and-Wing House Types, ca. 1840
Drawing by M. Margaret Geib. From Alan Noble, *Wood,
Brick, and Stone* (Amherst: University of Massachusetts
Press, 1984).

Perhaps the first major high or academic architectural style with a strong New England provenance to influence the Midwest was the last vestiges of the Federal quickly followed by the Greek Revival. Ohio and Michigan, then Indiana, Illinois, and Wisconsin, fell under the latter's popularity. Talbot Hamlin, who studied the Greek Revival movement in general, and Rexford Newcomb, who traced its pervasive influence throughout the Northwest Territory, both conclude that New Englanders expressed their love of the classics (literary and architectural) through their buildings in each of the five Midwestern states that evolved from the 1787 Territory.[17] Richard Campen has even shown how there are strong design parallels, in the Greek Revival mode, between specific buildings such as the Peleg Hancox House (1820), in Stonington, Connecticut, and the Mitchell-Turner House (1848), in Milan, Ohio.[18] similar parallels could be suggested from the New England concentration of Greek Revival buildings in a town such as Niles, Michigan.

Several of the Niles structures were designed by former Massachusetts carpenters who appear to have consulted sourcebooks such as *Rural Architecture,* by the Boston builder Edward Shaw. This work, published in Boston by James B. Dow in 1843, was one of a number of its kind in wide use.[19] Their local role in the larger drama of the transit of New England building preferences across parts of the Midwest landscape suggests at least two research opportunities for further study in American vernacular architecture: first, the need to trace the influence of New England pattern books in regions of known New England migration: and, second, the necessity of compiling a collective biography through more research on individual, native New England builders and carpenter-architects such as Colonel Joseph Barker of new Market, Connecticut, Benjamin Corp of Boston, and Jonathan Goldsmith of Milford, Connecticut, who left New England and contributed to the built environment of the Old Northwest.

American architectural history would also profit from scholarly studies of twentieth-century Midwestern builders—contractors, developers, and architects—who have given a distinctive New England flavor to the Colonial Revival that they have fostered in the region since the 1920s. Francis H. Underwood, for instance, designed a modern house (1954) for W. J. Martin in Rochester, Minnesota, based on two famous Massachusetts saltbox models: the John Adams House (1663) in which President John Adams was born and the Solomon Richardson House now sited on the green at Old Sturbridge Village. Underwood, like many other colonial Revivalists practicing in Midwestern suburbia since the building boom of post-World War II, has also made extensive adaptation of the Cape Cod house type, as in examples of his David McKenzie House (1956) and his J. H. Dobyns House (1953), whose prototype was the Atwood House (1752), the oldest extant dwelling in Chatham, Massachusetts.[20]

When New Englanders built public institutions rather than private residences in the Old Northwest, their historical identity usually survived. Such is true of Lemuel and Simeon Porter, two Waterbury, Connecticut, carpenters, who constructed "The Monumental Row" at Western Reserve College, Hudson, Ohio. Simeon Porter, for example, used the Yale chapel as the model for the chapel at Western Reserve; and the college founders similarly patterned their course of study, collegiate rituals, and form of governance after their New Haven prototype.[21]

All over the Northwest Territory graduates from Yale (known frequently as the "Yale Band" in Illinois and Iowa), as well as graduates of Harvard, Dartmouth, and Brown—many of them staunch members of the New England Society for Promotion of Collegiate Education at the West—brought with them their enthusiasm for higher learning, abolition, and moral reform.[22] One New England collegiate outpost almost immediately spawned another. Oberlin College, for example, was founded in 1833 by Philo Stewart and John Shipherd (classmates at the Academy at Pawlet, Vermont); and her academic progeny reads like a Genesis genealogy: in 1844, Oberlin begat Olivet College in Michigan which, in turn, begat Drury College (1846) in Illinois and Hinsdale College (1844) in Michigan. Oberlin graduates also helped build many of the colleges now gathered in the consortium called the Associated Colleges of the Midwest.

Yankees founded Presbyterian Illinois College at Jacksonville; and from that base, Professor J. B. Turner (who came from Templeton, Massachusetts) played a major role in establishing the University of Illinois at Champaign. Professor Caleb Mills, as first president of Wabash College in Indiana, developed that institution on the lines of his alma maters—Andover Academy and Dartmouth College. He deserves the credit for establishing the first free school system in Indiana—a public school system largely inspired by Horace Mann, Massachusetts educator and a president of Antioch College in Ohio. Finally, Beloit College, the work of the New England Emigrating Society in Wisconsin, was the parent to Carleton College, a sister institution in neighboring Minnesota.

Planning the Land

When the Beloit contingent of the New England Emigrating Society first arrived on the banks of Wisconsin's Turtle River from Colebrook, New Hampshire, they immediately took a characteristic New England step: they plotted a town. In good Yankee fashion they laid out village streets, naming one "College" as an indication of things to come. They set aside land for schools and an academy; and, of course, they soon erected a building for the Congregational Church Society. Such planning on the Midwest landscape went on wherever New Englanders settled.

Inasmuch as the Northwest Land Ordinance of 1785 had decreed that the principal method of land subdivision in the territory would be that of the cadastral grid, this planning configuration exerted an enormous influence on the shape and internal form of New England towns transplanted to the Midwest.[23] Exceptions would include areas like those occupied by the Ohio Company before the rectangular land survey was fully executed.[24] The federal land survey favored New England institutions, such as the township, over an alternative form of local governance, the county (a polity much preferred by Southern pioneers streaming into the lower regions of the Old Northwest). Through the instigation of New Englanders, Michigan became the first western state to adopt the township system and its attendant forum, the town meeting. Wisconsin, Illinois, and Minnesota quickly followed suit.

As John Reps has documented, most New England–planned towns in these states shared several general characteristics: "a system of outlots and town lots of ample size, one or more central greens, wide streets, moderate size, and a general air of order and repose." "The resemblance to New England communities," he concludes, "is as unmistakeable [sic] as it is understandable."[25] Mapped by Massachusetts minister Manasseh Cutler and designed by Rufus Putnam, Marietta on the Muskingum, the earliest "City and Commons" in the territory, also incorporated into its first town plan some of the extant geometrical earthworks left by the earlier mound-building Indians of the region. In an intriguing amalgam of Old World and New World antiquities, Putnam gave classical names to the open spaces formerly inhabited by the Erie tribes: Quadranaon, Capitolium, and Cecelia. The conical Indian mound became an elevated New England commons to be known as Conus.[26]

In 1796, Connecticut Land Company surveyors Moses Cleaveland and Seth Pease laid out a town on the banks of another Ohio river (the Cuyahoga) in the center of the Western Reserve (fig. 83). The public square, a hallmark of so many New England–inspired communities in the Midwest and still extant in the modern city, initially included some ten acres of ground. Streets 99 and 132 feet wide ran from the sides of the square. Other streets parallel and perpendicular to these formed a familiar grid pattern except for the irregular roads leading down the bluff to the river and lake banks. One street, then named "Bath Street" and bordering the Lake Erie shore, suggests that once the lake served as a public bath site.

In Cleaveland's town plan, town lots of two acres and outlots of up to one hundred acres were surveyed. Cleaveland, who thought that his

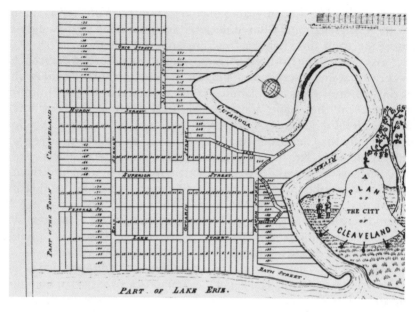

Figure 83.
Town Plan, Cleveland, Ohio, 1796
From John W. Reps, *Town Planning in Frontier America*
(Princeton: Princeton University Press, 1969), p. 355.

city might someday be "as large as Old Windham" in his native Connecticut, never anticipated the true future of the industrial metropolis. As Reps notes, "The Cleveland Plan of 1796 is simply a New England village transplanted to northern Ohio and in the process gaining something in regularity but perhaps losing part of its charm."[27]

Landscape features such as public squares, meetinghouse lots, and town greens in New England and in the Midwest have received the most attention by landscape historians. Less studied are other important artifacts (e.g., fencing types, schoolhouses, inns, and cemeteries) that deserve much more extensive research in the Midwestern communities founded by New Englanders.[28] On this research agenda might also be placed the systematic exploration and interpretation of the myth and symbol of the New England "village" as it was transported and translated into the American heartland in the nineteenth century and then idealized into one of the most powerful landscape symbols in the American cultural imagination. Assuredly, among the most famous landscapes in America is the scene of such a village embowered in great elms and maples. Here a slender steeple rises gracefully above a white wooden church facing the village green. Large, white clapboard houses surround the green; and they, like the church, show a simple elegance in form and trim. These few phrases are sufficient to conjure an instant mental image of a special kind of place in a very famous region. As the author of a recent guidebook confidently stated: "To the entire world, a steepled church, set in its frame of white wooden houses around a manicured common, remains a scene which says 'New England.' "[29]

The New England village as a landscape form traveled well beyond its source region. As D. W. Meinig and others have suggested, the romantic image of the New England village became a national symbol, a model setting for the American community.[30] This process of idealization has been bolstered by the diffusion of New Englanders and their landscape artifacts throughout the nineteenth-century Midwest. For example, researchers such as Joseph Wood have marshaled impressive evidence that it was precisely in the late eighteenth and early nineteenth centuries—the very time when New Englanders began naming, building, and planning on the Old Northwest landscape—that the historical reality of white-painted, classical style (Federal and Greek Revival) dwellings, churches, and stores abutting a tree-shaded green first existed in any substantial way in what might be called "Old" New England. That is, we are now realizing that many colonial New England settlements were not the tightly clustered nucleated communities that the conventional depictions of them once suggested. Rather, the formation of relatively compact settlements such as Sturbridge Center, Massachusetts, evolved and underwent centralization (usually around an earlier church or meetinghouse lot) and village beautification during the precise time that other New Englanders were moving west.[31] Moreover, the cultural diffusion of this relatively *recent* landscape assemblage (i.e., more a creation of the early nineteenth century than of the mid-seventeenth) of the *ideal* New England village was further propagated by numerous Yankees at home (Emerson, Bancroft, Hawthorne, Alcott, Mitchell, Channing) and abroad in the Midwest (Howells, Moody, Mills, Fuller), who through their histories, geographies, prose, and poetry bolstered this powerful myth and symbol.[32] Midwesterners such as Edgar Lee Masters and Vachel Lindsay celebrated it as well, with Lindsay even going so far as to hope that the United States would eventually become a "new New England of ninety million people."[33]

The overall impact of this New England culture, even when paralleled by a fair amount of extant material culture on the Midwest landscape, is difficult to measure in the aggregate. On one individual it appears to have been enormous. Henry Ford obviously revered New England artifacts *in situ,* for in 1922 he made three purchases: Henry Wadsworth Longfellow's celebrated Wayside Inn (figs. 84, 85) at Sudbury,

Figure 84.
"Red Horse Tavern," Sudbury, Massachusetts, 1905
Since publication of Henry Wadsworth Longfellow's 1863 *Tales*
this establishment has been known as "The Wayside Inn."
*(Courtesy The Collections of the Henry Ford Museum and
Greenfield Village)*

Massachusetts, the schoolhouse in Sudbury where Mary and her little lamb allegedly gamboled, and the shop of the "Village Blacksmith." He also sought to create a model nineteenth-century New England village near his mass-production, modern assembly-line, automobile manufacturing plant in Dearborn, Michigan.[34] Greenfield Village, named after the Michigan hamlet in which Ford's mother grew up, contained all the landscape elements that have made up the New England presence on the Midwest landscape. The village, designed by Ford's architect Edward J. Cutler, had an expansive grassy common around which were clustered a classical, white-spired church (directly modeled on the Universalist Church in Bradford, Massachusetts), a school, a town hall, a general store, and a colonial inn.

If what was important in New England had not already been replicated in the Midwest in the nineteenth century, Henry Ford would have supplied it. He transported all manner of Yankee artifacts to his recreated historical site in the twentieth century (see fig. 79). By rail, on barges, some dismantled, others shipped in toto, came Noah Webster's 1822 homestead from New Haven, Connecticut (see fig. 80); a vernacular

Figure 85.
"Wayside Inn" Interior, Sudbury, Massachusetts, 1924
Seated by the fireplace are Thomas Edison, Harvey Firestone,
and Henry Ford.
*(Courtesy The Collections of the Henry Ford Museum and
Greenfield Village)*

cottage (1645) from Plymouth, Massachusetts; windmills from Cape Cod;
and homes such as the Secretary Pearson's House (1750) relocated from
Exeter, New Hampshire, and Luther Burbanks' birthplace from Lancaster,
Massachusetts. From Mansfield, Connecticut, came the 1810 Hanks Silk
Mill (the shop that produced the first machine-made silk in America); from
Kingston, New Hampshire, a 1785 cooper's shop; from Phoenixville, Connecticut, a U.S. post office from 1830; from East Haverhill, Massachusetts,
the 1828 Whittier Toll House/Shoe Shop (fig. 86); and, finally, the Deluge
Fire House from Newton, New Hampshire. To complete his collection
of New England material culture, Ford also moved to Greenfield Village
an assortment of Midwestern Greek Revival structures whose inspiration,
if not actual building, had been influenced by the Yankee exodus of the
early nineteenth century.[35]

   The oldest extant structure in the city of Chicago, the Greek Revival
Henry B. Clarke House (1836), has a New England cast typical of
nineteenth-century Chicago construction. "*Checagou,*" place of the wild
onion to the Indians who used its portage, became Fort Dearborn (named
for a New Hampshire general) and then simply Chicago by the 1830s.

Figure 86.
East Haverhill Toll House (built in 1828)
Greenfield Village (ca. 1965), Dearborn, Michigan
*(Courtesy The Collections of the Henry Ford Museum and
Greenfield Village)*

The city's street-names recall New England places (e.g., Concord, Lexington, Cambridge), people (e.g., Hawthorne, Poe, Hancock), and promoters (e.g., Ogden, Clybourne, Elston). Furthermore, the Yankees who made up the city's economic and commercial hegemony included Long John Wentworth (Sandwich, New Hampshire), mayor and land developer; John S. Wright (Sheffield, Massachusetts), cartographer; Gustavus Swift (West Sandwich, Massachusetts) and Gurdon Saltonstall Hubbard (Windsor, Vermont), meatpackers; Marshall Field (Conway, Massachusetts), drygoods merchant; J. Young Scammon (Whitefield, Maine), newspaperman; Stephen A. Douglas (Brandon, Vermont), senator and a major stockholder in the Illinois Central Railroad, a Midwestern line largely financed by New England capitalists.

The impact of other transplanted Yankee entrepreneurs and philanthropists continued in the city's institutions: Walter L. Newberry's (Windsor, Connecticut) Library; Dwight Moody's (Northfield, Massachusetts) Bible Institute and Tabernacle; John Dewey's (Burlington, Vermont) Laboratory School at the University of Chicago; and Louis Sullivan's (Boston, Massachusetts) impressive Auditorium Building, modeled on the work of Boston architect H. H. Richardson.

The nineteenth-century cityscape of Sullivan's Chicago was indebted to New England builders and financiers. When Ellis Sylvester Chesbrough resigned his position as Boston's city engineer in 1855 to design Chicago's water supply and sewerage disposal systems, he probably did not realize that he, along with builder W. W. Boyington, would erect one of the city's most enduring symbols. Two other New Englanders changed the structural shape of the city's housing stock in their perfection and promotion of the balloon-framing construction technique. Historians debate whether it was George Washington Snow, a native of Keene, New Hampshire, or Augustine Deodat Taylor of Hartford, Connecticut, who deserved the credit as the "inventor" of the balloon frame.[36] There is no doubt, however, that transplanted New Englanders initiated the technique in Chicago. From there, thanks to the promotional efforts (articles, speeches, and books) of land speculators and town developers, such as Solon Robinson of Toland, Connecticut, this cheap, lightweight, and easy to assemble structural system swept across the plains and prairies, creating instant cities and greatly facilitating western settlement.

When the Chicago-based Illinois Central Railroad was chartered in 1851, two of its most active directors and heaviest investors were David A. Neal, who had made his initial fortune from Salem shipping in Massachusetts, and Robert Rantoul, a Bay State senator. Stephen A. Douglas from Vermont was among its promoters; and the railroad's chief counsel was James F. Joy, of Durham, New Hampshire. Its construction chief was a Yankee named Roswell B. Mason. One of the railroad's busiest publicists was Parke Godwin, son-in-law of William Cullen Bryant.

In order to develop, sell, and settle the lands adjacent to their railroad, the Illinois Central promoters purchased advertisements in newspapers in Vermont, New Hampshire, Connecticut, Maine, Rhode Island, and Massachusetts. They employed graphic artists, who created lithographs to prove that the words of Illinois Central poets were right. In one such advertisement, gorgeous trees shade a snug farmhouse—astounding, when one recalls that elsewhere in the pamphlet these fine prairie lands were said to be treeless. Everything is neatly fenced, in the best New England manner; and genteel horned cattle chew their cuds in the foreground. A staunch plow rests beside a superb field of truly gargantuan corn. The honest and happy husbandman himself is seen moving from house to barn, a splendid structure; and just at the far side of the cornfield is a train of cars, trailing a plume of smoke across the otherwise rustic and wholly charming scene. Such an image is followed by this injunction: "Look, ye sons and daughters of New England, look what a farm can be in Eden. Come down out of your granite hills, where only sheep can live. Come up out of your terminal moraines, which you foolishly call farms. Here in Illinois the life of the husbandman is fed by the bounty of the earth and sweetened by the air of heaven."[37]

Figure 87.
Monadnock Building, Wabash Avenue, Chicago, Illinois
The north half was completed in 1891, the south half, 1893.
Daniel Burnham and John Root, architects.
(Courtesy Chicago Historical Society)

New Englanders left their stamp on Chicago and the Midwest in one final way—with their money. When a comprehensive economic history of the states of the Old Northwest Territory is written, the influence of financiers in Boston, Hartford, Portland, and Newport will loom large. The enormous nineteenth-century New England investment in Chicago, for example, can be traced in the names of the city's highrise commercial buildings, merchandising blocks, and pioneering skyscrapers such as the Portland Block (1872), the Montauk Building (1881–82), the Old Colony Building (1894), the Boston Store (1905–17), or the Bay State Building (1872). Others without New England place-names in front of them but with ample Yankee capital (particularly of the Brooks Brothers' financial house in Boston) behind their real estate development were the Rookery Building (1885–86), the Marquette Building (1895), and the Monadnock Building (1888–93).[38] The latter stands on Chicago's South Dearborn Street as a massive parallel artifact symbolic of the New England–Midwestern cultural landscape interaction (fig. 87). Financed by Brooks Brothers, developed by Owen Aldis, and designed by Daniel Burnham and John Root, this monumental structure's four entrances were aptly named Kearsarge, Katahdin, Wachusett, and Monadnock, after New England mountain peaks. Monadnock, named after New Hampshire's 3,165 foot peak, is also the name of the entire building, which currently reigns as the tallest load-bearing commercial building still extant in the United States—another appropriate example of the New England presence on the Midwest landscape.

Notes

1. Alexis de Tocqueville, *Democracy in America,* ed. J. P. Mayer (Garden City, New York: Doubleday, 1969), 35. Howard A. Bridgman, *New England in the Life of the World* (Boston: Pilgrim Press, 1930).

2. As early as 1815, the elder Timothy Dwight, president of Yale, recognized the impact of the "forester class" from all six New England states (Maine, New Hampshire, Vermont, Massachusetts, Rhode Island, Connecticut) throughout the Old Northwest; see his *Travels in New England and New York,* 4 vols. (Cambridge: Harvard University Press, 1969), 3: 321–24; 2: 373; 4: 3, 18. The most authoritative modern assessment of the early history of the area is R. Carlyle Buley's two-volume study of *The Old Northwest, Pioneer Period, 1815–1840* (Bloomington, Ind.: Indiana University Press, 1950); Timothy Flint, *Recollections of the Last Ten Years in the Valley of the Mississippi* (New York: A. A. Knopf, 1932); Margaret Fuller, *Summer on the Lakes in 1843* (Boston: Charles C. Little & James Brown, 1844); Lois Kimball Mathews, *The Expansion of New England: The Spread of New England Settlement and Institutions to the Mississippi River, 1620–1825* (Boston: Houghton Mifflin, 1909); Stewart H. Holbrook, *The Yankee Exodus: An Account of Migration from New England* (Seattle: University of Washington Press, 1950).

3. Two works are excellent on the development of the Mormon landscapes out of New England: Dolores Hayden, *Seven American Utopias: The Architecture of Communitarian Socialism, 1790–1975* (Cambridge: MIT Press, 1976); Mark Leone, *The Roots of Modern Mormonism* (Cambridge: Harvard University Press, 1979). On Joseph Smith's New England background, see Fawn Brodie, *No Man Knows My History: The Life of Joseph Smith, the Mormon Prophet* (New York: A. A. Knopf, 1945). Because of limitations of space, the Mormons are excluded from this analysis despite the fact that Joseph Smith was born in Sharon, Vermont, lived for a while with his family in Lebanon, New Hampshire, and with fellow Vermonter, Brigham Young, contributed to the Mormon landscape all across the Midwest and throughout the Far West. Parenthetically, Smith, in his plural marriages, appears to have been particularly partial to New England women since six of his wives were Vermont natives, three were born in Maine, and two each were from New Hampshire and Massachusetts.

4. John Leighly, "Town Names of Colonial New England in the West," *Annals of the Association of American Geographers* 68 (June 1978): 233–48; Douglas R. McManis, *Colonial New England, A Historical Geography* (New York: Oxford University Press, 1975), vii.

5. See, for example, Fritz. L. Kramer, "Andover Moves West," *Names* 1 (1953): 188–91. For the revised edition of George R. Stewart's *Names on the Land* (Boston: Houghton Mifflin, 1958), Kramer supplied Stewart with a map that traces Winchester westward. See also Audrey R. Duckert, "Names Forever on the Land," *Names* 24 (1976): 124–27.

6. Thomas L. Clark, "Marietta, Ohio: The Continuing Erosion of a Speech Island," Ph.D. dissertation, Ohio University (1970), 145.

7. Because of the pillage and burning inflicted upon the Connecticut towns of New London, Groton, Danbury, New Haven, Fairfield, Norwalk, Greenwich, and Ridgefield by the British between 1777 and 1781, the General Assembly set aside the most western 25 miles of the Reserve (Huron and Erie counties) as a 500,000 acre tract for the benefit of the "sufferers" in these towns. Many towns in the Firelands derive their names from their ravaged namesakes in Connecticut.

8. Timothy Flint, *The Geography and History of the Western States* (Cincinnati: E. H. Flint, 1833), 2: 362. On Ohio place-naming patterns, also see William D. Overman, *Ohio Town Names* (Akron, Ohio: Atlantic Press, 1958) and Stuart Seeley Sprague, "The Name's the Thing: Promoting Ohio during the Era of Good Feelings," *Names* 25 (March 1977): 25–35.

9. David Lindsey, "New England Origins of Western Reserve Place-Names." *American Speech* 30 (February 1955), 245–49.

10. The first verse, as quoted in Mathews (p. 227) runs thus:

> Come, all ye Yankee farmers who wish to change your lot
> Who've spunk enough to travel beyond your native spot,
> And leave behind the village where Pa and Ma do stay,
> Come follow me and settle in Michigania—
> Yea, yea, yea, in Michigania.

11. Edward W. Barber, "The Vermontville Colony: Its Genesis and History," *Michigan Pioneer and Historical Collections* 28 (1900): 197–292. J. Harold Stevens, "The Influence of New England in Michigan," *Michigan Historical Magazine* 19 (Autumn 1935): 321–53.

12. Fred Kniffen and Henry Glassie, "Building in Wood in the Eastern United States: A Time-Place Perspective," *Geographical Review* 56 (1966): 40–65; Peirce F. Lewis, "Common Houses, Cultural Spoor," *Landscape* 19 (January 1975): 1–22; Wilbur Zelinsky, *The Cultural Geography of the United States* (Englewood Cliffs, N.J.: Prentice Hall, 1972).

13. Kniffen and Glassie, "Building in Wood," 64.

14. Hubert G. H. Wilhelm, "New England in Southeastern Ohio," *PAST* (Pioneer America Society Transactions, 1979): 24–29.

15. On the Mack House (1836), see Frederick Koeper, *Illinois Architecture from Territorial Times to the Present, A Selective Guide* (Chicago: University of Chicago Press, 1968), 256; on Western Reserve building types, consult Richard N. Campen, *Architecture of the Western Reserve, 1800–1900* (Cleveland: The Press of Case Western Reserve University, 1971).

16. See Francis H. Underwood, *The Colonial House Then and Now: A Picture Study of the Early American House Adapted to Modern Living* (Rutland, Vt.: Charles E. Tuttle, 1971), 2–29.

17. Talbot Hamlin, *Greek Revival Architecture in America* (New York: Oxford University Press, 1944), 159–86; 258–314; Rexford Newcomb, *Architecture of the Old Northwest Territory: A Study of Early Architecture in Ohio, Indiana, Illinois, Michigan, Wisconsin and Part of Minnesota* (Chicago: University of Chicago Press, 1950). Newcomb devotes a separate chapter to the impact of classicism in each of the Northwest Territory's five states: see pp. 74–137.

18. Campen, *Architecture of the Western Reserve*, 196, 220.

19. For example, Koeper in *Illinois Architecture* (p. 180) attributes the Anson Rogers House (1849) south of Marengo, Illinois, to Shaw's sourcebook. Historic American Buildings Survey's *Wisconsin Architecture* (Washington: U.S. Department of the Interior, 1965) traces (p. 22) similar Shaw influence via the Boston builder's later volume, *The Modern Architect, or Every Carpenter His Own Master* (Boston: Dayton and Wentworth, 1855).

20. Underwood, *The Colonial House*, 60–61, 66–67, 96–98, 105–6, 156–57.

21. Eric Johannesen, *Ohio College Architecture Before 1870* (Columbus: Ohio Historical Society, 1969), 21–23.

22. Brook Mather Kelly, *Yale: A History* (New Haven: Yale University Press, 1974); Roland H. Bainton, *Yale and the Ministry: A History of Education for Christian Ministry at Yale from the Founding in 1701* (New York: Harper, 1957). See Edward N. Kirk, *An Address before the Society for Promotion of Collegiate and Theological Education at the West* (Boston: n.p., 1851), p. 10; Nathan S. S. Beman, *Collegiate and Theological Education at the West* (New York: n.p., 1847), 13–22.

23. H. B. Johnson, *Order on the Land: The U.S. Rectangular Land Survey and the Upper Mississippi Country* (New York: Oxford University Press, 1976).

24. Wilhelm, "New England in Southeastern Ohio," 17.

25. John W. Reps, *The Making of Urban America, A History of City Planning in the United States* (Princeton: Princeton University Press, 1965), 230. Also consult Reps's two other volumes: *Town Planning in Frontier America* (Princeton: Princeton

University Press, 1965) and *Cities of the American West* (Princeton: Princeton University Press, 1979).

26.   The best treatment of the contemporary planning of Marietta is found in *The Records of the Original Proceedings of the Ohio Company,* ed. Archer B. Hulbert (Marietta, Ohio: Marietta Historical Commission, 1917) where the settlement is described (pp. 15–16) as follows:

> That within the said Tract and in the most eligible situation there be appropriated for a City, sixty squares of three hundred and sixty feet by three hundred and sixty feet each, in an oblong form. . . .
> That four of said squares, be reserved for public uses, and the remaining fifty six divided into house lots. That each square contain twelve house lots of sixty feet front, and One hundred feet depth. . . .
> That contiguous to, and, in the vicinity of the above trace there be laid off one Thousand Lots of Sixty-four acres each . . . which as the city lots, shall be considered a part of each proprietary share.

27.   Reps, *The Making of Urban America,* 230.

28.   See, for instance, John D. Cushing, "Town Commons of New England, 1640–1840," *Old-Time New England* 51 (January–March 1961): 86–94, and David B. Brodeur, "Evolution of the New England Town Common: 1630–1966," *The Professional Geographer* 19 (1967): 313–18; John R. Stilgoe, "The Evolution of the New England Town Common" in *Common Ground, A Conservation Handbook for New England Greens* (Cambridge, Mass.: Townscape Institute, 1982).

29.   Christina Tree, *How New England Happened* (Boston: Little, Brown, 1976), 135.

30.   D. W. Meinig, "Symbolic Landscapes: Some Idealizations of American Communities" in *The Interpretation of Ordinary Landscapes: Geographical Essays* (New York: Oxford University Press, 1979), 165–68; Samuel Chamberlain, *The New England Image* (New York: Hastings House, 1962), Hildegard B. Johnson, "Perceptions and Illustrations of the American Landscape in the Ohio Valley and the Midwest," in *This Land of Ours: The Acquisition and Disposition of the Public Domain* (Indianapolis: Indiana Historical Society, 1978), 1–38; John A. Jakle, *Images of the Ohio Valley* (New York: Oxford University Press, 1977).

31.   This important revisionist scholarship is perhaps best represented by Joseph S. Wood, "The Origin of the New England Village," Ph.D. dissertation, Pennsylvania State University (1978), 145–47; 203–85; and his essay, "The New England Village: Reality and Myth in Cultural Texts," presented at the Thirteenth Annual Meeting of the Society for Historical Archaeology, Albuquerque, New Mexico (January 1980), 7–8.

32.   Laurence M. Hauptman, "Westward the Course of Empire: Geography Schoolbooks and Manifest Destiny, 1783–1893," *Historian* 60 (May 1978): 423–40; Russell G. Handsman, "Machines and Gardens: Structures and Symbols of America's Past," unpublished paper delivered at American Ethnological Society (March 1978); David G. Russo, *Families and Communities: A New View of American History* (Nashville: American Association for State and Local History, 1974), 255.

33.   Vachel Lindsay, "The New American Village" as quoted in David Handlin, *The American Home* (Boston: Houghton, 1980), p. 236.

34.   Roger Butterfield, "Henry Ford, the Wayside Inn and the Problem of 'History Is Bunk,' " *Massachusetts Historical Society Proceedings* 77 (December–January

1965–66): 53–66. Thomas J. Schlereth, "The Historic Museum Village as a Learning Environment," *The Museologist* (June 1977): 10–17.

35. *The Book of Greenfield Village* (Dearborn, Mich.: Greenfield Village, n.d.); Geoffrey C. Upward, *A Home for Our Heritage: The Building and Growth of Greenfield Village and Henry Ford Museum, 1929–1979* (Dearborn, Mich.: The Henry Ford Museum Press, 1980), 111, 169–70. Interestingly enough, the most recent (1979) historic structure to be added to Ford's Greenfield Village is another New England structure, an eighteenth-century vernacular saltbox house with colonial furnishings donated to the Midwest site by Mrs. C. Gregory Wells, who first found it in Andover, Connecticut, in 1951, moved it to Union, Connecticut, and lived in it until 1977 when she gave it to Greenfield Village, where it now stands next to a Cape Cod windmill given to Ford in 1936 by the nationwide Ford dealers.

36. Compare John M. Van Osdel, "The History of Chicago Architecture," *Inland Architect* 1 (April 1883): 36–37; Walker Field, "A Re-examination into the Invention of the Balloon Frame," *Journal of the Society of Architectural Historians* 2 (October 1942): 3–29; and Paul Sprague, "The Origin of Balloon-Framing," *Journal of the Society of Architectural Historians* 40 (December 1981): 311–19.

37. Holbrook, *The Yankee Exodus,* 72–73.

38. *Summary of Information on South Half of Monadnock Block* (Chicago: Commission on Chicago Historical and Architectural Landmarks, 1972), 3. Here also consult Frank A. Randall, *History of the Development of Building Construction in Chicago* (Urbana: University of Illinois Press, 1947) and Carl W. Condit, *The Chicago School of Architecture, A History of Commercial and Public Building in the Chicago Area, 1875–1925* (Chicago: University of Chicago Press, 1964).

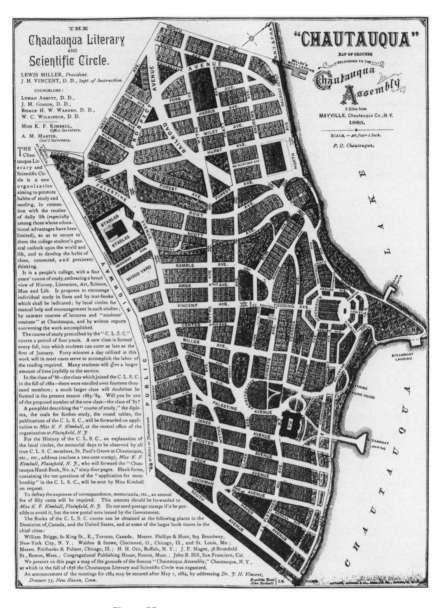

Figure 88.
Chautauqua Assembly, Map of Grounds, 1883
Chautauqua County, New York.
(Courtesy The Chautauqua Institution)

8

Chautauqua:
A Middle Landscape of the Middle Class

When I begin a course lecture on the Chautauqua movement in my sophomore survey course, American Thought and Culture I & II, few students in the 1980s know either where it was or what it is. I usually remark that if one discussed the topic with their collegiate counterparts a century ago, the reaction would be quite the reverse. By the late 1880s most middle-class Americans knew something about the original Chautauqua in Western New York State; many would have known or gone to its local imitators in their home regions.

Fortunately most American Studies students are familiar with Leo Marx's *The Machine in the Garden: Technology and the Pastoral Ideal* (1967), in which the philosophical and literary construct of "the middle landscape" is explored and on which this analysis is partially based. Although not stated so boldly below, I now argue in my *Transformations* volume that the middle-landscape concept may be the best covering term with which to explain several new landscape configurations of Victorian America.

What is missing in this essay is a clearer understanding of what I mean by the label "middle-class." Before attempting a brief definition of how I use the term, I should note how frequently this class's members appear in this book's chapters. We meet them as middle-class parents, along with doctors, teachers, and publicists, who discovered and developed the nineteenth-century's "cult of childhood." We encounter them as the class who founded and found new work in the spreading paper empire of late nineteenth-century business and government office. They urged city planning as progressive reform, backing the movement for new parks, playgrounds, settlement houses, and hospitals. The success of world expositions and history museums is due, if not to their leadership, certainly to their support. Finally, middle-class men and women lived in suburbs, went to colleges, and attended Chautauquas.

Here and elsewhere in the volume (pp. 9–10) I use the word class in a cultural sense, relying on occupational patterns, on how contemporaries saw social differences, and on real and perceived group traditions and ways of living. As many historians are quick to point out, the differences between working class and middle class in Victorian America were complex and continually shifting. Stuart Blumin argues

This article originally appeared in the Henry Ford Museum and Greenfield Village *Herald* 13.2 (November 1984): 22–31.

in his essay, "The Hypothesis of Middle-Class Formation in Nineteenth-Century America: A Critique and Some Proposals" (*American Historical Review* 90 [1985]: 292–338), both working class and middle class are problematic concepts because between 1870 and 1920 both groups underwent unprecedented statistical expansion, became more occupationally diverse, and simultaneously contended with and conciliated each other.

Americans who primarily did manual labor, worked for a daily wage, and lived at a modest income level populate all of my chapters. So do men and women employed at white-collar positions, who earned a weekly or monthly salary, and lived at a middle income level.

In comparison with the New England cultural hearth examined in chapter 7 (see fig. 81), we might say that the original Chautauqua, in part, continued the American lyceum movement begun in New England in the 1840s westward to New York in the 1880s. From this Mother Chautauqua the idea (with many additional programs) diffused throughout the Midwest to places such as Lakeside-on-the-Lake, Erie (Ohio) or Bay View (Michigan). While these independents were adminstratively separate and geographically diverse, most illustrate place-name diffusion. The majority carried the name Chautauqua as part of their identity.

This essay began as a lecture in a novel, three-day Chautauqua program hosted by the Michigan Council for the Humanities and the Henry Ford Museum. The council and the museum cosponsored a combined academic conference on the "Chautauqua in American Cultural History" and a two-day re-creation of a typical, Midwest, tent chautauqua on Greenfield Village's New England green. It took place in May 1984.

Our lectures were published in a special issue of the Henry Ford Museum and Greenfield Village's *Herald*. Two journals, both interested in regionalism and material culture, published my essay in other forms and with other graphics. *The Old Northwest* 12.3 (Fall 1986): 265–78 and *North American Culture,* the journal of the Society for the North American Cultural Survey 3.2 (1987): 3–18.

One appropriate way to describe the cultural environment that was Chautauqua is to call it a "middle landscape." This middle landscape had an enormous appeal to Americans in the period between the Civil and the First World wars for two important reasons: first, it drew upon an extensive tradition of normative and imaginative literature about the middle landscape ideal as well as the actual spatial evidence of that ideal created by Americans prior to the Civil War. Second, the cultural environment of the Chautauqua was not the only middle landscape in late nineteenth-century America; it had several cultural analogues that paralleled and reinforced its particular interpretation of the ideal. In turn, these institutions—suburbs, parks, college campuses, and world's fairs—augmented and reinforced the Chautauqua's middle landscape ethos.

Two parts of my title, "Chautauqua: A Middle Landscape of the Middle Class," need a word of clarification. *Chautauqua* was first a place name for a county, town, and lake in southwestern New York State (from the Seneca for "place of death," "place where one is lost," "foggy place"). Then in 1874 a Methodist minister, John Vincent, and an Akron, Ohio, businessman, Lewis Miller, established a Sunday school institute on a campsite on Lake Chautauqua. Soon this became a permanent summer colony offering a wide range of religious, cultural, and recreational activities, which taken together were called a *Chautauqua* (see fig. 88).

Inasmuch as it is an old idea—scholars trace the idea of the middle landscape ideal back to Shakespeare and even to Virgil—the concept is a complex one. Leo Marx, the most diligent student of the ideal in American literary and cultural history, defines it in several ways. In his classic study, *The Machine in the Garden: Technology and the Pastoral Ideal in America* (1967), he saw it as "a middle state between primitive nature and over-refined civilization." Marshaling evidence from Crèvecoeur to Jefferson, Emerson to Olmsted, Marx argued that the ideal environment that most Americans sought to create was a landscape that mediated between primitivism and civilization, a landscape posed between two metaphors: that of a wild, unspoiled Eden in which the Europeans thought they had first found the New York Senecas (who gave us the word *Chautauqua*) on the one hand, and the effete, rarified, decadent culture of the European cities they had left behind on the other.

Thomas Jefferson personified and publicized the ideal of the middle landscape. His dream of what Marx calls the "republic of the middle landscape" was an environment that was pastoral but not primitive. A dominant metaphor for this society of the middle landscape was the image of a garden: a self-contained, tranquil world of plantings and persons, largely removed from history, where nature and art were balanced and integrated. The garden of the middle landscape was thus an artifact of nature's artifice and of man's artisanry.

Jefferson's middle landscape, of course, was more than physical geography; it was, as Tench Coxe recognized, " a moral geography," a symbolic repository of economic, political, religious, and aesthetic values such as concern for self-education, the value of the arts, the self-enrichment of recreation, the moral precepts of Protestant Christianity, the impact of physical environment on human behavior.

In the eighteenth century, the ideal derived much of its persuasiveness from its anti-European posture. By the second half of the nineteenth century, the emerging urban American metropolis became a symbol of over-sophistication, over-civilization, and over-cultivation to be avoided. Americans set to shaping pleasure ground parks and vacation compounds, rural health spas and children's youth camps, and by the 1880s independent summer Chautauquas, to be followed at the turn of the century by tent circuit Chautauquas.

The Chautauqua has its origins as a middle landscape of the middle class in three spatial forebears: the American college campus, the outdoor religious camp meeting, and the communitarian settlement. The environmental influence of the early American residential campus was widespread. Again, Jefferson, himself a college planner and educational theorist, wrote the book on why American colleges should be middle landscapes. In his judgment, they should be located in the country, removed from the distractions of the city, where intellectual and moral maturation could best be nurtured. His own campus of the University of Virginia became the nation's norm: a rural setting, a planned physical environment that fused nature and art, one that nurtured faculty-student intellectual life and encouraged healthy recreation. By 1870, for example, Lewis Miller's Ohio had over one hundred such colleges; Galesburg's Knox College was but one of fifty similar colleges in John Vincent's Illinois.

Although not as indigenous an American middle landscape as the private, residential college, the religious camp meeting serves as another precedent for Chautauqua. I have in mind here famous nineteenth-century camp meetings like the ones that took place in Cane Ridge, Kentucky, in 1801 or on the campus of Ohio's Oberlin College, as well as those at thousands of other rural sites throughout the Upland South and the Midwest. Principally a Methodist institution in origin and influence, the rural camp meeting has various parallels to the Chautauqua movement. Both were located in rural or natural geographical settings, both sought some degree of spatial control over their participants, and both shared a belief in the beneficial auspices of a purifying and edifying environment of high thinking and natural living. Moreover, we should not forget that in creating the original Chautauqua, Methodist Bishop John Vincent and Methodist layman Lewis Miller were but transferring an early middle landscape into a new one since their first outdoor auditorium and fifty acres of land had formerly belonged to the Chautauqua Lake Camp Meeting Association of which Lewis Miller was a trustee.

One other pre-1870 American landscape also had some affinity with Chautauqua—the hundred or so communitarian experiments (see fig. 132) of the kind attempted by the Shakers, the Perfectionists, Harmonists, Fourierists, or the Owenites. "We are all a little wild here in America," wrote Emerson of these communities to his friend Thomas Carlyle in Britain, "Not a reading man but has a draft of a new community in his waist-pocket."

Dolores Hayden's *Domestic Utopias* is a recent attempt to analyze the spaces that these reformers sought to sculpt from the American countryside. Hayden's volume derives much of its documentary data from

Arthur Bestor's *Backwoods Utopias,* a classic study by a Midwest historian at the University of Illinois and, more important in this context, the president of the Chautauqua Board of Trustees and its program chairman for many years. Bestor Plaza at Lake Chautauqua is the landscape that honors his lifelong work on the movement's behalf.

How might we consider Bestor's Chautauqua as a middle landscape of the middle class? To begin with, the community is an intriguing spatial mixture of both formal and informal landscape planning. Parks abound: Lewis Miller Park, Bishop's Garden, Lincoln Park, College Hill Park, and, of course, Palestine Park—a topograpical visual aid to assist in the learning of biblical history and geography that dates from the 1880s (fig. 89). Chautauqua Lake, which gives the country, the town, the institution, the independents, the circuits, and this conference its name, affords all manner of water recreation. Middle-class pursuits such as music and art education also are ample (here you can learn the art of organ tuning). Tennis courts and croquet lawns, later playing fields and golf courses, were carefully integrated into this landscape (fig. 90).

As in most American suburbs, places of worship are in evidence at the Mother Chautauqua: nineteen churches representing eight major Protestant denominations. Jews and Catholics, excluded as they often were from various nineteenth-century middle landscapes, started their own Chautauquas. The Catholic Summer Chautauquas in Plattsburgh, New York, and in Watertown, Wisconsin, nonetheless assumed the basic characteristics of the generic Chautauqua: a rural enclave for self-improvement, a sylvan retreat away from the pressures of urban life, and a collective cultural enterprise for moral and intellectual rearmament.

Chautauqua and Other American Middle Landscapes

Many of the country's independent Chautauquas carry place names— Inland Park, Lincoln Park, Monona Lake, Red Oak, Mountain Park, Lakeside—that simultaneously evoke images of nineteen-century suburbs of similar ambience. Their site plans often look alike and they had similar town centers and formal entrance gates. Occasionally an Olmsted-planned suburb such as Riverside, Illinois (fig. 91), would have a hotel like the Athenaeum at Lake Chautauqua. In residential housing, the parallels are multiple. Chautauqua summer home architecture, as historian Pauline Fancher has traced, was largely synonymous with middle-class residential preferences from 1880 to 1920.

American Victorian suburbs were frequently developed around parks as well as named after them. Significantly, the first phase of the public parks movement in America—the era of the park type Galen Cranz has

Figure 89.
Palestine Park, ca. 1890
Chautauqua Assembly Grounds, Chautauqua, New York.
(Courtesy The Chautauqua Institution)

called "the pleasure ground park"—parallels the rise of the Chautauqua movement. In one sense, the great urban pleasure grounds created at New York's Central Park, Chicago's Lincoln Park, and San Francisco's Golden Gate Park were replicated, albeit in smaller scale, by the independent Chautauquas in their various permanent sites.

In the face of increasing urbanization, industrialization, and technological change, the late nineteenth-century American's love affair with nature is understandable. Some, such as John Muir, argued that American nature be left in the raw, wild state in which its creator had left it; others like Theodore Roosevelt (a perennial Chautauqua platform performer who considered the institution "the most American thing about America") insisted that only through national and state parks, that is, through man's deliberate artifice, could nature's art be preserved. While it would be wrong to claim that the new national parks of Yellowstone (1873) and Yosemite (1895) were true middle landscapes, part of the thinking behind their creation was. Moreover, the American national park movement received a sympathetic hearing among many Chautauquans.

In addition to being an environment for recreation, Chautauqua prided itself on its educational mission, espousing the perennial American

Figure 90.
Tennis Court Recreation Area, ca. 1890
Chautauqua Assembly Grounds, Chautauqua, New York.
(Courtesy The Chautauqua Institution)

ideal of democratic, popular, general education opportunities commensurate with the Jeffersonian dream of an educated people capable of self-culture and self-government. Such an ideal also was shared by the United States Congress (which legislated the Morrill Land Grant College Act of 1862) and by the state governments (which have supported such institutions of higher learning). Those who planned the great Midwestern land-grant colleges and universities did so largely as middle landscapes. They drew upon the campus ideal first promulgated by Jefferson, adding building types that, for example, the Chautauqua Institution also established as part of its spatial environment: dormitories, conservatories, art galleries, administration buildings, libraries, gymnasiums, and alumni halls. In this context of the summer Chautauqua as university campus, it is tempting—and I mean no irreverence here—to suggest that in one sense, the religious houses of the Methodists, Baptists, and Disciples of Christ act as do fraternity and sorority houses in the university environment.

Whether that be true or not, the Chautauqua Institution functioned, in name and in fact, as a university. Chartered by the state of New York, it offered numerous courses (one appropriately in landscape architecture)

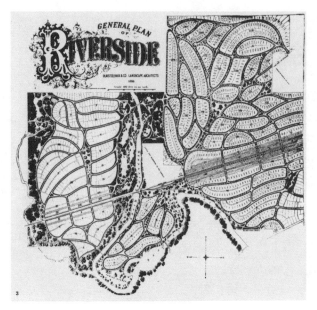

Figure 91.
Plan of Riverside, Illinois, 1869
Olmsted, Vaux and Company, Landscape Architects.
(Courtesy N. Barrett)

in the Schools of Philosophy, Education, and Theology; it established professorships; it initiated university extension course work, and it awarded degrees (fig. 92).

Although the land-grant colleges were the new kids on the higher education block in the post–Civil War era, private colleges also flourished. They likewise aspired to be middle landscapes. My own institution, the University of Notre Dame, landscaped its 4,000 acres, two lakes, and oak-and-sassafras forests into a sylvan environ that its founders thought conducive to learning. In the center of the campus, they laid out a 22-acre arboretum of every species of tree, shrub, and vine known to have been hardy in the northern Indiana climate (fig. 93). Surrounding this campus was a 2,400-acre university farm that raised all the foodstuffs for the school's dining hall tables with the surplus being sold in the grain and livestock markets of Chicago. Jefferson, I think, would have approved.

While most Chautauquas had no farms to augment their middle landscapes, they did have farmers and all manner of other folk to attend their lectures and programs. Of course, most farm people could not attend a resort Chautauqua for any extended length of time during the growing

Figure 92.
Graduation and Recognition Day, ca. 1890
Chautauqua Scientific and Literary Circle.
Chautauqua Assembly Grounds, Chautauqua, New York.
(Courtesy The Chautauqua Institution)

season. The tent Chautauqua, therefore, better served their needs since it only lasted but a week (sometimes three days) and usually had no residential facilities.

In this respect, the great world expositions of the nineteenth century offer a final parallel to the Chautauqua movement in that they were, in my judgment, another middle landscape of the American middle class. And, if the tent Chautauqua was a summer-long Chautauqua in miniature, the American world's fairs in Philadelphia (1876), Chicago (1893), St. Louis (1904), and San Francisco (1915) were Chautauqua on the world stage. (See chap. 10 of this volume.) A combination giant department store, art gallery and music hall, technological cornucopia, and huge municipal park, these world expositions celebrated the values of the moral, the mobile, and the middle.

Take, for instance, the World's Columbian Exposition in Chicago in 1893 (see figs. 99, 106, 107). Frederick Law Olmsted designed it—as he did so many other American spaces, like the Stanford University campus or New York's Central Park—as a middle landscape. Even throughout the interiors of the main exhibit halls of the machinery, manufacturing,

Figure 93.
University of Notre Dame Campus, ca. 1893
Bird's-eye view, Notre Dame, Indiana.
(Courtesy University of Notre Dame Archives)

and electricity buildings, palmetto palms were intermingled with power plants. It was as if Leo Marx's title had been inverted and now the garden was within the machine.

Finally, the 1893 fair was a moral enterprise akin to the Chautauqua movement. Many Chautauqua speakers participated in the summer-long series of world congresses devoted to literature, history, art, philosophy, and science. The massive World Parliament of Religions held in conjunction with the fair, turned out to be something of a national alumni reunion for many Chautauquans.

Chautauqua's Legacy to Contemporary Middle Landscapes

World's fairs, one of Chautauqua's sister institutions in the nineteenth century, continue as middle landscapes of the middle class in the twentieth century. Formalized in a somewhat similar spatial ethos of the middle landscape ideal, other contemporary American institutions are also, I think, heir to Chautauqua's legacy.

In the excellent special issue (Winter/Spring 1984) of *The Michigan Connection* devoted to Chautauqua, several authors allude to certain obvious parallels in our time: the State Humanities Programs, although usually lacking in actual physical landscape, are instances of continuing attempts to relate the teachings and insights of the humanities to adult public audiences.

The modern conference facilities such as the Kellogg Center for Continuing Education to be found on numerous Midwestern college campuses and the Johnson Foundation's Wingspread Center at Racine, Wisconsin, as well as the Aspen Institute in Colorado are other modern analogues. The Elderhostel movement, suggests Gordon Rohman, may be the Chautauqua reincarnate in our own day. Begun in 1975 by the University of New Hampshire administrator, Mary Knowlton, the Elderhostel idea also makes use of a traditional middle landscape—a college campus to run a summer school for persons of sixty or over at a university where faculty teach noncredit courses aimed at nonspecialist audiences. In 1984 the Elderhostel enrolled 40,000 adults in 450 colleges and universities in the United States and Canada.

The first Chautauqua Institution as well as several of its independent progeny continue to thrive. You can still go to a summer Chautauqua, for example, in Ocean Grove (New Jersey), Lakeside-on-the-Lake, Erie (Ohio), Monteagle (Tennessee), Fountain Park (Indiana), Colorado Association (Colorado), and Bay View (Michigan). Surviving fragments of the Chautauqua experience in the context of its middle landscape are also evident in the proliferation of summer music programs established in landscapes such as Tanglewood, Wolftrap, and Ravinia. And there are also the Historic Cooperstown Annual Seminars on American culture on Lake Otsego (New York), the Archaeological Programs at the Flowerdew Hundred Plantation in Virginia, and the Antiques Seminars of Colonial Williamsburg.

One of the greatest of all contemporary Chautauqua environments is that American outdoor living history museum, The Edison Institute's Greenfield Village in Dearborn, Michigan. Henry Ford, its creator, was a Chautauquan's Chautauquan, who publicly espoused the values of the Chautauqua experience and supported its aspirations.

I see The Edison Institute as a physical and spatial embodiment in the twentieth century of the Chautauqua ideal of the nineteenth century (fig. 94). Greenfield Village parallels several of the middle-landscape institutions we have examined. Is not its residential row a type of suburb

---

(*Overleaf*)
Figure 94.
Guide to Greenfield Village, 1988
The Edison Institute, Dearborn, Michigan.
(Courtesy The Collections of the Henry Ford Museum and Greenfield Village)

GUIDE TO GREENFIELD VILLAGE

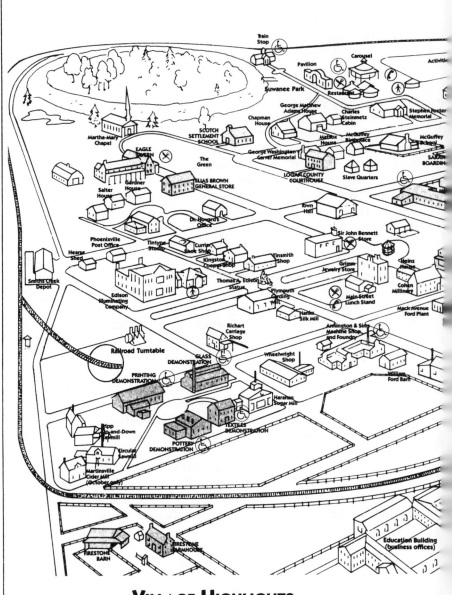

VILLAGE HIGHLIGHTS

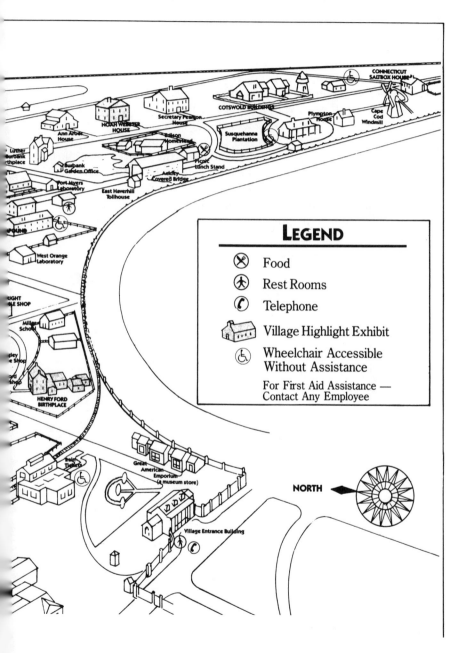

LEGEND

⊗ Food

🚻 Rest Rooms

📞 Telephone

🏠 Village Highlight Exhibit

♿ Wheelchair Accessible Without Assistance

For First Aid Assistance —
Contact Any Employee

CONNECTICUT SALTBOX HOUSE

COTSWOLD BUILDINGS

Plympton House

Cape Cod Windmill

Ann Arbor House

NOAH WEBSTER HOUSE

Secretary Pearson House

Edison Homestead

Susquehanna Plantation

Luther Burbank Birthplace

Burbank Garden Office

Picnic Lunch Stand

Fort Myers Laboratory

Ackley Covered Bridge

East Haverhill Tollhouse

West Orange Laboratory

WRIGHT CYCLE SHOP

Miller School

Sladey Tire Shop

Ford Shop

HENRY FORD BIRTHPLACE

Train Tickets

Great American Emporium (a museum store)

Village Entrance Building

NORTH

development? Does not the Suwanee Island evoke the ambiance of the lake vacation compounds? Inasmuch as the Educational Building complex has a library, classrooms, a swimming pool, and dormitories, are we not on a type of campus where education takes place at the elementary and secondary school level and, in recent decades, particularly among adult learners? Finally, we might consider Henry Ford Museum itself as one marvelous world's fair exposition pavilion since it contains a staggering array of technological wonders, domestic objects, and popular culture artifacts all housed in a replica of Independence Hall similar to those built at the 1893 and 1939 world's fairs in Chicago and New York.

The Edison Institute is thus heir to an enduring cultural tradition of beliefs and behaviors that can be summarized as the American middle landscape. This tradition, of course, did not begin with the Chautauqua. Yet, along with its analogous middle-class institutions of late nineteenth-century America, Chautauqua served as one of a network of interconnecting institutions which promoted and stabilized a middle-class value system that sought to reconcile morality and mobility, learning and living, enterprise and excess, art and nature.

Figure 95.
Fernand Janin, Front Elevation of Proposed Civic Center (detail)
Drawing. From Daniel H. Burnham and Edward H. Bennett, *Plan of Chicago*
(Chicago: The Commercial Club of Chicago, 1909), plate 131.

9

City Planning as Progressive Reform: Burnham's Plan and Moody's Manual

In chapter 6 we noted the great interest that men and women who styled themselves as Progressives in the early twentieth century took in shaping their urban environment. This coalition usually united those Republican insurgents and Democratic independents who formed the Progressive party in Chicago and supported Theodore Roosevelt for president in 1912. It also included individuals who demanded political reform and social uplift. These reformers came from the growing urban middle class representing its traditional vocations (lawyers, doctors, academics), as well as its new occupations (CPAs, engineers, corporate managers). Stow Persons, in *American Minds* (New York: H. Holt, 1958), called this diverse group "the neo-democratic mind."

Using Walter D. Moody's *Wacker's Manual of the Plan of Chicago* (1911) as an early (but neglected) classic in the history of American planning promotional literature, this chapter analyzes how Daniel Burnham's 1909 master plan for Chicago underwent popularization and promotion through the efforts of William D. Moody, drummer, adman, and business college teacher. It also sketches the effect of the urban planner, civic promoter, and public relations man on the city as artifact. I argue that Moody's manual, particularly its underlying tenets—belief in mass education, the efficient quest for order in metropolitan centers, the efficacy of public relations in modern life, and the influence (positive and negative) of the urban environment on human behavior—not only translates a landmark text in the normative literature on the American city into a more democratic medium, it also provides access to one version of the Progressives' vision for manipulating the urban built environment to implement their agenda of political and social hegemony.

What does all of this have to do with material culture? Actually a great deal. Simply put, it is a useful example of the axiom: "Artifacts have politics." Of course, some artifacts—public buildings, historic markers, parks and playgrounds, roads and highways, public utilities, civic art and sculpture—stir more immediate political debate than others. City plans fall into this category. Since I wrote this essay which only hints of this characteristic of material culture, other scholars have addressed the issue directly and persuasively. Here I recommend Robert Caro's massive biography, *Power*

This article originally appeared in the *Journal of the American Planning Association* 47.1 (January 1981): 70–82.

Broker: Robert Moses and the Fall of New York (New York: Random House, 1974) on the planning czar who changed the physical city scape of metropolitan New York in ways more drastic than anything D. H. Burnham and W. D. Moody accomplished in Chicago. One finds in Galen Cranz, *The Politics of Park Design: A History of Urban Parks in America* (Cambridge: MIT Press, 1982), a four-stage typology of city park design, each stage with a different spatial configuration and each with a separate ideology. In Roy Rosenzwieg's *Eight Hours for What We Will: Workers and Leisure in an Industrial City, 1870–1920* (Cambridge: Cambridge University Press, 1983), we learn how working-class and middle-class people contended with civic spaces such as urban playgrounds and public parks. Langdon Winner, "Do Artifacts Have Politics?" *Daedalus* (1980): 121–36, provides an overview of this aspect of material culture research.

Here, as so frequently throughout this book, Chicago serves as an evidential base and a case study. It is the American city I know best, historically and experientially. I have been riding the Chicago and South Bend South Shore Railroad (the nations's last major interurban) for three decades. Chicago's history (1870–1930) offers me, in an American Studies seminar I teach, an urban laboratory for doing cross-disciplinary material culture studies. My premise in this course, which includes examination of the Burnham plan and Moody's manual, rests on several assumptions. I see *fin-de-sièle* Chicago as a case study sliced off for the microscope, showing all the characteristics, tensions, and aspirations of the nation at large. None of the national struggles, problems and achievements, from 1871 through 1919, was missing in the area that James Bryce once called "the most American part of America." In Sam Bass Warner's estimate, Chicago during this period emerged as a prototype of "the total urban industrial landscape"; another urban historian, Zane Miller, sees Chicago as "a luminous illustration of how cities grew as a result of the simultaneous emergence of advocates of both the small and big community among builders of the twentieth-century city." Literary scholars have realized that in Chicago, from 1871 through 1919, there arose a "new poetry" and a "new American literature" in which a daring, younger generation would say new things in a new way. Finally, Louis Sullivan can be seen as the prophet of contemporary architecture and Frank Lloyd Wright as the first contemporary architect. I think Henry Adams writing in *The Education of Henry Adams* (1918) was right about Chicago in the 1890s when he said "one must start there" in order to understand "American thought as a unity."

Including this essay in a collection on material culture has a special personal meaning for me in addition to my fondness of Chicago history and my predilection for studying large landscapes. To begin with, the article has varied genealogy. Delivered first as a lecture at the Art Institute of Chicago upon the invitation of John Zukowsky, the AIC's curator of architecture, a short version of it appeared in the *Inland Architect* 24.3 (April 1980), and a longer adaption appeared in the *Journal of the American Planning Association,* where Donald Krueckeberg read it, liked it, and asked to include it in his anthology *The American Planner: Biographies and Recollections* (New York: Methuen, 1983). While not slighting any of these professional publications, the one that gave me the most personal satisfaction was the opportunity to contribute still another expansion of it to the festschrift, *Ideas in America: From Republic to Mass Society,* ed. Hamilton Cravens (Ames: Iowa State University Press, 1982). This volume was dedicated to my doctoral advisor and dissertation director, Stow Persons, upon his retirement from the department of history at the University of Iowa.

I enrolled in Iowa's Ph.D. program specifically to study American intellectual history with Dr. Persons. If I have sometimes ventured into other types of historical evidence such as material culture, I hope I have always done so with the seriousness of purpose and method he always taught us when investigating ideas—their creators, their contexts, or their manifestations. I hope this essay represents the research of a historian, ever mindful of intellectual history, as he probes material culture's inter-relation with cultural history.

To Chicagoan Walter Dwight Moody, "the completion of the Plan of Chicago was the most important civic event in the history of the city." Moody maintained that if implemented, the 1909 metropolitan plan prepared by Daniel H. Burnham and Edward H. Bennett[1] would enable Chicago to become nothing less than "the center of the modern world." No small claim for a city hardly seven decades old, but not atypical brag-gadocio for a midwestern metropolis already notorious for its special brand of civic and architectural boosterism.

Moody, a former general manager of the Chicago Association of Commerce and the first managing director of the Chicago Plan Commission (CPC), made his boast in a strangely titled, now largely unread work called *Wacker's Manual of the Plan of Chicago: Municipal Economy.*[2] First published in 1911, this curious volume in the history of American city planning literature went through several editions during the decade (1911–21) that Moody superintended the promotion of the Burnham/Bennett Plan. The book's misleading title prompted contemporaries as well as a few modern scholars mistakenly to attribute the work's author-ship to Charles Wacker, prominent Chicago brewer turned real estate developer, financier, civic leader, and first chairman of the CPC. Moody's middle and surname also occasionally prompted confusion with that of the popular Chicago evangelist Dwight L. Moody whose tabernacle and ancillary structures (bible college and institute, bookstore, radio station) still dot Chicago's near northside cityscape.[3]

The Manual's Author

Who was Walter Dwight Moody? Why did he write a bestseller and ascribe it to another man? What were the work's principal ideas? What might such ideas reveal about the philosophy and the practice of turn-of-the-century urban planning in Chicago and the nation? What might the intel-lectual history of this segment of the American city planning movement add to our understanding of the main currents of American history?

This chapter attempts to explore these questions through a textual analysis of Moody's widely promulgated book as an early classic in city planning promotional literature. While other historical data (e.g., correspondence, municipal archives, Chicago Planning Commission minutes) have also been consulted, the manual itself stands as the principal documentation that informs this essay. Thus the manual's ideas—belief in mass education, progressivism, the efficiency movement, and environmentalism—are the focus of the analysis that follows. Concentrating primarily on Moody's text rather than his context, on what he wrote rather than what he did, this study interprets the manual as an important document both in the intellectual history of the American city planning movement and in the history of the many-faceted reform movement known as progressivism.

The occasional mistaken identity of Walter Dwight Moody with Dwight Lyman Moody contains one clue to the former's character. In his efforts in "putting the Plan across," W. D. Moody openly acknowledged that he did so with all the zealotry of "the clergyman and the pedagogue."[4] In an era when many reformers had clerical backgrounds (e.g., Richard Ely or Graham Taylor) or personal religious motivations (e.g., John Bates Clark or Charles H. Cooley) behind their attempts to bring about social and political change,[5] his evangelical fervor to promote urban planning as the redemption of American cities puts Moody perfectly in step with many of his fellow progressives.

Moody's career began, however, not in salvation but in sales. The title of one of his early publications can serve as a capsule biography. On a 1907 book cover, he proudly proclaimed himself as one of those "men who sell things," the book being the *Observations and Experiences of Over Twenty Years as a Travelling Salesman, European Buyer, Sales Manager, Employer.*[6] Drummer, promoter, adman, business college teacher, showman, Moody personified the late nineteenth-century American whom Daniel Boorstin has symbolized as "the go-getter," and whom both Burnham and Wacker saw as "a hustler, a man who knows how to do things and to get the greatest amount of publicity out of a movement."[7]

To such a man the CPC entrusted the monumental task of making every Chicagoan fully plan-conscious. The objective was to reach the one and one-half million citizens who could not afford the prohibitively expensive ($25.00), lavish, limited first edition of two thousand copies of the plan published by the Commercial Club.[8] Handsome though it was, filled with evocative sketches in both color and black and white by Jules Guérin and Jules Janin (fig. 96), Burnham and his Commercial Club associates recognized that the plan of Chicago was little more than sagacious advice from people with no official power. In accepting one of the limited edition copies, Mayor Fred Busse, who would later create

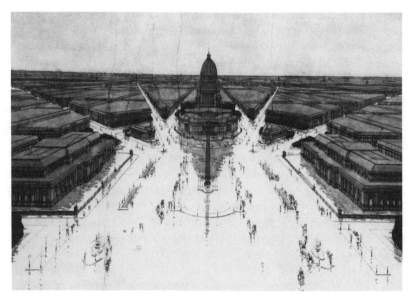

Figure 96.
Jules Guérin, View Looking West of Proposed Civic Center Plaza
Pencil and watercolor on paper. From Daniel H. Burnham and Edward H.
Bennett, *Plan of Chicago* (Chicago: The Commercial Club of Chicago, 1909),
plate 132.

the CPC, was careful to note that the plan's proposals were not "hard and fast" and would not necessarily result in immediate changes.⁹ The unofficial nature of the venture, however, inspired Charles Eliot, the retired president of Harvard, to write:

> That a club of businessmen should have engaged in such an undertaking, and have brought it successfully to its present stage, affords a favorable illustration of the workings of American democracy. The democracy is not going to be dependent on the rare appearance of a Pericles, an Augustus, a Colbert, or a Christopher Wren. It will be able to work toward the best ideals through the agency of groups of intelligent and public spirited citizens who know how to employ experts to advantage.¹⁰

To promote the plan that they had had experts produce, the Commercial Club members, through their control of the CPC,¹¹ employed another expert. Walter Moody, a professional organizer and one of the new breed of public executives who made careers out of managing civic organizations, assumed this responsibility. As early as 1909 Moody had been approached by Charles D. Norton (later Assistant Secretary of the Treasury under William Howard Taft) to publicize the plan as the exclusive promotional property of the Commercial Club. When the Plan was presented to the city, and The Chicago Plan Commission, a public agency, was created by municipal ordinance, Moody's talent was again solicited—this time by the CPC's first chairman, Charles H. Wacker. Moody accepted the task of mobilizing a comprehensive promotional campaign to match the sweeping metropolitan scope of the plan itself.[12]

Although he never pretended to be a practicing planner like Burnham or Bennett, Moody considered his task of "the scientifc promotion of scientific planning" to be equal in importance to whatever was accomplished on the drafting table or in the architectural office. He defined city planning as "the science of planning the development of cities in a systematic and orderly way." Furthermore, he divided city planning into "two distinct and widely separate scientific branches. The first, or technical branch, embraces architecture and engineering. The second, which is promotive, is likewise scientifically professional and could be truthfully termed the dynamic power behind the throne of accomplishment."[13]

The terms "scientifically professional" indicated another characteristic that Moody shared with many other thinkers of his era. As David Noble, Richard Hofstadter, and Charles Forcey have argued, many progressives believed strongly in the efficacy of the scientific method, guided by professional expertise, to achieve social change.[14] Walter Moody shared this assumption, not only in his promulgation of the Chicago plan but also in his promotion of city planning as a profession. The special identity that Herbert Croly claimed for architects, that Frederick Winslow Taylor coveted for industrial engineers, and Louis Brandeis wished firmly established for lawyers and businessmen, Moody sought for city planners.[15] Like Charles Mulford Robinson and John Nolen, his contemporary colleagues in city planning, he endeavored to contribute to what has been called the late nineteenth- and early twentieth-century "culture of professionalism." Moody's decade of work with the CPC, his numerous magazine and newspaper articles, and his two major books all were methods by which he sought to make the profession of city planning a vehicle of urban reform.[16]

The key to Moody's reformism was publicity. In debt to the social scientific advertising techniques he borrowed from the pioneering social psychologist Walter Dill Scott (a fellow Chicagoan who later became president of Northwestern University), Moody made his appeal for implementation of the 1909 Plan to each of the assorted interest groups and power blocs in Chicago.

Of the multiple constituencies to be persuaded of the necessity of the plan, Moody felt most confident of the city's capitalists. After all, had it not been an informal competition as to who would actually sponsor a city plan that encouraged the merger of Chicago's Merchants and Commercial Clubs? By the time the Commercial Club produced the Burnham Plan, its members had also invested over a half million dollars in the enterprise.[17] Moody was less sure of the general electorate. His first major publication as managing director of the CPC, therefore, sought to reach this citywide, adult audience. A ninety-page, hardbound reference work titled *Chicago's Greatest Issue: An Official Plan* was distributed to over 165,000 Chicago residents; these were property owners and tenants who paid $25.00 or more per month in rent. The booklet is usually credited with countering the initial critiques of the Plan (such as George Eddy Newcomb's caustic *Chicago Replanned* (Chicago: Privately printed, 1911) and the protests of the Twelfth Street Property Owners Association), and with securing support for the passage of the first plan bond issue (the widening of Twelfth Street) proposed to the Chicago voters in 1912.[18]

The Manual's Origins

Within the first six months of administering the CPC, Moody moved to institute a city planning study program in the Chicago schools. Daniel Burnham had suggested this move believing that for comprehensive urban planning to succeed "children must grow up dreaming of a beautiful city." Burnham, who had been extremely disappointed when his 1905 plan for San Francisco failed to be implemented because of inadequate promotion and subsequent citizen apathy, hoped to achieve this educational objective by lectures and the distribution of literature in the city schools.[19] Moody had bigger plans. Believing that "the ultimate solution of all the major problems of American cities lies in the education of our children to their responsiblities as future owners of our municipalities and arbiters of their governmental destiny," he proposed introducing an accredited course on the Chicago plan into the city's public school curriculum. The course would be a part of Moody's program for "scientific citizen making."[20]

To assist in such civic nurture, Moody wrote the first city planning textbook to be used in American schools. He named the text *Wacker's Manual,* because he believed that the people "should come to know intimately the individual who to a large extent held the destiny of the city in his hands." He felt it imperative for the populace to have the same confidence and knowledge about their plan leader, Charles Wacker (chairman of the CPC), as in their plan.

Influenced by the work of German educators who had been instructing children in urban planning since the 1880s, he designed his text and its accompanying teacher's handbook for use in the second semester of a civics course already operating in the final term of Chicago's public schools. The eighth grade was selected because many contemporary educational psychologists contended that at that stage of growth children were most impressionable. Also, after grammar school many would drop out of the system. While writing the manual, Moody sought help from the University of Chicago faculty, the staff at the Chicago Historical Society, and the Art Institute. He persuaded Ella Flagg Young, city superintendent of schools, to have the Board of Education officially adopt and purchase (at 34 cents a hardbound copy) the 1911 first edition for use in the spring of 1912. Eventually over fifty thousand copies of *Wacker's Manual* were printed. They were read not only by Chicago schoolchildren but also by their parents.

While by no means as stunning as the plan in terms of diversity of pictorial media or aesthetic quality, the manual aspired to make as powerful a visual impact. The manual included over 150 charts, maps, and pictures—many reproduced from the plan. (The plan had 142 illustrations.) Similar to the parent plan, nearly a third of the manual's graphics were of foreign urban design. Color renderings in both Burnham's treatise (where they were largely the work of Jules Guérin)[21] and Moody's textbook were hazy, subdued pastels, connoting a tranquil, sunlit, environment for Chicago which corresponds with an equally unreal absence of automobiles, pollution, and congestion in these visual utopias of Chicago's future.

Moody further modeled his 137-page primer along organizational lines roughly parallel to the 164-page, octavo-size Plan. He divided the textbook into four major topics: (a) general urban planning philosophy and nomenclature (chaps. 1–3); (b) a historical survey of city planning since antiquity (chaps. 4–7); (c) Chicago's historical, geographic, economic, and civic development, including the origins of the 1909 Plan (chaps. 8–10); and, (d) a detailed exegesis of the Plan's main components—transportation network, street system, Michigan Avenue and Chicago River redevelopment, park system (figs. 97, 98), and civic center (chaps. 11–16.)[22]

Of the four formats he produced in advancing the plan of Chicago,[23] Moody considered the manual to have the most long-range influence. Like previous American educational reformers Benjamin Rush, Horace Mann, Henry Barnard, and Francis Parker, he believed that the promise of a more enlightened, public-minded citizenry rested with the current school-age generation. Moody had been an educator for several years in Chicago's LaSalle Extension University, and he felt that his text "recognized the need for bringing out in the children of our cities a sharp, clear, vivid interest in those cities, in their history, their growth, in their present and

Figure 97.
View Looking North of the South Branch of the Chicago River, Showing
Suggested Arrangement of Streets and Ways
Drawing. From Daniel H. Burnham and Edward H. Bennett, *Plan of Chicago*
(Chicago: The Commercial Club of Chicago, 1909), plate 107.

their future.''[24] As a consequence, the manual can be considered one of
the earliest urban histories for use in the secondary schools. Moreover,
given its visual and verbal coverage of the American and European urban
built environment, the manual also introduced eighth graders to civic art
and public architecture—areas of the fine arts that progressive educators
usually found sorely neglected in most American classrooms.

Through his manual, Moody shared with fellow Chicagoans Francis
Parker and John Dewey the desire to create a larger classroom by relating
school and society. Like Parker and Dewey, Moody sought to adjust
education, through the discipline of city planning, to the interests of
young people and to tie what he called "civic learning" to the real world
outside the classroom.[25] The manual's injunctions to use the city itself
as a part of the curriculum were perfectly consonant with Dewey's principles of integrating *The School and Society*. Although in actual practice
he exhibited none of the innovative pedagogical techniques that Dewey
and his followers advocated,[26] Moody completely agreed in theory with
progressive education's concern to adapt schooling to fit the needs of
the child rather than to the demands of tradition.

Perhaps the greatest common ground shared by Moody (as a pro-

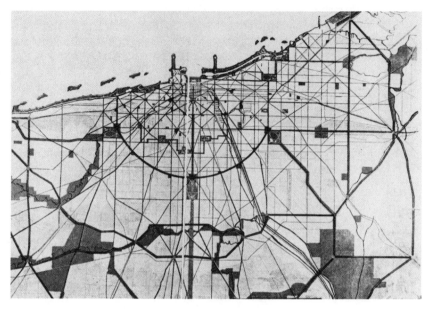

Figure 98.
General Map Showing Topography, Waterways, and Complete System of
Streets, Boulevards, Parkways, and Parks
From Daniel H. Burnham and Edward H. Bennett, *Plan of Chicago* (Chicago:
The Commercial Club of Chicago, 1909), plate 94.

moter of planning education) and Dewey (as a proponent of progressive
education) was the assumption regarding the correlation between education and politics. Just as Dewey in *Education and Democracy* (1916)—a
major educational manifesto of progressivism—wrote "we may produce
in the schools a projection in the type of society we should like to realize
and by forming minds in accord with it generally modify the larger and
more recalcitrant features of adult society"; likewise, Moody, in *Wacker's
Manual* (1911) proposed to "prepare the minds of our children to grasp
and lay fast hold upon the science of city planning for the future glory
of Chicago and the prosperity and happiness of all her people."[27]

The Manual's Ideas

Along with providing a pioneering pedagogy for disseminating "the principles and practices of scientific planning," Moody also wrote his primer,
quite unabashedly, in order to inculcate what he variously termed "community patriotism," "united civic interest," "civic patriotism," and

"community virtue." In the manual, building citizens and planning cities were synonymous since Moody saw the plan and its implementation across the cityscape as the artifactual evidence that "gave the people of Chicago a way to express in solid form their progressive spirit."[28]

In an article in the *Century Magazine,* "White City and Capital City," Daniel Burnham specifically identified himself and his city planning with the progressive movement.[29] Architectural historian Thomas Hines has pointed out the ramifications of Burnham's reformist liberal Republicanism, particularly its influence on the shape and substance of the 1909 Plan.[30] Such progressivism became further pronounced when Moody translated the plan into a manual.

By progressivism, Moody and Burnham meant something more than the Progressive (or Bull Moose) party formed in Chicago by the Republican insurgents who supported Theodore Roosevelt for the presidency in 1912. As contemporaries such as B. P. DeWitt (*The Progressive Movement* [New York: Macmillan, 1915]) almost universally recognized, progressivism was a pervasive, many-sided crusade of uplift and reform, often inconsistent, often naive, and sometimes palpably conservative. This broad impulse toward criticism and change was increasingly conspicuous after 1900 and had quite dissipated by the mid-1920s; as Richard Hofstadter states, progressivism was not so much the movement of any one social class, or coalition of classes, against a particular class or group as it was a rather widespread and remarkably good-natured effort of a significant segment of the urban middle class to achieve within their areas of expertise (e.g., law, academe, politics, social work) a societal self-reformation.[31] Accepting industrialization and urbanization as facts of twentieth-century American life, never seriously doubting the continued possibility of progress and prosperity, the majority of progressives sought the restoration of a type of modified economic individualism within a collective political democracy that was widely believed to have existed earlier in America and to have become threatened by greedy corporations, corrupt political machines, and apathetic citizens.

As representatives of what might be called main-line progressivism Moody and Burnham shared this political and social temper that was, paradoxically, innovative and reforming as well as traditional and conserving. Given this brand of progressivism, they understandably had an affinity with local Chicago reformers such as Charles Merriam (political scientist at the University of Chicago) or Mayor Tom L. Johnson (who first enlisted Burnham in comprehensive planning for the city of Cleveland). With moderate social progressives such as George E. Hooker and Jane Addams, Moody and Burnham's cautious reformism had only partial acceptance. More radical social progressives like Graham Taylor or Florence Kelly questioned Moody and Burnham's lack of concern in both plan and manual for adequate neighborhood housing and social welfare. Chicago labor progressives like John Fitzgerald and militant socialists like Lucy Parsons considered almost all progressive reforms, including proposals such as the plan and the manual, as but "band-aid" remedies designed to bolster the city's corporate capitalist interests.[32]

Moody, while basically a supporter of capitalistic individualism (he had been the Executive Director of the Chicago Association of Commerce before joining the CPC), also saw the need—perhaps in the interest of preserving capitalism—for greater social collectivization and municipal cooperation among individual citizens. Long-range, large-scale city planning would, he admitted, proscribe certain rights and prerogatives of the city dweller. Moody worried, however, that in early twentieth-century American cities such as Chicago, rampant individualism perhaps had gone too far and that the system's inherent atomism was rapidly destroying communal urban life.[33]

To meet this dilemma, Moody advocated major environmental and architectural change as a method by which to infuse his form of progressivism into the American city. Calling for planners to design a "New Metropolis"—an image bearing a striking resemblance to other "new" reform manifestoes being issued by fellow progressive publicists (e.g., Walter Lippmann's *New Republic* or Walter Weyl's *New Democracy*)— Moody espoused a politics that wished to conserve what was valuable from the past and also remain cognizant of the new challenges brought on by economic and urban concentration. In short, he argued both in the manual and in his later writings for a greater combination of central planning and voluntary individual cooperation. As his friend Bernard W. Snow summarized it in an address honoring the CPC in 1910: "Every generation has its burdens. To this is given the duty of curbing the individualism and establishing the collectivism of Democracy."[34]

Walter Moody promulgated a political progressivism that historian Stow Persons has labeled neo-democracy.[35] Nonpartisan, believing in the political role of public opinion, anxious to separate electoral politics from public administration, Moody's writings are a perfect case study of an early twentieth-century neo-democrat in action. With his fellow progressives, Moody was willing to revise his original ideal of social progress as achievable solely in individualistic terms and to concede to the state (particularly via a strong executive and numerous public commissions) the rapid expansion of its functions and powers. Moody saw in neo-democracy a political philosophy which did not threaten the prerogatives of the expert. Like Walter Lippmann, he did not fear either a big leader (especially if the leader were a Burnham) or bigness in business, labor, or government. The public relations man who translated the philosophy of a business client such as Burnham (who always insisted "Make no little plans") could hardly see bigness as a bogey.[36] Nor could he deny the power of the *word,* especially the printed word, in shaping democratic political thought and action. A reformer who had written a half dozen books, over forty pamphlets, position papers, reports, and newspaper and magazine articles would not think otherwise.[37] Finally, insistent that change would come about by working through the established political system, Moody concurred in the direct democracy principles of reformer Frank Parsons and maintained "that the ballot box always precedes the city planners."[38]

Since the ultimate implementation of the Burnham plan depended upon widespread voter acceptance of each of its specific proposals, Moody saw his task as identical to that of Frederick C. Howe, who in *The City, The Hope of Democracy* (New York: Charles Scribner's, 1905) had argued the necessity of linking all city planning reform with an extensive information and publicity program for adults and a comprehensive educational component for children.[39] Moody's *Wacker's Manual* and his adult primer *What of the City?* served these purposes. They also contain evidence of at least two other important intellectual currents of late nineteenth- and early twentieth-century America: a quest for efficiency and order in personal, commercial, industrial, and political activity, and the belief in the physical environment as a primary determinant of human behavior.

In a work subtitled "Municipal Economy," it comes as no surprise to find repeated pleas for greater centralization, the absolute necessity of eliminating all waste, the commercial value of beauty, and the civic efficacy of "good order, cleanliness, and economy."[40] In fact, many sections of Moody's tract could have been written by any number of Chicagoans—George Pullman, Marshall Field, Gustavus Swift—each of whom sought to impose an entrepreneurial system on the industrial and commercial landscape. This "search for order" as historian Robert Wiebe labels late nineteenth-century American history,[41] pervades the manual, a work that anticipates Walter Lippmann's *Drift and Mastery* in its demand for a "community patriotism to substitute order for disorder; and reason, common sense and action for negligence, indifference and inertia."[42] Moreover, Moody's incessant arguments for the efficient use of public space strongly parallel Frederick W. Taylor's similar claims (published in the same year as the manual) for *The Scientific Principles of Management* in the organization of industrial space.

Moody took the making of Chicago into a centralized city rather than a group of overcrowded villages to be a basic premise of the Burnham plan. Chicago's street and highway pattern, railroad network, and cultural and civic activities would each have a center and, in turn, be a component of a new central city. The linchpin on this new urban core was a monumental civic center that would be to Chicago what the Acropolis was to Athens, the Forum to Rome, and St. Mark's Square to Venice— the very embodiment of the reformed civic life that Burnham and Moody hoped to see come to pass in Chicago. Although we have understandably lost sympathy for neo-classical expressions of institutionalized political power, the progressives felt that neo-classicism's unity, permanence, balance, order, and symmetry best proclaimed both the symbolic role and the functional role of public buildings and communal spaces. A civic center (see fig. 95), a unified cluster of "vast civic temples" as Moody called Burnham's proposed building group dominated by a colossal municipal administration building,[43] would typify the permanence of the city, record its history, and express its aspiration for reform. In Moody's estimate, the civic center would "give life to the spirit of unity in the city."[44]

Congestion and waste would be eradicated in the process of centralization. In his manual, Moody warned his young readers that "the *elimination of waste is the World's Greatest Scientific Problem*" (emphasis original); and in his manifesto for adults he suggested various ways by which scientific planning would solve this international dilemma: zoning controls, public health regulations, uniform building codes, and standardized construction materials and designs.[45] A pet Moody project was a proposal he outlined in a pamphlet titled *Fifty Million Dollars for Nothing!* where he discussed how the people of Chicago could obtain thirteen hundred acres of lakefront parks, playgrounds, and watercourses by recycling the city's garbage and waste material—old bricks and mortar, excavation soil, street sweepings, cinders, and ashes. In twelve years, estimated Moody, Chicago taxpayers would have new parklands along the lakefront worth fifty million dollars, at no cost whatsoever.[46]

As both Samuel Haber and Samuel Hays demonstrate in their investigations[47] of the scientific management and conservation movements, progressives like Moody, Burnham, and their associates became enthralled with the principles of rationalization, standardization, and centralization in civic life because they had already attempted to implement such principles in business life. Although they looked to Europe for their aesthetic inspiration—particularly to that of Baron Georges Eugène Haussmann and the French Ecole des Beaux Arts[48]—their planning ideas reflected primarily the order and systematization they prized in their own businesses. For example, Frederic Delano, a Commercial Club Plan Committee member who had made his way up to the presidency of the Wabash Railroad at age twenty-two, maintained that, in his mind, "a comprehensive city plan represented a natural progression from his own idea of centralization of the Chicago passenger railroads."[49]

During a decade that produced studies on waste and scientific management in education, churches, and private homes,[50] it is hardly surprising that Moody should refer to the Chicago plan as an instrument of "the City Practical" as opposed to the City Beautiful with which it was often confused.[51] A rational, unified, efficient, scientific, practical plan, he insisted, was the sole way to order the chaos attendant to rapid urban growth.

To the elements of education and efficiency that have been suggested thus far as crucial to Moody's strategy for civic reform must be added a third feature: environmentalism. Like many of his generation, Walter Moody believed in a modified ecological determinism. He was taken with the emergence of American social science in the latter half of the nineteenth century and confident of its beneficial application to city planning. Thus, he maintained that the "physical conditions which make for good health, good order and good citizenship must be made clear to our children." Moody stated the conviction that "splendid material upbuilding" of the metropolis would yield "a social, intellectual and moral upbuilding of its people" as a simple environmental equation: "city building means man building."[52] Following an evolutionary analogue used earlier by Chicago novelist Henry Blake Fuller to explain the progressive development of "a higher type of Chicagoan" in cultural achievements, Moody predicted a parallel social evolution to follow upon the advent of social scientific urban planning in the "prairie city."[53]

Such city planning could not come too soon in Moody's judgment. "The physical condition of people in the cities as compared with the people of the open country is deteriorating," he warned his young readers, because "city life is an intense life, many times more wearing upon the nerves than country life." Quoting various social scientists, he also proposed that the unplanned and unkempt city "saps the energy of men and makes them less efficient in the work of life." Moreover, it was "this strain of city life which increases insanity and brings weaknesses of many kinds to shorten life and deprive people of their vigor."[54] Heady stuff for mere fourteen-year-olds but only one example of the manual's argument that the physical environment conditions public behavior.

Several of the manual's proposals to correct physical deterioration of urban dwellers bear a striking resemblance to the theories of American psychiatrist George M. Beard, discoverer of neurasthenia or "nervous weakness." Beard believed that environmental tensions, particularly when exacerbated by the stress of urbanization, modernization, and technological innovation, were the chief causal factors in the etiology of mental illness. In his most famous book, *American Nervousness,* Beard claimed that the incidence of mental disorders was unusually high (and growing even more so) in late nineteenth-century urban America. There had been no nervous exhaustion or physical deterioration, for example, in those cities of ancient Greece or Rome that Burnham and Moody held up as exemplary of ordered, planned, urban design. These ancient civilizations, Beard contended, lacked five characteristics peculiar to nineteenth-century civilization: steam power, the telegraph, the periodical press, the sciences, and the mental activity of women.[55] Beard felt America was a quarter century more advanced than any European country in each of these aspects of modernity.

Since at least the time of Benjamin Rush, American physicians had almost as a matter of course acknowledged that the unique pace of American life (e.g., its competitiveness, its religious pluralism, its lack of stability in social status) was somehow related to America's higher rate of mental illness. After the Civil War, two other ideas—the concept of evolution and the increase in the population and number of American cities—had been added to this traditional belief in the relationship between American civilization and psychological and physical health. Beard accepted and amalgamated both evolution and urbanization into his interpretation of American nervousness. He maintained that the conquest of neurasthenia need involve no change in man himself, just in his environment. The technology which had produced the telegraph, the railroad, and the factory had already begun to provide other technological innovations which helped to reduce the tensions of American experience. Beard cites as specific examples the elevator, the sewing machine, and the Pullman palace car.[56]

Although there is no evidence that he ever met or read Beard, Moody shared Beard's belief in evolution and in urban neurasthenia. Like Beard, he looked to the continued advance of material and technological progress to offset evils of the American urban environment. City planning, in Moody's view, naturally provided one panacea whereby urbanites could overcome, or at least mitigate, ecological determinism. In the school text that he also called "a physical geography," Moody (with an analogy he borrowed from Frederick Law Olmsted) made a special case for how urban parks (fig. 99) and forest preserves could be "compared with the lungs of a person, as the means by which the city and its people get the stimulus of fresh air so necessary to normal well-being."[57] Much like

Olmsted who argued for orderly park design as a method of social control and urban reform, Moody envisioned the parks of the 1909 plan as crucial components in alleviating stress, overcrowding, and congestion. In the Chicago city parks, the masses supposedly would find an environment conducive both to activity and to contemplation.[58]

The Manual's Deficiencies

Critics of Burnham's plan and Moody's manual complained, however, that the plan did not do enough to alleviate the social evils that afflicted numerous Chicagoans: lack of housing, schools, or adequate sanitation. Charges of elitism and lack of concern for public improvements at the neighborhood level were directed at a plan that, admittedly, dealt primarily with elaborate transportation systems, monumental aesthetic centerpieces, and symmetrical street façades. In several respects the Chicago that Burnham had planned and that Moody promoted was a metropolis for businessmen where, ironically, with the exception of the central business district, there were no carefully designated areas for commercial expansion throughout the rest of the city. Nor were there any model tenements for workers, much less model neighborhoods.

Not that Moody was oblivious to Chicago's housing or social problems. Slums were mentioned in both the manual and the plan but only briefly. Once in the plan, for example, it was suggested that "it is no attack on private property to argue that society has the inherent right to protect itself (against) gross evils and known perils" by imposing restrictions on overcrowding, enforcing sanitary regulations, and limiting lot coverage.[59] As Mel Scott has discovered, there is even assertion in the plan that if private enterprise cannot rehouse persons forced out of congested quarters, the city itself may have to do so "in common justice to men and women so degraded by long lives in the slums that they have lost all power of caring for themselves."[60] But this daring idea only appears as an afterthought in the Burnham/Moody philosophy of the city, tucked away surreptitiously, at best a very minor chord in a grand symphony of magnificent boulevards, imposing structures, and splendid parks. The housing concerns of other progressives in other cities (e.g., Lawrence Veiller and Jacob Riis in New York) did not exist in most of their counterparts of the Burnham/Moody persuasion in Chicago.[61]

Moody, as his writings reveal, had many of the myopias of the contemporary neo-democratic mind. He had little notion of the racial changes

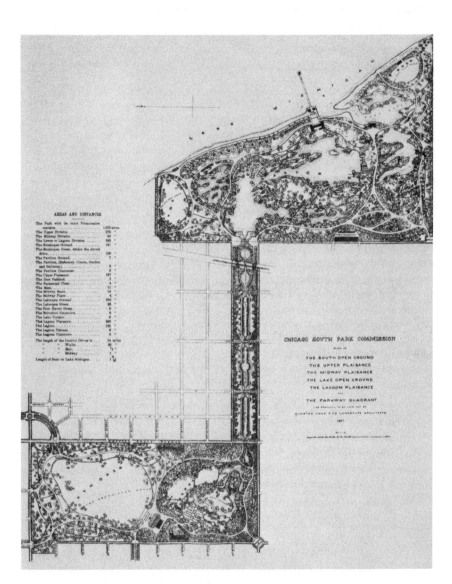

Figure 99.
Site Plan, Jackson Park, Chicago, Illinois, 1871
Designed by Olmsted, Vaux and Company, Landscape Architects.
(Courtesy National Park Service, Frederick Law Olmsted National Historic Site)

that were going to sweep over neighborhoods in a city such as Chicago. He was far too sanguine about the coexistence of the city and the automobile. Furthermore, he tended to exaggerate the beliefs that the conservation of wasted energy and resources alone would solve urban problems, or that ordered civic spaces, efficient circulatory systems, and grandiose natural landscapes would yield contented, prosperous, virtuous citizens. Had social problems been stressed more directly in Moody's translation of Burnham's plan, however, as they were in the St. Louis City Plan of 1907,[62] perhaps nothing of the Chicago 1909 Plan would have been implemented. So argues historian Robert Akeley, who is persuaded that if Moody had not played down the social reform dimension of what would have eventually had to accompany any genuine municipal rejuvenation, the success of the physical proposals and the image of the plan as a comprehensive program of civic renaissance would have been seriously jeopardized. Akeley also feels that "Chicago planning salesmanship was based upon enthusiasm and commitment, rather than on calculated exploitation."[63]

The Manual's Legacy

Moody assuredly was an enthusiast. "No one has ever equaled him in promoting city planning, convincing an entire metropolis of its value, and winning support of a particular plan from voters and public officials alike."[64] An ingenious and skillful propagandist, he promulgated the necessity of scientific city planning in ways other than through *Wacker's Manual*. Thousands of pamphlets, mailings, and circulars with titles like "Chicago Can Get Fifty Million Dollars for Nothing!" "Reclaim South Water Street for All the People," "Pull Chicago Out of the Hole—United Action Will Do It!" and "Economic Readjustment from a War to a Peace Basis" were his work.

As adroit with other communications media as he was with publications, he developed an extensive stereopticon slide library illustrating all aspects of the Burnham Plan and many examples of city planning throughout the world. Over the ten years that he gave slide-lectures on city planning all over Chicago and around the country, he estimated he had talked to approximately 175,000 people. Under his direction, the Chicago Plan Commission even made its own movie, *A Tale of One City,* a two-reeler contrasting the existing conditions of Chicago with the 1909 Plan proposals. The first documentary film on city planning ever produced, it opened in Chicago (a city that in 1915 still hoped to become the movie capital of the country) to a sell-out crowd at the Majestic Theater. In fifty theaters in the Chicago metropolitan area and then in other U.S. cities, over 150,000 people saw the film during its premier year of 1915.[65]

Finally, in 1919 Moody wrote a 440-page treatise titled *What of the City?* where much of the history of the Chicago Plan Commission as well as his own history in the planning movement was recounted. Probably his most sophisticated analysis of Chicago city planning within the context of the national urban planning movement, the book's highly autobiographical content also reveals much about Moody the plan promoter; along with the manual it summarizes his main political and planning ideas. Whereas the manual had proselytized on the local level, *What of the City?* sought converts throughout the nation. Moody designed the former publication to reach the generation of the future, still occupying Chicago's classrooms; he prepared the latter book for the continuing adult education of his own generation throughout the country's cities.

To talk of converts and proselytizing recalls an initial characterization of Walter Moody made earlier in this chapter. W. D. Moody, it will be remembered, was occasionally confused with fellow Chicagoan D. L. Moody. A later historian of American city planning, while not mistaking the two men, aptly calls Moody an "evangelist of planning" whose "bible" was the 1909 Plan, and who sought to spread that gospel of municipal reform "with the aggressiveness of a salesman and the fervor of a religious zealot."[66]

Within this context Moody might also be compared to William Thomas Stead, editor of the Anglo-American *Review of Reviews,* who a decade earlier had written another municipal reform tract, *If Christ Came to Chicago!* Stead's bestselling exposé of municipal corruption and his program for urban reform included in a final chapter a comprehensive city plan to implement comprehensive civic reform.[67] A detailed comparison of Moody's primer and Stead's intriguing city plan for making Chicago "the ideal city of the world," while pertinent to this discussion, will not be done here; mention is made merely to suggest that Moody's techniques were by no means novel to the Chicago reform effort that sought to improve the city by altering the cityscape.

Moreover, W. T. Stead, a Congregational minister who preached civic and social reform at rallies in the city's Central Music Hall in the wake of the World's Columbian Exposition,[68] could only have smiled with approval at one of Moody's last official acts to promote the Burnham Plan. In early 1919, Moody wrote *Seed Thoughts for Sermons,* a seven-page appeal to the city's clergymen to recognize the humanitarian and social value of the *Plan of Chicago* that had been written a decade earlier. Numerous clergy followed Moody's injunction to preach the value of comprehensive planning to their congregations on 19 January 1919, the date chosen as "*Plan of Chicago* Sunday" throughout the city. Later that day was alluded to as "Nehemiah Sunday" because so many ministers had used Nehemiah's description of the rebuilding of Jerusalem and the temple as their text; many congregations also displayed the Chicago flag on their churches while others sang hymns such as "Work, for the Night Is Coming!"[69] W. T. Stead would have loved it.

The British reformer would also have endorsed Moody's career as a propagandist, particularly Moody's crucial role in effecting the transition whereby a private plan drawn up by a private club became a public ordinance to be implemented by a public commission which, in turn, hired as its managing director a former publicist for private enterprise who became a public civil servant who wrote a public school textbook. Stead, had he lived to see a copy,[70] would have also approved of Moody's manual, a book that can serve the historian as a tracer element in order to reveal some of the less familiar intellectual history of the vast effort surrounding the 1909 Plan.

Thus the legacy of the Burnham Plan and Moody's promotion of it is assuredly multiple (fig. 100). Simply in terms of actual alteration of Chicago's cityscape, it has been estimated that over three million dollars in public construction can be directly attributed to the inspiration of the plan and its purpose.[71] Every major subsequent planning enterprise in the city of Chicago has had to react to its premises and its presence. For example, in the struggle to keep the city's lakefront, "forever, open, clear and free," historian Lois Wille credits Burnham, Wacker, and especially Moody with launching 'the most energetic public information effort in the city's history.'"[72]

While Moody's enthusiastic promotion of the changing, building, regrouping, and restructuring the face of the American's urban landscape on the Chicago model did assume the dimensions of a real reform movement (or at least a significant planning and architectural arm of that movement), his progressivism in planning was not without its inadequacies. For instance, his own myopias (e.g., his overreliance on the premise that structured, orderly, public buildings, circulatory systems, and civic landscapes would result in an enlightened citizenry) and his unquestioned support of Burnham's retreat to the safety of the neo-classical womb as the recommended style for the new urban America reminds us of the strong conservative strain in his progressivism and the high degree of caution in that reform movement generally. This inconsistency, ambiguity, and paradox were also bequeathed to posterity via the 1909 Plan and the 1911 manual.

On balance, however, Moody's numerous publications contributed positively to the early literature of the city planning profession. His prolific corpus, but especially the manual and his most mature work (*What*

Figure 100.
"Michigan Avenue"
Detail of museum exhibition, "Chicago Architecture, 1872–1922,"
The Art Institute of Chicago; John Zukowsky, chief curator; Stanley
Tigerman, designer.
(Courtesy The Art Institute of Chicago)

of the City?), sought consciously to provide the professional city planner with personal inspiration for the work in the decades ahead.[73] The manual also prompted an increased demand for the services of city planners in cities all over the nation thereby giving the emerging profession even greater visibility through the actual practice of its craft.[74]

Finally, because of Moody's salesmanship of Burnham's idea, the Burnham Plan became the paradigm for the American city planning movement for the next generation, the model of the City Practical that future planners and politicians in Chicago[75] and elsewhere built on, adapted, or rebelled against in their collective task of what Moody called the science of city planning and citizen building.[76]

Notes

1. Daniel H. Burnham and Edward H. Bennett, *Plan of Chicago Prepared under the Direction of the Commercial Club during the Years 1906, 1907, 1908,* ed. Charles Moore (Chicago: The Commercial Club, 1909); hereafter cited as *Plan of Chicago.* A modern edition, with an introduction by W. R. Hasbrouck, has been issued in the DaCapo Press Series in Architecture and Decorative Arts, No. 29 (New York: DaCapo Press, 1970).

2. Walter D. Moody, *Wacker's Manual of the Plan of Chicago: Municipal Economy* (Chicago: Chicago Plan Commission, 1911), 3; hereafter cited as *Wacker's Manual.* As an example of a full-blown instance of Moody's proposed economic and cultural hegemony for Chicago, see his essay "Chicago Destined to Be the Center of the Modern world," *Municipal Engineering* 43.3 (September 1912): 49–61, and also in *The Bank Man* 7 (November 1912): 307–24.

3. See James Findlay, *Dwight Moody* (Chicago: University of Chicago Press, 1969).

4. Walter D. Moody, *What of the City? America's Greatest Issue—City Planning, What It Is and How to Go about It to Achieve Success* (Chicago: A. C. McClurg and Co., 1919), 3; hereafter cited as Moody, *What of the City?*

5. Henry May, *The Protestant Churches and Industrial America* (New York: Harper & Row, 1949), 182–234.

6. (Chicago: A. C. McClurg and Co., 1907). This handbook of "modern salesmanship" went through seventeen editions.

7. Daniel Boorstin, *The Americans: The Democratic Experience* (New York: Random House, 1973), 5–88. When Moody accepted the position of Managing Director with the CPC, R. W. Butler, a member of the CPC, wrote Daniel Burnham that "from this time forward the work will be pushed by the 'Chief of all Pushers'—Mr. Moody." Butler to D. H. Burnham (20 January 1911), Burnham Papers, Art Institute of Chicago.

8. The origins, underwriting, and unveiling of the plan have been copiously documented; see Ira Bach, "A Reconsideration of the 1909 'Plan of Chicago,' " *Chicago History* 2 (1973): 132–41; Francoise Choay, *The Modern City, Planning in the 19th Century* (London: Studio Vista, 1969); Patrick Geddes, *Cities in Evolution* (London: Williams and Norgate, 1915); Werner Hegemann and Elbert Peets, *The American Vitruvius: An Architect's Handbook of Civic Art* (New York: The Architectural Book Publishing Co., 1922); Vilas Johnson, *A History of the Commercial Club of Chicago*

including the First History of the Club by John J. Glessner (Chicago: Commercial Club of Chicago, 1977); Lewis Mumford, *The City in History, Its Transformations; and Its Prospects* (New York: Harcourt, Brace and World, 1961); John Reps, *The Making of Urban America* (Princeton: Princeton University Press, 1965); and Lois Wille, *Forever Open, Clear and Free: The Historic Struggle for Chicago's Lakefront* (Chicago: Henry Regney, 1972).

9. Helen Whitehead, *The Chicago Plan Commission, A Historical Sketch, 1909–1960* (Chicago: Chicago Plan Commission, 1960), 3–9.

10. Charles W. Eliot, "A Study of the New Plan of Chicago," *Century Magazine* 79 (January 1910): 418; also see Perry Duis, *Chicago: Creating New Traditions* (Chicago: Chicago Historical Society, 1976), 49.

11. On the complicated machination whereby "an alliance of businessmen, planners and politicians, by persuasion, pressure and politics" set the 1909 plan in motion, consult Michael P. McCarthy, "Chicago Businessmen and the Burnham Plan," *Journal of the Illinois State Historical Society* 63.3 (Autumn 1979): 228–56.

12. Moody, *What of the City?* 329–32; *Chicago Tribune* (7 July 1909): 3; *Chicago Record-Herald* (2 November 1909): 2.

13. Moody, *What of the City?* 21–22.

14. David Noble, *The Paradox of Progressive Thought* (Minneapolis: University of Minnesota Press, 1958); Richard Hofstadter, ed. *The Progressive Movement 1900–1915* (Englewood Cliffs, N. J.: Prentice-Hall, 1963); Charles Forcey, *The Crossroads of Liberalism, Croly, Weyl, Lippmann and the Progressive Era, 1900–1925* (New York: Oxford University Press, 1961).

15. Chap. 2, "The New Profession—City Planning," *What of the City?* 18–27.

16. Robinson (1869–1917) and John Nolen (1869–1935) also contributed to the literature of American city planning and the city planning profession. Robinson, who wrote three important books—*The Improvement of Towns and Cities* (New York and London: G. P. Putnam's Sons, 1901), *Modern Civic Art* (New York and London: G. P. Putnam's Sons, 1903), and *City Planning* (New York and London: G. P. Putnam's Sons, 1916)—was the first appointee to the first university chair of civic design (Harvard) in the United States. Nolen, a founder and later president of the American Institute of Planners, wrote *Replanning Small Cities* (New York: American City Bureau, 1912), *City Planning* (New York and London: D. Appleton and Co., 1916), and *New Ideals in the Planning of Cities, Towns and Villages* (New York: American City Bureau, 1919). On the quest for professionalism, see Burton J. Bledstein's *The Culture of Professionalism: The Middle Class and the Development of Higher Education in America* (New York: W. W. Norton, 1976), 80–128 and 287–332.

17. The most comprehensive assessment of the business community's involvement in the Chicago Plan is chronicled in Neil Harris's *The Planning of the Plan* (Chicago: The Commercial Club of Chicago, 1979), and Michael McCarthy's previously cited "Chicago Businessmen and the Burnham Plan," 228–56.

18. W. D. Moody, *Chicago's Greatest Issue: An Official Plan* (Chicago: Chicago Plan Commission, 1911); Executive Committee, CPC, *Proceedings* (19 June 1911): 237. Robert Akeley ("Implementing the 1909 Plan of Chicago: An Historical Account of Planning Salesmanship," master's thesis, University of Texas [1973]) calculates (pp. 185–87) that there were eighty-six separate bond issues, totaling $233,985,000 falling within the recommendations of the plan.

19. *Chicago Daily News* (26 October 1910):1; on Burnham's disappointment with the inadequate promotion of the San Francisco Plan, see D. H. Burnham to Willis Polk, 22 April 1909, Burnham Papers, Art Institute of Chicago.

20. W. D. Moody, *The Work of the Chicago Plan Commission during 1911* (Chicago: Address to the Commercial Club of Chicago, 1912), 10; *What of the City?* 50; "City Planning and the Public Schools," *American City* 6 (May 1912): 720.

21. On the visual pedagogy of the plan's illustrations, see Robert Bruegmann, "Burnham, Guérin, and the City as Image," in *The Plan of Chicago, 1909–1979*, ed. John Zukowsky (Chicago: Art Institute of Chicago, 1979), 16–28.

22. Historians of American city planning have traditionally interpreted the 1909 Burnham Plan to have had six basic objectives: (1) improvement of the Chicago lakefront from Winnetka on the north to the Indiana state line on the south, (2) creation of a beltway/highway system on the rim of the city, (3) relocation of railway terminals and development of a complete freight and passenger traction system, (4) acquisition of an outer park system and of parkway transport circuits, (5) systematic arrangement of streets within the city to facilitate movement to and from the central business district, and (6) promotion of centers of intellectual life and civic administration so related as to provide coherence and unity for the metropolis. Carl Condit, "The Chicago Plan," in his *Chicago, 1910–29; Building, Planning and Urban Technology* (Chicago: University of Chicago Press, 1973), 59–88.

23. In his highly autobiographical *What of the City?* (pp.107–8), Moody listed his major educational achievements in advancing the plan as his work with the daily and the periodical press, his book on *Chicago's Greatest Issue,* the various lecture series he coordinated, and, of course, the *Wacker's Manual.*

24. *Wacker's Manual,* 3–4. One product of Moody's teaching efforts was his ten-volume research series on *Business Administration: Theory, Practice and Application* (Chicago: LaSalle Extension University, 1910–11.)

25. On Parker's progressive pedagogy see Jack K. Campbell's well-researched life, *Colonel Francis W. Parker, The Children's Crusader* (New York: Teachers College Press, 1967) and Merle Curti's assessment (pp. 374–95) in his *The Social Ideas of American Educators* (Paterson, N.J.: Littlefield Adams, 1965); for Dewey's impact in Chicago, consult Katherine Mayhew, *The Dewey School: The Laboratory School of the University of Chicago, 1896–1903* (New York: Oxford University Press, 1966).

26. Moody's inclusion of study questions (as many as sixty-seven in chap. 4), at the conclusion of each of the seventeen chapters, gave his text a highly catechetical tone reminiscent of the predetermined memorization, disciplined recitation, and rote learning that the progressive educators wished to eradicate.

27. John Dewey, *Education and Democracy,* 100–2; *Wacker's Manual,* 10. Another example of the progressives' interest in education and city planning reform can be seen in Randolph Bourne's discussion of the curriculum unit, "The City: A Healthful Place to Live" in *The Gary Schools* (Boston: Houghton Mifflin, 1916), 117–19.

28. *Wacker's Manual,* 4, 8, 97.

29. D. H. Burnham, "White City and Capital City," *Century Magazine* 63 (February 1902): 619–20; also see Burnham's speech, "A City of the Future under a Democratic Government," *Transactions of the Town-Planning Conference, Royal Institute of British Architects* (October 1910): 368–78.

30. Thomas S. Hines, "The Paradox of Progressive Architecture," *American Quarterly* 25 (1973): 427–48. For Hines's extended treatment of this facet of Burnham see his biography, *Burnham of Chicago: Architect and Planner* (New York: Oxford University Press, 1974), chaps. 8, 14.

31. Richard Hofstadter, *The Age of Reform, From Bryan to F. D. R.* (New York: Vintage, 1955), 5–6.

32. William J. Adelman, "Robber Barons and Social Reformers," *Inland Architect* 24.3 (April 1980): 12–15.

33. *Wacker's Manual,* 140–45; *What of the City?* 412–30; also see McCarthy, "Chicago Businessmen and the Burnham Plan," 233.

34. Commercial Club of Chicago, *The Presentation of the Plan of Chicago* (Chicago: Chicago Plan Commission, 1910), 29.

35. Stow Persons, *American Minds, A History of Ideas* (New York: H. Holt, 1958), 349–52.

36. Burnham's famous credo—"Make no little plans, they have no magic to stir men's blood and probably themselves will not be realized. Make big plans; aim high in hope and work, remembering that a noble, logical diagram once recorded will never die"— is but another example of what David Burg calls "The Aesthetics of Bigness in Late-Nineteenth-Century American Architecture" in *Popular Architecture,* ed. Marshall Fishwick and J. Meredith Neil (Bowling Green, Ohio: Bowling Green University Popular Press, 1978), 108–14.

37. Consult Hofstadter, *The Age of Reform,* on the role of print in progressivism, 186–97.

38. *What of the City?* xi, 4; on Parsons, see Persons, *American Minds,* 366–68. Other theorists of public opinion discussed in this context include A. Lawrence Lowell, *Public Opinion and Popular Government* (New York; Longmans, Green and Co., 1913), Walter Lippmann, *Public Opinion* (London: G. Allen and Unwin, 1922), and Edward L. Bernays, *Crystallizing Public Opinion* (New York: Boni & Liveright, 1923).

39. *Wacker's Manual,* 45. Moody was particularly taken with Howe's critical study on Dusseldorf, Germany, because, in addition to insisting on constant publicity of plan purposes and educational programs, the Dusseldorf plan (like the Burnham Plan) planned for city life a half century in the future and, perhaps best of all, it was a plan originally sponsored by the city's businessmen.

40. *Wacker's Manual,* 4.

41. Robert H. Wiebe, *The Search for Order, 1877–1920* (New York: Hill and Wang, 1967); an earlier study that buttresses the Wiebe thesis is Samuel P. Hayes, *The Response to Industrialism* (Chicago: University of Chicago Press, 1957).

42. *Wacker's Manual,* 4, 17, 104, 8.

43. Burnham's proposed municipal building (see *Plan,* p. 115–18) was modeled, in part, after Richard Morris Hunt's administration building at the 1893 world's fair and the building that prompted Henry Adams to muse:

> One sat down to ponder on the steps beneath Richard Hunt's dome almost as deeply as on the steps of Ara Coeli and much to the same purpose. Here was a breach of continuity—a rupture in historical sequence! Was it real, or only apparent? One's personal universe hung on the answer, for, if the rupture was real and the new

American world would take this sharp and conscious twist towards ideals, one's personal friends would come in, at last, as the winners in the great American chariot race for fame. (*The Education of Henry Adams* [New York: Modern Library, 1931], 340–41.)

44. *Wacker's Manual,* 135–37.

45. Ibid., 13, 66–70; *What of the City?* 38–60. Moody was also something of a historic preservationist in that he opposed the destruction of old structures having aesthetic, historic, and functional utility. He always argued for "the value of permanency in city building," especially since there were "many sites within Chicago that, within the space of seventy years, have been occupied by three, four, or five different buildings." *Wacker's Manual,* 69.

46. *Fifty Million Dollars for Nothing!* (Chicago: Chicago Plan Commission, 1916).

47. Samuel Haber, *Efficiency and Uplift: Scientific Management in the Progressive Era, 1980–1920* (Chicago: University of Chicago Press, 1964); Samuel P. Hayes, *Conservation and the Gospel of Efficiency* (Cambridge, Mass.: Harvard University Press, 1959).

48. On Haussmann see Howard Saalman, *Haussmann: Paris Transformed* (New York: G. Braziller, 1971).

49. Michael P. McCarthy, "Businessmen and Professionals in Municipal Reform: The Chicago Experience, 1887–1920," Ph.D. dissertation, Northwestern University (1970), 106.

50. John Dewey, "Waste in Education," in *The School and Society,* ed. Jo Ann Boydston in *John Dewey: The Middle Works,* Volume I: 1889–1924 (Carbondale, Ill.: Southern Illinois University Press, 1976), 39–56; Shailer Mathews, *Scientific Management in the Churches* (Chicago: University of Chicago Press, 1912); Charlotte Perkins Gilman, "The Waste of Private Housekeeping," *Annals of the American Academy of Political and Social Science* 48 (July 1913): 91–95.

51. On the differences between these two modes of planning see John W. Reps, *The Making of Urban America: A History of City Planning in the United States* (Princeton, N.J.: Princeton University Press, 1965), 331–39, and William H. Wilson, *The City Beautiful Movement in Kansas City* (Columbia: University of Missouri Press, 1964), 40–54; Moody's argument for the Burnham Plan as primarily one of the "City Practical" can be found in *What of the City?* 15, 93.

52. *Wacker's Manual,* 4, 145, 80–81.

53. Henry Blake Fuller, "Chicago's Higher Evolution," *The Dial* (1 October 1892): 205–6; *Wacker's Manual,* 80–81.

54. *Wacker's Manual,* 133.

55. *American Nervousness* (New York: G. P. Putnams' Sons, 1881), 96; also see Beard's *Sexual Neurasthenia (Nervous Exhaustion): Its Hygiene, Causes, Symptoms, and Treatment, With a Chapter on Diet for the Nervous,* ed. A. D. Rockwell (New York: E. B. Treat, 1884), 238n.

56. Charles E. Rosenberg, *No Other Gods: On Science and American Social Thought* (Baltimore: The Johns Hopkins University Press, 1976), 107.

57. *Wacker's Manual,* 97.

58. Geoffrey Blodgett, "Frederick Law Olmsted: Landscape Architecture of Conservative Reform," *Journal of American History* 62.4 (1976):869–89; Michael McCarthy, "Politics and the Parks: Chicago Businessmen and the Recreation Movement," *Journal of the Illinois State Historical Society* 65.2 (1972): 158–72; Peter J. Schmitt, *Back to Nature: The Arcadian Myth in Urban America* (New York: Oxford University Press, 1969).

59. *Plan of Chicago*, 105.

60. Scott, *History of American City Planning*, 108; *Plan of Chicago*, 109.

61. Roy Lubove, *The Progressives and the Slums: Tenement House Reform in New York City, 1880–1917* (Pittsburgh: University of Pittsburgh Press, 1962), 217–56.

62. Civic League of St. Louis, *A City Plan for St. Louis* (St. Louis: Civic League of St. Louis, 1907).

63. Akeley, "Implementing the 1909 Plan," 52, iii.

64. Scott, *History of American City Planning*, 139.

65. *What of the City?* 108.

66. Scott, *History of American City Planning*, 140.

67. William T. Stead, *If Christ Came to Chicago!* (Chicago: Laird & Lee, 1894), 421–42. Akeley, "Implementing the 1909 Plan" (p. 31), recognizes one similarity between the two reformers in noting that both saw the Chicago citizenry as "full of a boundless elan and full of faith in the destiny of their city."

68. On Stead in Chicago, see Joseph O. Baylen, "A Victorian's 'Crusade' in Chicago, 1893–1894," *Journal of American History* 51.3 (December 1964): 418–34; also "Stead in the Slums," *Chicago Sunday Tribune* (12 November 1893): 1.

69. *Chicago Tribune* (19 January 1919): 1.

70. Stead perished aboard the *Titanic* when it sank in 1912.

71. Robert L. Wrigley, Jr., "The Plan of Chicago: Its Fiftieth Anniversary," *Journal of the American Institute of Planners* 26 (February 1960): 37.

72. Wille, *Forever Open*, 88.

73. Moody, *What of the City?* x.

74. Chappell, "Chicago Issues: The Enduring Power of a Plan," 14; Scott, *History of American City Planning*, 139.

75. In Chicago, some of the most important progeny that have followed in the wake of the 1909 Burnham Plan are: *Harbor Plan of Chicago* (1927); *The Outer Drive along the Lake* (1929); *The Axis of Chicago* (1929); *Building New Neighborhoods: Subdivision Design and Standards* (1943); *Master Plan of Residential Land Use of Chicago* (1943); *Planning the Region of Chicago* (1956); the *Comprehensive Plan* (1966); *Chicago 21* (1973); and *Riveredge Plan* (1974). A summary of several of the post-1909 plans are also found in a report written by J. T. Fink, entitled *Grant Park Tomorrow* (1979). (All works listed here published by the Chicago Plan Commission.).

76. *Wacker's Manual*, 8.

Figure 101.
George Ferris' Revolving Wheel, 1893
The Midway Plaisance, World's Columbian Exposition, Chicago, Illinois.

10

The Material Universe
of American World Expositions, 1876–1915

World fairs periodically figure in my personal history as well as my professional writing. My parents spent part of their honeymoon at the 1939 New York Fair. As a child I poured over their snapshot scrapbook on the World of Tomorrow. A quarter of a century later, as a young assistant professor teaching in Bridgeport, Connecticut, I made several excursions to Flushing Meadows during the 1964 New York Fair. In the following decade, I discovered Chicago's Columbian Exposition as I developed my Chicago course, and as several essays in this volume attest, I have been writing about the 1893 event ever since. Fair history also entered other courses, beginning with an early material culture seminar that devoted a semester to the study of Philadelphia's 1876 Centennial celebration in 1976. A discussion of that seminar can be found in "The 1876 Centennial: A Model for Comparative American Studies" in *Artifacts and the American Past,* chapter 6. Fairs serve as bellwethers in my survey course, American Thought and Culture I & II, including, in addition to those in 1876, 1893, 1939, the New York Crystal Palace Fair in 1853 and Chicago's Century of Progress in 1933.

Between 1876 and 1916 nearly one hundred million people visited a dozen major international expositions held in the United States. Organizers of these events hoped to promote the economic development of the cities and regions in which they were held. Fairs showcased mass-produced goods available for mass consumption. They showed off technological innovations, particularly for the work place and the home. They displayed artistic resources, influenced architectural style, and offered models for urban planning. Fairs also presented new forms of entertainment.

World expositions evolved into important nineteenth-century cultural institutions. Writing in *The Education of Henry Adams* (1918), historian Henry Adams "professed the religion of world's fairs, without which he held education to be a blind impossibility." Modern historians agree. John Cawelti surveying "America on Display, 1876, 1893, 1933" (in *America in the Age of Industrialism,* ed. Frederic C. Jaher [New York: Free Press, 1968]), comments: "Because it brings together many different aspects of civilization under, so to speak, a single roof, a world's fair can give us much insight into how people view the unity of their culture, how they understand the structure of its means, achievements, and aspirations."

Here I use three fairs—the 1876 Centennial in an eastern city, the 1893 Columbian exposition in the Middle West's largest metropolis, and the 1915 Panama-Pacific Exposition on the Pacific coast to summarize trends in past everyday life and to suggest contours of future cultural history. Within the compass of a half century, Americans witnessed the rise of corporations and trade unions. Technology, evident in ever-expanding halls of machinery influenced every aspect of daily life from traveling to consuming, from birthing to dying. Agriculture and industry, often with their exhibit halls facing each other, contended as to which would triumph as the nation's economic base. Victorian concern for learning at all levels was exhibited in specific pavilions devoted to liberal arts (1893) and education (1915). And, of course, the American belief in progress permeated every fair. President William McKinley summarized the conventional wisdom: "World's fairs are the timekeepers of progress." Tragically McKinley died of an assassin's bullet at the 1901 Buffalo Pan-American Exposition, an event devoted to fostering hemisphere peace and good will.

I look at fairs because they provide striking material culture contrasts. The monumental and genteel Courts of Honor faced the spontaneous and mass entertainment of the Joy Zones. Despite the fairs' exuberant new urbanism, much exposition art evoked nostalgia for a rural, frontier America. As Jack London wrote of the 1915 fair, it juxtaposed "the new San Francisco with old, wild 'Frisco.' " Racial and ethnic minorities had neither administrative roles nor sympathetic representation in exhibits that Frederick Douglass called "white sepulchers" rather than white cities. Fairs designed to foster domestic and international peace ironically took place during summers of Indian uprisings (Custer's Last Stand), economic and labor turmoil (Depression of 1893) and, in 1915, World War I.

Americans attending expositions at Philadelphia and San Francisco witnessed changes along a diverse cultural spectrum. In 1876 they enjoyed soda water and patent medicines and took multicourse noon meals; by 1915, they preferred white flour, cold-cereal breakfasts, and fast-food lunches. Hand-rolled cigars of the Gilded Age's early Brown Decades yielded to machine-made, white cigarettes of the Progressive Era. In the Centennial's Machinery Hall, individual artisans crafted horse saddles, completing one every two days; at the Panama-Pacific Exposition industrial laborers, working on an assembly line, built a new Ford every half-hour. In 1893 electricity contended with steam as the dominant energy source only to be challenged by oil in 1915. Queen Anne houses yielded to California bungalows as the nation's residential ideal. Perhaps most significant of these changes was a transformed middle-class culture, expanded by increasing bureaucratization, fueled by consumer abundance, promulgated by communications technology, and motivated to hold power without property and to maintain hegemony with education and expertise.

The 1876 Centennial Exposition

At dawn on 10 May 1876, the tower bell in Philadelphia's Independence Hall began to ring. Ringing the city's chimes and church bells, including the Liberty Bell, expanded the clamor. All proclaimed the beginning of a Centennial Exhibition to celebrate a century of American independence. The 186,672 visitors to the fairgrounds (figs. 102, 103) that first day began a stream of almost ten million people who saw the exposition. Before the exhibition's conclusion in mid-November, nearly one fifth of the U.S. population passed through its automatic, self-registering turnstiles, making its attendance greater than that of any previous fair.

President U. S. Grant officially opened the Centennial. After the ceremonial odes, marches, and hymns, he, along with Emperor Dom Pedro of Brazil, processed to the exposition's symbol of the age, the Corliss Steam Engine (fig. 104), in Machinery Hall. There, after receiving instructions from the engine's designer, George Corliss, the two heads of state turned levers and the mechanical behemoth sprang to life. Thereafter the Great Corliss commanded enormous public attention as the world's largest steam engine. Visitors marveled at its fifty-six ton flywheel revolving without noise or vibration. People lined up to watch this mechanical prime mover go into action, twice a day, as it energized the seventy-five miles of belts and shafts driving shining rows of humming, clicking machinery—lathes and saws, drills and looms, presses and pumps—that increasingly characterized the American work place.

Previous world fairs housed all of their exhibits within a single building complex. Philadelphia introduced a multiple-building plan that reflected the enormous expansion of the nineteenth century's material universe—what Lewis Mumford later called "the goods revolution"— and the specialization of function in Victorian life (fig. 105).[1] In addition to Machinery Hall, the Fairmount Park site included six other major structures. Visitors could also explore nine foreign pavilions and seventeen state buildings. Separate corporation buildings, like that of Singer Sewing Machine, appeared for the first time. H. J. Schwartzmann, who had planned much of Philadelphia's Fairmount Park, and its zoo (the first in North America in 1874), became the Centennial's Engineer of Design and the architect of several fair structures. In using part of the Fairmount site (236 acres within a park of 800) for the Centennial grounds, he employed many of the landscape features typical of the urban pleasure park: informal ornamental plantings, an arboretum, and parterre gardens.[2]

Several fair buildings had everyday-life analogues: the manufacturing hall resembled the new department stores such as Wanamaker's in

Figure 102.
View of Grounds and Buildings, International Centennial Exposition,
Fairmount Park, Philadelphia, Pennsylvania, 1876
Lithograph by A. L. Weiss, Philadelphia, Pennsylvania.
(Courtesy The Library of Congress, Division of Prints and Photographs)

Philadelphia; the machinery building paralleled the rise of industrial factories, while the agriculture palace recalled county or state fairs.[3] Horticultural Hall represented the Victorian love of exotic gardens enshrined in glass conservatories. New metropolitan museums of art drew part of their inspiration from exposition art galleries. The Centennial's layout of intersecting grand avenues anticipated the Progressives' fascination with city planning, particularly as evidenced at the Chicago or San Francisco fairs (see fig. 103). Finally, the suburban quality of the smaller state pavilions, including their Queen Anne styles, recalled current American residential patterns.

The fair operated under two restrictions indicative of 1870s cultural attitudes. The exposition's directors first sought to have the fair open weekday evenings and Sunday. Sabbatarians lobbied successfully to keep the Centennial closed on Sundays, and fear of possible fire from night gas lighting of the exhibit halls meant a daily 6:00 P.M. curfew. Prohibitionists banned the sale of beer and spirits from the fair's concession stands except its indoor restaurants. In 1876, the first time Congress entertained

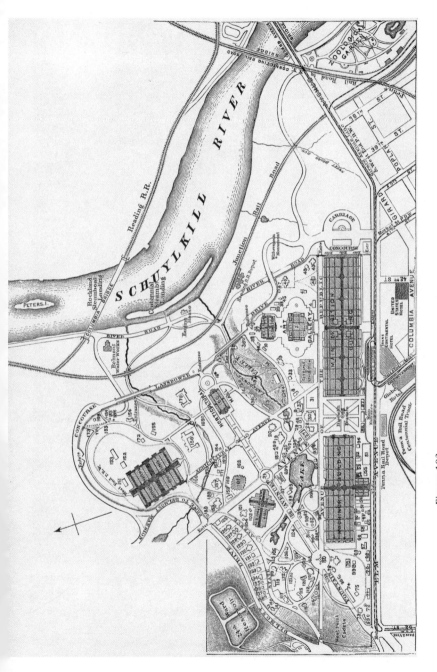

Figure 103.
Map of Grounds, International Centennial Exposition, Philadelphia, Pennsylvania, 1876

Figure 104.
The Centennial Steam Engine, 1876
George R. Corliss, manufacturer. Machinery Hall, International Centennial
Exposition, Philadelphia, Pennsylvania.

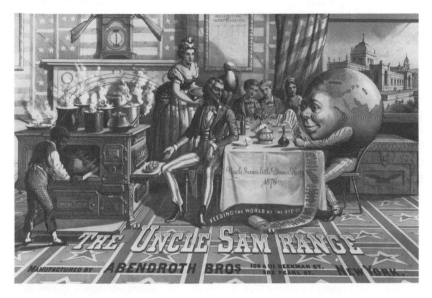

Figure 105.
"The Uncle Sam Range"
Chromolithograph by Schumacher and Ettlinger (1876) for Abendroth
Brothers, New York City.
(Courtesy The New-York Historical Society, New York City)

a prohibition amendment to the Constitution, antiliquor reformers also
made their point in statuary throughout the grounds with public fountains such as those erected by the Sons of Temperance and the Catholic
Total Abstinence Union.

Laborers usually had to take time off from their typical six-day work
week to attend the Centennial. In a few instances, companies such as Yale
Lock Company and the Baltimore Cotton Mill owners paid the way for
several thousand of their hands. Such excursions paralleled, on a much
larger scale, the use of the annual company picnic to maintain factory
loyalty and employee morale. In the immediate aftermath of the Molly
Maguire troubles in the Pennsylvania coal fields, the Reading Coal and
Iron Company arranged for 1,100 miners, wives, and children to receive
a free railroad trip to and a dinner at the Philadelphia fair. The House
of Representatives at one point formulated plans, never implemented,
to provide travel funds for one skilled mechanic from every Congressional
district to visit the Centennial.

Americans traveled to Philadelphia by all manner of locomotion. At
the fair they encountered a transportation network of efficient, regulated
flow—a trait soon championed as desirable in industrial production,

energy allocation, and goods distribution. U.S. railroads arranged special trains and reduced fares to Philadelphia. Two lines, the Pennsylvania and the Reading, built special tracks to the site. Although the Centennial management did not construct a separate transportation building (as would be done in Chicago and San Francisco), the fair's Bureau of Transportation anticipated much modern transport planning by providing several modes of access: horse-drawn streetcar, carriage, steamboat, and railroad. People arriving in carriages or buggies could park in "Carriage Repositories" for a fifty-cent charge. When these visitors wished to leave, they telegraphed the hostlers to prepare their teams. While scores of locomotives and passenger cars displayed at various places confirmed railroads as the dominant form of long-distance land transport in America in 1876, a separate Carriage Building, with its several hundred vehicles, affirmed the principal means of transport for everyday affairs and local travel.[4]

Within the grounds, a narrow-gauge railroad circled the site for a nickel fare. An elevated monorail carrying sixty people shuttled across the Belmont Ravine between the Agricultural and Horticultural halls. One could travel vertically as well as horizontally: either outdoors in the Belmont Hill Tower elevator that carried forty people 185 feet up to an observation platform for a bird's-eye view, or at one of the elevator companies exhibiting their steam and hydraulic mechanisms for hoisting and lowering goods and people. One could also arrange personal transport. Relaxing in a rolling chair, pushed by a porter, Walt Whitman took in the fair site and its sights. Such devices rented for 60 cents an hour or $4.50 for the day.

Visitors admiring the modes of mobility, whether push chairs or phaetons, could locate them within a classification scheme that reveals the Victorian fascination with systems of order and control. In the context of world's fairs, classification meant the proper arrangement of objects in an exhibition so that they could be conveniently located, examined, compared, judged, and cataloged. Geologist William Blake proposed that the material universe of the Centennial be organized in ten departments which could be divided and subdivided into 100 groups and 1000 classes. While Blake's major departments were later modified to seven, his concept of decimal notation prevailed. More important, the notation system influenced how Americans would find books in their public libraries. Melville Dewey apparently used, but failed to acknowledge, Blake's system as the basis for his own decimal arrangement of books, first published as a pamphlet in June 1876.[5]

Classification schemes (table 10.1) also codified exposition competition. Awards served as advertisements, emblazoned on company letterheads, produce labels, and salesmen's trade-cards. Who won what

Table 10.1.   The Categories of Exhibits at World's Fairs

Fair		Number of Major Categories	Raw Materials	Heavy Machinery	Food Products	Liberal Arts	Agriculture and Horticulture	Fine Arts	Decorative Products	Chemical Products	Oil and Electricity	Transportation and Communication	Education, Health and Social Life
1851	London	4	1	1				1	1				
1855	Paris	9	1	1		1		1	3	1			1
1862	London	4	1	1				1	1				
1867	Paris	10	1		1	2	2	1	2				1
1873	Vienna	26	1	4	1	4	1	3	6	1			5
1876	Philadelphia	7	1	1			2	1	1				1
1878	Paris	9	1	1	1		2	1	2				1
1889	Paris	10	1	1	1		2	1	2				2
1893	Chicago	13	1	1		1	5	1	1		1	1	1
1900	Paris	18	1	3	1	1	3	1	3	1	1		3
1904	St. Louis	16	1	1		1	5	1	1		1	1	4
1915	San Francisco	11	1	1		1	3	1	1			1	2
1933	Chicago	11	*	*		1	2	1	*	*	1	2	2
1937	Paris	14		2		2		2	3			1	3
1939	New York	8	*	*		*	1		*	*		2	3
1958	Brussels	8	*	*			1	1	*	*	1	1	3
1967	Montreal	5		†			1	1			†		2
1970	Osaka	9	1	1		*			*	*	1	1	4

* At these fairs manufactures were put together in a single category that would include Heavy Machinery, Liberal Arts, Decorative Arts, Chemical Industries, etc.
† Matter and Energy were in a single category.

From: Burton Benedict, *The Anthropology of World's Fairs* (Berkeley: Solar Press, 1983).

counted and was, in turn, counted. General Francis A. Walker, the chief of the Centennial Bureau of Awards, said that American's had "a strong passion for statistics."[6] The Centennial management affirmed his claim. Because of their records, we know how many persons were admitted at each of 106 gates during each hour on every day, and the meteorological data for every hour of every day. Also documented are the age of the oldest person who received medical treatment (96 years) and the youngest (2 weeks), plus the number of arrests made by the Centennial Guards (675) for offenses ranging from larceny (160) to fornication and bastardy (1). Statistics survive as to telegrams sent and received (151,428) and miles run by public messengers (49,034), and that 7,760,720 strokes of the pumping engines supplied 389,373,019 gallons of water. Four people died at the exhibition.

We do not know exactly how many people saw which exhibits among the 22,742 that displayed both the commonplaces of their culture—machine-made shoes, reed organs, bone corsets, cooking ranges (see fig. 105), folding chairs, ingrain carpets, sewing machines—and the recent innovations—ready-made clothing, linoleum floor coverings, refrigeration processes, canned foods, dry yeast, mass-produced furniture—that would influence everyday life. A shrewd observer could point to artifacts that signed the times and others that signaled the future. For example, several Centennial displays foreshadowed an aborning communications revolution, Alexander Graham Bell's telephone and Christopher B. Sholes's Remington typewriter being only the most famous harbingers of things to come. Scattered throughout the grounds were separate offices housing the *Philadelphia Times,* the *Boston Herald,* and the *New York Tribune,* evidence of the expanded presence of the metropolitan press. The Women's Pavilion published its own weekly, *The New Century for Women.* Photographic Hall and the Centennial Photographic Association exhibited advances in visual communication.[7]

The U.S. Government Building and the Women's Pavilion typified other important themes of Victorian America: the slow but steady expansion of the nation-state and the continual debate over women's rights. Washington's presence in Fairmount Park ranged from the Post Office's new envelope and penny postcard-making machine to the formidable fifteen-inch guns of the Navy Department's iron-clad monitors pointed ominously in the general direction of the Women's Pavilion. The Patent Office, celebrating its fortieth anniversary at the Centennial, displayed approximately 5,000 patent models that had accompanied patent applications, unaware that between 1876 and 1915, the government would grant over 60,000 patents—the largest number in American history. The Treasury Department (first federal office to employ women in large numbers as clerical workers) had a place in the Government Building as did the Smithsonian Institution. The latter bureau, in conjunction with the Department of the Interior, mounted an immense array of Indian "curiosities"—everything from tepees to pottery, saddles to weaponry, beaded moccasins to totem poles—designed to portray the Native American and his culture. Unfortunately the exhibition, premised on the assumption that Indians were unassimilable savages expendable in the wake of American expansion, depicted them as relics of an earlier evolutionary stage.[8] William Dean Howells, an observer for the *Atlantic Monthly* reinforced this stereotype: "The red man, as he appears in effigy and in photograph in this collection, is a hideous demon, whose malign traits can hardly inspire any emotion softer than abhorrence."

The Women's Centennial Executive Committee amassed evidence of the far-ranging activities of nineteenth-century women in a special building, the first such structure in international exposition history. The Women's Pavilion and its exhibits owed its existence to a characteristic American institution: the private voluntary association that takes as its purpose some civic betterment or common cause. The WCEC, led by Elizabeth D. Gillespie, a great-granddaughter of Benjamin Franklin, sold exposition shares, commissioned Schwartzmann to design their building, and filled it with a working steam engine (run by Emma Allison), several power looms, and a printing plant. More than 75 women displayed examples of patents they had obtained on new inventions. Implements used in laundering (Margaret Calvin's Triumph Rotary Washer), ironing (Mary Potts's patented flat-iron), food preparation, and cooking represented the traditional sphere of homemaking. Other material culture hinted at the economic fact that by 1876 women constituted close to 20 percent of the American labor force outside the home. Mary Nolan exhibited a model house made of her patented interlocking bricks of a composition she called Nolanum. Elizabeth Stiles presented a multi-functional desk, only one of a dozen examples of the rage for patented furniture. Mary Whitter manufactured a new type of stereoscope, a necessity of the Victorian parlor. Female workers ran the pavilion's telegraph office, carpet loom, quill wheel, ribbon loom, spooling machine, Jacquard loom, cylinder printing press, and sewing and knitting machines. In the Government Building and Machinery Hall, women operated virtually every kind of machine for manufacturing articles of wood, metal, leather, and cloth, for wages averaging $1.25 a day.

The novel Women's Pavilion represented different things to American women active in the struggle for equal rights. To more radical suffragists like Elizabeth Cady Stanton and Susan B. Anthony, it did not say or do enough; on the Fourth of July, they and others staged a counterdemonstration by reading a "Women's Declaration of Independence" at the other end of the official celebration in downtown Philadelphia. To moderate advocates of women's rights such as Elizabeth Harbert and Elizabeth Gillespie, the fair building provided a beginning; a gathering of women of many persuasions whose political awareness had been heightened at least in a symbolic way.

Other symbols intrigued Americans as they toured their Centennial. Some, such as battle-scarred Civil War eagle, "Old Abe," of the 8th Wisconsin Regiment or the thirty-six foot granite sculpture of "The American Volunteer," reminded visitors, as did absence of all but two Southern state buildings (Arkansas and Mississippi) at the fair, that they were a generation that had fought a Civil War but a decade ago. Outside of Machinery Hall stood a symbol in the making. Known variously as "Bartholdi's Electric Light" or the "Colossal Arm of Independence," the arm and torch of the Statue of Liberty created by French sculptor Frédéric Bartholdi provided a major fair attraction. For a small charge, tourists could stand in the gallery at the base of the torch.

Touring, no matter how exciting, has its everyday necessities. At the Department of Public Comfort, tired fairgoers found many services free or modestly priced: chairs and sofas, writing and reading rooms, a message center, barber shops, lavatories, changing rooms, post office, newsstands, rolling chairs, theater ticket reservations desk, and lunch counters. The Centennial Medical Department gave free medical and surgical care to some 6,463 people.

New food and beverage preferences surfaced at the 1876 exposition. Americans ate bananas (separately packaged in tin foil and costing ten cents) in large numbers for the first time. Hot popcorn, known to Native Americans and rural folk for centuries, became a favorite snack food for urbanites who, after the fair, demanded it when attending baseball games, vaudeville shows, and nickelodeons. Vienna bread had its debut as did Hires Root Beer. Cigars, as evidenced by the six separate concession stands devoted to their sale, continued their popularity, although plug chewing had numerous advocates. Soda fountains, both inside the fairgrounds and on its commercial perimeter, were everywhere. Ice cream sodas became a national institution thanks to the Tufts Arctic Soda Water Company, which paid $50,000 for the exclusive right to make them at the fair. One of their fountains, a thirty-foot ornamental marble structure, possessed seventy-six syrup dispenser tubes.

The Philadelphia Centennial opened in the trough of the depression of 1873 and closed shortly before the massive railroad strikes of 1877, the first outburst of nationwide industrial labor conflict. It, like the period it inaugurates, was rife with paradox. Ostensibly it commemorated 1776, yet only a few colonial relics were exhibited: Washington's false teeth, a few colonial army uniforms, and the contents of a "New England Kitchen of 1776." In 1876 Americans looked forward, not backward. In that year, they participated in the most disputed presidential election ever, heard U. S. Grant apologize for the scandals of his administration, and witnessed the first national convention of the Greenback party. They also took in the National League's first baseball season, made John Habberton's pulp novel, *Helen's Babies,* the year's bestseller, and banned Mark Twain's *The Adventures of Tom Sawyer* at the Brooklyn and Denver public libraries.

The 1893 Columbian Exposition

Chicago launched its first world's fair with rituals similar to those that opened the Centennial. Following a Columbian hymn, ode, and march, President Grover Cleveland, first Democrat elected to the White House since 1856, read the required presidential address. Shortly thereafter he pressed a gilded button, sending electricity pulsating through the fair site. Instantaneously visitors heard machinery rumble; water gushed from the Columbian Fountain in the Court of Honor; banners and flags unfurled from atop twelve major exhibit halls, while on the U.S.S. Michigan, anchored off shore in Lake Michigan, cannons boomed in military salute. A shroud fell from Daniel Chester French's giant (seventy-five foot), gilded Statue of the Republic and, since the U.S. had no official national anthem, an orchestra played "America, the Beautiful."

Whereas the Philadelphia fairgrounds could be compared to a pleasure park, the Chicago setting (fig. 106) evoked a planned, albeit idealized, urban environment. Its scale, building density, and municipal services all suggested a model metropolis (table 10.2). As the first "City Beautiful," it influenced the next two decades of American urban design as well as the planning for subsequent U.S. fairs.

The 685-acre fairgrounds resulted from massive transformations of the physical environment. For example, to convert Chicago's Jackson Park site from a dune wasteland into an instant city in less than three years required moving millions of tons of earth, constructing hundreds of miles of avenues and railroads and installing even more miles of telephone and electrical cables, plus erecting over two hundred structures. More than 10,000 construction workers, often working night shifts under electric lights, built Chicago's White City at the cost of 700 accidents and 18 deaths.

The Columbian site had several components, most of which came dressed in the architecture of Beaux Arts classicism (figs. 107, 108).

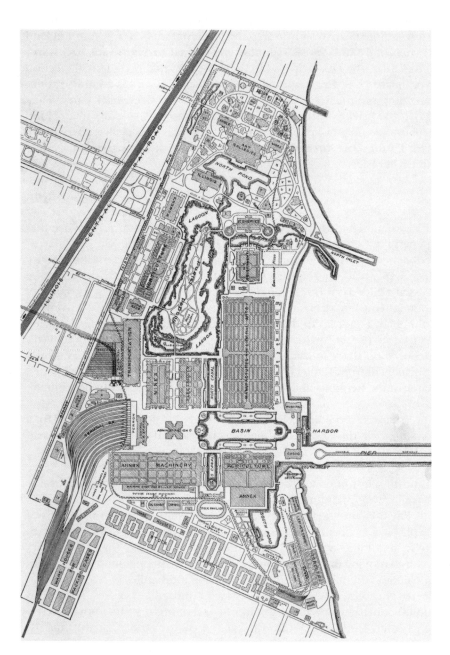

Figure 106.
Map of Grounds, World's Columbian Exposition, Chicago, Illinois, 1893

Table 10.2.   The Development of Buildings at World's Fairs

Fair		Total Number of Buildings*	Major Exhibit Halls	National Pavilions	State or Regional Pavilions	Commercial Exhibitors' Buildings	Art Palaces or Museums	Agriculture and Livestock Displays	Colonial Pavilions
1851	London	1							
1855	Paris	4	2				1		
1862	London	2	2						
1867	Paris	ca.70	1	20		ca.10		yes	2
1873	Vienna	ca.50	2	7	6	9	1	yes	
1876	Philadelphia	48	6	8	17	6	1	yes	
1878	Paris	25	2	17		2	1	yes	1
1889	Paris	50	4	31	2	2	3	yes	18
1893	Chicago	77	9	17	37	3	1	yes	
1900	Paris	73	16	32	1	2	2	yes	14
1904	St. Louis	75	11	19	40		1	yes	
1915	San Francisco	68	11	21	26	7	1	yes	2
1933	Chicago	33	6	6	2	9		yes	
1937	Paris	130	4	38	25	6	2	no	16
1939	New York	112	6	22	26	34	1	no	
1958	Brussels	83	6	39		15	1	yes	1
1964	New York	114	2	34	19	37		no	
1967	Montreal	86	†8	40	6	27	1	no	
1970	Osaka	71	†5	38	5	22	2	no	

SOURCE: This table has been derived from many sources and from scrutinizing site maps. The figures are approximations and do not take into account size and importance of buildings.

* Excluding service buildings, kiosks, restaurants, amusement zone buildings.

† Major buildings for these fairs were "theme pavilions" rather than general exhibit halls.

From: Burton Benedict, *The Anthropology of World's Fairs* (Berkeley: Solar Press, 1983).

Figure 107.
Frances Johnson (photographer), The Court of Honor, World's
Columbian Exposition, Chicago, Illinois, 1893
*(Courtesy The Library of Congress, Division of Prints
and Photographs)*

Around a formal court with its central Administration Building clustered
buildings housing what Americans, in the 1890s, deemed basic to their
economy: Railroads, Machinery, Manufactures, Agriculture. Two
buildings, Mining (fig. 108) and Electricity (fig. 109), signaled the expansion of the extractive industries and also the growing utilization of a new
power source. Encircling a miniature park called The Wooded Island,
one found Louis Sullivan's Transportation Building with its gilded entrance, a Women's Building and its adjoining Children's Building, a Horticultural Hall, plus two massive structures of state: the Illinois Building
and the United States Building. An Art Palace formed the nucleus of
another ensemble, with forty-four state buldings dotted around its circumference. Finally, to the west stretched the Midway Plaisance, a milelong recreational corridor that some bemoaned as "a colossal den of
vulgar and exotic displays" while others claimed it to be "the most interesting, hurly-burly, and exciting part of the whole darn fair."[9]

Although the White City contained few residences, many exhibits
displayed trends in domestic life. For example, the growing competition
between gas and electricity as home utilities could be seen by visiting
model kitchens in the Women's, Electricity, and Horticultural buildings.

Figure 108.
Palace of Mining, World's Columbian Exposition, Chicago, Illinois, 1893
S. S. Beman, architect.

New stoves, hot-water heaters, refrigerators, coolers, and dishwashers came in both power sources. In the Manufacturers and Liberal Arts Building, a consumer could examine every type of home furnishing, period room settings of furniture, display cases of tablewares, and showrooms of textiles.[10]

While many states contributed extensive housekeeping exhibits, New York constructed a life-size ideal American residence. Katherine Davis, a Rochester social reformer, coordinated the designing and furnishing of the Workingman's Model Home. She imagined a young engaged couple—a laboring man earning $500 a year and a woman, a house servant making $3 a week and board—as its future residents. Their house, a two-story, wood-frame dwelling, built at a cost not to exceed $1000, contained a front parlor about 13 feet square, a slightly smaller kitchen, and a bath with a tub and water closet. The upstairs had a front bedroom and two smaller children's bedrooms. A range, parlor fireplace, and room stoves heated the house. In the two-year engagement Davis conjectured for her hypothetical couple, she calculated that two could amass $400, of which $100 would be kept as savings, leaving $300 for furnishing their mortgaged dwelling. Lists of what such household items cost were posted

Figure 109.
Interior, Palace of Electricity, World's Columbian Exposition, Chicago,
Illinois, 1893

next to the objects throughout the home-as-exhibit. Similarly, Davis
meticulously priced and displayed all the clothing that her experimental
family (to which she added an eight-year-old boy, a five-year-old girl,
and an infant) would need over a year. Finally she researched feeding
this "average" family, calculating both food costs in Chicago markets and
the nutritional content of her purchases. Davis prepared daily meals during a month of the fair and served them to a policeman and an Irish widow
with three children.[11]

In the Electricity Building, another model home suggested the future
material culture of domestic science: electric stoves, hot plates, washing
and ironing machines, dishwashers, carpet sweepers, plus electric door-
bells, phonographs, fire alarms, and innumerable lighting fixtures. The
Westinghouse Electric Company's mammoth dynamos symbolized to
Henry Adams a new energy force whose application to common life
seemed unlimited. As the telegraph and telephone dramatized electricity's potential at Philadelphia, now phonographs and kinescopes suggested
still newer types of communication at Chicago. Here, too, were the
Holreith calculating machines used to tabulate the 1890 census. Devices
such as electric time clocks, resistance welding machines, and portable
motors of all sizes indicate changes in the work place. Electric streetcars,

elevators, railways, and street lights transformed urban place and purpose. The exterior and interior illumination (using over 100,000 incandescent bulbs, 5,000 arc lights, and 20,000 glow lights) of the fair buildings awed visitors. Walter Besant, an English novelist not usually prone to hyperbole, thought the spectacle comparable only to the "new heaven and new earth" foretold in the Book of the Apocalypse.

Electricity illuminated miles of consumer-goods displays in the forty-four acre Manufacturers and Liberal Arts Building, the largest department store the world had ever seen. Many wares were exhibited with price tags so that visitors could do comparison shopping. Among the most popular items were Morris chairs, the "Clasp Locker or Unlocker for Shoes" (the world's first slide fastener or zipper), garden furniture, bathroom fixtures, baby carriages, and rural telephones. As Burton Benedict has pointed out in *The Anthropology of World's Fairs,* "Such products could be used as fences or bridges. In world's fairs exhibitors were mostly building bridges, expanding their markets, but they, as well as their customers, recognized the importance of goods as fences marking off one status group from another."[12] The enormous range of goods at the Chicago fair provided a cornucopia of material culture that catered to middle-class taste and helped to form that taste. Not only were Americans educated as to what to buy but also they were taught to want more things, better quality things, and quite new things.

"One of the manias dearest to Americans consists in meeting in groups and founding societies apropos of everything and apropos of nothing," wrote French composer Jacques Offenbach after a tour of the nation in 1877. "Any pretext is good, and associations abound in the United States." World's fairs especially served the middle-class penchant for the associative life; they provided a forum for confirming the class's cultural hegemony for extending the nation's corporate, professional, and scientific leadership. Philadelphia hosted national gatherings of Odd Fellows, Superintendents of Asylums for the Insane, Knights Templar, the American Banking Association, and the Socialist Party. Chicago established a separate World's Congress Auxiliary of 14,000[13] members who organized 139 national conferences attracting more than 700,000 participants. The most popular were on education (where G. Stanley Hall, David Starr Jordan, and John Dewey spoke), labor (with addresses by Henry Demarest Lloyd, Samuel Gompers, Clarence Darrow, and Henry George), women (Julia Ward Howe, Lucy Stone, Jane Addams, and Frances Willard as featured speakers), and religion. The World's Parliament of Religions, lasting seventeen days, reflected both American pluralism and the country's anxiety over the future of belief in an age of increasing materialism.[14] By 1915, the United States was truly "a nation of joiners" who went to 928 conferences and conventions (a world record) at San Francisco's Panama-Pacific Exposition. Several of these meetings reflected new trends in everyday life: the National Congress on Recreation, Rotary International, the National Funeral Directors Association, the Motion Picture Exhibitors League, plus 172 professional educational societies and 105 fraternal organizations.

Chicago's Midway Plaisance, in a summer's course, became "the midway," a new term subsequently applied to commercial entertainment zones common to county fairs, tent Chautauquas, or trolley parks. Unlike Philadelphia's "Centennial City"—an Elm Avenue strip of restaurants, ice cream parlors, dioramas, beer gardens, and medicine shows located just outside the 1876 fair's main entrance—Chicago's midway achieved a degree of official status. Fair organizers classified it under the Department of Ethnology.[15] The polyglot midway presented a diverse counterculture to the moral earnestness of the White City. Here the Court of Honor (see fig. 107) and the Statue of the Republic gave way to the Streets of Cairo and George Ferris' wheel. Fairgoers, on foot or in hired chairs, made their way through a riot of attractions: Turkish bazaars, Hawaiian volcanoes, Hagenbeck's circus animals. Flesh was flaunted: by world heavyweight Jim Corbett, by hootchy-kootchy dancer "Little Egypt"; by body builders Bernard MacFadden and Eugene Sandow. The show careers of Flo Ziegfeld, Sol Bloom, and Harry Houdini were launched.

Visitors could ride several types of railroads, make a 1,500-foot ascent in a captive balloon, or, for fifty cents, purchase two revolutions on the Ferris Wheel (see fig. 101), the unofficial icon of the dynamic, heterogeneous midway. Chicago's answer to Paris's 1889 Eiffel Tower, Ferris' 264-foot bicycle wheel in the sky dominated the landscape. With thirty-six cars, each larger than a Pullman coach or a New York brownstone and capable of holding sixty people, the wheel, when fully loaded, rotated with 2,160 people in the air.[16]

Following the example of colonial villages introduced at the 1889 Paris fair, Columbian Exposition organizers featured living ethnological displays of nonwhite cultures. These exhibits of people, rather than goods, appeared on the midway juxtaposed with wild animal acts, joyrides, and other side shows. The village displays frequently reinforced American racial prejudices and ethnic stereotypes (fig. 110). Often depicting people as curiosities (the Javanese) or trophies (the Sioux) the exhibits were staged along what one contemporary called "a sliding scale of humanity." Nearest to the White City were the Teutonic and Celtic races as represented by the two German and two Irish enclaves. The Midway's middle contained the Mohammedan and Asian worlds. Then, continued the observer, "we descent to the savage races, the African of Dahomey and the North American Indian, each of which has its place" at the remotest end of the midway.[17] Blacks repeatedly petitioned Congress for Afro-American exhibits in both the fair's main structures and the state pavilions, but the only official display mounted presented the Hampton Institute's education program. While Chicago had a growing black population, discrimination barred them from the fair's construction crews and clerical staffs. In a remarkable pamphlet published privately by Ida Wells during the fair, T. L. Barnett noted the extreme irony in White City officials designating 25 August as "Colored People's Day."[18]

Others noticed other tensions at the fair, paradoxes emblematic of the American culture at large. For example, Daniel H. Burnham's Beaux Arts prescription for the model American metropolis seemed at odds with his architectural firm's downtown (in Chicago and elsewhere) skyscrapers—awesome vertical towers that would radically alter urban life by 1915. The displays in the Women's Building contrasted with activities in the World Congress of Beauty ("40 Girls From 40 Countries"). Buffalo Bill's Wild West shows drew sell-out audiences, while a young Wisconsin professor named Frederick Jackson Turner told his colleagues in the American Historical Association that frontier America was over.

A greater paradox was yet to come. In 1893 Americans honored the Duke of Veragura and the Spanish Infanta as the diplomatic representatives of the country that, four hundred years earlier, had dispatched Columbus on his epic voyage across the Atlantic; five years later, many of those same Americans cheered the military humiliation of Spain in what Secretary of State John Hay would call "that splendid little war."[19] Burnham, imperial planner of the White City, went on to redesign the United States's colonial capitol of Manila in the conquered Philippines.

Burnham, with typical Chicago bravado, claimed the Columbian Exposition as the third greatest event in American history, the other two having occurred in 1776 and 1861. Unlike at the Centennial, Americans in 1893 reveled in their historical identity. At the fair, the Colonial Revival style characterized many state pavilions, the first commemorative postage stamps and coins were issued, and historical pageants dramatized the American past. The new nationalism added a new holiday and ritual to everyday life. Francis J. Bellamy, an editor of *Youth's Companion,* de-

---

(*Overleaf*)
Figure 110.
"Darkies' Day at the Fair"
From *Puck* (1893).
(*Courtesy The Library of Congress, Division of Prints and Photographs*)

PART I.

THE EVENTS of the Great World's Fair
　　Impressive went their way.
Time rolled around ; at last it was
　　The Colored People's Day !
The Sons of Ham from far Soudan
　　And Congo's Sable Kings
Came to the Fair with all their hosts,
　　Their wives, their plumes, their rings.
From distant Nubia's torrid sands,
　　From far-famed Zanguebar,
Together with their Yankee friends,
　　The Darkies all were dar !

PART II.

But a Georgia coon, named Major Moon,
　　Resolved to mar the day,
Because to lead the whole affair
　　He had not had his way.
Five hundred water-melons ripe,
　　(The Darky's theme and dream,)
He laid on ice so cool and nice
　　To aid him in his scheme.

PART III.

The plans are laid for a big parade
　　Of great impressiveness ;
With bands, so grand, on every hand,
　　And gorgeousness in dress.
　　No eye to right must show the white,
　　　Each head must poise erect,
　　With proud reserve each must preserve
　　　His dignity circumspect.

'T is a glorios
　　The ranks s
Until at a tu
　　Those melo
　　　Teeth
　　　　Fo
　　He c
　　　'T

ICE
COLD
WATER
MILLIONS

J. Opper

PART V.

With one loud whoop, with one fell swoop,
　　They swarm down on the stand ;
The sons of Ham in the foremost jam,
　　With a big slice in each hand.

And
　　Gi
As th
　　Ar

DARKIE

(A

L'Envoi.
But Major Moon is a saddened Coon ;
For his melons he got no pay.
His successful spite was a boomerang quite —
But it busted up Darkies' Day.

FAIR.

vised a plan for the fair's dedication (12 October 1892) where schoolchildren across the country could participate in the Exposition's quadricentennial liturgy by celebrating it in their schools. To make the event truly national, Bellamy drafted the Pledge of Allegiance to the flag of the United States. The federal Bureau of Education circulated copies to teachers nationwide. At the Chicago ceremonies schoolgirls dressed in red, white, and blue formed a living flag. As a hundred thousand people witnessed the fair's dedication and the pledge's recitation, millions of children around the country also promised their allegiance, thus beginning a ritual thereafter repeated daily in the nation's public schools.

In addition to Columbus Day and the flag pledge, Chicago in 1893 introduced Americans to Cream of Wheat cereal, Aunt Jemima pancake mix, Postum, Juicy Fruit gum, Shredded Wheat, and Pabst Blue Ribbon (a fair award) beer. That year rural telephone companies proliferated as the 1876 Bell patents expired, *McClure's* magazine began at fifteen cents a copy, the country maintained the gold standard with the repeal of the Sherman Silver Purchase of 1890, Sears, Roebuck sent out its first five-hundred-page catalog, and the "Sooners" and thousands of other would-be Oklahomans staked out the Cherokee Strip. The murder trial of Lizzie Borden, a thirty-two-year-old Fall River (Massachusetts) spinster, monopolized the gossip of fairgoers as did a children's street chant: "Lizzie Borden took an axe / And gave her mother forty whacks. / And when she saw what she had done / She gave her father forty-one."

In Washington, D. C., Charles T. Kelly's Industrial Army chanted, 1,500 strong, to demand relief for the unemployed as the country's worst economic depression to date deepened due to the era's continuing boom-bust business cycles. Wall Street stocks plunged on 5 May, with the market all but collapsing on 27 June. Six hundred banks closed their doors, more than 95,000 business firms failed, and seventy-four railroads (including the Philadelphia and Reading, the Northern Pacific, Erie, and the Santa Fe) went into receivership. As the Columbian Exposition closed on 29 October—its flags lowered to half-mast to mourn the brutal death of Chicago's five-term mayor, Carter Harrison, by an assassin's revolver at his home the night before—four years of social violence, widespread unemployment, labor protest, farm foreclosures, business bankruptcies, and economic turmoil were only beginning.

The 1915 Panama-Pacific Exposition

While 150,000 people waited in balmy San Francisco on 20 February 1915, President Woodrow Wilson, at his White House desk in Washington, pressed a button that signaled an aerial tower at Ruckerton, New Jersey, which, in turn, relayed a wireless radio message across

Figure 111.
Panoramic View, Panama-Pacific International Exposition, San Francisco, California, 1915

the continent to an antenna atop a 435-foot Tower of Jewels (fig. 111) at the entrance to the Panama-Pacific International Exposition. Within the fairgrounds, the wheels of a gigantic Busch-Sulzer Diesel engine began rotating. Throughout the city, factory whistles blew. Overhead, aviator Lincoln Beachey circled the Exposition, performing side-spirals in his Curtis biplane.

Although Portland (1904) and Seattle (1909) had staged earlier regional fairs, San Francisco's P.P.I.E. represented the Pacific coast's first major international exposition. It signaled the increased role of the nation's western states (Arizona and New Mexico, joining the union in 1912) and its newly acquired Pacific territories (Alaska by purchase in 1867 and Hawaii by conquest in 1898). Many Californians viewed the fair's landscaping and architecture as emblematic of a region often called the "American Mediterranean"; other residents considered its educational, medical, and welfare exhibits as the triumph of their state's political and social Progressivism. San Franciscans saw it as a civic triumph over a devastating 1906 earthquake and as a chance to play host to the nation, displaying despite the spreading world war, the United State's abundance and altruism in a marble mantle of empire and expertise.[20]

The opening salvos of the awesome Krupp guns of August, prominently exhibited at Chicago and Philadelphia, ended the Victorian epoch, not the British queen's death in 1901. Similarly, although less violently, the Panama-Pacific Exposition concluded a major period in the common culture of the United States. San Francisco's long summer simultaneously summed up two generations of past experience and manifested new trends in everyday life. Like the Centennial, it revealed many Americans mesmerized by movement, infatuated with consumer goods, and concerned to make it in (or into) the middle class. San Francisco in 1915, however, also suggested Americans played more, put greater stock in education and engineering, and found themselves living in a culture more national and urban, more incorporated and interdependent, than had their counterparts who visited Philadelphia in 1876.

The fair's walled city plan (fig. 112), reinforced a sense of global intimacy and urban density. An inner core of eight main structures tightly clustered around five courts formed its nucleus, creating what Bernard Maybeck saw as a gigantic "Golden Brooch." Individual buildings (Art, Music, California) and gardens bordered this ensemble. At the fair's opposite ends were state and foreign pavilions and an entertainment sector called "The Joy Zone." Unlike Philadelphia and Chicago, San Francisco had no building specifically devoted to electricity (considered too common to everyday life); to women (hoping to achieve parity with eventual passage of the Eighteenth Amendment); or to the federal government (adequately represented by the adjacent thousand-acre U.S. Presidio).[21]

Vivid polychromy and brilliant illumination enthralled visitors. Unlike the cast-iron grey of the Centennial or the hygienic uniformity of the White City, the Jewel City exuded the region's pastel pinks, ultramarine blues, chaparral browns, and hibiscus reds. Jules Guerin, the Director of Color, splashed the four golds of California—wheat, oranges, gold, and wild poppies—over the entire landscape. Like a master chromolithographer or department store decorator, he color-coordinated everything: attendants' uniforms, banners, admission tickets, souvenir autochromes. He even roasted the sugary Monterey sand on the footpaths to a rich cinnamon brown as a final touch to the harmonized environment.

Fair architects manipulated other materials and colors.[22] Instead of Chicago's plaster staff façades, San Francisco cladded its main buildings with manufactured travertine, a chemical composition first used by McKim, Mead, and White in parts of their 1910 Pennsylvania Station in New York when true stone proved too expensive. The manufactured travertine faked marble's substance and antiquity's patina. Another foreshadowing of the American fascination with synthetics could be seen in the Varied Industries Building where Bakelite plastic was displayed in a rainbow of colors.

Color merged with illumination, giving fairgoers a brilliant demonstration of the night life now typical of cities. W. D. Arcy, electrical engineer for the Panama Canal and head of General Electric's research and development department, lit up every interior and exterior space of the P.P.I.E. including the sky. Flood, underwater, and especially indirect lighting created a nocturnal newness. Three evenings a week, a company of Marines manned the Scintillator, a battery of forty-eight searchlights off the marina, creating an hour-long visual extravaganza, part *son et lumière,* part aurora borealis, and part Hollywood film premiere night. The Tower of Jewels, the walled city's centerpiece, received special lighting effects. Festooned with over 102,000 "Novagems"—large-faceted, colored "jewels" backed with mirrors and hung by wires to gyrate and flash continually with the slightest breeze—the illuminated tower seemed, to one observer, as a vibrant "living film of light."

Appropriately in the state that would become the world's cinema capitol, the Panama-Pacific Exposition featured film as a medium for shaping cultural values. "To a degree never seen before," observed newspaper columnist Ben Macomber, "the moving picture has taken a place in this exposition as an exhibition adjunct." Lewis J. Selznick, vice-president of the World Film Corporation, distributed promotional films of the Panama-Pacific International Exposition to 3,500 theaters across North America. Seventy-seven movie theaters on the fairgrounds bombarded fairgoers with films on topics ranging from immigration to city planning to state politics. Here one could see movies on Americans working in mines, factories, and offices. Newsreels reported the latest European war developments, while travelogues beckoned Americans to non-European vacations. Several feature-length films, for example, Carl Laemmle's *The World to Come,* used the fair as their setting.

The Joy Zone (fig. 113) had twenty-five theaters offering dance, light opera, vaudeville, and movies. Popular culture assumed both predictable and unprecedented forms. For example, "Stella" played to standing-room-only crowds. For a dime, patrons could ogle an electrically lighted nude painting of a well-endowed young lady delicately veiled with translucent fabric. Unlike the nudes found on saloon walls, Stella possessed the added attraction of an automated bosom. The concession, with neither overhead costs nor seats, grossed $75,000. Others, like the Dayton Flood, the Jester's Palace, Frederic Thompson's Toyland, and the Eden Musée, made

---

(*Overleaf*)
Figure 112.
Map of Grounds, Panama-Pacific International Exposition, San Francisco, California, 1915

BAY OF SAN FRANCISCO

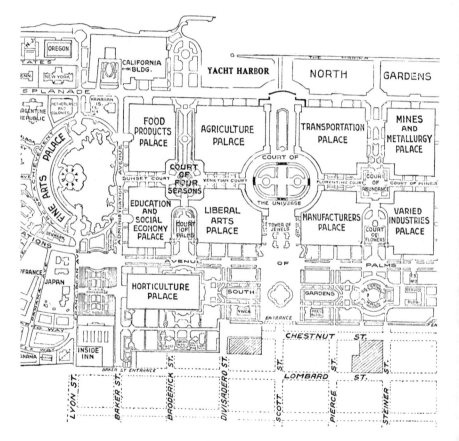

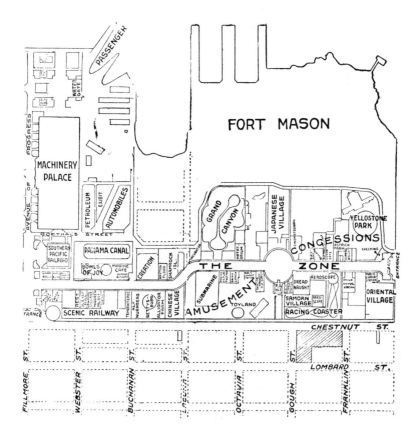

Figure 113.
Joy Zone Concessions, U.S. Dollar Watch Company, Panama-Pacific
International Exposition, San Francisco, California, 1915

less. In the Zone, many Americans first experienced eating in a cafeteria
(Y.W.C.A. Building), bought a dollar watch (U.S. Pocket Watch Company), or drank pineapple juice (Hawaiian Pavilion).

Motion dominated the Zone. The relaxed pace of the motorized
"Fadgl" (five cents for a fair train tour), the Universal Bus System (ten
cents a ride), and the "Electriquette" battery-powered wicker chairs (a
dollar an hour) could be accelerated if, as a spectator, one paid to watch
cars and motorcycles careen around the open Autodrome at 100 miles
per hour or, as a participant, one rode the Auto Race at half the speed.
(Sufficient visitors came to San Francisco in their own cars to necessitate
four parking lots equipped with service stations operated by Shell Oil of
California). The ultimate in speed trials meant height: either a ride (fifty
cents) in the Zone's Strauss Aeroscope, a massive arm of a bascule bridge
with propeller blades or a brief (ten dollars for ten minutes) barnstorm-
ing flight in the Yacht Harbor's Lockheed airplanes.

The western railroads, each erecting a corporation pavilion, promoted vacation travel by recreating American scenic wonders in the Zone:
the Sante Fe miniaturized the Grand Canyon, the Union Pacific showed
the Old Faithful Inn at Yellowstone (fig. 114), and the Great Northern
reproduced Glacier National Park. One could also be conveyed, via a

Figure 114.
Advertisement, Old Faithful Inn, Union Pacific System-Yellowstone Park, Panama-Pacific International Exposition, San Francisco, California, 1915

mobile platform capable of carrying 1,200 people, around a working model of the Panama Canal. An automated system of phonographs and telephones described the canal's operations.

Other Zone displays indulged the Victorian's persistent (but ofttimes prejudiced) interest in faraway places. As Native Americans and Afro-Americans had been caricatured in the 1876 and 1893 fairs, Asians were similarly misrepresented in 1915. New imperial conquests, the Filipinos and the Samoans, appeared as the nation's "little brown brothers," while the Zone represented old immigrants to America, the Chinese and the Japanese, with disgraceful displays such as the Underground Chinatown and the Oriental Joy Garden. Racism surfaced elsewhere, for example, at the exhibits of the Race Betterment Foundation. Here eugenicists, through the use of large plaster casts of Atlas, Venus, and Apollo and printed materials espousing I.Q. tests, advertised their "scientific judgement for the human race at its best."[23]

In the Education Palace and its companion Liberal Arts Building, Americans saw other social issues displayed, particularly two of Progressivism's most hallowed beliefs: (1) democratic education meant a reformed politics and (2) a reformed politics meant social improvements. In addition to kindergartens, public schools, the work of state agricultural colleges, industrial and vocational schools, and the centralized urban high schools could be examined. Three model schools operated within the grounds: a Commercial Business College, the Palmer School of Penmanship, and Maria Montessori's preschool. Informal education also demonstrated the Victorian American's penchant for striving. Both the Y.M.C.A. and the Y.W.C.A. had separate buildings. The Chautauqua crusade and the social settlement movement were represented. While there was no counterpart, at least in size, to the Columbian Exposition's World Parliament of Religions, a World Bible Congress and a Social Christianity Congress took place. Utah exhibited the tenets of Mormonism, and Christian Science had displays in the Liberal Arts building.

Within Liberal Arts, the social sciences (particularly economics, political science, and anthropology) contended for a place in the academic curriculum and the national culture. Fair congresses—a new world's record of 928, averaging ten a day—preset courses such as teaching hygiene, biology, and civics in the nation's schools or improving public welfare programs. Other meetings pressed their cause (with ample supporting statistics) for public health, social welfare legislation, and federal income taxation.

The world's first Insurance Congress, seen as the "era's latest combination of economics and social service," mirrored changes in American demography and health. The insurance industry also mounted a seventy-five-company collective exhibit, published a daily paper during the fair, and bombarded visitors with statistics on mortality as related to gender, race, marital status, occupation, weight, disease, and seventy-seven other variables. Anthropometry, manifested in graphs, charts, maps, models, and diagrams ran riot. The Prudential Company, assuring visitors (via its trademarked slogan and logo) that only Prudential possessed the "strength of Gibraltar," also provided a calculus of living and dying statistics specific for the generation of 1886–1912 and advertised the benefits of the "social providence" of life, home, and car insurance.[24]

Government bureaus, along with private reform groups, also monitored life's rites of passage, with particular interest in youth and health. The Y.W.C.A.'s day care center, the U.S. Government Children's Bureau, and the displays of the Boy Scouts and Girl Scouts documented the Victorian discovery of childhood and adolescence. A separate Food Products building—a "temple of the tin can and food package"—displayed the latest offerings in convenience food and nutritionist's claims. Exhibits on hospital care, on the nation's chronic afflictions (yellow fever, tuberculosis), and on new pharmaceuticals (aspirin, Bromo-seltzer) reflected the growing effect of institutional and prepackaged medical care.

American corporations mounted many displays. Beginning in 1876 with separate pavilions by companies such as Singer and Goodyear, the corporate presence expanded at each subsequent fair. Multinational firms such as Ford, Heinz, and U.S. Steel controlled a large portion of the economy by 1915. A quest for control, particularly through education, expertise, and engineering also characterized much of what Americans saw at San Francisco. Not only did the engineering triumph of the Panama Canal's completion serve as the rationale for the West Coast fair, but many of the nation's "new managers" administered the P.P.I.E.'s bureaucracy. For example, Charles C. Moore, president of one of the nation's hydroelectrical engineering firms, chaired the Exposition's board of directors, a group that included Herbert Hoover, the first engineer to become President of the United States. As James Beniger argues in *The Control Revolution* (1986), massive changes generated by the industrial revolution in manufacturing, transportation, and communications—evident at the 1915 fair in Ford's assembly line, exhibits on wireless telegraphy and radio, and displays of scientific management methods—also heralded "a revolution in social control."[25]

Elsewhere others questioned or confronted such control or sought to impose their own hegemony. On 19 November 1915 the state of Utah executed, by firing squad Industrial Workers of the World organizer Joe Hill. Earlier that year, racial tensions flared over the showing of D. W. Griffith's *The Birth of a Nation.* On Thanksgiving night atop Stone Mountain near Atlanta, William Simmons revived the Ku Klux Klan to promote "white supremacy." Prolonged labor strikes took place in Pittsburgh, Gary, and Seattle. The U.S. Senate passed legislation requiring literacy tests for all immigrants, while the House moved to adopt the Eighteenth Amendment prohibiting the manufacture, sale, import, or export of liquor in the United States.

The Panama-Pacific International Exposition epitomized American society at its first twentieth-century fault line. It revealed Americans in one of their typical Janus-like postures: it was "conceived in optimism and carried through despite the outbreak of World War I," and "its great palaces and courts dripping with allegorical statues and murals" reflected a final, sentimental, opulent display of American Victorianism.[26] The fair also suggested future modernity. It asserted the growing importance of California and the American West while also turning national attention toward the Pacific and South America. It adumbrated the everyday life to come, both in mundane ways like processed Kraft cheese, Pyrex glass, and Carrier air conditioning, and also in the ways (and wishes) of the middle class: white-collar work, wider leisure, consumer abundance, information access, and social reform.

Notes

1. Lewis Mumford, *Technics and Civilization* (New York: Harcourt, Brace, 1934).

2. John Maass, *The Glorious Enterprise: H. J. Schwartzmann and the 1876 Centennial* (Watkins Glen, N.Y.: American Life Foundation, 1973).

3. Maurice F. Neufeld, "The Contribution of the World's Columbian Exposition of 1893 to the Idea of a Planned Society in the United States," Ph.D. dissertation, University of Wisconsin (1935).

4. Robert Post, ed. *1876: A Centennial Exhibition* (Washington, D.C.: National Museum of American History, 1976).

5. John Maass, "Who Invented Dewey's Classification?" *Wilson Library Bulletin* 47 (December 1972): 335–41.

6. Francis A. Walker, *The World's Fair* (New York: A. S. Barnes, 1878).

7. William D. Andrews, "Women and the Fairs of 1876 and 1893," *Hayes Historical Journal* (1977): 173–83; Virginia Grant Darney, "Women and World's Fairs: American International Expositions, 1876–1904," Ph.D. dissertation, Emory University (1982).

8. Robert A. Trennert, "A Grand Failure: The Centennial Indian Exhibit of 1876," *Prologue* 6 (1974): 118–29; Judy Brown, "The North American Indian Exhibits of the 1876 and 1893 World Expositions: The Influence of Scientific Thought on Popular Attitudes," master's thesis, George Washington University (1975).

9. Alan Trachtenberg, *The Incorporation of America* (New York: Hill and Wang, 1982), chap. 7, 208–34; Rodney Reid Badger, *The Great American Fair: The World's Columbian Exposition and American Culture* (Chicago: Nelson-Hall, 1970).

10. Neil Harris, "Museums, Merchandising, and Popular Taste: The Struggle for Influence," in *Material Culture and the Study of American Life,* ed. Ian M. G. Quimby (New York: W. W. Norton, 1978): 141–74.

11. Joseph W. Barnes, "How to Raise a Family on $500 a Year," *American Heritage* 133 (December 1981): 91–95.

12. Burton Benedict, *The Anthropology of World's Fairs—San Francisco's Panama-Pacific International Exposition of 1915* (Berkeley: Scoler Press, 1983), p. 2.

13. Jacques Offenbach, *A French Traveler in America;* David F. Burg, *Chicago's White City of 1893* (Lexington: University of Kentucky Press, 1976).

14. Kenten Druyvesteyn, "The World's Parliament of Religions," Ph.D. dissertation, University of Chicago (1976).

15. Robert Rydell, *All the World's a Fair* (Chicago: University of Chicago Press, 1984); Edo McCullough, *World's Fair Midways: An Affectionate Account of American Amusement from the Crystal Palace to the Crystal Ball* (New York: Exposition Press, 1966); Sol Bloom, *The Autobiography of Sol Bloom* (New York: G. P. Putnam, 1948).

16. John A. Kouwenhoven, "The Eiffel Tower and the Ferris Wheel," *Arts Magazine* 54 (February 1980): 170–73.

17. Rydell, *All the World's a Fair,* 64–68; John C. Eastman, "Village Life at the World Fair," *Chautauquan* 17 (1893): 602–4; *Midway Types: A Book of Illustrated Lessons*

about the People of the Midway Plaisance (Chicago: American Engraving Company, 1894); *Oriental and Occidental: Northern and Southern Portraits: Types of the Midway Plaisance* (St. Louis: N. D. Thompson Co., 1894).

18. Elliot Rudwich and August Meier, "Black Man in the 'White City': Negroes and the Columbian Exposition, 1893," *Phylon* 26 (1965): 354–61; Robert Rydell, "The World's Columbian Exposition of 1893: Racist Underpinnings of a Utopian Artifact," *Journal of American Culture* 1 (1978): 253–75; Ann Massa, "Black Women in the White City," *Journal of American Studies* 8 (1974): 319–37.

19. Justus D. Doenecke, "Myths, Machines, and Markets: The Columbian Exposition of 1893," *Journal of Popular Culture* 6 (1972): 535–44.

20. Frank Morton Todd, *The Story of the Exposition* (New York: G. P. Putnam and Sons, 1921).

21. John D. Barry, *The City of Domes* (San Francisco: John J. Newbegin, 1915).

22. William H. Jordy, *American Buildings and Their Architects: Progressive and Academic Ideals at the Turn of the Twentieth Century* (Garden City, N.Y.: Anchor Books, 1976), 275–300.

23. Benedict, *Anthropology of World's Fairs,* pp. 34, 41, 49–52.

24. Frank M. Todd, *The Story of the Exposition, Being the Official History of the International Celebration Held at San Francisco in 1915,* 5 vols. (New York: G. P. Putnam, 1921), 5: 90–97.

25. James Beniger, *The Control Revolution: Technological and Economic Origins of the Information Society* (Cambridge: Harvard University Press, 1986).

26. Benedict, *Anthropology of World's Fairs.* p. 60.

Part Three

Museums as Artifacts

If I could do it, I'd do no writing at all here. It would be photographs; the rest would be fragments of cloth, bits of cotton, lumps of earth, records of speech, pieces of wood and iron, phials of odors, plates of food and of excrement. Book sellers would consider it quite a novelty; critics would murmur, yes, but is it art; and I could trust a majority of you to use it as you would a parlor game.

—James Agee

(*Opposite page*)
Figure 115 (*above*).
Charles Willson Peale and Titian Ramsay Peale, *The Long Room, Interior of Front Room in Peale's Museum,* 1822
Watercolor.
(Courtesy The Detroit Institute of Arts)

Figure 116 (*below*).
"Phineas T. Barnum's Museum," Ann Street and Broadway, New York City, 1851–52
Lithograph by G. W. Lewis.
(Courtesy The New-York Historical Society, New York City)

Figure 117.
"First Class Museum for Ladies, Gentlemen, and Children," Chicago, Illinois,
ca. 1895
(Courtesy The Chicago Historical Society)

The History behind, within, and outside the History Museum

By a fortuitous coincidence, I, a historian trained in and for teaching in the academy, became interested in American history museums about the same time such institutions and the historians working in them were reviewing their approaches to exhibition presentation. The National Endowment for the Humanities pressed history museums for greater interpretation in their exhibitions. Museum education and museum studies programs in colleges and universities sent a new type of graduate into the field. Men and women, possessing recent doctorates in the so-called "new" urban, ethnic, and social history as well as fields like demographic, family, and women's history, took their first jobs in history museums. It was a heady time, a propitious one for an outsider to listen in and, on occasion, to contribute a few words to the conversation.

Many scholars facilitated my entry into museums. In addition to Harold Skramstad, Ken Ames, and John Zukowsky, Martin Sullivan, a deputy director at the NEH and now the director of the New York State Museum, provided introductions to many people and places. So did John Herbst at the Western Pennsylvania Historical Society, William Alderson at Old Salem Village, and Pete Daniel, Curator of Agriculture, and Gary Kulik, Assistant Director for Academic Programs at the National Museum of American History. John encouraged my ideas on dealing with historical conflict in museums; Bill assisted my publishing efforts, particularly *Material Culture Studies in America;* Pete helped immensely during my stay as a Fellow at the Smithsonian Institution with advice on my material culture research. Gary invited me to participate in the NMAH seminar on exhibition design criticism that he and Jim Sims organized in November 1988; he has also offered counsel about appropriate reviewers for my history museum exhibition section in the *Journal of American History.*

Peer review of history exhibitions now happens more routinely and in more professional journals than when I first complained about the paucity of scholarly critique several years ago. I have been on the stump about it when any one would listen. I think it especially imperative now for several reasons. Museum exhibitions and their related elements are a distinct medium for identifying, organizing, comparing, analyzing, and communicating historical information and interpretation. They shape much

This article originally appeared in *Curator* 23.4 (December 1980): 255–74.

of the public's perception of the past. Museum exhibition catalogs now represent an important, albeit neglected, source of scholarly historical writing. Finally, the history museum in the contemporary United States serves as an institutional context in which an increasing number of professionally trained historians now conduct their research and present their scholarship.

Exhibition reviewing, however, presents special problems for both editors and reviewers. Unlike "portable" historical presentations such as monographs or microprints that can be easily mailed to a reviewer, exhibitions require a visit. Many history museum exhibitions also tend to be ephemeral. Their limited public life-span necessitates that reviewers evaluate them within the relatively brief period (three months to two years) during which many are mounted or traveling. Major historical exhibitions are usually collaborative endeavors, involving the works of exhibition committees, curatorial and research departments, designers, and consultants. It is thus much more difficult to identify professional responsibility for the strengths and weaknesses of such collective enterprises than, say, in the case of a typical monograph written by an individual author. Museum audiences are extremely diverse, and exhibitions must be judged against the visitor clientele that the sponsoring museum had in mind. A final complicating factor in exhibition reviewing is how to learn when, where, and what new history exhibitions are being mounted by museums throughout the country. At present, no national register, funding aid, or professional association provides, in a systematic and comprehensive fashion, information that constitutes a bibliography of past, present, and projected history exhibitions in the United States. A beginning attempt at providing such a research service, however, is the American Association for State and Local History Registry of History Exhibits that appears at various times in the Association's newsletter, *History News Dispatch.*

Acknowledging these obstacles, I still think we need several forums for the professional review of history exhibits. What should be the criteria for the selection of exhibits to be reviewed? What should be the criteria for the selection of exhibits to be reviewed? What type of guidelines should we use for appraising those exhibits? As the editor in charge of such reviews for the *Journal of American History,* I made my case in two places. See "Why We Must Review History Exhibits," *History News,* 43.3 (May–June 1988), 30–33 and "Reviewing History Museum Exhibits," *Journal of American History,* 76.1 (June 1989): 192–95.

The George Washington University sponsored the first hearing of this article in fall 1980 during a visit hosted by the departments of museum studies, museum education, and American studies. The general idea led to an NEH grant, a miniconference on the history behind, within, and outside the history museum at Colonial Williamsburg, a publication titled *Historians/Artifacts/Learners: The Working Papers,* and the friendship of three new museum colleagues—Carol Stapp, Barbara Fertig, and Susan Nichols—who were responsible for the success of all of the above.

Family photograph albums, attic trunks, and certain household drawers contain numerous artifacts of what we value during our lives. History books and history museums represent a similar attempt to collect, keep, and interpret communal memories.

History museums in America have been around for a fairly long time—at least as long as Charles Willson Peale's famous institution (see fig. 125) now so patiently reconstructed in a book by his descendent, the late Charles Coleman Sellers.[1] Although many of their individual histories and, assuredly, their collective story over the past two hundred years have yet to be written, I think history museums may be entering upon what Cary Carson, writing about the new plans for *Teaching History at Colonial Willamsburg,* has described as a new era of growth and change.[2]

I share his optimism about the "future of the past," particularly after seeing how the past is coming to be interpreted in a number of history museums. Much work remains to be done, however, in making the history museum into a vital research, educational, and cultural institution that recognizes history, not as nostalgia, nationalism, or nativism, but as an accumulated record of past change which we use to fashion our strategies for coping with the present and future. I would like to take up three broad issues that all of us in the history field, regardless of our institutional affiliations, will be confronting in the next decade. Here I direct my discussion largely toward the men and women who work in the historical museum profession, those individuals whom E. McClung Fleming identifies as "museum historians" as opposed to someone such as myself who is often called an academic historian.[3] My remarks here also apply to historians in the schools, grammar through graduate. I would like to propose three tasks to the present and the next generation of history museum professionals.

The first task is to define the purpose and conduct of the history museum profession as a profession, or, in my title's formula, "the history *behind* the history museum." The second involves exploring the problems and possibilities of history teaching where the museum is used as "an educational setting,"[4] or, in the scheme of this paper, "the history *within* the history museum." I would then like to conclude by suggesting some possibilities for investigating present-day material culture, or what I call the "history *outside* the history museum." In brief, the three responsibilities that we must shoulder in the 1980s with even greater dedication than in the past are: 1) an increased responsibility to the history museum profession and the discipline of history; 2) a responsibility for the teaching of history in a variety of institutions and with an assortment of learning strategies; and 3) a responsibility to develop programs in which local and community history becomes the province of all people, not just the prerogative of an academic elite.

The History behind the History Museum

My first concern is that history-museum historians simply do not do enough museum history. Historical museums and many of the historians who work in them, while devoted to the cause of expanding the public's historical consciousness, are often curiously inattentive to their own histories. Although we have a few historical treatments of nineteenth-century historical societies (largely depositories of archival rather than artifactual records),[5] little attention has been paid to the origins, development, and influence of history museums as part of both the history of American museums and American cultural history. The recent works of Edward Alexander, Melinda Frye, Dianne Pilgrim, and Katharine Rich are an encouraging beginning,[6] but I am convinced we need a great deal more careful research—at the level of the individual history museum—before we can assess how American museums over the past two centuries have depicted American history. In short, we need to develop a thorough historiography of American-history-museum history (fig. 118) in all of its genres (e.g., period rooms, gallery exhibitions, historic houses, outdoor villages) just as we have historiographies of other major cultural institutions in the United States. One model to imitate is D. R. Rickeson's *Western Canadian History: Museum Interpretations,* a publication which contains an excellent historical overview of the parallels and polarities of western Canadian academic and museum history. The Rickeson anthology recognizes that, just as the writing of history reflects the interests, predilections, and even prejudices of a given generation, so does the exhibiting of history.[7]

The recent *Museum News* series on the "Pioneers of American Museums" is another start in the right direction; but where in the history field are the comprehensive biographies of Henry Mercer, Charles Montgomery, Justin Winsor, Harold Shurtleff, or Malcolm Watkins?[8] Why have not scholars of folklore analyzed the historical-museum profession the way Alan Dundes, in the very funny book *Urban Folklore from the Paper Empire* (1976), scrutinized American business professionals? How have the personalities and political ideologies of certain museum historians affected the exhibitions they mounted? Has there been a consensus school and a conflict school of history-museum interpretation? Was there a proto-Marxist or Socialist trend in the 1930s? What has the increase of professional design firms (fig. 119) meant for museums in the 1970s? Do we now have a "modern school" and a "clutter school"?

Ironically, other types of museums—particularly American art museums—have been far more conscientious in keeping and telling their histories.[9] In so doing they have occasionally been willing to subject their collection policies, administrative decisions, and, perhaps most important, the purpose, scope, and interpretations of their collections and exhibitions to historical interpretation. The historical-museum profession, I am persuaded, needs more critical interpreters who in public print and

Figure 118.
Plummer Hall, Essex Institute Museum Gallery (1916), Interior
View
(Courtesy Essex Institute, Salem, Mass.)

professional forum will offer careful, scholarly critiques of historical
museums from a historical perspective.

Museum and academic historians alike have pointed out that one excellent way to evaluate the historical museum and its interpretation of
the past is the exhibition review. Historian Wilcomb Washburn has been,
perhaps, the most continuous and most vocal scholar advocating the absolute necessity of such a review practice among serious scholars of
history in the history museums.[10] Yet today, most historical exhibitions,
if reported at all, are so reported only as cultural events in the society
pages where more attention is paid to those who attended the opening
than to the exhibit itself. Usually no indication is given that anyone created
this interpretation of history; it is as if the exhibition emerged, like Athene,
fully armed from the head of Zeus.

Professional museum historians should not tolerate such shoddy treatment. Nor should they tolerate their institutions' usurping the total credit
for the enormous time and energy that they expended in researching,
organizing, and creating what is, in fact, their "historical publication."[11]
Museum historians must step out from *behind* the history museum, out
from the closet of anonymity, and into the professional place of recogni-

Figure 119.
The Chicago History Galleries, 1979
Chicago Historical Society.
(Courtesy Staples and Charles, Designers, Washington, D.C.)

tion they deserve. In so doing, they must be prepared for the considered, published judgment of their peers so that standards for historical-museum exhibitions might continually improve and that innovations in exhibition techniques receive thorough discussion and dissemination.

Fortunately, a few hopeful signs suggest a growing awareness of the necessity of the exhibition review. In addition to the early reviews pioneered by Thomas Leavitt in *Technology and Culture* and by Kenneth Ames in the *Decorative Arts Society Newsletter*,[12] we now see an occasional detailed critique like Jay Cantor's of the Metropolitan Museum's "19th-Century America" exhibition in the *Winterthur Portfolio*.[13] The AASLH's *History News,* in its recently expanded format, has begun to devote a regular section of its pages to extended exhibition reviews. I hope that *History News* will follow the review guidelines of the Canadian National Museum of Man's *Material History Bulletin,* where the editors print commentaries by the museum curators and designers who prepared the exhibition in addition to the exhibition review by an outside critic.[14] In order to make my own American-material-culture students into more perceptive historical-museum visitors, I've devised an exercise that they can use as a set of critical guidelines where I launch them into a semester of "reviewing history museums along with reviewing history books."[15]

As historians, we should find the general lack of critical apparatus in the history-museum profession particularly distressing, given the fact that most exhibits, even so-called permanent ones, are a relatively singular and ephemeral type of history. Even the most esoteric historical monograph usually has a press run of at least five hundred to a thousand copies, whereas the exhibition "The Growth of the United States," mounted some years ago at the National Museum of History and Technology was the only "copy" of that historical research. Now it, like so many other history exhibits, is gone forever to historians. No one sought to preserve its totality in any systematic, scholarly way; no one tried to capture its essence in a critical exhibition review. I hope some scattered evidence (e.g., a catalog, a film, floor plans, still photography, a list of artifacts displayed, research reports, and notes) survives to aid in a historical reconstruction. I fear, however, that such historical data are usually collected and conserved in only the most haphazard fashion.

Ironically, we save an exhibition's artifacts but neglect to preserve, in some appropriate archival format, the context that gave these objects historical meaning. Outside of a usually cursory photographic depiction of gallery highlights, the art of properly documenting a historical exhibit remains in a primitive state. I am not proposing the wholesale preservation of history museum and historical exhibitions; that is neither feasible nor worth doing. I do laud, however, the experiments being tried by the staff of the Shelburne Museum, the Oakland Museum, and the Virginia Museum of Fine Arts to preserve and then re-use certain earlier museum settings as historiographical teaching tools.

Developing a feasible documentation system for historical-museum exhibitions for future study along with establishing a national network of exhibition reviews ought to heighten our understanding of the exhibition process as an intellectual activity. The exhibition process, suggests Harold Skramstad, has yet to receive the scholarly attention that the curatorial and research aspect of artifact study has. Literature concerned with the exhibition process has largely been left to art critics whose primary interest lies with the individual objects, or to social scientists whose concern is more with the behavior patterns of individual visitors than with the content and meaning of the exhibition. This is unfortunate, argues Skramstad,

> because it neglects a basic fact of life for museums: that the selective arrangement of artifacts and other related information in a public display is a museum's most fundamental means of communication, and that such displays or exhibitions are the basic building blocks for exploring the intersection of material culture and its larger constellations of meaning. Perhaps more than anything else a museum's exhibition environment is an accurate index of its attitude toward material culture.[16]

I have argued elsewhere that there are epistemologies behind historical-museum exhibitions.[17] Every historical exhibit is, in short, a manifestation of a historian's method. In the historical exhibition, as in the historical monograph, there should be a continual quest for the appropriate explanatory method, model, or metaphor. However, museum historians shy away from questions of historical epistemology—how they know what they know about the past and how they communicate that knowledge through the techniques of the exhibition. Historical epistemology is basic for the exploration and discovery of the world of material culture in history museums.

Nicholas Westbrook, coordinator of exhibitions in the education services division of the Minnesota Historical Society, recently struggled with those difficult questions in one of the few articles that I know of where a museum historian candidly and critically examined the historical methodology behind an exhibition he had conceived of and had constructed. His little essay, aptly titled "Decisions, Decisions,"[18] illuminates the kinds of research designs, collateral reading, and scholarly choices that must be made in analyzing and "translating" (to use Westbrook's word) an enormous 10,000-piece collection into a historical display for a modestly sized gallery. A history exhibition, like a history book, happens in the historian's mind as much as in a library or an artifact collection. The historical profession needs more of Westbrook's type of methodological scrutiny and intellectual rigor. Historical exhibitions, like history books, are reconstructions of the past. At their best, they are not the past recaptured; they are carefully conceived, thoroughly researched attempts to give the past a present form.

The History within the History Museum

The communal and primary task of those who teach history in the history museum is to help others think historically, or, as the title of one of Carl Becker's most famous essays proposes, to make "Everyman His Own Historian."[19] This is not to say that everyone should necessarily become a professional historian. Rather, one should acquire the skills of reading critically and intelligently history books, and of visiting history museums with perspicacity and pleasure.

A corollary to this teaching objective is an acceptance of both the provisional and contingent nature of history; history books are rewritten every generation and even permanent galleries are torn down every few decades.

The intriguing method of *remembering*—both individually and collectively—is what we seek to understand and to nurture in history education, whether we do it in communities, schools, or museums. Classroom students and teachers at present make up ten to fifteen percent of the annual attendance of most American museums. Education programs for this school audience take many forms—exhibitions, escorted tours, teacher education and curriculum workshops, and active participation by both teachers and students in the study of artifacts, documents, photographs, and historic sites. However, for most history museum staffs, as Barnes Riznik points out, "museum education is a new and unfamiliar responsibility which calls for rethinking many aspects of the traditional museum and requires special training."[20]

What might such rethinking entail? For one, I would suggest the exploration of some historical topics still largely unexamined by museum and academy historians. I think by now most of us are painfully aware that for generations, American history was something that happened primarily to prosperous white males in the middle years of life. Fortunately, we are increasingly sensitive, in exhibitions and books, to the role that gender and race have played in the past. But what do we know of the role of anxiety, pain, disease, sex, and death in American history?

We still need artifacts, exhibitions, and skillful history-museum historians to help us experience something of the isolation, the monotony, the scarcities, the boredom, and the high mortality rate of a frontier prairie existence. How does one convey the overwhelming dread of blizzard or drought? the fear of mortgage foreclosure? the anxiety of frequent childbirth? the uncertainty of fluctuating grain prices? the depression and loneliness? the instances of insanity and suicide that also characterized nineteenth-century American rural life? Might there be a *Wisconsin Death Trip* for every *Little House on the Prairie*?[21]

Recent trends in American religious historiography likewise have yet to be carefully and critically pursued by history museums (figs. 120, 121). To be sure, religion is present in many museum settings, particularly in historic churches and in outdoor historical villages, which invariably contain a single Georgian or Federal white clapboard church, but which are hardly suggestive of the extensive religious pluralism (and conflict) that existed in most American communities. Has the Great Awakening in eighteenth-century New England, the middle colonies, and Virginia ever been accurately portrayed in an American history museum? Is the acute social and religious radicalism of the Shakers (now ironically organized into a National Historic Communal Societies Association) very often depicted in the twentieth-century museum restorations of their way of life? I fear that the once bitterly maligned countercultures of earlier eras have been reconstructed into homogenized, respectable, middle-class cultural establishments. Museum historians must not let these simplistic interpretations continue.

Another task is to remember those whom Carl Sandburg's poem calls

Figure 120.
"Collections at the University of Notre Dame, 1870–1970"
Museum exhibition, University Archives (1989).
*(Photograph by Kevin Knepp. Courtesy University of
Notre Dame Archives)*

the "losers" in American history—those men and women who tried but
failed, aspired but did not achieve.

Fernand Braudel, the French scholar of the material culture of early
modern Europe, reminds us that "victorious events come about as the
result of many possibilities" and that "for one possibility which actually
is realized, innumerable others have drowned." Usually these others leave
little documentary trace for the historian. And yet Braudel adds, "it is
necessary to give them their place because the losing movements are
forces which have at every moment *affected* the final outcome."[22] We
tend to forget that the Wobblies and Molly Maguires, Knights of Labor
and Socialists, the Cherokee Nation and the "Celestial" Chinese were also
part of American history. In the city of Chicago, for instance, much attention is lavished on the remaining historic house museums of Prairie
Avenue's merchant princes, while the scene of one of the bitterest labor
conflicts in the 1877 national railroad strikes, a few blocks away, goes
largely unnoticed.[23]

A final topic that I would put on our research agenda for the 1980s
is consumer history. Most American history museums possess an abundant cache of consumer goods, the artifacts of a nation whom David

Figure 121.
Re-enactment of the Nineteenth-Century Harvest Festival, St. Mark's Chapel
of Ease, 1989
King's Landing Historical Settlement, St. John River, New Brunswick, Canada.
(Courtesy A. Gregg Finley, King's Landing Historical Settlement)

Potter has called a "people of plenty." Colonial Williamsburg, argues Cary Carson, may "well be the unique survivor, the last, best place to conjure up in people's imaginations the strange, *new* world of eighteenth-century consumerism."[24] A recent Minnesota Historical Society exhibition, *The Wishbook: Mail Order in Minnesota,* offers another example of the contribution that museum historians can make to our historical understanding of American consumerism—in this case, the time frame being the nineteenth century.[25] Mail order merchandising, catalogs (see figs. 25, 29, 31), and goods provide us with a range of historical data that enables students to grasp what an enormous "economic transformation," to use Robert Heilbroner's phrase,[26] took place in America between the Civil War and World War I—an overwhelming change involving mass production, mass marketing, mass advertising, mass transportation, mass communication, and mass consumption. Researching the consumer history of the twentieth century will be possible if imaginative projects like those conceived by Edith Mayo and Barbara Riley, two museum historians with an eye for the "connoisseurship of the future," continue to gather the artifacts of current everyday life.[27]

If these are a few of the new topics that might be pursued in education programs within history museums, might there be a characteristic method to the pursuit? I would propose a simple model focused on three objectives: 1) using the *inquiry approach* to history teaching; 2) concentrating research efforts on the *museum's collections;* and 3) developing a cadre of intelligent, perceptive *museum users.*

I anticipate that many historians know the inquiry approach, pioneered in this country by Francis Parker and John Dewey at the turn of the century and revived again in the 1960s by a third generation of progressive educators. The inquiry pedagogy sees every environment—school, museum, community—as a learning environment. Dewey, who is still worth re-reading on the role of history museums in public education, saw the museum as a learning laboratory where "experiments in history teaching" should take place.[28] This is a most appropriate analogy for the institutional context in which history-museum educators work, for it considers that learning environment as one where the original Greek meaning of the word "history" (to investigate, to inquire) applies in its fullest sense.[29] Teach technique, I would urge upon all of us who teach history. Or, to say it another way, teach method, historical method. Impart to students, whether they be eight or eighty, learning skills that will enable them to acquire historical knowledge and understanding for the rest of their lives.

To be sure, such history teaching is going on in schools and museums. I would, however, complain there is not enough of it and what there is is hard to discover. For example, in the historical profession there is no counterpart (other than Susan Lehman's valuable *Programs for Historic Sites and Houses*) to *The Art Museum as Educator,* [30] a sort of whole earth catalog of current innovations in the teaching of art in museums and schools. Speaking of catalogs, has any one ever tried to teach, say, a two-semester U.S. history survey course based entirely upon history-museum catalogs? I venture it could be done; the Smithsonian's 670-page *A Nation of Nations* catalog alone is certainly as large as any current history textbook.

To those of us who see great potential in a stronger alliance of historians teaching in the schools and those teaching in museums, I would impose a second imperative: we must teach all those who come to us to learn history how to *use* the history museum and how to *use* its unique asset: the museum's collections.

Collections are crucial to museum identity—tools, paintings, furniture, clothing and other artifacts make the history museum a novel depository for the study of the past. Such uniqueness should not be sacrificed. Museums occasionally have been too willing to respond to various demands of educational systems for satisfying experiences for their students solely on the school's terms. Unfortunately, some museums have taken on the undesirable function of becoming a mere extension of the traditional classroom. It would be a tragedy to watch history museums lose their special identity by becoming a tool for the schools to manipulate and mold to fit their needs.

I fear, however, that the history museum's unique identity and special resources remain misunderstood and underused. "If Public Libraries, Why Not Public Museums?" asked Edward S. Morse writing in the *Atlantic Monthly* in 1893.[31] Why not? Why do we historians teach our students how to use the library and archive so that they can forever return to explore its riches for fun and profit, but provide them with little museum training (only a few finding aids) and little sense that a history museum is a reference and research center? Nor, as I have suggested earlier, do we equip them with methods for critically evaluating the various forms of historical publication—exhibitions, simulations, demonstrations, walking tours—that they will encounter in the history museum. Ellie Caston, coordinator of interdisciplinary programs at the Carnegie Museum of Natural History and Art, goes right to the heart of the matter by insisting that "museums, in addition to everything else they may do, must be concerned with educating people about museums as museums . . . [with] developing audiences for museums—as multifaceted resources for use."[32]

Most visitors to a history museum, unlike visitors to an open-stack library, have little idea of the vast amount of historical evidence stored and cared for in history museums. They do not, and I acknowledge cannot, see all of the collections. But they should be able to see more than they do now and, within the limits of proper security and conservation practice, they should have access to *using* that material culture evidence that is part of their past (fig. 122). For example, Alexander Wall at Old Sturbridge Village and Karen Grochau at the Western Reserve Historical Society have encouraged intelligent visitor use of their museums.[33] In a *Roundtable Reports* issue some time back, I offered specific proposals—in the case of living history farms—of how history museums might afford the interested individual greater access to the history *within* the history museum.[34] Even if those ideas prove impractical for many museums, I would maintain that history museums should demonstrate to their patrons how they, as the history museums, do history; that is, the various stages of researching, classifying, designing, fabricating, mounting, and evaluating that are involved in a museum historian's practice of the historical method.

The History outside the History Museum

Such historical understanding can also be discovered *outside* the history museum. Already a wide assortment of historians with all sorts of titles—neighborhood historians, public historians, backyard historians, preservation historians—are rummaging around in what may be the largest, uncataloged, unclassified, unedited, and still largely uninterpreted collection of historical data that lies all around us, ever accessible, ever inexhaustible, ever changing.

The American landscape, despite all our celebration of it in verbal language (prose to poetry) and in visual expression (painting to photography) remains largely unresearched by professional historians. Yet the landscape, in all its variety, is an amazing historical document (figs. 18, 51, 70, 71). In fact, in his classic study of *The Making of the English Landscape,* W. G. Hoskins has gone so far as to insist the land and its artifacts are "the richest historical record we possess." To be sure, the language of any landscape is so dense with evidence and so complex and cryptic at times that we can never be certain we have read it all or that we have read it all right. Yet it is "a rich and beautiful book always open before us," argues J. B. Jackson. "We have but to learn to read it." We need only devise appropriate "looking strategies" to begin to understand its artifactual evidence.[35] In short, I propose we investigate this landscape as a gigantic, open-air historical archive, library, and museum wherein local and community history can be discovered, identified, classified, and interpreted by people in a personal and novel way. In such a context,

Figure 122.
Study Collections: Ceramics and Silver
The Margaret Woodbury Strong Museum
(Courtesy The Strong Museum, Rochester, N.Y.)

the rural agrarian countryside, the suburban tract development, or the central city core can be examined as a material culture collection, an assemblage of artifacts that includes every tangible, physical object of human ingenuity found extant on the land.[36]

How might such diverse historical evidence be examined? What shall we call this type of historical study? I have used the neologism, "above-ground archaeology," to identify my method, and I have called its study that of "the history on the land."[37] We have already used its approach in programs at the Indianapolis Museum of Art and the Chicago Historical Society. This past summer and fall we launched similar history projects *outside* the Cincinnati Historical Society and the Delaware Museum of Art.

The concept of above-ground archaeology is simple. Like the below-ground, prehistorical or historical archaeologist,[38] the *above*-ground archaeologist concentrates on using material objects and physical sites as primary evidence; on employing extensive fieldwork as a fundamental research technique; on adapting anthropological explanatory concepts (e.g., typology, diffusion, space-time patterns)[39] where feasible; and, on acquiring historical knowledge and understanding about humankind as the principle objective of any research investigation. The above-ground archaeologist simply does his or her "digging" into the past above-ground.

In the past decade, archaeologists themselves have endorsed such an approach in studying the American landscape. "A coherent and unified body of subject matter entirely appropriate to the archaeologist," writes James Deetz, "is the study of *all* the material aspects of culture in their behavioral context, regardless of provenance."[40] Historical and cultural geographers concur with this assumption. "The student of the cultural landscape is a kind of contemporary archaeologist," suggests Peirce Lewis; "with somewhat different materials, but very similar methods, and nearly identical motives, we are all trying to understand the human condition—nothing less."[41]

In addition to its obvious debts to archaeology as traditionally conceived, above-ground archaeology borrows much of its theory and practice from related fields such as art history, geography, architectural history, history of urban and town planning, folkways research, and the history of technology. Above-ground archaeology also goes by various synonyms—environmental history, material-culture studies, backyard history, urban archaeology, history under foot, nearby history, landscape archaeology.[42] In Great Britain, the undertaking is often called landscape history or history on the ground. In fact, the British have been the pioneers of such an approach to local history in the world's English-speaking countries.[43]

Above-ground archaeology has, likewise, been heavily influenced by American scholarship. The ideas of landscape historians such as Grady

Clay and J. B. Jackson are invaluable to any environment interpreter; cultural geographers such as John Fraser Hart and Fred Kniffen, along with historical geographers like Peirce Lewis and John Stilgoe are required reading for anyone anxious to pick up clues for evaluating the landscape.[44]

A common denominator uniting these assorted above-ground archaeologists is their recognition that a diverse collection of American material culture survives in our everyday environment and is usually not found within the confines of our historical museums or historical societies. Here I would like to propose a few ways in which this approach to using local artifacts as indices to local history can be applied to a community's natural and built environment outside the history museum.

From the creation of the first New England commons and the earliest town-planning designs such as that by Pierre Enfant for Washington, D.C., Americans have been creating all sorts of town plans and public landscapes that are significant historical data to the above-ground archaeologist (see figs. 83, 91, 98, 99). The placement, size, design, and vegetation of city parks, market malls, arboretums, public gardens, and other planned civic open spaces reveal to the landscape historian an amazing amount of information about a town's social, political, cultural, recreational, and even medical history.

Each of these artifacts has been studied separately by naturalists, botanists, and a new breed of historians calling themselves environmental or ecological historians.[45] It is possible, as Galen Cranz has demonstrated in researching the history of American city parks, to construct a typology by which to interpret this material-culture form in a particular locale.[46] Phoebe Cutler has done the same for the living evidence of numerous WPA and CCC projects that were planted in the 1930s and 1940s.[47]

An indefatigable explorer of both natural and man-made urban artifacts, Grady Clay, author of *Close-Up: How to Read the American City,* prompts us to ferret out the historical information implicit in the assorted streets and street names—be they boulevards or parkways, avenues or roads, simple lanes or byways—found in most American urban environments. Clay has made a special study of "alleys," as has James Borchert in Washington.[48] Clay acknowledges, as do street historians Anthony Vidler and Bernard Rudofsky,[49] that to be able to understand city streets as historical markers, the above-ground archaeologist should classify them by a simple typology; for just as there are ceramic and house types, so there are street types: trader trails and toll roads, main streets of business districts, linear ribbon developments, commercial/highway strips, and limited access and interstate systems.

When the above-ground archaeologist walks the city's streets, I suggest watching for what I call "time collages" and what below-ground archaeologists call a "tell." Often one will find a series of artifacts from different eras in a community's history lined up along a single streetscape or clustered about a civic space (fig. 123). As an above-ground researcher, one can discover architectural styles "layered" vertically just as the below-ground archaeologist searches for potsherds in a horizontal stratigraphy.

In doing landscape-history fieldwork, consider every building as a historic site. For example, whatever has been added is important; whatever was removed tells a tale; whatever was never completed (such as the second half of Chicago's Newberry Library, halted in construction by the panic of 1893) raises historical questions for the explorer of urban artifacts. When "reading" a house, the smallest details can yield ideas: an archway in Philadelphia or an ice box on a façade in Alexandria, Virginia, are clues to the building's former use as a stable or a slaughterhouse now transformed into a residence and an apartment building. Such conversions abound on the landscape: one-room Indiana schoolhouses and interurban stations made over into private homes; breweries turned into shopping centers; public liveries in Chicago converted into gas stations.

Above-ground archaeology takes a particular interest in American vernacular building in its multiplicity of forms: the hall-and-parlor, the shotgun, the bungalow, the four-over-four, the row house or the Georgian I-house. These structures are crucial primary evidence for identifying and interpreting the local history of a community through its surviving residential environment.

Inasmuch as architectural historians have tended to concern themselves only with the so-called high or academic styles, the other ninety-five percent of surviving American domestic buildings has gone largely uninvestigated and unappreciated. Fortunately, settlement geographers, folkways experts, popular-culture enthusiasts, and historians like Dell Upton have become intrigued with how and where average Americans live.[50] The above-ground archaeologist freely borrows from their pioneering field study and archival research in order to construct working definitions and tentative typologies. Vernacular building—be it Mormon central-hall housing in the West, dog-trot homes of the South, cobblestone structures of the country's heavily glaciated regions, the upright-and-wing buildings of New England and the Midwest (see fig. 82), or the ubiquitous, prefabricated, catalog architecture of mail-order houses such as Sears, Roebuck—remains a vital artifactual collection for urban-history museum research (see figs. 32, 33).

Thinking in terms of commonplace, statistically representative housing prompts us to be cognizant of a community's neighborhoods: who has lived where, when, and why. Local material-culture evidence often

Figure 123.
"Time Collage," Government Center, Boston, Massachusetts, 1980
Faneuil Hall, 1740–42 (*center, rear*); the nineteenth-century Crescent Office
Building (*right*); and the Brutalist architecture of 1969 Boston City Hall (*left*).
(*Photograph by author*)

identifies the ethnicity of a place through its churches, place-names, types
of businesses, and communal institutions. For instance, numerous artifacts
immediately impress a visitor as to how heavily Germanic was the
nineteenth-century "Over-the-Rhine" district in Cincinnati, the *Nord Seite*
of Chicago, or any number of Teutonic enclaves in Indianapolis. In 1893,
when the Germans built their cultural activities center at 401 East Michigan
Street in Indianapolis, they called it *Das Deutsche Haus,* a fact that the
structure's iconography makes very clear. However, one is puzzled by
the imposing, out-of-scale, classical marquee, that appears to have been
added later, and proclaims the building to be "The Athenaeum." A bit
of further research clears up the mystery first raised by the artifactual
evidence: the name change is the result of strong anti-German prejudice
during World War I when many Germans altered their surnames and those
of their institutions to avoid ethnic discrimination. Population shifts in
ethnic neighborhoods, as in the Pilsen area of Chicago (originally Czech,
now Hispanic), can also be spotted in changes in the names of parishes
and businesses, and also in the presence of distinctive street mural art.
    Industrial archaeology, of course, must be included in any approach

to exploring the history outside the history museum. Research by Robert Vogel, Larry Lankton, Theodore Sande, and Kenneth Hudson provides models for an area of study still almost virgin territory for the professional and amateur alike.[51] Mine shafts, canal segments, trolley and streetcar lines, abandoned factories, old sewer systems, water towers, quarries, workers' housing, and numerous other artifacts lie about on the land, waiting for identification, classification, and interpretation to help us better understand local and community history and the history of technology, labor, business, and government.

American technology and industry have produced all forms of material-culture evidence, but few of their progeny have had such a widespread impact as the automobile. This movable artifact (fig. 124) has practically reoriented the nation's countryside and cityscape. The horseless carriage has nurtured what historian James Flink calls "the American car culture." Or, as Marshall McLuhan puts it, "The car, in a word, has quite refashioned all of the spaces that unite and separate men."[52]

Some historians, preservationists, and museum curators may scoff at the American highway and its artifacts as a source of historical study and museum exhibitions, but to anyone interested in probing the attitudes of the typical American—who now changes his address every five years, drives more than 10,000 miles annually, and eats every third meal outside his home—the omnipresence of gasoline stations, tourist camps, shopping centers, and drive-ins looms as a significant cultural phenomenon.[53] On the commercial strip where buildings are diminutive, neon or electric signs are gigantic and expensive. Has not the huge graphic sign in space become the monumental architecture of the American highway landscape? Is it not possible, as Robert Venturi has argued, "to learn from Las Vegas?"[54] Should we not, as Peter Smith and Chester Liebs of the Society for Commercial Archaeology argue, give serious attention to identifying and interpreting (perhaps even collecting?) the pluralistic, eclectic, vernacular, regional manifestations of this "neon culture"?

As is probably apparent by now, these suggestions for greater recognition of the history that is outside the history museum have a strong populist flavor. This is the avowed objective of the above-ground archaeology, for this historical approach considers the "city as a museum," the "city as an artifact." As urban historian Sam Bass Warner proposed, "Every city and town is a living museum of the past. . . . Given the nature of urban growth, somewhat in the manner of rings of a tree, the artifacts of the past are all around us. Moreover, these artifacts reflect some of the most important forces governing the development of the future city."[55] I, like Warner, would like to see us value "people's history" as

Figure 124.
Studebaker Champion, 1939
Advertising and publicity photograph for Studebaker Corporation.
(Courtesy National Studebaker Museum, South Bend, Indiana)

a primary agenda for history teachers and history museum curators, that is, to show average citizens various ways of knowing themselves and their communities through an understanding of their own past and the past of others.

Conclusion

This tripartite job description for the museum historian parallels that to which I also aspire as an academic historian. I research, lecture at scholarly meetings, write and publish specialized research with and for other professionals. I am persuaded that this component of my work as a historian is absolutely crucial to the other two aspects of my professional responsibilities as a teacher and as a citizen. Museum historians, no matter what their institutional tasks, also need an intellectual life of their own, a significant area of the past in which they are expert and to which they contribute new knowledge and understanding. I am convinced that if a historian is to be genuinely creative in stimulating intellectual discovery and learning in others, he or she must concurrently be involved in some type of intellectual quest and original research on his own or with other professionals.

Yet as Alfred Kazin correctly reminds us, "history must be felt by many people, not just admired by individual connoisseurs."[56] Hence, in addition to my work with professional peers, I also research, lecture, and write history for and with a wider constituency—university students, usually within the classrooms of the academy but increasingly (with the gracious indulgence of museum historians) also in the galleries of history museums. Most museum historians, whether or not they work in a museum education department, are also involved in the formal education business.

John Dewey's famous dictum that "the aim of education is to enable individuals to continue their education" should also inspire our mutual aspiration to nurture a historical sensitivity among our fellow citizens who, unlike us, spend most of their lives outside the history museum. I consider it my obligation as a professional historian and as a university teacher to share both my techniques of inquiry into the past and my understanding of that past with those whom the George Washington University Center for Museum Education publication identifies as *Lifelong Learning/Adult Audiences* and whom I know as community members.[57] Museum historians do such public teaching day in and day out. Fortunately, the education, the entertainment, and the enrichment of the democratic populace have always been among the purposes of the American history museum ever since Charles Willson Peale opened his doors in Philadelphia in 1785.

In our own time, we historians are slowly realizing that, as Warwick in Shakespeare's *Henry IV* told us long ago, "there is a history in all men's lives." To discover the full significance of that poignant epigram we should look at the history behind, within and outside the history museum.

Notes

1. Charles Coleman Sellers, *Mr. Peale's Museum: Charles Willson Peale and the First Popular Museum of Natural Science and Art* (New York: W. W. Norton 1980).

2. Cary Carson, et. al., *Teaching History at Colonial Williamsburg: A Plan of Education* (Williamsburg: The Curriculum Committee, 1977), 60. I am particularly indebted to Dr. Carson for sharing a copy of this innovative document with me.

3. E. McClung Fleming, "The Period Room as a Curatorial Publication," *Museum News* 50.10 (1972): 39–43.

4. *Program for Museum Education Studies* (Washington, D.C.: George Washington University School of Education and Allied Services, 1979), 2.

5. Walter Muir Whitehill, *Independent Historical Societies* (Boston: The Boston Athenaeum, 1962); Leslie W. Dunlap, *American Historical Societies, 1790–1860* (Madison, Wis.: Wisconsin Historical Society, 1944).

6. Edward Alexander, *Museums in Motion: An Introduction to the History and Functions of Museums* (Nashville: American Association for State and Local History, 1979); Melinda Young Frye, "Charles Wilcomb, Museum Pioneer," *The Museum of California* 1.5; Dianne H. Pilgrim, "Inherited from the Past: The American Period Room," *The American Art Journal* 10.1: 5–23; Katharine Rich, "Beacon," *Old-Time New England* 66 (1976): 42–60.

7. D. R. Rickeson, *Western Canadian History: Museum Interpretations,* History Division Paper No. 27 (Ottawa: National Museum of Man, Mercury Series, 1979).

8. On Mercer, see Donna G. Rosenstein, "Historic Human Tools: Henry Chapman Mercer and His Collection, 1897–1930," master's thesis, University of Delaware/Winterthur Museum, (1977).

9. Nathaniel Burt, *A Social History of the American Art Museum* (Boston: Little, Brown, 1977); Daniel M. Fox, *Engines of Culture: Philanthropy and Art Museums* (Madison, Wis.: Wisconsin State Historical Society, 1963).

10. Wilcomb Washburn and Gordon Gibson, Letter, *Museum News* 42.6 (February 1964): 7; Wilcomb Washburn, "The Dramatization of American Museums," *Curator* 6.2: 109–24.

11. Fleming, "Period Room as a Curatorial Publication," 39–40.

12. Thomas W. Leavitt, "Toward a Standard of Excellence: The Nature and Purpose of Exhibit Reviews," *Technology and Culture* 9 (January 1968): 70–75 and his "The Need for Critical Standards in History Museum Exhibits: A Case in Point," *Curator* 10.2 (June 1967): 91–94.

13. Jay Cantor, "When Wine Turns to Vinegar: The Critics' View of 19th Century America," in *Winterthur Portfolio 7,* ed. Ian M. G. Quimby (Charlottesville: University Press of Virginia, 1972), 1–27.

14. For example, see Zane Lewis's exhibition review of "The World of Children: Toys and Memories of Childhood" with a commentary by Ivan Sayers in *Material History Bulletin* 9 (Fall 1979): 51–60.

15. Consult app. II, "American Material Culture Technique: The Historical Museum Exhibition Review," in Thomas J. Schlereth, *Artifacts and the American Past: Techniques for the Historian* (Nashville: American Association for State and Local History, 1980), 233–34.

16. Harold K. Skramstad, Jr., "Interpreting Material Culture: A View from the Other Side of the Glass," in *Material Culture and the Study of American Life,* ed. Ian M. G. Quimby (W. W. Norton, 1978), 175–76.

17. Thomas J. Schlereth, "It Wasn't That Simple," reprinted in this volume as chapter 13.

18. Nicholas Westbrook, "Decisions, Decisions: An Exhibit's Invisible Ingredient," *Minnesota History* 45.7: 292–96.

19. Carl Becker, "Everyman His Own Historian," *American Historical Review* 37 (1932): 221–36.

20. Barnes Riznik and Deborah Pope, *Hawaii's Museums and the Schools* (Honolulu: Hawaii Museums Association: Paper Number 8, 1979), 7.

21. Michael Lesey, *Wisconsin Death Trip* (New York: Pantheon Books, 1973); Laura Ingalls Wilder, *The Little House on the Prairie* (New York: Harper & Row, 1971).

22. Fernand Braudel, *Capitalism and Material Life, 1400–1800* (New York: Harper & Row, 1978), xiv–xv.

23. Compare, for example, the extensive coverage of the Prairie Avenue capitalists in Victor Dyer, *Prairie Avenue* (Chicago: Chicago Architectural Foundation, 1977) and William Adelman, *Pilsen and Chicago's West Side* (Chicago: Illinois Labor History Society, 1984).

24. David Potter, *People of Plenty: Economic Abundance and the American Character* (Chicago: University of Chicago Press, 1954); Carson, *Teaching History at Williamsburg,* 8.

25. Joan Siedl and Nicholas Westbrook, *The Wishbook: Mail Order in Minnesota—An Exhibition at the Minnesota Historical Society* (St. Paul, Minn.: Minnesota Historical Society, 1978).

26. Robert Heilbroner, *The Economic Transformation of America* (New York: Harcourt, Brace, 1977).

27. Edith P. Mayo, "Connoisseurship of the Future," unpublished paper, Division of Political History, Smithsonian Institution, n.d.; Barbara Riley, "Contemporary Collecting: A Case History," *Decorative Arts Newsletter* 4.3: 3–6.

28. Peter Martorella, "John Dewey, Problem Solving, and History Teaching," *Social Studies* 69.5: 190–94; Randolph S. Bourne, *The Gary Schools* (Boston: Houghton Mifflin, 1916), 24–26; Stephen Botein, *Experiments in History Teaching* (Cambridge, Mass.: Harvard–Danforth Center for Teaching and Learning, 1977).

29. Thomas J. Schlereth, "A Question is an Answer: An Experimental Inquiry in American Cultural History," *The History Teacher* 6.1 (1974): 97–106. Examples of excellent collaborative history teaching between schools and history museums would include projects such as Dolly Sherwood, "Historical Goodies Crammed in Old Camelback Trunks," *Smithsonian* (June 1977): 106–13 and Martin E. Sleeper's article, "Teaching about Work in History: A Museum Curriculum for the Schools," *The History Teacher* 11.2: 159–74.

30. Barbara Y. Newsom and Adele Z. Silver, eds., *The Art Museum as Educator* (Berkeley: University of California Press, 1978); Susan Lehman, *Program for Historic Sites and Houses Sourcebook #3* (Washington, D.C.: Center for Museum Education, 1978). A British study by John A. Fairly, *History Teaching through Museums* (London: Longman, 1977) and a Canadian one by J. Patrick Wohler, *The History Museum as an Effective Educational Institution* (Ottawa: National Museum of Man, Mercury Series, Paper No. 4, 1976) are of use in this context.

31. Edward S. Morse, "If Public Libraries, Why Not Public Museums?" *Atlantic Monthly* 72 (July–December 1893): 112.

32. Ellie Caston, "An Interdisciplinary Approach to Education," *Museum News* 57.2 (1978): 52.

33. Alexander J. Wall, "The Case for Popular Scholarship at Old Sturbridge Village," *Museum News* 47.5: 14–19; Karen Grochau, *"To See"* A Museum—A Guide to the Western Reserve Historical Society (Cleveland: Western Reserve Historical Society, n.d.); Leni Buff, Laurie Kaplowitz, and Ken Yellis, *Include Me In* (Washington, D.C.: Smithsonian Institution, National Portrait Gallery, 1977).

34. Thomas J. Schlereth, "Collecting Ideas and Artifacts: Common Problems of History Museums and History Texts," *Roundtable Reports* (Summer/Fall 1978): 11–12.

35. W. G. Hoskins, *The Making of the English Landscape* (London: Hodder and Soughton, 1963), 14; J. B. Jackson, *Landscape* 1.1 (Spring 1951): 5.

36. D. W. Meinig, "Introduction," *The Interpretation of Ordinary Places* (New York: Oxford University Press, 1979), 6.

37. Borrowing from archaeologist John L. Cotter's slightly similar use of the term in an essay titled, "Above-Ground Archaeology" (*American Quarterly* 26.3 [August 1974]: 266–80), I first argued for the methodology in a short study, "The City as Artifact," *American Historical Association Newsletter* 15.2 (1977): 7–9. In this context, see also Bert Salwen, "Archaeology in Megalopolis," in *Research and Theory in Current Archaeology,* ed. Charles L. Redman (London, New York: John Wiley and Sons, 1973), 151–63; David R. Goldfield, "Living History: The Physical City as Artifact and Teaching Tool," *The History Teacher* 8.4: 535–56.

38. Definitions of these three archaeological perspectives on three major chronological periods can be found in James B. Griffin's "The Pursuit of Archaeology in the United States," *American Anthropologist* 61 (1959): 379–88; Douglas Schwartz, "North American Archaeology in Historical Perspective," *Actes du Congres International d' Histoire de Sciences* 2 (Warsaw and Cracow, 1968): 311–15; Gordon Wiley and Philip Phillips, "Method and Theory in American Archaeology, II: Historical-Developmental Interpretations," *American Archaeologist* 57: 723–819; and Gordon R. Wiley and Jeremy A. Sabloff, *A History of American Archaeology* (San Francisco: W. H. Freeman, 1974).

39. Perhaps the most useful introduction to the principles, practices, and problems of modern archaeological study is James Deetz's *Invitation to Archaeology* (Garden City, N. Y.: Doubleday/Natural History Press, 1967).

40. James Deetz, "Archaeology as a Social Science," *Bulletin of the American Anthropological Association* 3.3 (Part 2): 115–25.

41. Peirce Lewis, "Axioms of the Landscape," *Journal of Architectural Education* 30 (September 1976): 8.

42. For example, Michael Aston and Trevor Rowley, *Landscape Archaeology: An Introduction to Field Work Techniques on Post-Roman Landscapes* (London: David and Charles, 1974); Henry Glassie, *Pattern in the Material Folk Culture of the Eastern United States* (Philadelphia: University of Pennsylvania Press, 1968); David Weitzman, *Underfoot: An Everyday Guide to Exploring the American Past* (New York: Charles Scribner's Sons, 1976); David Kyvig and Myron Marty, *Nearby History* (Arlington Heights, Ill.: AHM Publishing Corporation, 1980); John R. Kinard, "The Neighborhood Museum and the Inner City," *Architecture Yearbook* 14 (1974): 108–11; Zora Martin Felton, *A Walk Through "Old" Anacostia* (Washington, D.C.: Smithsonian Institution, Anacostia Neighborhood Museum, 1975).

43. Penelope Lively, *The Presence of the Past: An Introduction to Landscape History* (London: William Collins and Sons, 1976); Maurice Beresford, *History on the Ground: Six Studies in Maps and Landscapes,* rev. ed. (London: Methuen, 1971): and W. G. Hoskins, *The Making of the English Landscape.*

44. Grady Clay, *Close-Up: How to Read the American City* (New York: Praeger, 1973); John Leighly, ed., *Land and Life: A Selection from the Writings of Carl Ortwin Sauer* (Berkeley: University of California Press, 1963); John Fraser Hart, *The Look of the Land* (Englewood Cliffs, N.J.: Prentice-Hall, 1975); Fred Kniffen, "Louisiana House Types," *Annals, American Association of Geographers* 26 (1936): 179–93; Pierce Lewis, *New Orleans: The Making of an Urban Landscape* (Cambridge, Mass.: Ballinger, 1976); John R. Stilgoe, "Jack-o-Lanterns to Surveyors: The Secularization of Landscape Boundaries," *Environmental Review* (1976): 14–32.

45. See, for instance, the recent scholarship of Roderick Nash, *The American Environment: Readings in the History of Conservation,* 2d ed. (Reading, Mass.: Addison-Wesley, 1976); and the literature published in *Environmental Review,* the quarterly journal of the American Environmental History Society.

46. Galen Cranz, "Changing Roles of Urban Parks: From Pleasure Gardens to Open Space," *Landscape* 22.3 (1978): 9–18.

47. Phoebe Cutler, "On Recognizing a WPA Rose Garden or a CCC Privy," *Landscape* 20.2 (1976): 3–9.

48. Grady Clay, *Alleys: A Hidden Resource* (Louisville, Ky.: Grady Clay and Company, 1978); also see James Borchert, "Alley Landscapes of Washington, D.C.," *Landscape* 23.3 (1979): 3–10.

49. Anthony Vidler, "The Scenes of the Street: Transforming Ideal and Reality, 1750–1871," *On Streets* (Cambridge, Mass.: MIT Press, 1978), 29–112; Bernard Rudofsky, *Streets for People: A Primer for Americans* (Garden City, N. Y.: Doubleday, 1969).

50. Dell Upton, ed., *Vernacular Architecture Newsletter,* Department of Architecture, University of California, Berkeley, California 94720.

51. Robert Vogel, ed., *A Report of the Mohawk-Hudson Area Survey: A Selective Recording of the Industrial Archaeology of the Mohawk and Hudson River Valleys in the Vicinity of Troy, New York, June–September, 1969* (Washington, D.C.: Smithsonian Institution Press, 1973); Theodore A. Sande, *Industrial Archaeology: A New Look at the American Heritage* (Brattleboro, Vt.: Stephen Green Press, 1976); Donald E. Sackheim, *Historic American Engineering Record Catalog* (Washington, D.C.: National Park Service, 1976).

52. James T. Flink, *The Car Culture* (Cambridge, Mass.: Harvard University Press, 1975); Marshall McLuhan, *Understanding Media: The Extension of Man* (New York: New American Library, 1964), 201; also see John B. Rae, *The Road and the Car in American Life* (Cambridge, Mass.: Harvard University Press, 1971).

53. Bruce A. Lohof, "The Service Station in America: The Evolution of Vernacular Form," *Industrial Archaeology* 2.2 (Spring 1974):1–13; John A. Jakle, "The American Gasoline Station, 1920–1970," *Journal of American Culture* 1.3: 520–42; David I. Vieyra, *Fill 'Er Up: An Architectural History of America's Gasoline Stations* (New York: Macmillan, 1979).

54. Robert Venturi, Denise Scott Brown, and Stephen Izenour, *Learning from Las Vegas* (Cambridge, Mass.: Massachusetts Institute of Technology Press, 1972).

55. Sam Bass Warner, "An Urban Historian's Agenda for the Profession," *History and the Role of the City in American Life* (Indianapolis: Indianapolis Historical Society, 1972), 56–58.

56. Alfred Kazin, *New York Review of Books* (23 October 1963): 25.

57. Center for Museum Education, *Lifelong Learning/Adult Audiences, Sourcebook #1* (Washington, D.C.: George Washington University, 1978).

Figure 125.
Charles Willson Peale, *The Artist in His Museum*, 1822
Oil on canvas.
(Courtesy The Pennsylvania Academy of the Fine Arts, Philadelphia.
Gift of Mrs. Sarah Harrison, The Joseph Harrison, Jr. Collection)

Pioneers of Material Culture:
Teaching History with American Things

I have had continuing qualms about being considered as an appropriate individual for this Masters series. I have no hesitation, however, about the five individuals whom I discuss below. Without question, they produced masterworks in material culture studies. They are a cross-section of notable and influential history teachers who early on recognized the value of artifactual evidence and included it in their researching and understanding of the past. They are among my personal role models although I never met any of them.

Charles Willson Peale connects me with my early interest in the eighteenth-century Enlightenment. He also represents, in my judgment, the first American to think of museums as artifacts. Charles P. Wilcomb, a cultural historian, in addition to pioneering the period room as a material culture form, promoted history education in schools and museums. To John Dewey, I am indebted for the inquiry method, the hands-on approach, and his recognition of the abundant history-outside-the-history-museum. Thomas J. Wertenbaker was one of the first traditionally trained historians to integrate vernacular architecture, historical archaeology, and the decorative arts in his research and writing. Charles Montgomery, whose many students I know from Winterthur and Yale, developed the material culture exercise of connoisseurship to a high art.

In the five vignettes of these genuine masters of the artifact, I resort again to intellectual history, particularly one of its subgenres known as intellectual biography. A longer version of the study appeared in *Historians/Artifacts/Learners* (p. 304) which we affectionately called *HAL,* thinking of the computer in Arthur Clarke's *Space Odyssey: 2001.* An early draft also acted as dress rehearsal for the eventual survey I did of the intellectual history of the material culture movement in *Material Culture Studies in America.*

Several other scholars have recently contributed important research in the historiography of history museums and are not found in this chapter's endnotes. For example, Edward Alexander's *Museums in Motion: An Introduction to the History and Functions of Museums* (Nashville: American Association for State and Local History, 1979) and his *Museum Masters: Their Museums and Their Influence* (Nashville: American Association for State and Local History, 1983) survey several

---

This article originally appeared in *History News* 37.9 (September 1982): 28–32.

American institutions. I have also learned much from Neil Harris, "Museums, Merchandising, and Popular Taste: The Struggle for Influence," in *Material Culture and the Study of American Life,* ed. Ian M. G. Quimby (New York: Winterthur-Norton, 1978), 140–74; Melinda Young Frye, "The Beginnings of the Period Room in American Museums: Charles P. Wilcomb's Colonial Kitchen, 1896, 1906, 1910," in *The Colonial Revival in America,* ed. Alan Axelrod (New York: Winterthur-Norton, 1985), 217–40; Michael Wallace, "Visiting the Past: History Museums in the United States," *Radical History Review* 25 (1981): 63–96; and Jo Blatti's *Past Meets Present* (Washington, D.C.: Smithsonian Institution, 1987). Simon Bronner's *Folklife Studies from the Gilded Age: Object, Rite, and Custom in Victorian America* (Ann Arbor: UMI Research Press, 1987) provides an excellent historical overview of late nineteenth- and early twentieth-century folklorists and their interest in material culture.

In "Designing the Past: History Museum Exhibitions from Peale to the Present," published in *History Museums and Historical Societies in the United States,* ed. Warren Leon and Roy Rosenzwieg (Urbana: University of Illinois Press, 1989), Gary Kulik provides a critical analysis of several museums. Kulik approaches the topic in a way similar to the technique of intellectual biography I use here. We both like Emerson's suggestion that certain institutions are but the lengthened shadow of an individual. Kulik writes perceptively of George Brown Goode's Smithsonian and R. T. H. Halsey's American Wing at New York's Metropolitan Museum of Art and, concludes with the hero of his piece, Louis C. Jones, at Cooperstown. In a coda, Kulik provides us with a brief and insightful overview of the contemporary American museum scene since the appearance of the endowments (the National Endowment for the Humanities and the National Endowment for the Arts) and the professional design firms.

The American historian Carl Becker once defined history simply as "that memory of things said and things done in the past." Within the formal history establishment, the work of most historians has been primarily based on "things said," especially from literary sources like newspapers, congressional debates, and presidential edicts. Even when depicting history as "things done," verbal evidence such as treaties, governmental legislation, or court decisions provides the basis of perspective. Words and deeds appear to be the hallmark of the historian's craft. On first glance, there appears to have been little attention paid to "things"— physical objects such as food, clothing, or shelter—as evidence in historical research and teaching.

Simply paging through recent issues of *History News* reveals that a considerable amount of fascinating work has been going on in teaching American history using material culture. For example, we have Fred Schroeder's "Schoolhouse Reading" (April 1981), Betty Doak Elder's "Mid-South Teachers Take the Local Route to American History" (September 1980), Ann Nickerson's "Teaching Hometown Heritage" (September 1981), and Linda Lange's "Learning to Care" (July 1980), to mention but a few articles on innovative activity in the field.

In short, the disciplinary perspectives of historical archaeology, social history, cultural and historical geography, history of technology, art and decorative arts history, cultural anthropology, and folklife studies are all making valuable pedagogical contributions to history education. Teachers in these fields recognize that American things deserve a place in American history interpretation and that without looking at material culture, historical awareness and understanding can be incomplete, distorted, or quite wrong.

Has this perception always been so? Is there a history of material culture history? Or, is there a history of *teaching* history with material culture? To all of these questions the answer is both yes and no. Contemporary interest in teaching history using artifactual data does seem quite widespread. *History News* and other publications such as *Social Education, Museum Roundtable Reports,* and *The History Teacher* contain many examples of this interest. And *Historians/Artifacts/Learners: The Working Papers,* available through the proceedings of a colloquium of history-museum professionals, museum educators, and university and secondary school teachers held at Colonial Williamsburg, reflects future directions in teaching with material culture. Many other scattered examples of past history instruction employing American artifacts exist. Over the past decades, there have been exemplary teachers who have used material culture in their teaching of American history.

I have deliberately highlighted individuals rather than institutions because I believe that most good teaching is a personal art. Behind the obvious and impressive contributions to the field of teaching material culture at a place such as the Smithsonian lie the achievements of individuals such as a Spencer Baird or a Malcolm Watkins. In limiting the selection to but a few representatives, I recognize that I have neglected many others. For the moment, my heuristic handful of past history teachers who have recognized the value of artifactual evidence will have to stand as symbolic figures for the many other similarly motivated individuals who have worked, unknown and unappreciated, in schools, museums, historical societies, and agencies.

Charles Willson Peale: Exhibits as Historical Explanation

The American interest in material culture originated in the assorted borderlands and hinterlands of the early nineteenth-century's expanding universe of knowledge. The first people to realize its didactic potential were an eclectic mélange of museum founders, curators and benefactors as well as early antique collectors, historic preservationists, antiquarians, and local history enthusiasts. Charles Willson Peale (see fig. 125), the founder of perhaps the first great collection of material culture in America and one of the nation's earliest museums, personified many of the interests of these dilettanti. An avid collector of every type of object—Indian artifacts, wax effigies of all the human species, the Great Mastodon exhumed from upstate New York—Peale's particular insight into teaching history with objects came from his pioneering work as a museum exhibitor and designer.

Peale recognized two important, if somewhat contradictory, functions of artifacts in teaching history. First, he made use of material culture in order to promote visual and tactile responses to the past. To see, to touch a fragment of the past firsthand, to experience directly a surviving historical activity, remains one of the obvious pedagogical strategies to which we all turn when using material culture data. On a basic level, this affective mode of knowing prompts intellectual curiosity and creative wonder; on another level, the technique often allows us to measure our own cultural perspective in time and place. For, as art historian Jules Prown has suggested, by undertaking cultural interpretation through artifacts, we can begin to comprehend another culture not with our minds—the seat of many of our cultural biases—but with our senses. "This affective mode of apprehension," writes Prown, that allows "us to put ourselves, figuratively speaking, inside the skins of individuals who commissioned, made, used or enjoyed these objects, to see with their own eyes and touch with their hands, to identify with them emphatically, is clearly a different way of engaging the past than abstractly through the written word. Instead of our minds making intellectual contact with minds of the past, our senses make affective contact with the senses of the past."

From what we know of his exhibits from 1786 to 1827 at the Peale Museum in Philadelphia and from his writings, Peale had a sense of this use of the past. He, with a sophistication practically unknown among his peers, also recognized that a history museum's exhibition environment itself was one of its more vital teaching tools. He was aware that objects collected unsystematically or without any particular intellectual framework would provide little insight into the past. Peale realized that the raw data in the historical collections could not be properly understood or effectively used unless it was organized in such a way that one object would be seen in the context of others, and in conjunction with additional information. As historians Harold Skramstad and Charles Sellers have pointed out, people recognized that perhaps the highest interpretive level of a historical exhibition of past material culture is its visual storage and arrangement. In short, museum exhibits are historical publications, and the exhibiting process is a highly creative activity just like writing a history text.

Finally, ardent democrat that he was, Peale saw historical museums as history books for the general populace. The very process by which historical materials are brought together, classified, organized, displayed, arranged, and rearranged in the mode of communicating history—commonly known as public interpretive exhibits—is part of his legacy to modern historians.

Charles P. Wilcomb: Taking Objects to the Schools

One of Peale's late nineteenth-century heirs was Charles P. Wilcomb, a New England collector-scholar transplanted to the west coast and the founding curator of the Golden Gate Park Museum and the Oakland Public Museum. During an all-too-brief professional life of some twenty years (1895–1915), Wilcomb personified several of the traits of an emerging cadre of professional scholars impressed with the explanatory potential of material culture. As a self-taught ethnographer of California's Indian civilizations and as a decorative arts historian of his native New England's colonial past, Wilcomb's two research interests represent the first two American academic disciplines (cultural anthropology and art history) to take artifacts seriously and to embrace them as vital to teaching their subject matter. For example, Wilcomb participated in archaeological excavations on the shore of San Francisco Bay, consulted with visiting ethnologists, and formed a working relationship with the famed University of California anthropologist A. L. Kroeber. By 1899 he had developed a study collection of North American ethnology with more than 400 basketry specimens.

Wilcomb's work in colonial art history led to the development in 1896 of what some museum historians consider the first "period room" setting in the United States (figs. 126, 127). Not satisfied with the traditional "cabinet of curiosities" or the typical narrow corridor of glass cases for the exhibition and interpretation of the Colonial objects he had collected, Wilcomb sought to install them "in a room of sufficient capacity, finished in the Colonial style" so that the collection would form a most impressive and instructive exhibit. "Our Colonial Department," boasted Wilcomb, "will be the most complete, and from an educational standpoint, the most valuable in the United States."

History education at all levels remained an avowed objective of Wilcomb's extensive school program. More than 19,000 schoolchildren came for formal lectures in the initial five years of his museum's operation. Museum lecturers visited another 16,000 in the classroom. The museum frequently loaned duplicate material culture artifacts through a variety of public outreach programs to schools and other agencies. The city's Free Library and its branches mounted special exhibits. When the

Figure 126.
"Colonial Kitchen" (undated)
Planning sketch by Charles P. Wilson.
(Courtesy Oakland Museum, Oakland, California)

number of visitors grew too large for the exhibition galleries, Wilcomb
added a 150-seat hall with lantern-slide projection facilities. Recognizing the symbiotic relationship between material culture evidence and
documentary sources in teaching history—and learning—with artifacts,
he fastened a copy of Alice Morse Earle's then recently published book,
Home Life in Colonial Days, to a small reading table in the colonial
galleries. Reference materials were available in all exhibition spaces, as
well as in an adjacent museum library. In short, Wilcomb established
several of the teaching techniques and curriculum practices now traditional to many contemporary departments of education in American
historical museums, as well as in university museum studies programs.

Although he began as an antiquarian, Charles Wilcomb matured into
a perceptive cultural historian with a wide vision of the American past.
As historian Melinda Young Frye suggests, he came to regard material
culture "primarily as a means of education." In an annual report prepared
midway through his years at the Golden Gate Park Museum, he delivered
a statement that might serve as a summary of his teaching credo: "The
test applied to each [object] when its admission to the museum was con-

Figure 127.
Colonial Kitchen (1910)
Oakland Museum, Oakland, California.
(Courtesy Oakland Museum, Oakland, California)

templated has been: Is it interesting? Does it move thought and appeal to the higher reaches of the imagination, or, in a word, is it 'educational'?''

John Dewey: Theorist of Experiential Learning

With a few exceptions—such as Bronson Alcott's Temple School or Friedrick Froebel's Kindergarten at the 1876 Philadelphia Centennial—the nineteenth-century American educational establishment used few objects in history teaching. Words dominated the history curriculum. Reading, 'riting, and recitations preoccupied the student's learning experience.

Moreover, the American history subjects taught in most nineteenth-century schools, from grammar to graduate level, dealt almost solely with politics, war, and diplomacy. History texts paid no significant attention to the role of art, architecture, technology, costumes, or any of the components of what we now call cultural history. American education saw little heuristic value in American things. Nothing important, it was thought, could be learned from such commonplace objects.

John Dewey, epistemologist and educator, strongly disagreed. He was distressed by a kind of intellectual snobbery deeply rooted in Western culture that defined the physical as inferior to the abstract. Dewey sought to redress the imbalance in the distinctions we tend to make between the material and the theoretical, between doing and thinking, between the concrete and the abstract, between words and things. His early twentieth-century educational philosophy, often labelled "progressive education," stands as an important benchmark in the development of teaching history with artifacts (fig. 128). The inquiry approach, which Dewey pioneered while teaching at the Laboratory Schools at the University of Chicago and at the Teachers College of Columbia University, considered every artifact—a student's textbook, school room, home, museum, community—as a learning environment. As Peale and Wilcomb were innovative practitioners of material culture history teaching, Dewey was one of the approach's most provocative early theorists.

Dewey's many contributions to the theory and practice of history education have yet to be fully explored, but at least three merit brief mention. One is epistemological, another curricular, and the third might be classified as administrative.

Undoubtedly Dewey's greatest theoretical contribution to material culture studies was his championing of the inquiry method in approaching historical evidence, whether it was verbal or visual. In *How We Think* (1933), Dewey outlined the steps that should prompt progressive and systematic inquiry on the part of the learner. The inquiry method confronts the learner with new or primary data in order to promote thinking about what he or she already knows as well as to nurture the discovery of brand new ideas and insights. Dewey argued that conclusions or hypotheses about the past resulted from interaction with actual data (not abstractions), the problems posed by such data and the task of finding the most plausible explanations for such problems created by the data. Dewey found that having students confront objects such as pottery, maps, and paintings often stimulated the learning pattern more readily than rote memorization or historical chronologies. In his laboratory school projects, he included such activities as re-creating historical foodways, manufacturing simple tools, and even building various forms of shelter.

Such a "hands-on" history approach to learning naturally widened the subject matter covered in the schools. In fact, Dewey's model curriculum, in addition to being both multidisciplinary and interdisciplinary, embraced most of the fields we now include under the umbrella of material culture studies: art, architecture, decorative arts, folklife, cartography, agriculture, technology, geography—all taught from a historical perspective. Dewey considered each area as vital to the child's total learning experience.

Figure 128.
Mathematics Class, Washington, D.C., 1912
(Courtesy The Library of Congress, Division of Prints and Photographs)

In order to pursue such topics and their special evidence, Dewey advocated what might be called "history outside the history classroom." Libraries and archives housed resources for cognitive learning, but the data for the inquiry method also existed elsewhere—in museums, in historical agencies or in situ, out on the landscape. In *The School and Society* (1899), Dewey recommended that history teachers make extensive use of such community resources. In Chicago, for instance the Laboratory School took students to the site of the Chicago portage, the Art Institute, local industries, and, of course, the Chicago Historical Society. Progressive education, in both theory and practice, urged teachers to take their history classes wherever the history had taken place.

Thomas Jefferson Wertenbaker: Material Culture in Academe

Dewey's pedagogy had its greatest impact at the elementary and secondary school level. With a few exceptions—such as Abner Bushnell Hart's pioneering work with cartography or Dixon Ryan Fox's research in social history—most American collegiate and university history courses lacked any material culture perspective. Hence the isolated career of Thomas

J. Wertenbaker, professor of colonial history, is all the more striking. During his long years (1910–66) at Princeton University, Wertenbaker preached a brand of material culture history in his classroom and practiced it in his numerous books on colonial, urban, cultural, and social history.

His courses and seminars were novel not in method but in content. Beginning his teaching career in the traditional—and highly respected—field of American political history, Wertenbaker soon widened his vision to what he came to call the neglected "field of Colonial culture." His courses were titled "American Civilization," and Princeton offered them through its early interdisciplinary program in American Studies. In such courses, Wertenbaker exposed students to Quaker vernacular architecture, Swiss barn types, American highboys, New England field patterns, transportation artifacts, and recent archaeological excavations at sites such as Jamestown and Williamsburg.

In 1947 Wertenbaker completed his trilogy, *The Founding of American Civilization,* which demonstrated an impressive knowledge of seventeenth- and eighteenth-century Anglo-American artifacts. In documenting both his classroom teaching and his published research, Wertenbaker was the first established university historian to use extensively the Historic American Buildings Survey (fig. 129), the Pictorial Archives of Early American Architecture at the Library of Congress, and the in-house research reports prepared at Colonial Williamsburg. In a field report he authored for the Smithsonian Institution, *The Archaeology of Colonial Williamsburg* (1964), he urged his fellow historians, especially colonialists, to recognize the importance of archaeological material culture to historical study.

Wertenbaker was practically alone among established university American historians in recognizing the value of material culture as resource material for teaching and writing American history. His professional odyssey is almost archetypal of the generation of material culture historians, both in universities and museums, that followed him. Those historians shared several common characteristics. Like Wertenbaker, most post–World War II university teachers who became interested in doing American history with American things came to material culture research via some other discipline or vocational route. With the exception of those with anthropological training, such as Fred Kniffen, geographer at Louisiana State University, or C. Malcolm Watkins, curator of cultural history at the Smithsonian, or those with a familial interest in antiques such as University of Pennsylvania art historian Anthony Garvan, few were specifically trained in interpreting the artifactual record of a literate society. In short, like Wertenbaker, in working with artifacts this generation

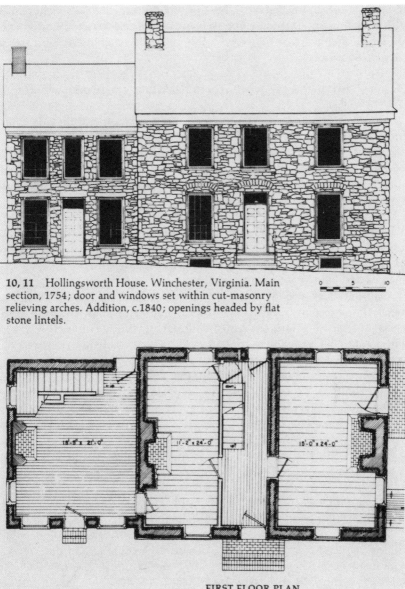

10, 11 Hollingsworth House. Winchester, Virginia. Main section, 1754; door and windows set within cut-masonry relieving arches. Addition, c.1840; openings headed by flat stone lintels.

0   5   10

18'-5" x 21'-0"   11'-2" x 24'-0"   15'-0" x 24'-0"

FIRST FLOOR PLAN

Figure 129.
Hollingsworth House, Winchester, Virginia
Main section built in 1754, additions, ca. 1840.
(Historic American Buildings Survey)

of material culture scholars was largely self-taught usually through their personal research in the history, art or technology, museum collections with which many of them came to be affiliated and, of course, through the years of their own fieldwork. Like all good teachers, they learned a lot on the job.

Charles Montgomery: A Mentor of Artifact Professionals

Charles Montgomery is representative of the next generation that came into its majority by the late 1950s. With a degree in history from the University of Illinois, Montgomery became director and senior research fellow at the Winterthur Museum (fig. 130) from 1954–1970 and curator of the Garvan and Related Collections of American Art and professor in the history of art department at Yale University from 1970–1978. He contributed to the material culture studies movement in many ways—as an avid and perceptive collector, particularly of American pewter; as a careful researcher—his volume on *American Furniture: The Federal Period* (1966) remains the definitive work; as a diligent curator; and as an artistic, imaginative, and zealous museum teacher.

Montgomery was also largely responsible for the idea of joining together a muscum collection—Winterthur—and a university—Delaware—for research and teaching. That partnership developed into the pioneering educational experiment now known as the Winterthur Program in Early American Culture. For many years Montgomery was its administrator, taskmaster, guru, promoter, and most respected teacher. Former students, protégés, and colleagues all recall his unbridled energy and enthusiasm. He was famous for rigging up multiple slide projections with nine screens for optimum visual teaching impact, for his perennial willingness to experiment (he encouraged students to use computers in their art history research) and for his unabashed love of objects—their texture, ornament, aesthetic proportions, and cultural and historical significance.

Montgomery set down the "art and mysterie" of connoisseurship in a primer that beginning material culture students still find valuable. He, like Peale, knew the affective power of objects in teaching. He would ask his Winterthur students, for example, to look long and quietly at a double-arm candlestand and then ask them, "Does it *sing* to you?" As his fellow historian and associate E. McClung Fleming recalled, Montgomery's teaching objective remained singular throughout his career no matter what learning strategies he employed. His constant aim was to encourage the historical understanding and enjoyment of the American arts and the artisans who fashioned them.

Figure 130.
Federal Parlor from the Phelps-Hatheway House, Suffield, Connecticut
Winterthur Museum, Winterthur, Delaware.
(Courtesy Winterthur Museum)

In order to do so, he tried a number of new ideas. He connected the artifact with the tools that made it and began Winterthur's Dominy family exhibition workshops. He joined the artifact and the word, helping to create one of the finest museum libraries in the country. He connected the artifact with the image, creating a collection that grew to 85,000 photographs and 72,000 slides. He joined the artifact with its culture, resulting in the *Index of American Cultures,* launched at Winterthur and then moved to the University of Pennsylvania. He insisted on using scientific methods to identify artifacts, which led to Winterthur's wood analysis and X-ray fluorescence laboratories—and to its conservation training program. One of his innovations led to what some Winterthur curators still consider to be "the most revolutionary of all his projects—having his students actually *sit on* museum *chairs* to experience their effect on the body."

Charles Montgomery trained a significant number of the current generation of American history teachers who include artifacts in their own teaching. His influence at Winterthur and then later at Yale runs parallel to other mentors who have influenced the material culture teaching and research of the last decades: Fred Kniffen at Louisiana State University, Louis C. Jones at the Cooperstown Graduate Program, Anthony Garvan at the University of Pennsylvania, J. B. Jackson at the University of California, John Kouwenhoven at Columbia, Eugene Ferguson at the Hagley Museum, and many others.

These students of the artifact, their students, and now their students' students share, I think, several characteristics with their past counterparts. For example, like Peale and Dewey, the current generation of historians working with material culture sees it as a way to make American history more *populist.* They argue that only a small percentage of the world's population is and has been literate and that individuals who write literature or keep diaries are quite atypical. Artifacts, used by a much broader cross-section of the population, offer a potentially more wide-ranging, more democratic source of information than words. Material culture evidence may afford a way to understand the minds of the great majority of people in the past who were nonliterate and who remain otherwise inaccessible except through impersonal records.

Contemporary material culture historians also recognize and aspire to contribute to a more *pluralistic* history that ancestors like Wilcomb and Wertenbaker helped to forge. Those who advocate including artifacts in the acceptable canon of historical data insist they have not only widened the historian's pool of evidence, but they have also expanded the traditional boundaries of historical knowledge. Resorting to material culture data has often made for a more heterogeneous and expanded version (and vision) of the American past.

Finally, past and present devotees of the artifact have a common cause in their mutual dedication to *public* history, a history that reaches beyond scholarly journals and graduate seminars. Such history seeks to pervade our common and communal lives. It is a history, as Dewey hoped, found in both the school and the society. Teachers, from Peale to Montgomery, have found the artifact an extremely effective tool in creating this kind of popular historical understanding.

In short, doing American history with American things is one approach to helping individuals move from their store of personal experience to a wider knowledge, to a human identification with communities and people once remote from them in time as well as space.

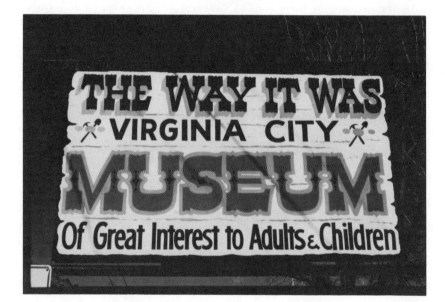

Figure 131.
Outdoor Sign Advertisement, 1988
Virginia City Museum, Virginia City, Nevada.
(Photograph by author)

13

It Wasn't That Simple

This critique originated thanks to three museum historians: Peter Cousins and Larry Lankton at the Henry Ford Museum in Michigan and Barnes Riznik at Old Sturbridge Village in Massachusetts. Cousins and Lankton took me in tow in the early 1970s and showed me the complexities of museum site interpretation. If I developed a critical eye, it was they who first showed me how and where to look. We used the Greenfield Village site for this analytical target practice. Although the following essay cites examples from other outdoor living history sites—Colonial Williamsburg, Shakertown at Pleasant Hill, Old Sturbridge Village—it grew out of my Greenfield Village visits and from the Cousins/Lankton tutelage.

Barnes Riznik, Deputy Director at OSV in 1977 and a member of the program committee for the Society of Architectural Historians for its national meeting, accepted my proposal to present a paper titled: "Historic Homes and Historic Sites" at the SAH meeting in Boston. Afterward Barnes encouraged me to expand the paper, and the following chapter resulted in first form as "The Historic Museum Village as a Learning Environment" in *The Museologist* 141 (June 1977): 10–18.

It was simple to write about oversimplification in museums then as it is now; yet several of the themes explored here demand perennial reexamination of how history museums interpret issues of gender, race, conflict (see chap. 14), religion, or radicalism. Many museum historians had said as much both privately in staff meetings and, occasionally, in publications. I merely said what many had long known and were anxious to change. *Museum News* flattered me by reprinting the essay in their special sixtieth-year anniversary issue and by asking me to add a brief afterword. Jay Anderson, himself a scholar of living history sites, has included it in his anthology, *The Living History Reader* (Nashville: American Association for State and Local History, 1989).

While greater sensitivity to the nuances of historical interpretation assuredly has increased in many history museums, historians working there still need additional scholarly apparatus to advance the empirical base and the methodological rigor of material culture studies. Computerization will help, as will technologies for preserving and manipulating visual data. In this enterprise, perhaps the Common Agenda for History data-base project will integrate documentary, statistical, and artifactual

This article, with afterword, originally appeared in *Museum News* 62.3 (February 1984): 61–65.

data in a national or regional archive that will be easily accessible to historians no matter what their institutional affiliation.

I also think it imperative not only that historians give serious thought to the documentation of extant material culture collections in various institutions, but also that we attempt to formulate some guidelines for the documentation of contemporary history museum exhibitions and sites. Some argue that exhibit catalogs provide sufficient documentation of the intellectual creativity of the historians involved in an exhibit project. I would answer many exhibits have no catalog, sometimes not even a gallery brochure or guide. Others say that a file of exhibit reviews from several professional journals will indicate its import. Perhaps, but catalogs (no matter how comprehensive) and reviews (no matter how many are done) are only two forms of an exhibition's intellectual record. We need to think about how would be the best way(s) to document systematically the three-dimensional spatial artifact that an exhibit usually is. We need to find techniques for recording (photography, videotape, documentary files) not only the final *product* that results as a historical exhibit, but also the historical *process* that originates and produces it. Whom would such comprehensive documentation serve? Certainly our students in the present and our counterparts in the future. If advanced students working in our graduate programs in material culture could study the historical exhibition practice across the country on a particular topic over a period of a decade or two, they could acquire familiarity with the efforts of previous historians in a way not possible at present. In addition to the historiography they master on a particular topic or period through reading bibliographies and monographs in material culture research, they could review parallel scholarship as presented on the same topic or period in history museum exhibitions. Historians working fifty years from now would have similar advantages as well as an excellent data base from which to write the history of history museums.

Edward P. Alexander once called the historical museum village "a huge textbook of three-dimensional American history." Outdoor historical museums, like history textbooks, have proliferated in almost a geometric progression in the past three decades. Despite competition from numerous other forms of popular history—historical novels, films, television programs—historical texts and historical villages continue to exert an enormous influence on the average American's perception of the national past and on his or her understanding of history as a way of knowing.

An analysis of a typical outdoor historical museum as a "textbook" of American history demonstrates the obstacles that curators must overcome when using this museum format to interpret historical knowledge. It also partially accounts for the traditional indifference that most professional historians have had toward museums as potential research and teaching resources. To some academic historians, the "museumization" of American history produces many of the same distortions, inaccuracies and oversimplifications that result from history textbooks.

Figure 132.
"The United States Senate, A.D. 1850," 1855
Engraving by Robert Whitechurch. Henry Clay presenting his program
of compromise to the Senate in 1850, over which Vice-President Millard
Fillmore presides. John C. Calhoun appears to the right of Fillmore and
Daniel Webster is seated on the left, head in hand. The engraving was
based on an oil painting by Peter Frederick Rothermel, who used
daguerreotypes to produce highly accurate portraits of the members.
(Courtesy United States Senate Collection)

Authors of history texts generally follow a chronology of the American past based primarily on the events of political (fig. 132) or military
history. Despite an excess of artifactual survivals that should force an extensive study of social, economic, and cultural history, historical museums
are prone to similar timeline interpretations that define all their activities
as being either before or after the Revolutionary War or the Civil War.

Modern history textbooks, moreover, often betray a second chronological fallacy to which historical museums also succumb: the assumption that American history is singularly progressive. Since their origins
in the nationalistic fervor of the early nineteenth century, American textbooks have been the histories of winners, of individuals who succeeded
in *The March of America, The Victory of Freedom,* or *The Triumph of
Democracy* (current text titles). Given their origins in the isolationism
of two post–world war eras, the 1920s and the 1950s, it is not surprising

that historical museum villages have been equally addicted to what Walter Muir Whitehill calls the "celebration rather than the cerebration of the American past." Villages, perhaps biased by the associational aura of the houses of the "great white men" that often form the nucleus of their sites, tend to champion an inevitable evolution of democratic principles, a glorious series of technological advancements, and a continual rise in the American standard of living. Museum villages are not highly populated with Loyalists or Luddites, Anti-Federalists or Wobblies (see fig. 138), Molly Maguires or Copperheads.

Various observers naturally accuse both textbooks and museum villages of being overly patriotic. Of course, sophisticated curators are aware that cultural nationalism is probably endemic to their sites.

They might also consider their installations as evidence of what Robert Bellah and other sociologists define as the "American civil religion." Outdoor museums are historical shrines to which visitors are beckoned to make pilgrimages, particularly on national holy days (Memorial Day, Independence Day, Thanksgiving) when the American democratic faith is reiterated in numerous secular homilies. Historical villages often inculcate, in ritual and symbol, a worship of the national scriptures (the Declaration of Independence, the Constitution) as well as the republic's civic saints, prophets, and martyrs (Revolutionary and Civil War heroes). The folk religion that Will Herberg summarized as "the American way of life" pervades many exhibits and much interpretation.

When Williamsburg's restorers decided in the 1930s that colonial history terminated in 1800, and all structures or additions built thereafter had to be stripped away, a museological practice of enormous influence was inaugurated (fig. 133). Selective preservation, restoration, and reconstruction in a museum village, like selective arrangement of chapters and the number of pages allotted in a textbook, promote a discontinuous perspective on the past. Moreover, this practice often deliberately denigrates the excluded historical epochs as inferior and unworthy of study and understanding. Consider, for instance, how little attention is given, either in textbooks or in historical museum villages, to the era from 1660 to 1730, the so-called "glacial age" of American history.

Plotting change across time—the historian's raison d'être—is done in textbooks and historical museums with a dogmatic certainty that unnerves the professional historian. Textbook authors rely on the simple linear order of their chapters to show change across time; museum curators resort to simplistic, single-factor explanations (see fig. 131) in exhibitions designed to demonstrate historical change. Both historical genres are methodologically prejudiced to show only development, not decline; neither is informed by the abundant literature on the difficulties

Figure 133.
Duke of Gloucester Street, Williamsburg, Virginia, ca. 1890
(Courtesy Colonial Williamsburg Foundation)

of explaining and communicating historical change currently surfacing among historiographers and philosophers of history.

Curators rely too heavily on craft demonstrations to give a visitor some sense of change, of history as process. Unfortunately such demonstrations are often themselves static, providing the viewer with little awareness of shifts in technology, materials or what Page Talbott calls the changing "ethnography of the artisan."

Change in history is often caused by conflict (see chap. 14). Yet textbooks and museums remain lodged in the "consensus" historiography of the 1950s. Historical museum villages are still, with a few exceptions, remarkably peaceable kingdoms, planned communities with over-manicured landscapes or idyllic small towns where the entire populace lives in harmony. The visitor to such sites, who usually does not see the artifacts of convict laborers, domestic servants, hired hands, or slaves in the statistical proportion in which such material culture would have cluttered most communities, comes away from the museum village with a romanticized, even utopian perspective of the popularly acclaimed "good old days."

Deliberate utopian ventures (fig. 134) constitute an inordinately large proportion of American outdoor history museums. There are more Shaker villages in the United States than there are Shakers. Unfortunately the acute social and religious radicalism (and ostracism) of these and other dissenters (now ironically organized into a National Historic Communal Societies Association) is never adequately portrayed in the twentieth-century restorations of their lifestyles. In fact, more often than not, the once bitterly maligned countercultures of earlier eras have been homogenized into respectable middle-class cultural establishments.

Homogeneity pervades American history textbooks, in part because of pressure from school boards, in part because their authors tend to plagiarize from one another, but particularly because they have tradition-ally omitted large, usually documentarily inarticulate, components of the population in their historical surveys. The same holds true for museum villages. Despite the increased scholarship and availability of materials on racial and ethnic minorities, both historical texts and villages are still largely populated by white, Anglo-Saxon, nondenominational Protestant males.

Similarly, trends in American religious history have not been translated into museum village installations that, while they invariably have a single Georgian or Federal white clapboard church, are hardly sug-gestive of the extensive religious pluralism and conflict that existed in most American communities.

To be sure, women's work (fig. 135) has been depicted, but only that centering around the home and hearth, particularly in kitchens furnished with more equipment than any cook could ever have used. If it is any comfort to museum curators, textbooks have been even more resistant to women's studies.

Museum curators, like textbook writers, do not have access to the highly developed scholarly apparatus of systematic, collective research procedures common to most professional disciplines. Primary research is ongoing in museum villages with research divisions and in museum-university related graduate programs. Unpublished inventories, cor-respondence, account books, and other manuscript materials are now used frequently in museum interpretation. Unfortunately those who do this research do not always mount the exhibit or determine how much of their research is to be used and in what fashion. Nor is this research sufficiently shared. There is no national network for collecting, catalog-ing, publishing, and distributing it; there is no abstracting service to con-dense it to manageable format, convenient to distribute and to retrieve. Since many studies in American material culture are master's degree theses, the extensive graduate research done in programs like those at

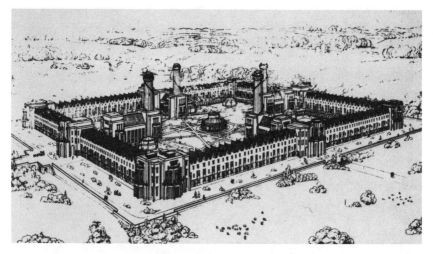

Figure 134.
"A Bird's-Eye View of One of the New Communities at Harmony, in the State of Indiana, North America," ca. 1825
Stedman Whitwell, architect.

Winterthur, Cooperstown or Hagley is not listed in *Dissertation Abstracts* and consequently is not available in either microfilm or photocopy.

Historical museum villages and textbooks lack both footnotes and bibliographies. Neither the historical scholar nor the curator, much less the interested museum visitor, is encouraged in most outdoor museums to consult the elaborate (and generally unavailable) staff research reports, laboratory analyses of artifacts, minutes of curator-designer meetings, or registrar's records that are the documentation on which the interpretation of a historical environment is based.

There are still no regular scholarly mechanisms whereby individuals can get behind the façade of an exhibit, restoration, or reconstruction. The credibility and historical authenticity of such background research cannot be adjudicated by professional peers; it cannot be a base on which other scholars might build further research; it cannot be a cross-reference to parallel work in the field. Although historical museum village installations are indeed curatorial publications, they have no footnotes and are never used as footnotes to other publications.

Curators may argue that their guidebooks, research studies, or craft demonstration leaflets perform this function. Although some local research studies and craft series do have bibliographical leads, there is no comprehensive, documented catalog or interpretive analysis of a major historical museum village and its study collections. At best, most

Figure 135.
Nineteenth-Century Foodways at the Lint House, 1989
King's Landing Historical Settlement, St. John River, New Brunswick, Canada.
(Courtesy A. Gregg Finley, King's Landing Historical Settlement)

guidebooks are mementos rather than monographs, souvenirs rather than reference and interpretive works for the library shelf.

Historical museum villages, like most textbooks, do not have prefaces, forewords, or introductory statements. In fact, for all the public knows, historical museum installations are self-generating since curators are not usually credited with authorship. No standard vehicle exists that allows the textbook historian or historical curator to explain his objectives, delineate his hypotheses, or articulate the problems he may have encountered in researching the data, organizing it, and communicating it to a wider audience. Neither author has an appropriate public forum in which to admit his reservations about certain aspects of his interpretation or to explain the documentation that supports controversial judgments or unfamiliar facts. Consequently village visitors, as well as their volunteer guide interpreters, have no clues as to the methodological difficulties or evidential gaps in an exhibition, and almost inevitably regard the published result as the definitive study on the subject.

Professional historians, of course, are not as easily convinced. In their work they depend on peer review in order to appraise completed scholarship and stimulate further research through constructive criticism. If the historical museum profession were to follow suit, it would escape another of the critical comparisons made here with history textbooks, which do not usually receive professional peer review.

Peer review prompts interpretation revision. Without such revisionism, museums and textbooks lack both a historical tradition and a tradition of historical analysis. Both genres of historical interpretation would profit if their practitioners thought more seriously about their philosophical assumptions and professional practices. If museum curators took more time to explore the epistemological questions of chronology, causation, periodization, and generalization, the quality of interpretation in historical villages would be more sophisticated, but still comprehensible to the average visitor. As curators can learn from the methods of academic historians, teaching historians can profit from the scholarship of museum professionals.

Before both professions is what American historian William Hesseltine, in *The Present World of History* (1958), called "the challenge of the artifact." "[How can] artifacts be made into historical facts? By what method can they be examined? What internal evidence can they produce to aid in the search for historical truth?" For, as Hesseltine rightly saw, "until artifacts can be subjected to internal criticism and made to bear their witness, the task of historical methodology is unfinished."

It Won't Be Easy: An Afterword (1984)

I wrote the preceding essay in the wake of the American Bicentennial. I prepared this brief coda in the early years of a decade devoted to the 200th anniversary of the American Constitution. Anticipating some of the chauvinistic manifestations that the next bicentennial will undoubtedly elicit, I again find myself wondering how history museums and history textbooks will portray the Constitutional era in particular, and American history in general, during the decade of the 1980s.

I am persuaded that history museums will do their work with increasing sophistication. Not so textbooks. Their authors seem almost forever doomed, much like Sisyphus, to roll their hard little rock of historical dogma up and down the minds of bored students everywhere. Many history museums, on the other hand, are venturing forth onto new interpretive frontiers (fig. 136; see also figs. 152, 156) and demonstrating the intellectual openness and methodological savvy that I called for in 1978.

How and why is this happening? In brief, many history museums are now seriously reexamining both their professional activities and the philosophical assumptions involved in their conceptualization and communication of the past. In professional terms, new forums such as the *Museum Studies Journal* have appeared, joining the ranks of publications such as *Museum News* and *History News* in a common aspiration to publish more rigorous museological research and more analytical museum history. In addition to this growing liveliness in professional literature, exhibit catalogs are occasionally evolving into major research publications. The Boston Museum of Fine Arts' three-volume catalog, *New England Begins: The Seventeenth Century* (1982), is an example. History museums still need, however, more critical peer review of their publications in all forms—exhibits, monographs, catalogs. My hope for a regular exhibition review section in each major museum journal has yet to be realized.

Reevaluation of philosophical premises, I suppose, has been largely a result of the social history juggernaut. In fact, many institutions are becoming as deeply committed to the social history gospel as they once were to a political history ideology. Colonial Williamsburg, for example, an institution of which I was critical in 1978, now contends to be the major museum research center for the interpretation of eighteenth-century colonial society. At nineteenth-century sites such as Sturbridge, Conner Prairie (fig. 137), Greenfield Village (see fig. 156), and Old World Wisconsin, we now see a perspective on the past that is more diverse in human motivation, more representative of actual human populations, and more complex in its explanation of human behavior.

Figure 136.
Experimental Archaeology in Agricultural Mechanization
Sawing firewood with a double horse tread mill, 1989.
King's Landing Historical Settlement, St. John River, New Brunswick,
Canada.
(Courtesy A. Gregg Finley, King's Landing Historical Settlement)

Despite these achievements, interpreting certain dimensions of the American experience is still problematic for many history museums. The complicated and often controversial role of religion, for instance, is not researched or communicated in ways appropriate to its importance. The presentation of difficult historical issues such as conflict, failure, dissent, or prejudice also continue as interpretive challenges that we have not adequately met. And questions perennial to the historian's craft—the nature of causation, the rationale for periodization, the differing velocities of change or the limits of historical explanation—still haunt our best efforts.

Finally, I think my earlier insistence that one of the most urgent tasks of contemporary historical scholarship is to explore, both in the museum and in the academy, the full potential of material culture evidence, remains as demanding an imperative now as it was six years ago. If museum and academic historians, with American history museums as research laboratories, can join in expanding historical understanding through a sensitive and systematic study of the past's objects, this may be the history

Figure 137.
Nineteenth-Century Funeral Re-enactment, 1986
Conner Prairie Pioneer Settlement, Noblesville, Indiana.
(Courtesy Conner Prairie Pioneer Settlement)

museum's most vital contribution to historical methodology in the remaining decades of this century. However, I should add that just as we have come to realize that the past wasn't that simple, we can be certain that the effort to comprehend the measure and the meaning of its material universe won't be easy.

Figure 138.
Patterson Pageant Strike Committee Poster, 1913
(Courtesy The American Labor Museum)

14

Causing Conflict, Doing Violence

In 1983 the editors at *Museum News* asked me to contribute to a special issue that they wished to do on controversial issues in historical interpretation in museums.

To frame the discussion, I reused a format similar to the one I adopted in chapter 13, that is, contrasting how historians worked with words and things. In chapter 13, it was history textbooks and outdoor living history sites; here it is history monographs and history museum exhibitions. In both comparisons, I see historiographical myopia.

In writing both essays, but especially this one, I realized how the extant historical record, whatever its evidential form, favored winners. Past losers in conflicts or at the hands of violence often lost a second time. Frequently any record of the roles they played in the drama of their own lives or in that of their communities was purged, suppressed, or abandoned. Perhaps it is a curse of modernity. "Modern men are afraid of the past," wrote Walter Lippmann in 1914. "It is a record of achievement, but its other face is human defeat."

Material culture research also tends to investigate and to exhibit the delightful rather than the deviant. As I detail in chapter 15, we often overemphasize products that "make it" due to their monetary worth (gold and silver wares), historical association, technological innovation, or avant-garde style. As I have argued in *Material Culture: A Research Guide* (1984), we who study artifacts can easily exaggerate human efficacy in the past if we fail to remember the fecklessness of historical preservation.

Failures in artifacts and in actions deserve the historian's attention for, in one sense, "to lose is not to lose all." As I quoted French historian Fernand Braudel above (p. 312), those who struggle and yet do not win often affect history's outcome nonetheless. By their resistance, their opposition, their violence, losers influence winners in subtle ways, many not immediately known to either side. Part of a historian's responsibility is to ascertain, if possible, this interaction and to assess the import of both sides.

Unfortunately, much of this aspect of the human past is lost forever. Despite our current research using court records, police files, and institutional archives, many *other* sides of American history remain elusive. While we can do only so much about

This article originally appeared in *Museum News* 63.5 (October 1984): 45–52.

the past, we can take a more active part in collecting contemporary evidence documenting conflicts we estimate to be historically significant.

Museum historians, like most decent people, usually try to avoid conflict. Physical violence is likewise abhorred. Yet the history we collect and curate is shot through with social, cultural, generational, economic, and psychological conflicts; the past that we examine and exhibit is, if the truth be told, racked with much individual and collective violence.

To be sure, most of us recognize that group violence and ideological conflict attended both our national birth in the American Revolution and our national preservation and the expurgation of slavery in the Civil War. These tumultuous events provide the rationale for many of our most popular museums. Even in these museums, however, many types of human conflict are not always adequately portrayed. Moreover, the extent and impact of *domestic* conflict and violence in American history are almost totally ignored. We have been victims of what members of the National Commission on the Causes and Prevention of Violence have called "a historical amnesia" regarding "the sheer commonplaceness of conflict and violence in our past."

Why is this so? We historians, whether we work in the museum or the academy, are at least partially to blame. Until a decade ago, the topic received little attention. While Progressive historians such as Charles Beard, Carl Becker, Frederick Jackson Turner, and Vernon Parrington did depict the American past in terms of conflicting economic and political interests—Patriots versus Tories, Federalists versus Anti-Federalists, Democrats versus Whigs, populists versus plutocrats—the vast majority of American historiography is consensual. Only since the 1960s have we admitted to the drama and the dimensions of personal conflict and public violence in the historical American psyche.

In addition to the fact that conflict and violence usually produce equally unsavory and unsettling reactions in us and our audiences, the interpretation of these historical phenomena poses nettlesome institutional and methodological problems for museum historians. Interpretation is problematic because the topic lacks cohesion. In America, conflict and violence have largely lacked both a geographical and an ideological center. As Richard Hofstadter once pointed out in *American Violence,* very little of public conflict in this country has been insurrectionary. That is, most of our public violence has taken the form of action by one group of citizens against another group, rather than a group of citizens against the state.

Political history long dominated our interpretive focus. For political historians, conflicts between groups of citizens, no matter how murderous and destructive, have been forgivable; attacks upon state power, no matter how transient and ineffective, win historical attention—and perhaps exaggeration. But in this country's history, violence against the government has been minor compared to that found in other nations. This may explain why low-key and almost charmingly benign episodes such as the Boston Tea Party always find a place in our histories; other episodes, often of startling savagery, like the suppression of the slave revolt in New York in 1712 or the anti-Chinese riot in Los Angeles in 1871, frequently do not appear.

In American history, conflict and violence have also been too various, diffuse, and spontaneous to be interpreted by any one perspective. They have been committed by isolated individuals, by small groups, and by large mobs; they are directed against individuals and crowds alike; they are undertaken for a variety of purposes (and at times for no discernible rational purpose at all) and in a variety of ways ranging from assassinations, murders, and lynchings, to duels, brawls, feuds, and riots; they stem from criminal intent and from political idealism, from antagonisms that are entirely personal and from antagonisms of large social consequence.

My interest here is basically *domestic* conflict and violence in American history museum interpretation. I have not forgotten that war is by far the most pernicious form of conflict and the most destructive of all forms of violence. I am aware that historical military sites (many of them devoted to the interpretation of warfare) are the most abundant of all historic sites in the United States. But I have excluded discussion of this extremely important museum type for two reasons. First, the topic of conflict and violence in military museum interpretation deserves a separate and more extended treatment; second, military sites and structures are already everywhere to be seen on the museum landscape; they need no new advocate, since military history has long been a traditional strand of American history.

My brief here is simply that many (nonmilitary) history museums need to review and, where the historical evidence merits it, revise their interpretations so that their visitors come to understand the legacy of domestic turbulence and violent conflict that Richard Maxwell Brown has described as "the dark side of the American tradition." I have used gerunds in my essay's title to emphasize this imperative. I wish to have us "do" violence and "cause" conflict where they are historically appropriate in our interpretations; I want us to explore more carefully their causes and, in turn, what they cause. In short, I believe conflict and its most tangible physical manifestation—violence—deserve our attention as possible explanatory factors in our attempt to understand the various meanings of the American past.

The historical forms of domestic conflict and violence in America are many. Our past includes both personal violence (the 1804 Hamilton-Burr duel or the 1881 gunfight at the O.K. Corral) and group conflict (the 1921 Tulsa race riot or the 1887 Louisiana sugar strike). There are numerous instances of political conflict (Bleeding Kansas in the 1850s) and economic conflict (New Jersey tenant riots of 1745–54). Racial violence has included slave revolts and their suppression (Nat Turner in 1831), race riots (East St. Louis in 1917), and ghetto riots (Watts in 1965). Our past has had religious and ethnic conflict (Philadelphia nativist riots in 1844 or the New Orleans anti-Italian riot in 1891) as well as antiradical and police violence (Centralia, Washington, in 1919 or the Dearborn massacre in 1932). Finally, we have had violence in the name of law, order, and morality (the San Francisco vigilance committee of 1856 or the infamous Paris, Texas, lynching in 1893).

How might museums interpret such chaos and conflict (fig. 139)? Are there any particular and perennial conflicts inimical to certain types of museum interpretive formats? What might we do to infuse our exhibitions with the tension, contention, passion, and, where the historical record warrants it, violence that our understanding of a certain period, place, or personality demands?

Why not, for instance, consider the period room as one possible museum setting for the interpretation of conflict. Courtrooms, such as the one built for Saint Joseph County in 1854 and now part of the Northern Indiana Historical Society, while ostensibly designed to adjudicate conflict, were also places of violent harangue and bitter discord. Do we usually interpret them so? City council chambers and state legislatures, like the one preserved in the old State Capitol in Iowa City, were frequently alive with acrimonious debate, political in-fighting, personal contention, and strong passions. We usually interpret them as hallowed halls of statesmanship and civic virtue. Jail cells or prison blocks can be found in various museum settings, but do we ever seriously interpret the assorted human behavior—other than a few remarks about a notorious gangster or Western Bank robber who may once have been incarcerated there—that took place within their confines day after day?

Police stations, as the precinct headquarters of the television series "Hill Street Blues" attests, are theaters of continual human conflict and crisis. Historians such as Sidney Harring know that such has always been the case in most American cities. As Harring's provocative study, *Policing a Class Society,* suggests, the police station and its ancillary artifacts—the patrol wagon, signaling system, and squad car—have been extremely significant facets of late nineteenth- and early twentieth-century American urban history. Yet how many police museums do we have in America, say, in comparison with firehouse museums?

Figure 139.
Robert Koehler, *The Strike*, 1886
Oil on canvas.
(Courtesy Lee Baxandall, Green Mountain Editions, Oshkosh, Wisconsin)

Typical American historic house museums usually do not suggest to visitors any of the conflicts that may have raged around their dining room tables, not to mention in their kitchens or bedrooms. While much domestic discord is trivial, some of it can be extremely consequential to family history and, therefore, to the museum interpretation of family history.

Take, for example, the classic house-barn conflict evident in the material culture of many American farmsteads. Family arguments between husbands and wives often erupted over which site deserved the family's financial priorities: a new tractor or a new kitchen stove; painting the corncrib or wallpapering the front parlor. The size of most American barns (especially when compared to their European counterparts) and the machinery in and around such structures, when compared to a site's farmhouse and its household furnishings, may reflect some such domestic tensions.

House museums, where their histories demand it, might also reveal the marital conflicts of their former occupants such as suggested by one spouse's insistence on separate bedrooms. Sibling rivalry might be shown in the special decor and toys given one child and not another. If we know there to have been child or spouse mistreatment, alcohol or drug abuse (more widespread among nineteenth-century middle-class Americans than we once realized) or prolonged illness that, in turn, strongly affected life as lived in the historic house, we need to explore how best to interpret such manifestations of what social historian Gary Nash calls "the private side of American history."

Social historians, understandably, urge us to pay attention to past behavior during the especially traumatic moments of the life cycle—birth, puberty, marriage, prolonged illness, death. Until the twentieth century, most of these events took place at home. Many also produced conflict, some even violence. Occasionally a historic house will be interpreted as the site of a marriage, but I have yet to see a parlor exhibited, on even a temporary basis, as a funeral site (see fig. 137). All that we are learning, for example, about nineteenth-century funerary art, artifacts, and activities ought to be applied to the interpretation of a historic site where death is a crucial factor in its social history (fig. 140). And, when conflict surrounds a death in the family in the form of will contests or inheritance disputes over the division of household goods, lands, and perhaps the house itself, we need to consider the proper interpretive devices to depict this internal (possibly factious) history of the place and its people.

Suicide and murder are also the untold story of some American historic houses. If a violent death occurred in such a house, it is usually either sensationalized or ignored. No adequate explanation is given of its specific historical context or its place in the historical patterns of personal mortality of the time. Not that such interpretation is easy. How, for example, should the curators of the Vachel Lindsay House in Springfield, Illinois, interpret the poet's suicide? Shortly after drinking Lysol, Lindsay decided he had made a grievous mistake and did not want to take his own life. His violent death—crawling up stairs on hands and knees, running through the second-floor hallway in agony and anguish—is a poignant, if painful, part of his (and his homestead's) biography.

The family blood feud is a final manifestation of American domestic violence. The feud appears dramatically in Kentucky and West Virginia as well as in Central Texas and New Mexico in the era between the Civil War and World War I. This is the period that produced the famous Hatfield-McCoy feud (1873–88) of the Kentucky–West Virginia border as well as the Sutton-Taylor conflicts (1869–77) of DeWitt and other counties in Texas, and the Pleasant Valley War between the Graham and Tewksbury families in Arizona from 1886 to 1892. Of course, these are only the nation's most notorious and deadly feuds. Anyone familiar with the country's local history knows it to be filled with similar antagonisms, vendettas, bitterness, and, on occasion, violence to both person and prop-

Figure 140.
Harvey Andrews Family, 1887
This photograph shows the family at the grave of their child, Willie
Andrews, age 19 months, on their farm near New Helena and
Victoria Creek in Cedar Canyon, Custer County, Nebraska.
*(Courtesy Solomon D. Butcher Collection, Nebraska State
Historical Society)*

erty. We have yet to tell this part of our familial and communal history
in its proper perspective.

Our regional history museums still need to explore historical phenomena such as lynching and vigilantism. Although this is especially the
case for museums that interpret the post–Civil War South, Southwest,
and parts of the West, there are only four states—Massachusetts, Rhode
Island, New Hampshire, and Vermont—that have never had a lynching.
Lynching and vigilantism have so few parallels or equivalents elsewhere
that political scientists and historians tend to regard them as distinctive-
ly American institutions. Incomplete records show more than 4,950
lynchings in this country from 1882 to 1927. Many more were attempted
but stopped. During the nineteenth century a significant minority of
lynching victims were white; after the turn of the century, almost all were
black. Is this story told in a representative and analytical format in our
museum exhibitions?

Vigilantism, argues Brown in *Strain of Violence*, also appears to be native to America. Brown suggests there are at least two major types of vigilantism. Both, however, operate on the premise that groups can be formed to create and enforce (by violence, if necessary) laws of their own interpretation (or making) in the supposed absence of adequate law enforcement. The first type of American vigilantism—often a specific concern with the classic frontier problems of horse thieves and counterfeiters—is usually found in regional museum interpretations where the vigilantes are more often than not portrayed as local heroes. One finds the second form of vigilantism less frequently in museum interpretations, although it is one of much greater historical consequence than the first. This new vigilantism, a symptom of the growing pains of the post–Civil War era, broadened its scope to include a variety of antagonisms connected with the tensions of industrial and urban America, particularly prejudice and violence against Catholics, Jews, blacks, immigrants, laboring men and labor leaders, political radicals, advocates of civil liberties, and nonconformists in general. Representatives of this new vigilantism would include groups such as the Night Riders, White Cappers, Bald Knobbers, and, of course, the Ku Klux Klan (see fig. 142)—organizations more often than not left out of historical exhibits.

Urban museums have likewise often neglected the scale and significance of riots in the history of American cities. Civil War battles are reenacted with painstaking precision, but we seldom consider restaging the massive Civil War draft resistance riots that raged for three days in New York City in 1863. Nor do we usually portray any one of 35 major riots that occurred in Baltimore, Philadelphia, New York, and Boston from 1830 to 1850 or any one of the 22 major interracial riots in American cities during the four years between 1915 and 1919. The modern urban police force (the history of which, I maintain, is shockingly ignored by most city museums and historical societies) was created in response to the sustained urban rioting prior to the Civil War, as the National Guard system of arsenals was established in reaction to the uprisings of the postwar decades.

Violent American group conflict has by no means been restricted to the urban sector, with its manifold racial, ethnic, and economic antagonisms. The countryside, too, has been the domain of relentless violence growing out of our agrarian history. Yet how many living history farms are populated with residents that might have participated in the Whiskey Rebellion in western Pennsylvania in the eighteenth century, the Farmers' Alliance in Texas in the nineteenth century, or the Farmers' Holiday Association in the Midwest in the twentieth century? How many Grangers, Greenbackers, or Populists do we encounter in a typical American museum of our rural past?

The labor movement in American history—like that of the farmers—reveals some of the same mixture of noble ends and violent means. It has been better documented, however, than other forms of large-scale group conflict. We recognize the impact, for example, of the Haymarket riot in Chicago, the Homestead strike in Pittsburgh (fig. 141), or the Ludlow massacre in Colorado. The latter conflict in 1914 concluded what has been called Colorado's Thirty Years War (1884–1914) of strikes and violence that typified the economic, class, and ethnic tensions of what many historians see as the most violent era in American labor history.

Site markers are the interpretive strategies to which we most frequently resort in order to designate the historical importance of a riot, civil disturbance, or other form of conflict. Sometimes, as at Chicago's Near West Side Haymarket, a historical monument is erected. The policeman statue at the Chicago Haymarket site has, over the years, itself precipitated further conflict as radicals have sought to destroy and replace it with their own version of the past; the establishment, in turn, has continually rebuilt the monument in an effort to have its view of history prevail. Thus a historical marker of a violent nineteenth-century urban conflict has also become something of an outdoor living history museum of twentieth-century urban conflict.

Much of Chicago's other violent past, however, goes largely undocumented and uninterpreted. To be sure, the St. Valentine's Day massacre and other gangster exploits are included in museum interpretations, but there is little mention of the chaos of the 1877 railroad strike in the city, the Pullman strike of 1894, the bloody race riots of 1919 and 1967, the eviction riot of 1931, the Memorial Day massacre of 1937, or the battle of Balboa Drive in 1968.

What might we do to overcome our common neglect of conflict and violence in American history museum practice? I would like to suggest three general ways whereby we might attempt to be more cognizant of this factor in the past and better communicate its role and relevancy to our visitors in the present. I would, therefore, recommend we, first, do more reading in the current historical scholarship on American conflict; second, be appreciative (and imitative) of contemporary museum exhibitions that successfully deal with violence and conflict; and, third, experiment with techniques of reenacting past group behavior.

First, I would recommend several studies on the topic that should be in every museum historian's reference library. They would include Hugh D. Graham and Ted R. Gurr, *Violence in America;* Norman S. Cohen, *Civil Strife in America;* and Bernard Sterusher, *Consensus, Conflict, and American Historians.* In addition to this professional literature, we need, periodically, to "reread" whatever historical time period,

Figure 141.
"Homestead: Story of a Steel Town," 1989
Museum exhibition, Historical Society of Western Pennsylvania,
Pittsburgh, Pennsylvania.
(Courtesy Historical Society of Western Pennsylvania)

topical interest, or geographical area we are responsible for interpreting. Such a critical review should be done with an eye particularly attentive to aspects of our interpretation where we may have either overlooked or underemphasized the historical role that domestic violence and civil conflict may have played in promoting or hindering change. Here, too, we need to be especially careful to be as precise as possible in communicating what we know about violence in a certain historical era. This means watching our words when labeling: how, for example, should we distinguish between a rebellion, a riot, and a revolution? This also means trying to interpret both quantitative (e.g., number of participants, duration of incidents, casualties) and qualitative (e.g., emotional impact on participants, reaction of bystanders, historical legacy) dimensions of violent conflict.

Several history museums are already striving for well-researched interpretations where conflict and violence are integral to the human behavior they are trying to understand in historical terms. They deserve our applause and imitation. The Allen County–Fort Wayne Historical Society in Indiana faced squarely the issue of how to exhibit the impact of the Ku Klux Klan in a northern Midwestern city in the 1920s. The Mississippi State Museum took on the Klan question as well as several other powerful themes in its exhibition on the history of civil rights in Mississippi (fig. 142). The Minnesota Historical Society's *Where Two Worlds Meet* grapples with the cultural conflict inevitable in the seventeenth-century French and Indian fur trade (fig. 143).

Other museums promise to deal with the conflict-violence issue in future exhibitions. The Department of Social and Cultural History at the National Museum of American History aspired to make conflict, along with the themes of everyday life and diversity, a central interpretive skein of its new *After the Revolution* installation, which opened in 1985. The curators intended to depict the rapidity and ubiquity of change in an era (1780–1800) that most of the American public now regards as static, almost mythic. Persuaded that all change involves conflict, the museum historians researching and presenting this exhibition hoped to show how "fundamental transformations in family dynamics and living spaces, in patterns of work and consumption, and in how communities organized themselves characterized this time."

In Texas, the Dallas County Historical Foundation, with the assistance of the Staples and Charles design firm, has converted the sixth floor of the Dallas County Administration Building (formerly the Texas School Book Depository) into a historical exhibit area (fig. 144). The exhibition offers a thoughtful look at this national tragedy. The carefully researched installation combines photographs (some of which have never been on public display), film clips (including rare footage of international tributes to JFK), and documents concerned with times and events of the 1960s. Prominent elements of the exhibition are two evidential areas—the corner window where the sniper's perch was discovered and the stairway area where the assassin's rifle was found.

To interpret the events surrounding the assassination of President John F. Kennedy in 1963 and the official and unofficial investigations of perhaps the most controversial act of political violence in our contemporary history is an interpretive challenge indeed. It is, however, the kind of museological problem that museum historians with research stamina and methodological verve should welcome.

In our concern to understand and depict conflict and violence in the past, I think we should also be receptive to the attempts being made by various museum research staffs to engage visitors in role playing, simulations, first-person interpretation, and historical dramatizations. None of these techniques are new. Museums such as Colonial Williamsburg, the Old Cowtown Museum in Wichita, Kansas, and the Tryon Palace in New Bern, North Carolina, have been doing what is often called "theatrical

Figure 142.
"The Struggle for Equal Rights," 1986
Permanent exhibition, State Historical Museum, Jackson, Mississippi.
(Courtesy Mississippi Department of Archives and History)

living history" for several years now. Using techniques derived from the theater and scripts well grounded in historical fact, this approach seems especially promising for including conflict and violence in interpretive strategies.

First-person interpretation can, of course, be a powerful way to dramatize what an individual may have felt in a certain historical context. You can invoke the terror of being part of a lynching mob or a near victim of a race riot. You can relate your life outside the law as an eighteenth-century runaway indentured servant, as actor Harvey Credle has done at Colonial Williamsburg. In order to keep your audience with you as you attempt to relive the conflict and violence of past experience, you can "break character" (using your twentieth-century persona to provide introductions and conclusions that explain what is going on) in your interpretation of your historical existence as a caustic abolitionist agitator in Kansas, as a religious sister in the Ursuline convent in Charlestown, Massachusetts, when it was sacked and burned by a mob of laborers, or as a Detroit policeman at the Dearborn Ford plant confrontations in 1932.

Interpreting past conflict in this intimate way may help provide visitors with some sense of one of conflict's truest terrors: the uncertainty

Figure 143.
"Where Two Worlds Meet," 1986
Museum exhibition, Minnesota Historical Society.
(Courtesy Minnesota Historical Society)

Figure 144.
"The Sixth Floor," 1989
Museum exhibition, Dallas County Historical Foundation, Dallas, Texas.
(Courtesy Staples and Charles, Washington, D.C.)

of its outcome. We historians tend to forget that we usually know what happened in the past, even though we may be unclear as to why it happened. We know, for instance, who was killed in the Hamilton-Burr duel in 1804. The participants, at the time of that conflict, did not know who would die or be wounded.

The unknown continually lurks around all the corners of past human conflict. Will the county court rule against my claim contesting my brother's inheritance of the family homestead? Will I be the victim of vigilante racial violence? Should I join my union's protest march? What might happen if I do? If I don't?

With larger settings and added characters, museums can perform something akin to what historian Rhys Isaac, in *The Transformation of Virginia,* calls "historical dramaturgy." The concept of dramaturgy recognizes that each culture and subculture has its own settings, props, costumes, roles, script formulas, and conflicts. The role of the historian is to recreate such dramas (see fig. 138). The model of the theater is often an excellent vehicle, especially if the historical facts demand a portrayal of persons or forces in strong opposition. In such a context, we might more vividly and more accurately communicate our historical understanding of group conflicts such as Indian-white confrontations, ethnic rivalries, religious vendettas, clan feuds, urban riots, agrarian uprisings, and labor-versus-industry struggles.

Such museum interpretations of conflict and violence may provoke some conflict (but I hope no violence) among visitors and boards of trustees. The experience of those who have ventured into interpreting these difficult themes, however, has not been overly distressing and is often quite the opposite. People are much taken with the museum's candor and courage, despite the fact that the subject matter being presented may have been disturbing, even disgusting.

I realize that many museum historians, while they may concur in my critique of our previous treatment of conflict and violence, will not agree with my conclusions that we should think of history museums as places of emotion as well as entertainment. I would simply answer that history museums, like human history itself, must be engaging repositories of past anguish and anxiety as well as happy storehouses of memories and expectations if the complexity of past experience is to be faithfully served and honestly presented.

Using the theater metaphor a final time, let me say that visitors deserve some warning about the past they are going to see interpreted, just as they do when they attend a musical, an opera, or an off-Broadway play. Occasionally we may have to warn them that what they are about to see is violent, depressing, and recommended only for mature audiences.

History is consensus and conflict, virtue and violence. We need not, as the line of an old vaudeville refrain admonishes, "Always leave 'em laughing." To some aspects of our past and to some of our history museum exhibits, thoughtful silence, inquisitive anxiety, or a quiet cry might be the most appropriate mode of response. In addition to presenting a view of American history that has its parallel in Busby Berkeley musical extravaganzas and Neil Simon Broadway comedies, museums also need to depict, where appropriate, a perspective on the past analogous to the poignant American dramas of Tennessee Williams and Eugene O'Neill.

Figure 145.
Sanford Thayer, *The Connoisseurs*, 1845
Oil on canvas.
(Courtesy the painting collection of the Onondaga Historical Association, Syracuse, N.Y.)

15

History Museums and Material Culture

I hope this final essay does two things: provide an appropriate closure for the chapters that preceed it and, conversely, suggest some future directions that cultural history, material culture, and history museums might take by the end of this century. It has much in common with my introduction and prologue in that many of my perennial hobbyhorses are ridden again. For example, my long-standing interest in who has done and who is doing what in material culture studies surfaces early in this article. Here I provide a player depth chart of sorts so that readers can keep score themselves. Many recent students of material culture are not listed on this heuristic roster (see table 15.1) first drawn up in 1980. Their achievements and publications can be found, in part, in many of my post-1980 citations that document the essays in this collection. As I repeat below, I have great expectations for this cadre of scholars.

I hope they will tackle methodological questions such as how should the material culture of the present (sometimes called "collecting the contemporary" or "contemporary collecting") be gathered, documented, and preserved? How should the creative processes and the public response to history museum exhibitions be documented and preserved for researchers in the future? I complained about this problem in chapters 11 and 14 and I bemoan this ahistoricism here again. Ironically, we save and pamper an exhibition's artifacts but seem totally indifferent to preserve, in some appropriate archival format, the spatial design and physical context that gave these objects historical meaning. It is as if after I had researched, written, revised, and assembled the text, graphics, and structure of this volume, I would display it somewhere for six months to a year and then rip up its dust jacket, tear off its binding, scatter its format and graphics, and toss much of the rest of it away. Its totality as an artifact (of considerable interest to scholars in such subspecialities as the history of printing, graphics, design, and bookmaking) would be gone forever. Some might say, "Good riddance," but that is not the point. The issue is how do we document and preserve as much as is possible of the multidimensional totality of the material culture assemblages in a systematic, scholarly way.

History museum exhibition documentation may develop more quickly if historians take an active role in the peer review of museum exhibits interpreting American history.

This article originally appeared as a chapter in *History Museums in the United States: A Critical Appraisal,* ed. Warren Leon and Roy Rosenzweig (Urbana: University of Illinois Press, 1989), 294–320.

Fortunately a dozen professional journals are presently doing such reviews. I have agreed to coordinate the *Journal of American History's* efforts in reviewing history exhibits because I believe that museum exhibits and their related elements are a distinct medium for identifying, organizing, comparing, analyzing, and communicating historical information and insight.

Once we have done a decade or so of peer reviewing we will have a corpus of one type of exhibition documentation. I hope such reviewing will also prompt debate over issues such as authorship and sponsorship, design and content, method and evidence in history museum exhibitions. I also hope it might stimulate sustained discussion about what material culture research might contribute to explanatory theory in cultural history.

On the other hand, we need to probe the limitations of material culture in historical inquiry. Below I briefly examine five problems: the randomness of artifact survival, the difficulty of access and verification, the exaggeration of human efficacy, the progressive determinism of much artifact scholarship, and the proclivity to synchronic interpretation. Others have noticed these challenges as well as suggested new directions in a collection of essays commissioned by Warren Leon and Roy Rosenzweig titled *History Museums in the United States: A Critical Appraisal.* I recommend this for a more detailed assessment of the interconnections between history museums and material culture. The essay that follows is a slightly expanded version of a similar article I wrote as the final chapter in the Leon-Rosenzweig volume.

The relationship between American history museums and material culture studies is both an old and a new one. It is old in the obvious sense that the collection, preservation, and display of artifacts have been traditional tasks of history museums. It is new in that the term *material culture* has only been in use since the late nineteenth century,[1] when anthropologists first employed the phrase in an effort to distinguish three types of cultural data: ideational (found usually in oral or written data), sociological (documented by fieldwork observation of human behavior, such as child rearing or kinship patterning), and material (found in the work of people, such as ceramics, tools, houses, and the like). In the twentieth century, the meaning of *material culture* has undergone various redefinitions and reformulations.[2]

In chapter 1, I assessed the assets and liabilities of three terms— material history, material culture, and material life—now used in artifact study nomenclature. I suggested that each is problematic in certain ways and that each betrays certain scholarly predilections, institutional affiliations, and intellectual temperaments of its proponents. Here I prefer the label *material culture* for several reasons: common use in several disciplines in both the humanities and social sciences; a historical lineage of scholarship dating back to the nineteenth century; evocation of both human behavior and belief; embodiment of the culture concept, and an increasingly widespread usage, at least in the past decade, among both "museum historians" and "academic historians."[3]

To understand the history of American material culture as a scholarly enterprise, I once divided it (table 15.1) into three chronological phases: a collecting or classifying period (1876 to 1948); a descriptive or connoisseurship era (1948 to 1965); and an analytical or explanatory period (1965 to the present). To be sure, the three periods overlap and were never as distinct as my Procrustean outline might suggest. For example, the earlier interest in collecting artifacts and arranging them in appropriate topologies has continued with vigor into the present. Similarly, R. H. Halsey, L. V. Lockwood, and others occasionally practiced the careful connoisseurship of material culture evidence before World War II. Important analytical studies by J. Kouwenhoven, C. M. Watkins, and J. B. Jackson also appeared before the mid-1960s. The classification scheme nevertheless provides a shorthand to the history of material culture research. If one examines the biographies of the scholars whom I claim to be representative of their time, one finds that almost three-fourths of the key contributors to the American material culture movement had some museum experience.

This essay assesses the complex and reciprocal relationship between museums and material culture, focusing particularly on the past two decades. Using the three categories of the classification scheme—collection, description, and interpretation—it asks how material culture research has affected public presentations in museums as well as how history museum presentations and programs have influenced the public's understanding of the scope and significance of object research. It concludes with some observations on the future course of material culture studies and American history museums.

History Museum Collecting: Gathering Material Evidence

Most American history museums acknowledge the collection of the physical past as one of their functions. In this century, and particularly since the 1950s, they have become the major repositories for most extant, moveable, pre-1850 American artifacts. Thus anyone pursuing object research on a pre–Civil War historical topic must work in museum collections. As a result, the future of a large segment of material culture studies, be they communicated in essays or exhibitions, will be determined by the content of American history museum collections. Although historical archaeology may add some objects, collections of pre-1850 data

Table 15.1. The Shifting Paradigms: A Brief Historical Overview of Material Culture Studies in America

Character	Age of Collecting (1876–1948)	Age of Description (1948–1965)	Age of Analysis (1965–)	
Pioneering Scholars	I J. Henry C. Dana C. Wilcomb W. Nutting G. Goode W. Appleton L. Lockwood I. Phelps Stokes H. Cahill S. Clark H. DuPont R. Halsey H. Mercer	II J. C. Harrington L. Jones C. Watkins J. Kouwenhoven T. J. Wertenbaker F. Kniffen J. B. Jackson C. Peterson J. Cotter J. Downs E. Ferguson W. Whitehill C. Montgomery	III B. Hindle C. Hummel I. Noël Hume D. Yoder P. Lewis W. Roberts G. Kubler J. Schlebecker E. Dethlefsen A. Gowans A. Garvan A. Ludwig J. Deetz	IV D. Kelsey H. Marshall C. Carson S. Bronner M. Jones J. Prown M. Leone J. Vlach J. Anderson P. Marzio C. Gilborn K. Ames R. Cowan C. Kidwell R. Trent H. Glassie
Typical Intellectual Emphases	Historical associationism; primacy fascination; search for artistic uniqueness	Cult of connoisseurship; taxonomy fascination; search for American uniqueness	Vernacularism, typicality, methodology fascination; search for artifact's evidential uniqueness	
Principal Research Concerns	Collecting, salvaging, preserving, hoarding high-style, unique, or elite artifacts	Preparing descriptive typologies, chronologies, classifiction systems of artifacts	Seeking to use artifacts to analyze human behavior in societal context	
Interests in Artifacts and Artifact-Makers	Objets d'art: An artiste creating art	Results of craft processes: A technician working in a tradition of artisanry	Consumer goods and services: A citizen involved in community life	
Main Disciplinary Specialties	Art history, architectural history; anthropology; archaeology	History of technology; folk art and folklife studies, cultural and historical geography; cultural history; historical archaeology	Social history; industrial, commercial, experimental archaeology; museum studies; social and environmental psychology; folkloristics; cognitive anthropology	

Table 15.1. The Shifting Paradigms *(continued)*

Character	Age of Collecting (1876–1948)	Age of Description (1948–1965)	Age of Analysis (1965–)
Professional Institutions	The Walpole Society; College Art Association; Society of Architectural Historians	Society for History of Technology; Decorative Arts Society; American Association for State and Local History	Pioneer America Society; Society for Industrial Archaeology; Society for a North American Cultural Survey
Research Centers Established	Smithsonian Institution; Colonial Williamsburg; Index of American Design; Henry Ford Museum	Winterthur Museum-University of Delaware; Cooperstown Program SUNY-Oneonta; National Park Service Index of Early American Culture	George Washington University; University of Pennsylvania; American Folklife Center; Boston University; Indiana University
Typical Serial Publications	*Antiques; The Antiquarian; Art in America*	*Technology and Culture; Winterthur Portfolio* (annual); *Pennsylvania Folklife; Contributions from MHT*	*Material History Bulletin; Winterthur Portfolio* (quarterly); *ALHFAM Bulletin; Journal of Interdisciplinary History; Journal of American Culture*
Historiographical Assessments	W. Kaplan, "R. H. Halsey: An Ideology of Collecting American Decorative Arts" (1980)	C. Montgomery, "Classics and Collectibles" (1977)	S. Bronner, "Concepts in the Study of Material Aspects of American Folk Culture" (1979)
Representative Publications	I. Lyon, *Colonial Furniture of New England* (1891) C. Wissler, "Material Cultures of North American Indians" (1914) H. Mercer, *Ancient Carpenter Tools* (1929) F. Kimball, *Domestic Architecture of the American Colonies* (1922) R. Burlingame, *March of the Iron Men* (1938)	J. Kouwenhoven, *Made in America* (1948) J. Lipman, *American Folk Art* (1948) S. Giedion, *Mechanization Takes Command* (1948) C. Montgomery, *American Furniture: The Federal Period* (1966) A. Gowans, *Images of American Living* (1964)	H. Glassie, *Folk Housing in Middle Virginia* (1975) L. Ferguson, *Historical Archaeology and the Importance of Material Things* (1977) K. Ames, *Beyond Necessity* (1977) M. Jones, *The Hand-Made Object* (1975) P. Benes, *The Masks of Orthodoxy* (1977) J. Fitchen, *The New World Dutch Barn* (1968)

are now largely closed. Curators' preferences, donors' demands, museum size, conservation practices, and collecting fads have shaped the surviving evidence.

The utility of historic museum object collections is limited. Often the provenance of objects within the museum's confines is not known. Their historical and cultural contexts have vanished or were never recorded. For example, tools have been separated from the craftsman and his tool chest or kit, from the shops where they were used, and from the products fabricated with their help. "Out of site" can mean "out of sight." Without a documented context, many artifacts remain little more than historical souvenirs. History museums are not the only institutions saddled with anonymous artifacts. The material culture holdings of many anthropological museums, as Nan Rothschild and Anne-Marie Cantwell have shown, are similarly problematic.[4] History museum exhibitions might, however, introduce the public to what it does not know about their holdings. Visitors would, I think, welcome such intellectual candor and learn much from it. An extended discussion among museum historians about the research problems of their previously gathered collections would be a contribution to material culture methodology.

The public would also profit from knowing more about the randomness of material culture survival and what this means for historical interpretation. More research should be done on the complex process of selection by which some artifacts survive and others perish. In their interpretation of the past, history museums must attempt to establish some quantitative sense of what has been lost in relation to what they have saved.[5] We have no adequate awareness of how wide the gap is between the former reality of the physical past and its present reality as extant objects in our collections.

Greater accessibility for scholars and the interested public to museum collections and techniques for their verification are a must for the mutual sophistication of both history museum interpretation and material culture research. Unlike most documentary data stored in libraries and archives, material culture evidence cannot be easily duplicated, microfilmed, published, or made widely available to other scholars for further interpretation and verification. Most historical institutions do not engage in regular object-study loans, as is common among anthropology and science museums. Nor is there any adequate finding aid to material culture collections comparable to the National Union Catalogs of Books, Serials, and Manuscripts.

Wilcomb Washburn has proposed reducing many artifacts now in museum collections to photographs, drawings, and other more portable, quantitative, and storable forms of data as a way to improve access. Such extracted evidence would then permit the disposal of many, although not all preserved objects.[6]

Modern artifacts—computers, holographs, video discs—may assist in duplicating and manipulating material culture in research inquiries involving large aggregates of data, as the efforts of several history museums (St. Mary's City, the Strong Museum, Plimoth Plantation, Sleepy Hollow Restorations, and the Smithsonian Institution) have suggested. Robert Chenall's scheme, *Nomenclature for Museum Cataloging: A System for Classifying Man-Made Objects* (1978), first developed at the Strong Museum in Rochester, continues to prompt useful debate about this issue in the methodology of material culture research and collection management.[7]

Finally, history museums that claim to cover all of American history must confront the question of contemporary material culture (figs. 146, 147). Yet many refuse, because of limitations of space and time, lack of personnel and funds, and the complexity of selection and documentation. The first two objections are real but not insurmountable. The third is pertinent to the interrelation of material culture and the history museum. Many historians, in the academy and in the museum, have been reluctant to become aggressive, purposeful collectors. Instead they are content to wait and accept whatever objects or documents chance happens to place in their hands. This laissez faire policy of collecting leaves the selecting of the material culture evidence to private collectors, antique promoters, and collectible entrepreneurs.

A cadre of material culture researchers would have it otherwise. They argue that history museums should take an active, deliberate, analytical approach to the collection of contemporary objects. Some espouse the program developed by the historical museums of Sweden called SAMDOK (an acronym for the Swedish word *samtidsdokumentation,* or "same-time documentation"); others promote the work of American projects, such as the Society for the North American Cultural Survey or the Contemporary Collections of the American Folklife Center.[8] At least a few museums, including the Oakland Museum (fig. 148) and the National Museum of American History, have followed this lead and have revised their collection policies to recognize the historical present.[9] Such purposeful collecting can reduce the bias that makes the study of material culture a kind of Whig history in which it is assumed that certain artifacts were destined to survive.

Because museums' collections of past objects are currently so unrepresentative, Dell Upton has argued that the best samples of material culture evidence are "contemporary artifactual landscapes" that still exist outside the museum in their full density and complexity. He similarly

Figure 146.
United Klans of America, ca. 1960
Broadside.
(Courtesy Mississippi State Historical Museum, Jackson, Mississippi)

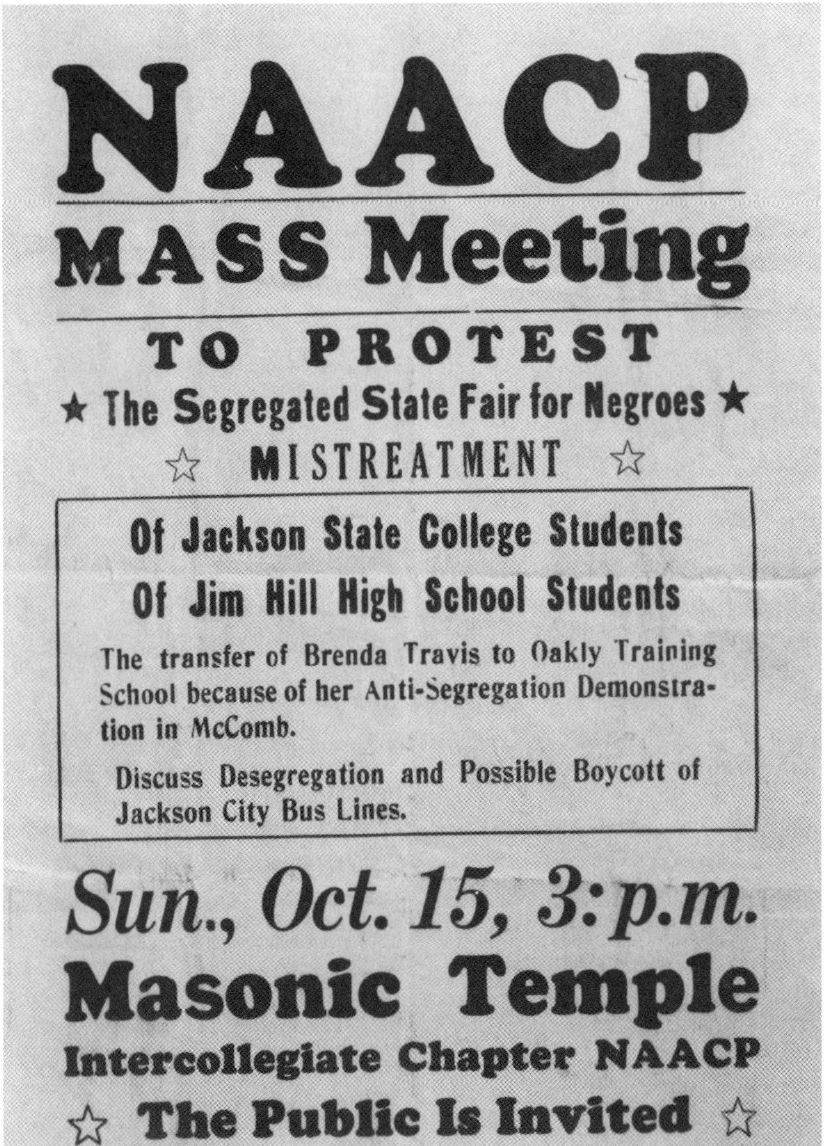

NAACP
MASS Meeting
TO PROTEST
★ The Segregated State Fair for Negroes ★
☆ MISTREATMENT ☆

Of Jackson State College Students
Of Jim Hill High School Students

The transfer of Brenda Travis to Oakly Training School because of her Anti-Segregation Demonstration in McComb.

Discuss Desegregation and Possible Boycott of Jackson City Bus Lines.

Sun., Oct. 15, 3: p.m.
Masonic Temple
Intercollegiate Chapter NAACP
☆ **The Public Is Invited** ☆

Figure 147.
NAACP Mass Meeting, ca. 1960
Broadside.
(Courtesy Mississippi State Historical Museum, Jackson, Mississippi)

Figure 148.
"Challenging the System"
Detail of exhibition: "California: A Place, A People, A Dream," 1985.
Permanent exhibition, Oakland Museum, Oakland, California.
(Courtesy Oakland Museum, Oakland, California)

points out that study of objects being fabricated and used right now (figs. 149, 150)—if the testimony of their makers and users is also collected and studied—may offer the most potential for theoretical and methodological advances in material culture analysis. Only by careful collecting of present-day objects can museums ensure that their collections will be seen as useful by future scholars.[10]

Contemporary collecting (see figs. 146–49) can also make it easier for exhibitions and other public presentations to connect past and present. A few material culturists have gone even further and have used exhibitions on recent American history to collect additional contemporary material culture. For example, in three important exhibits, David Orr interpreted artifacts of the Vietnam War, Barbara Riley placed modern consumerism in historical perspective, and Joan Siedl and Nicholas Westbrook examined the Midwest history of mail-order catalogs.[11]

History Museum Connoisseurship: Describing Material Evidence

Although many history museums have resisted collecting contemporary data on a large scale, they have paid increasing attention to the care and classification of their collections. This curatorship of artifacts has been principally a task of authentification, classification, and conservation. As such, this involvement with material culture has been principally descriptive, emphasizing connoisseurship (see fig. 145) and conservation, rather than analytical.[12]

Those in charge of artifacts in natural history, physical science, or anthropology museums are usually called scientists, whereas the comparable person in most American history museums is generally identified as a curator, not as a historian. This identification has often isolated the curatorial staff of many history museums from the American history profession, which became increasingly entrenched in the nation's colleges and universities in the late nineteenth and early twentieth centuries.[13] Excluded from the associations, conferences, and journals of the American history establishment, historians in museums understandably took little interest in the historiographical concerns, methodological techniques, and theoretical models erected by those who claimed to speak for the "history profession." Many history museum curators, whose job descriptions focused on connoisseurship and conservation, therefore had little time or inclination to make original contributions to historical research as defined by academic historians. Some came to see themselves as essentially librarians or archivists maintaining objects for the use of other scholars or the museum staff who mounted exhibits.

Figure 149.
Manufactured Housing Brochure, 1989
Skyline Corporation, Elkhart, Indiana.

Figure 150.
Tupperware Party, Tallahassee, Florida
Postcard.
(Courtesy Florida Historical Society)

The "compiler-describer-collector," as Cary Carson calls this type of artifact scholar, has both advanced and retarded material culture research. The principal labor of such scholars has been to explain why man-made objects look as they do. All have a common devotion to objects as both starting points and destinations for their scholarship. But, as Carson notes, "however far afield they forage in written records, graphic sources, and oral histories to collect information they deem useful, they always come back to the object literally of their quest." Yet, continues Carson, the collector-compiler-describer "provides an essential preliminary service without which there can no more be a history of material life than there could be economic history without reliable statistics or biography without authentic personal papers.[14]

Those principally concerned with taxonomic questions have enriched object studies in several ways. One early experiment in developing a comprehensive methodology for describing and cataloging an enormous number of artifacts was the Index of Early American Culture at the Winterthur Museum. It was based on the principles of the human relations files developed by anthropologist George Murdock and codified in 1950 in the *Outline of Cultural Materials*.[15] The published object checklist and the study collection are formats that history museums have occasionally borrowed from their counterparts in the art museums to describe and delineate classes of objects. Numerous exhibit catalogs exemplify this approach, as do comprehensive study collections, such as those on permanent display at the Strong Museum, in Rochester, New York (see fig. 122), and in the Henry Luce Study Center of the American Wing in the Metropolitan Museum of Art.

Historians at American museums have also augmented the techniques of object description. In the past decade there have been several attempts to develop strategies that could be claimed as indigenous to material culture research. I have noted them above in the prologue (pp. 18–32).

While connoisseurship and conservation do not normally have a public face (such work is done in offices and laboratories out of sight from a museum's public areas), they have an effect on public presentation of material culture. Called "object fetishism" by its critics, "object primacy" by its advocates, the reverential treatment curators often accord single objects is translated to museum visitors in what might be called "the enshrinement syndrome." For example, a West Virginia post office that had been neglected for more than one hundred years was dismantled and rebuilt in the National Museum of History and Technology (now the National Museum of American History). As Harold Skramstad notes, by moving this artifact into the museum it became, instantaneously, a revered national treasure—so revered, in fact, that there was serious talk of removing the original shutters and replacing them with exact replicas since the originals contained carvings of the names of Civil War soldiers. The ennobling effect of the museum environment affects not only visitors but staff perceptions as well. When asked what great historical treasures the museum possessed, one curator at the National Museum responded that anything was a national treasure simply by being in the collection.[16]

Kenneth Ames points out other dangers of an overemphasis on merely describing objects: creator worship (concern for who made it or an exhaustive study of an object's maker rather than its user); primacy fascination (concern for who made it first or a high valuation being automatically assigned to an artifact's novelty or innovative elements); and excessive normative evaluation (asking what it is worth on the artifact—often read antiques—market as opposed to its possible social, cultural, or ideological significance). Ames also alludes to another issue that history museums and material culture studies must address: How representative is the material evidence that has been collected? How many instances of an object on display are to be found in a history museum's collections behind the scenes? How many exist in other museum collections? How many are one of a kind? How many were truly commonplace in their time?[17]

Historians who espouse the use of material culture evidence in order to counter the biases of documentary and statistical sources must also recognize its methodological limitations. The charge that many verbal records of American history have been generated by a small group of mostly white, mostly upper- or middle-class, mostly male, mostly urban, and mostly Protestant individuals could also be levied against many history museum collections. The influx of social history topics (for example, demographic history) and techniques (for example, quantitative methods) into both material culture research and history museum interpretation may further alert us to the liabilities imposed by the gender, race, ethnic origin, and socioeconomic status of the makers and users of objects.[18]

History Museum Interpreting: Analyzing Material Evidence

Over the past two decades, history museums and material culture scholars have gradually acknowledged the need to move beyond the simplistic claim that objects were important in and of themselves. Museums have had to interpret as well as gather and describe objects. National Endowment for the Humanities funding requirements made *interpretation* a buzzword among museum professionals in the 1970s. The American Association for State and Local History and other organizations sponsored seminars on museum interpretation throughout the United States. Book reviewers of American material culture studies demanded "explanatory models." Manifestoes for a new analytical vision of artifact research appeared. Theorists claimed that to achieve intellectual substance and academic respectability, defensible techniques and theories had to be applied to the material culture evidence that previous generations had collected and classified.

Institutionally, North American history museums contributed to this effort by publishing two of the three material culture journals in North America: *Winterthur Portfolio: A Journal of American Material Culture* by the Winterthur Museum and *Material History Bulletin* by the National Museum of Man.[19] Numerous national and international conferences on the subject also received strong museum sponsorship and support.[20] Institutions, such as the Smithsonian, established fellowships in material culture research, and occasionally a museum, such as the Colorado Historical Society, advertised for a curator of material culture.[21]

Intellectually, North American history museums have only begun to explore the explanatory power of the artifact. While several provocative advances (reviewed below) have been made, the present state of the art in object interpretation in historical explanation is still largely derivative. But this is also the case within the multidisciplinary material culture movement as a whole (see pp. 27–32). In material culture theory, students of the object have been consumers rather than producers. In an assessment of how widespread and diverse this borrowing has been, I once came up with several conceptual positions on which American material culture scholarship was modeled (table 15.2).[22] One might ask what role have history museums played in the development or diffusion of these explanatory paradigms? Which of these intellectual frameworks have been most influential in contemporary history museum interpretation?

One way of answering the last question is to set aside two material culture approaches—the structuralist and the behavioralist—that have been least congenial to historians working in museums.[23] Although the monographic literature applying structuralism in material culture research is growing, the theory, to my knowledge, has yet to inform a major history exhibition. Similarly, the behavioralistic approach advocated by Michael Owen Jones surfaces principally in folk art and craft demonstrations.[24] History museums have, however, benefited from and contributed to four other identifiable forms of material culture interpretive theory: national character; functionalist; cultural reconstructionist, and social history.

The national character approach to material culture interpretation uses particular objects to explain the collective ethos of an entire nation. Its advocates have produced such classics as John Kouwenhoven, *Made in America* (1948); Alan Gowans, *Images of American Living* (1964); Alan Trachtenberg, *The Brooklyn Bridge: Fact and Symbol* (1964); and Daniel Boorstin, *The Americans* (1958–73). Its manifestation in the history museum can be documented in several blockbuster exhibitions mounted at the time of the nation's Bicentennial. For example, the National Museum of American History made American pluralism the chief American character trait in its "A Nation of Nations" exhibition. Although this focus on the collective character is most frequently applied to explain the total national experience (particularly by demonstrating what is "American" about American artifacts), it has also informed permanent gallery installations on a regional level (for example, the New York State Museum's plans for its Upstate Gallery) and a local level (for example, the Fort Worth Museum of Science and History exhibition, "Images of Fort Worth").

In the New York State Museum's permanent gallery, the museum historians plan to organize part of their artifact assemblage around a sense of self-definition by opposition ("We are what New York City is *not*") to demonstrate how upstate New York historically has had a distinctive regional identity, one claiming to be nonmetropolitan, rural-oriented, and independent. In the Fort Worth exhibit, curators attempt to prove that Fort Worth is the state's "Texasmost" city by documenting its several

Table 15.2. The Current Research Trends in American Material Culture Scholarship (Part I)

	Art History	Symbolist	Cultural History
Main disciplinary perspectives	Architectural history; decorative arts history	American Studies, American literature	Historical archaeology; cultural anthropology; experimental archaeology; folklore
Usual artifact interest	Masterpieces of art and decorative arts	Public monuments, civic totems, icons, popular culture	Preindustrial, agrarian material culture of communities
Definitions of history	Biography of individuals and their works	History of ideas, myths, symbols, and the imagination	Past is real; it can be recreated, rebuilt, reassessed, in the present
Interpretive objectives	Depict the historical development and intrinsic merit of art objects	Portray the abstract as well as the concrete meanings of past artifacts	Muster all empirical resources in the recovery of certain historic pasts
Frequent research methods	Analysis of the established canon of Western art	Discover dual life of objects as both facts and symbols	Fieldwork; historical archaeology; folklife interviewing
Publication and presentation formats	Museum exhibit catalog; single artifact exhibit; biography; period room	Monograph; historic battlefield site; temporary exhibits	Field work report; historic house restoration; outdoor historic museum village/community re-creation
Typical scholarship	J. Kirk, *American Chairs: Queen Anne and Chippendale* (1972) C. Montgomery, *American Furniture: The Federal Period* (1966) J. Lippman and A. Winchester, *The Flowering of American Folk Art* (1973) J. Prown, "Style as Evidence," *Winterthur Portfolio* (1980)	A. Tractenberg, *The Brooklyn Bridge: Fact and Symbol* (1965) A. Ludwig, *Graven Images: New England Stonecarving and Its Symbols, 1650–1815* (1966) R. Rudsill, *Mirror Images: Influence of the Daguerreotype* (1971) R. Venturi, *Learning from Las Vegas* (1972)	J. Cotter, *Archaeological Excavations at Jamestown* (1957) I. Noël-Hume, *Here Lies Virginia: An Archaeologist's View of Colonial Life and History* (1973) J. Deetz, *In Small Things Forgotten* (1977) R. Schuyler, *Historical Archaeology* (1978)

Table 15.2. The Current Research Trends in
American Material Culture Scholarship (Part II)

	Environmentalist	Functionalist	Structuralist
Main disciplinary perspectives	Cultural and historical geography; regional ecology; cultural anthropology	History of technology; cultural anthropology; folklife studies, experimental archaeology	Folklife studies; enthnography/linguistics; cultural anthropology
Usual artifact interest	All landscape features, especially housing	All components of a technological system	Vernacular folk housing; popular culture data
Definition of history	Cultural change revealed in cultural landscape	Rational development, adaptation, transmission and function of artifacts as "tools"	Past behavior discovered in previous communication systems
Interpretive objectives	To depict cultural adaptations across space	To explain the evolution of human technologies over time	To ascertain basic universal patterns that structure human consciousness
Frequent research	Fieldwork to test the concept of diffusion of artifacts in a region	Fieldwork and experimentation to test "usefulness" and "practicality" of objects	Comparative fieldwork to find the "artifactual grammar" of physical data
Publication formats	Folklife/anthropology museums; monographs; cultural atlases	Craft demonstrations; technology museum exhibits; experimental archaeology	Monographs; single-genre artifact exhibits
Typical scholarship	F. Kniffen, "Folk Housing: A Key to Diffusion" (1963) J. B. Jackson, "The Westward-Moving House" (1957) P. Lewis, "Common Houses Cultural Spoor" (1975) *North American Cultural Survey Atlas* (1982)	W. Roberts, "Folk Architecture in Context," *Pioneer American Society Proceedings* (1973) J. Anderson, "Immaterial Material Culture," *Keystone Folklore* (1977) R. Howard, "Interchangeable Parts, Re-Examined," *Technology & Culture* (1978) E. N. Anderson, "Folk Art of Landscaping," *Western Folklore* (1972)	H. Glassie, *Folk Housing in Middle Virginia: A Structure Analysis of Historic Artifacts* (1975) H. White, "Structuralism and Popular Culture," *Journal of Popular Culture* (1974) E. Wilson, "Form Changes in Folk Houses," *Geoscience and Man* (1974) B. Herman, "The Whole Cloth of Ethnography," *American Material Culture and Folklore* (1982)

Table 15.2. The Current Research Trends in
American Material Culture Scholarship (Part III)

	Behavioralistic	National Character	Social History
Main disciplinary perspectives	Folkloristics; folk-life science; psycho-history; cognitive anthropology; environmental and social psychology	Philosophy of history; history of technology; Whig history/Marxist history	Family history; women's history; labor history; black history; urban history
Usual artifact interest	Folk art, foodways; spatial constructs; domestic artifacts; photographs	Entire material culture corpus but especially technology	Artifactual remains of non-elite groups; probate data; inventories, wills
Definition of history	Biography; contemporary activity	National character; ideology	Evolution of collective biographies within social structures
Interpretive objective	To investigate the life stages and the social processes of behavior	To understand the ideological configurations of any national culture	To investigate the common activities of common people in social groups, classes, institutions
Frequent research methods	Fieldwork observations; oral history interviewing; historical psycho-analysis; hypothesis testing	Synthesize previous scholarship (documentary, graphic and artifact evidence) into a broad, interpretive overview	Statistical articulation of quantitative data; test explanatory concepts such as modernization
Publication and presentation formats	Folk art demonstrations; informant interviews; social/psychological statistics	Multi-volume history textbooks; block-buster museum exhibits; permanent gallery installations	Monographs; living history farms; historic house museums
Typical scholarship	M. Jones, *The Hand-Made Object* (1975) E. Hall, *The Hidden Dimension* (1966) D. Upton, "Toward a Performance Theory in Vernacular Architecture," *Folklore Forum* (1979) S. Bronner. "Investigating Identity and Expression in Folk Art," *Winterthur Portfolio* (1981)	J. Kouwenhoven, *Made in America* (1948) A. Gowans, *Images of American Living* (1964) D. Boorstin, *The Americans* (1958–1973) R. Burlingame, *March of the Iron Men* (1938)	J. Demos, *A Little Commonwealth* (1970) P. Benes, *Masks of Orthodoxy* (1977) C. Clifford, "Domestic Architecture," *J. Interdisciplinary History* (1976) K. Ames, "Meaning in Artifacts," *J. Interdisciplinary History* (1978)

"border lives"—as a frontier line in the 1850s, a cattle kingdom in the 1870s, a commercial gateway to the West in the 1890s, to meatpacking after 1910, to the West Texas oil fields of the 1920s, and to the aviation industry in the 1940s—as emblematic of "Texasness" as a whole.[25]

A national character approach, whether communicated in monographs or museums, can be prone to the fallacy of progressive determinism, a tendency that has been enormously influential in both American history and material culture research. Often the American past is depicted as one material success after another in an ever-upward ascent of more goods and services for all the nation's citizens. George Basalla and others have traced this tendency in the history of technology and in technical museums. Such museums, notes Basalla, are often dominated by a "technological cornucopia" mentality in their celebration of American progress. Michael Ettema sees the same problem in the American decorative arts as does Dell Upton in American vernacular architecture.[26] Examples of this perspective's influencing exhibitions would be those at the National Air and Space Museum and "In Praise of America: American Decorative Arts, 1650–1830" mounted in 1980 by the National Gallery of Art.[27]

A national character emphasis in a history museum exhibition need not be uncritical or insensitive to changes that were unsuccessful or to points of view that did not prevail. Exhibitions around several 1980s historical anniversaries—the opening of the Brooklyn Bridge, the completion of the Statue of Liberty, the ratification of the U.S. Constitution, the adoption of the national flag, the opening of Ellis Island—could explore not only the continuity and consensus surrounding these national symbols but also the complexities, contradictions, and controversies they have engendered among Americans, whom historian Michael Kammen has aptly described as a "people of paradox."[28]

Even a minor revision of a traditional national character exhibition can promote more sophisticated understanding of nationhood and a more perceptive understanding of the national past. When an exhibition is different in tone, subject matter, or point of view from what they expect, visitors will be surprised and take notice. For instance, Barbara Clark Smith of the National Museum of American History has suggested revising its exhibit, "The Star Spangled Banner" by alternately playing a traditional nineteenth-century rendition of the national anthem and Jimi Hendrix's 1960s version of the song. Many visitors would be taken aback, but they would also think critically about the presentation.[29]

A special interest in the material culture of technics unites the advocates of national character research (who see such artifacts as skyscrapers, assembly lines, and balloon-frame houses as quintessentially

American) and those who follow a functionalist interpretation. Functionalists hold that culture is primarily a means of adapting to environment, with technology being the primary adaptive mechanism. With strong advocates in fields of cultural anthropology, the history of technology, and folklore, the functionalists in material culture research are especially concerned with explaining two processes: how an object was "worked" (how its maker acted in order to make it) and how the object itself "works" (how it actually functions in a sociocultural context).[30]

History museums with institutional ties to natural history collections often have a strong functionalist orientation that is evident, for example, in the use of habitat groups to show stages of economic evolution and the development of technological skills. Many American Indian history museums, despite recent calls for broader interpretation, have a similar focus.[31] The ubiquitous craft demonstrations found at practically all outdoor living history sites and agricultural museums are often other examples of functionalism. Finally, the approach is personified in such organizations as SWEAT (Society of Workers in the Early American Trades) and, of course, in the ever-growing reenactment movement.[32]

Although history museums have become enormously proficient in demonstrating how an artifact was actually worked—Old Sturbridge Village and Conner Prairie Settlement, for example, pride themselves on their accurate replication of the processes of how things were made— most history sites and exhibitions pay less attention to how objects functioned in a social, cultural, or political context. The traditional emphasis of so much material culture research on the makers of objects rather than the users encouraged this neglect. Moreover, the extensive literature on this the second half of the functionalist equation (that is, the magical, religious, regional, national, social, and ideological functions of artifacts) has received only limited attention from museum historians.[33]

Historians, sensitive to how ideologies function, recognize that objects mediate power relationships between people. Artifacts do have politics (fig. 151).[34] And curators interpreting government buildings, churches, civic structures, recreational spaces, public sites, and history museums must not neglect this important function of material culture, past and present.

Functionalists are eager to demonstrate that material culture reflects the rationality and practicality of participants in a culture. A person's description of his own motives often helps the researcher establish a functional explanation. Thus oral history fieldwork is a frequently employed research tool. But often such information is not available. Then the researcher is left to probe "the mind of the maker," particularly the functional sequence that existed in the fabrication and use of an artifact.

Figure 151.
Vice-President Nixon's "Kitchen Debate" with Nikita Krushchev, 1959
(Courtesy World Wide Photos)

To explore the cognitive processes involved in the production of past material culture, researchers in a number of American history museums have engaged in "experimental or imitative archaeology." Experiments in seventeenth-century brewing have been done at Plimoth Plantation and in early nineteenth-century kiln construction and ceramics manufacture at Old Sturbridge Village (fig. 152).[35] In a summary of such research, Jay Anderson notes that "experimental archaeology was developed as a means of (1) practically testing theories of past cultural behavior, especially the technological processes involving the use of tools, and (2) obtaining data, not readily available from more traditional artifact and historical sources."[36]

A strict functionalist interpretation of material culture can exaggerate human efficacy. The aura and physical presence of certain types of things still so tangibly present centuries after their actual making can seduce the researcher into overemphasizing what anthropologists call "the culture of agency"—the self-defining or self-assertive activities of their original makers. The history that is written or exhibited from such material culture is prone, therefore, to champion only the activities of the movers and shakers of the past. More triumphs than tragedies survive in the extant physical record.

Figure 152.
Early Nineteenth-Century Kiln Reconstruction, Old Sturbridge Village,
Sturbridge, Massachusetts

Functionalist-oriented exhibits in museums often promote a view of history as a story of success and achievement. For example, the Cooper-Hewitt Museum's 1986 exhibition, "Milestones: Fifty Years of Goods and Services," chronicled five decades of consumer "small wonders and big deals" without much attention to consumer fraud, protection, or rejection.[37]

In these contexts, documentary and statistical records (rather than the artifactual) may prove especially helpful to the researcher since people could and did write about the dark and unpleasant side of their existence; that is, the uncertainties, the false starts, the halfway measures, the intentions that failed. But object study also requires analyses of material culture pathology so that we might know more about what things, in various historical periods, did not work, which consistently broke down or were quickly junked in favor of other products. We need a greater appreciation of the losers (people and products) in American written and material history. For insights as to how this might be pursued see Denis Donoghue's provocative 1976 essay, "The American Style of Failure."[38]

John Demos, for example, notes that *New England Begins: The Seventeenth Century,* an exhibition and three-volume catalog produced by the Department of American Decorative Arts and Sculpture of the Boston Museum of Fine Arts (BMFA), depicts New England settlers as uncommonly active, effective, and forceful in coping with the circumstances of their lives.[39] This viewpoint contrasts sharply with a generation of scholarly opinion on seventeenth-century New England life, which has emphasized the unanticipated and the unwelcomed effects of seventeenth-century life in a new environment. Americans arrived with plans, expectations, and assumptions as to what they were about, but environmental circumstances transformed most of these.[40] The artifacts analyzed by the BMFA research team of archaeologists, decorative arts specialists, and social historians lead to a quite different conclusion. New Englanders were in control of their lives and their actions, artifice, and artifacts show them so.

A number of cultural anthropologists, folklike scholars, historical archaeologists, and historic preservationists take what might be called a "cultural reconstructionist" view of material culture. This approach is evident in small institutions like Turkey Run Farm in Virginia and larger operations such as Historic New Harmony in Indiana. Cultural reconstructionists believe, with varying degrees of fervor, that the past is real, that much of its reality can be resurrected, often physically rebuilt, through patient empirical research. Their imperative is no less than to document, study, and communicate as holistic a view of the past as is possible. In this attempt at reconstructing a total sense of the past, artifacts are seen as vital building blocks.[41]

American historical reconstructionists have found certain pasts more in need of rebuilding than others. To date, most of their work has focused on America's preindustrial craft villages, rural agrarian communities, and military garrisons. Deliberate utopian ventures constitute an inordinately large proportion of American cultural reconstruction interpretations.

Although cultural reconstructionists may seem more intent on historic preservation than historical analysis, their approach is strongly research-oriented. In their background preparation (and sometimes in their exhibitions) they examine extensive documentary, statistical, and especially archaeological evidence before articulating an interpretive framework. This analysis is revised as new data become available. Although such an approach is used by some historic house museums and historic sites, the paradigm finds its largest following in outdoor living history museums.

Plimoth Plantation represents one epitome of the cultural reconstructionist model since, as is stated in its mission statement, its goal is to re-create a complete portrait of life in the colony in the year 1627. Its staff has painstakingly researched every detail of clothing, speech, work habits, house construction, furnishings, diet, livestock, and family life. Interpreters bring these details to life by acting out roles of actual settlers. Because the museum is stocked entirely with reproductions, visitors are encouraged to open cupboards, sit on benches, and pick up food containers. The result, unlike many overtidy, immaculate, and manicured outdoor villages, is a decidedly unromanticized view, complete with the filth, hard labor, and lack of privacy typical of the early seventeenth century. The museum's planners have made every effort to avoid presenting the Pilgrims as the courageous and visionary founding fathers celebrated in modern stereotypes. Indeed, Pilgrim lives seem restricted, difficult, and mundane; the reconstruction of their past lifestyle strikes one as sensitive, convincing, and accurate.

And yet, as Michael Ettema has argued, the restoration gives few clues about why it is important for us to know that information. Because this "time travel" approach allows for no anachronistic questioning about life after 1627, the past is severed from the present. Ettema writes,

> The visitor is discouraged from questioning how social and material conditions in the Plimoth colony contributed to the social and material conditions we face in the present. But then, the role-playing interpreters would not be allowed to address such questions anyway. Theoretically, visitors might at least explore the social and cultural relations of Plimoth in 1627, but in practice, the very success of the reconstruction militates against it. The complete and seductive nature of the recreated material environment leads the visitor only to explore what can be seen and touched. The history of life in Plimoth becomes the history of its material conditions. Modern people may

find such a technologically crude environment appealing in its rusticity or appalling in its backwardness, but in any event the primary conclusion most will draw is that progress has brought us many material comforts. Through its elaborate and enjoyable scheme, the Plantation simply reinforces the ideas that modern technology results in a superior existence and that it is the only logical course for humanity. The only real choice in life is to sustain progress, and that is best done materially.[42]

Outdoor living history museums tend to pay attention to the spatial and environmental contexts of material culture. They are interested in various landscape features (particularly houses and barns) and how such artifacts depict cultural adaptations across space. An assumption, sometimes explicit, sometimes not, underlying much of their research is a concept of regionalism, especially the idea that a region's diverse material culture is, at its core, integrative; that is to say, all the culture manifested in a region's material culture can be considered to be an integrated whole.[43]

Cultural reconstruction, despite its many adherents in history museums and material culture research, is not without its pitfalls. An obvious dilemma is its tendency to present the past as static. Uniformity and homogeneity can also characterize these interpretations, particularly if the material culture of those outside its mainstream—laborers, slaves, women, agitators—is underrepresented in a museum's collections. An example of a history museum overcoming this problem is a 1979 New York Gallery Association exhibit at the Cooper-Hewitt Museum, "Resorts of the Catskills," which used cottage architecture, hotel advertisements, and promotions for resort activities directed at various ethnic and racial groups to explain different views of vacationing, nature, ideas of leisure, and experiences of ethnic identity.[44] Finally, perhaps because of the romantic but influential notions of early cultural reconstructionists such as Jared Van Wagener and Henry Chanlee Forman, who viewed the past as primarily a harmonious agrarian existence that was supposedly destroyed by technology and urbanization, the approach has never been applied in any systematic way to urban material culture.[45]

Perhaps material culture students with a social history orientation will one day make significant contributions to urban history (fig. 153). A number of American city museums—for instance, Cincinnati, Brooklyn, Chicago, and Pittsburgh—are attempting to analyze urbanization as a cultural process. They are also committed to exploring the material culture ramifications of the social history agenda: widening the conventional parameters of historical study to include day-to-day experiences (working, child rearing, schooling, playing, marrying, dying) of large aggregates of the population (minorities, women, workers, ethnic groups) that have previously been excluded from many museum interpretations.

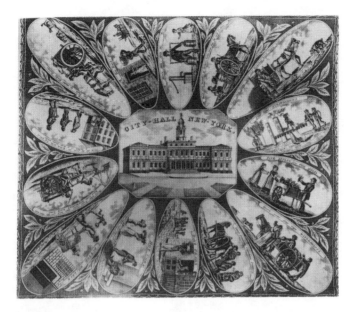

Figure 153.
New York City Hall, Surrounded by Fourteen Street Cries, ca. 1814
Printed toile.
(Courtesy Museum of the City of New York)

Social historians and certain students of material culture have much in common: a mutual concern for historical explanation of human behavior over time and place; a wish to challenge the older view of history as solely past politics; an interest in the heterogeneity of the American people and their life ways; and a desire to expand the traditional boundaries of American historical scholarship. Each frequently has been considered by other historians as a maverick approach to the past, yet each has claimed to hold a key to a more democratic and populist history.

Several topical areas—residential spaces, domestic life, women and children, working and workers, life cycles, and community landscapes—have been of interest to researchers with a social history orientation working in history museums and material culture.[46] Social history's interest in the everyday lives of ordinary people, plus its concern for a higher degree of representativeness in the evidential basis of all historical explanation, has been its major influence in history museums. Such interest has been evident in exhibits dealing with workers (the Essex Institute's "Life and Times in Shoe City: The Shoe Workers of Lynn," the National Museum of American History's "Symbols of American Labor" [fig. 154]), women (the Strong Museum's "Light of the Home"), and immigrants (the

Figure 154.
"Labor's Choice"
Cigar box label (ca. 1900).
(Courtesy Division of Political History, National Museum of American History)

Balch Institute's "Freedom's Doors").[47] Significant social history exhibits have also dealt with life-cycle history, from infancy and childhood (the Strong Museum's "A Century of Childhood") to death and mourning (the Museums at Stony Brook, "A Time to Mourn").[48] Adolescence and senescence still await comprehensive history museum interpretation.

Among some material culture students, social history has helped foster an increasing self-consciousness about methodological strategies: What type of data (written, statistical, oral, artifactual) produce the highest degree of causal explanation? How does the historian of objects measure change and depict it intelligibly to a public audience? Which questions that are worth asking about past human behavior are answerable with material culture?[49]

Social historians have frequently asked about the causes and consequences of human conflict, but neither history museums nor material culture studies have yet offered convincing explanations in response.[50]

Only a few museums and scholars have collected and interpreted the material culture of this aspect of the American past.[51] There are several reasons for this. One is professional. Social, as opposed to political, conflict has been a topic of interest to American historians for only a few decades.[52] Some are practical. Many museum staff members and their boards of trustees worry how visitors will react to presentations on ethnic tensions or religious conflicts.[53] Some are political. Some museum historians, like some social historians, avoid issues of conflict because they are uncomfortable with questions of power. Here the broader criticism leveled against social history by Eugene Genovese and Elizabeth Fox-Genovese and others applies. In their quest to understand group behavior, social historians often ignore relationships between groups. Like much social history writing, therefore, social history as presented in museums is depoliticized. We may learn much about the details of everyday life, but not, as Genovese and Fox-Genovese put it, "who rides whom and how" in the political and economic arena.[54]

Social history's most significant influence on American history museums has been in prompting reinterpretation of the material culture of domestic life. For example, the social history possibilities of the period room have been explored. Permanent and temporary exhibitions on American domesticity (figs. 155, 156), particularly in the nineteenth century, have made significant contributions to the work of both material culture students and social history researchers.[55]

The social history approach to history museum interpretation and material culture research has enjoyed wide acceptance. Young scholars trained in the 1960s and 1970s are particularly attracted to its explanatory potential. Many of these men and women took advanced degrees in social history and instead of pursuing careers in academic institutions joined the staffs of American history museums. The full effect of this important occupational shift and intellectual reorientation probably will not be known for another decade or two. I would suggest, however, that its ramifications for more sophisticated museum interpretation and more rigorous artifact study are auspicious.

History Museums and Material Culture: Future Possibilities

What else might be ventured as to the future of material culture, cultural history, and the history museum? In conclusion, I want to discuss: (1) possible topics for future museum exhibitions; (2) aspects of the relationship between museums and material culture scholarship in the next decade or so; and, (3) the growing interest, among both historians in the academy and historians in museums, in the theory and practice of the history exhibition as a distinct mode of communication. With regard to topics that might be opportunities for further studies, I would propose that consumerism, foodways, childhood (already in vogue), recreation, and

Figure 155.
Noah Webster House Study Installation, early 1960s
Greenfield Village, Dearborn, Michigan.
*(Courtesy The Collections of the Henry Ford Museum and
Greenfield Village)*

creativity will be subjects of mutual interest.[56] On the last topic—the
historical origins, dimensions, and ramifications of human innovation and
invention—we are already seeing research combining traditional
documentation and material culture evidence.[57] If the current arguments
of Jules Prown and Dell Upton are heeded, there will be a return—despite
the influence of the social history juggernaut—to elite material culture,
particularly high-style decorative arts, architecture, and the fine arts. The
strategy suggested here (at least by Upton) is to study high-style objects
along with common material culture in a total "landscape approach" to
artifact research.[58] An exemplar of this concept in history museum exhibition was the cooperative interpretation of the Lambert Castle–Botto
House program, "Mill Owner/Mill Worker," in Paterson, New Jersey.[59]

Although there is renewed interest in material culture scholarship
among some anthropologists, it remains to be seen whether or not the
founders of the movement (or their museums) will make any serious
claims to take over as its institutional or intellectual home base.[60] It is
also difficult to predict the institutional future of the American material
culture movement. Some suggest it could be lodged in universities within

Figure 156.
Noah Webster House Study Installation, 1988
Greenfield Village, Dearborn, Michigan.
(Courtesy The Collections of the Henry Ford Museum and Greenfield Village)

multidisciplinary programs called departments of material culture.[61] Others argue for its organization through a consortium of history museums (with university affiliations) concentrating their efforts regionally or chronologically.[62]

If history museums are to play a larger role in material culture research, they need to amplify their voice in the scholarly forums that cover the field. An alarming trend, however, prompts doubt about whether this will happen. In the 1984 American Association for State and Local History national survey of the history museum profession, institutions were asked to identify their most important concern. Fund raising and public relations ranked first for almost half of them (43.1 percent), with management, preservation, conservation, and acquisition of collections next in order of priority. In contrast, those activities related to the interpretation of material culture ranked lowest: exhibitions were the most important concern for only 2.2 percent; publications for 2.0 percent; educational programs for 1.8 percent; and improved interpretation for 1.3 percent. Most worrisome of all, research ranked last, with only 0.2 percent of the respondents listing it as their major concern.[63]

In surveying the major national journals of the history museum field over the past decade, one is struck by how few articles address methodological or conceptual issues in material culture research.[64] However, parallel review of the two American material culture publications indicates a similar neglect of the museum interpretive potential of artifacts. Whereas these journals review material culture scholarship when published in book form, only hesitantly have they or the history museum journals been willing to establish a systematic policy of exhibit review and evaluation.[65]

What are occasionally reviewed in both material culture and history museum publications are exhibition catalogs. Although a thorough study of the catalog as a device for the communication of material culture research has yet to be written, the genre is maturing as a standard vehicle for disseminating important analyses of artifacts. In this sense, certain catalogs have become helpful reports of work in progress or, where their data have been fairly comprehensive, useful reference tools.[66] A few daring scholars have used the medium to speculate about the interpretive message of artifacts in a wider cultural context.[67]

The problems and potential of the medium that generated the two-dimensional catalog—that is, the three-dimensional history exhibition—deserve much more serious research. Literature concerned with the exhibition process has been largely left to the art critics whose primary interest lies with individual objects, or to social scientists whose concern is more with the behavior patterns of the visitor. In addition, we need studies that view the history museum exhibition as a type of publication and that recognize the selective arrangement of artifacts and other related information in a public display for an audience to be a museum's special mode of communication. Such displays are one of the media for exploring the intersections of material culture and its larger constellations of meaning. As Harold Skramstad observes "perhaps more than anything else a museum's exhibition environment is an accurate index of its attitude toward material culture."[68]

We have had some preliminary discussion of the history exhibit as a distinct form of cultural discourse. Nicholas Westbrook and others have suggested that the complexities of the exhibition processes be given wider public acknowledgment.[69] Fath Davis Ruffins argues that we need to think of every exhibition as a spatial, often nonlinear, interactive, visual form, a complicated material culture assemblage that is more than the sum of its parts. In her estimate, every exhibition is an approximation of the past and should therefore be best thought of as a "metaphor about the past" as well as a "cultural argument" in the present.[70] Barbara and Cary Carson have proposed that one might think of the historic house, site, or setting as a material culture theater, furnished with appropriate and accurate artifacts, where what Rhys Isaac, in *The Transformation of Virginia,* calls "historical dramaturgy" might be enacted either by visitors or for them.[71]

Jim Sims, senior designer at the National Museum of American History, suggests we turn to the history of the theater for insights as to how exhibition design might better communicate an understanding of the past. Sims recommends we keep Aristotle's six principles of theater (plot, character, thought, diction, music, and spectacle) in mind when creating certain types of artifactual narratives; as a counter model, he proposes museum historians might find aspects of the Brechtian drama of confrontation to be useful for telling quite different stories.[72]

These historians regard the history museum environment as a public forum where the exploration and evaluation of material culture can be presented in both an intellectually stimulating and visually legible manner comprehensible to a wide audience. They see exhibits as cultural arguments that are the vehicles for communicating the best insights of material culture research. They recognize that those who study material culture have a mission that includes but also extends beyond the marshaling of objects or the description of artifacts. The mission—to integrate the three-dimensional remnants of our past with documentary, oral, and statistical resources—remains an engaging future task for both museum and academic historians.

Brooke Hindle, a scholar who has contributed to both institutional contexts, is optimistic about the future of material culture in the history museum. Although written a decade ago, his words still hold true. "The mission," he notes, "is a great one. Even the beginnings registered so far are exciting. They point to the fulfillment of the deep-running need of this generation and those to come for a better history of their past that is both true and useful. It will be truer and more useful than the present histories," concludes Hindle, "precisely because its abstractions will be tied by an intricate web to the real world of material culture."[73]

Notes

1. For example, in 1875, A. Lane-Fox Pitt-Rivers, in his essay "On the Evolution of Culture," urged his fellow anthropologists to consider material culture as "the outward signs and symbols of particular ideas in the mind." See J. L. Meyers, ed., *The Evolution of Culture and Other Essays* (Oxford: Clarendon Press, 1906), 6.

2. A sampler of these definitions can be found in Thomas J. Schlereth, "Material Culture and Cultural Research," in *Material Culture: A Research Guide,* ed. Thomas J. Schlereth (Lawrence: University Press of Kansas, 1975), 2–5.

3. E. McClung Fleming, "The University and the Museum, Needs and Opportunities for Cooperation," *Museologist* 111 (June 1969): 10–18.

4. Anne-Marie E. Cantwell and Nan A. Rothschild, "The Research Potential of Anthropological Museum Collections," *Annals of the New York Academy of Sciences* 376 (December 1981): 1–7.

5. John E. Fleming, director of the Wilberforce Museum in Ohio, recognized this in his recent survey of artifact collections at thirty historical institutions; see his essay "Taking Stock of Afro-American Material Culture," *History News* 40.2 (February 1985): 15–19.

6. Wilcomb Washburn, "Collecting Information, Not Objects," *Museum News* 62.3 (February 1984): 5–15.

7. Sandra Elkins, "What's in a Name?" *History News* 40.8 (August 1985): 6–13.

8. Goran Rosander, *Today for Tomorrow: Museum Documentation of Contemporary Society in Sweden by Acquisition of Objects* (Stockholm: SAMDOK Council, 1980); Maria Papageorge, "Collecting the Present in Sweden," *Museum News* 60 (September/October 1981): 13–18; John Rooney et al., *This Remarkable Continent: An Atlas of United States and Canadian Society and Cultures* (College Station: Texas A & M University Press, 1982).

9. L. Thomas Frye, "The Recent Past Is Prologue," *Museum News* 53 (November 1974): 24–26; Candace Floyd, "Too Close for Comfort," *History News* 40.9 (September 1985): 9; Edith Mayo, "Connoisseurship of the Future," in *Twentieth-Century Popular Culture in Museums and Libraries,* ed. F. E. H. Schroeder (Bowling Green, Ohio: Bowling Green University Popular Press, 1981), 13–24.

10. Dell Upton, "The Power of Things: Recent Studies in American Vernacular Architecture," in Schlereth, *Material Culture: A Research Guide,* 72. For an oral history study investigating the significance of material possessions in contemporary family life, see Mihaly Csikszentmihalyi and Eugene Halton-Rochberg, *The Meaning of Things: Domestic Symbols and the Self* (Cambridge: Cambridge University Press, 1981).

11. David Orr and Mark Ohno, "The Material Culture of Protest: A Case Study in Contemporary Collecting," in Schroeder, *Twentieth-Century Popular Culture,* 37–54; Barbara Riley, "Contemporary Collecting: A Case Study," *Decorative Arts Newsletter* 4 (Summer 1978): 3–6; Nicholas Westbrook and Joan Siedl, *The Wishbook: Mail Order in Minnesota—An Exhibition of the Minnesota Historical Society* (St. Paul: Minnesota Historical Society, 1977).

12. Charles Montgomery, "Some Remarks on the Practice and Science of Connoisseurship," *American Walpole Society Notebook* (1961): 7–20.

13. David Nicandi, "Museums, Scholars, and Popular History," *Pacific Coast Forum* 3.4 (1978): 25–29.

14. Cary Carson, "Chesapeake Themes in the History of Early American Material Life," paper presented at "Maryland, A Product of Two Worlds" Conference, St. Mary's City, Maryland (19 May 1985), 77. For a Canadian discussion of this issue, see Gregg Finley, "Material History and Museums: A Curatorial Perspective in Doctoral Research," *Material History Bulletin* 20 (Fall 1984): 75–79, and Finley, "Material History and Curatorship," *Muse* 111.3 (Autumn 1984): 36–39.

15. Anthony Garvan describes the index and its anticipated application to material culture research in his essay "Historical Depth in Comparative Culture Study," *American Quarterly* 14 (Summer 1962): 260–74. On the potential of a more recent research

tool being developed at the Smithsonian, see Rita Cipalla, "The Video-Disc Advantage," *History News* 40.8 (August 1985): 18–21.

16. Harold K. Skramstad, Jr., "Interpreting Material Culture: A View from the Other Side of the Glass," in *Material Culture and the Study of American Life,* ed. Ian M. G. Quimby (New York: W. W. Norton, 1978), 180.

17. Kenneth Ames, *Beyond Necessity: Art in the Folk Tradition* (New York: W. W. Norton, 1977), 297–301.

18. Thomas J. Schlereth, "Social History Scholarship and Material Culture Research," *Journal of Social History* 16.4 (June 1983): 111–43; Shomer Zwelling, "Social History Hits the Streets," *History News* 35.1 (January 1980): 10–12.

19. The third scholarly publication, *Material Culture,* is published by the Pioneer Society of America at the University of Akron in Akron, Ohio.

20. "Canada's Material History—An International Conference," sponsored by the National Museum of Man, Ottawa, Ontario, March 1979; "Material Culture and the Study of American Life," sponsored by the Winterthur Museum, Winterthur, Del., 23 March 1980; Simon J. Bronner, ed., *American Material Culture and Folklife: A Symposium* (Cooperstown, N.Y.: Cooperstown Graduate Associate Proceedings, 1981); "Material Culture, A Conference," sponsored by the Bay State Historical League, Bradford, Mass., 20–22 June 1980; North Carolina Department of Cultural Resources, "The Material Culture of Black History: Problems and Methods," Durham, N.C., 13 December 1980; "North American Material Culture Research: New Objectives, New Theories," sponsored by Winterthur Museum and Memorial University of Newfoundland, St. John's Newfoundland, 19–21 June 1986.

21. The curator of material culture at the Colorado Historical Society administers "the material culture department of CHS with responsibility for planning, developing, implementing and supervising programs to aid in the cultural and historical heritage of Colorado." *History News* 35.4 (May 1980): 19.

22. Thomas J. Schlereth, *Material Culture Studies in America* (Nashville: American Association for State and Local History, 1982), 32–75. Peter Rider has applied the topology to Canadian scholarship in his essay "Concrete Clio: Definition of a Field of History," *Material History Bulletin* 20 (Fall 1984): 93–94.

23. For a detailed discussion of the structuralist and behavioralistic approaches to material culture research, see Schlereth, *Material Culture Studies in America,* 55–57, 58–63.

24. Henry Glassie's *Folk Housing in Middle Virginia: A Structural Analysis of Historic Artifacts* (Knoxville: University of Tennessee Press, 1975) is an example of American structuralism; on behavioral approaches to material culture, see Michael Owen Jones, "Bibliographic and Reference Tools: Toward a Behavioral History," unpublished paper presented at the American Association for State and Local History Folklore Conference, New Orleans, 4–6 September 1980.

25. Patrick Norris, "A Primer of Place," *History News* 40.6 (June 1985): 11–16.

26. George Basalla, "Museums and Technological Utopianism," in *Technological Innovation and the Decorative Arts,* ed. Ian M. G. Quimby and Polly Anne Earl (Charlottesville: University of Virginia, 1974), 360; Michael J. Ettema, "History, Nostalgia, and American Furniture," *Winterthur Portfolio* 17. 2, 3 (Summer, Autumn 1982): 135–44; Upton, "The Power of Things," 72.

27. Wendy Cooper, *In Praise of America: American Decorative Arts, 1650–1830* (New York: Alfred A. Knopf, 1980).

28. Michael Kammen, ed., *The Contrapuntal Civilization: Essays toward New Understanding of the American Experience* (New York: Alfred A. Knopf, 1971) and *People of Paradox: An Inquiry Concerning the Origins of American Civilization* (New York: Alfred A. Knopf, 1973).

29. Barbara Clark Smith, paper on the National Museum of American History exhibition, "After the Revolution," presented at the Organization of American Historians annual meeting in Los Angeles, April 1984.

30. Richard Dorson, *Folklore and Folklife* (Chicago: University of Chicago Press, 19XX), 20–21; Simon Bronner, "Concepts in the Study of Material Aspects of American Folk Culture," *Folklore Forum* 12 (1979): 145–46; Siegfried Giedeon, *Mechanization Takes Command* (New York: Oxford University Press, 1948); Lynn White, *Medieval Technology and Social Change* (New York: Oxford University Press, 1964); Carl Condit, *The Chicago School of Architecture* (Chicago: University of Chicago Press, 1964); Warren Roberts, "Folk Architecture in Context: The Folk Museum," *Pioneer American Society Proceedings* 1 (1973): 34–50.

31. On American Indian museum interpretation, see David Lowenthal, *The Past Is a Foreign Country* (Cambridge: Cambridge University Press, 1985), 55, 278, 276.

32. Data on SWEAT can be secured from its national headquarters: 606 Lake Land Blvd., Auburndale, Fla. 33823. On the reenactment movement, see Jay Anderson, *Time Machines: The World of Living History* (Nashville: American Association for State and Local History, 1984).

33. For a classic statement of an artifact's multiple functions based on Peter Bogatyrev, *The Functions of Folk Costume* (1937, 1971), see Henry Glassie, "Structure and Function, Folklore and the Artifact," *Semiotica* 7 (1973): 313–51. In his *All Silver and No Brass: An Irish Christmas Mumming* (Dublin: Dolmen, 1976), Glassie proposes several applications of the functionalist perspective.

34. Landon Winner, "Do Artifacts Have Politics?" *Daedalus* (1981): 121–36.

35. Jay Anderson, "Foodways Program on Living History Farms," in *Association for Living Historical Farms and Agricultural Museums Annual* 1 (1975): 21–23, 23–26.

36. Jay Anderson, "Immaterial Material Culture: The Implications of Experimental Research for Folklife Museums," *Keystone Folklore* 21 (1976–77): 1–13; Robert Saher, "Experimental Archaeology," *American Anthropology* 63(1961): 793–816; John Coles, *Archaeology by Experiment* (New York: Scribners, 1973).

37. The catalog *I'll Buy That* (New York: Cooper-Hewitt Museum, 1986) also celebrates the magazine *Consumer Reports,* which celebrated its fiftieth anniversary in 1986.

38. Denis Donoghue, "The American Style of Failure," in *The Sovereign Ghost: Studies in the Imagination,* ed. Denis Donoghue (Berkeley: University of California Press, 1976).

39. John Demos, "Words and Things: A Review and Discussion of 'New England Begins,' " *William and Mary Quarterly* 40. 4 (October 1983): 584–97. See also Christopher M. Jedrey, "New England Begins: The Material Origins of American Culture," *Reviews in American History* 12 (September 1984): 363–71.

40. Bernard Bailyn, *Education in the Forming of American Society: Needs and Opportunities for Study* (Chapel Hill: University of North Carolina Press, 1960); Oscar Handlin, "The Significance of the Seventeenth-Century," in *Seventeenth-Century America: Essays in Colonial History,* ed. James Morton Smith (Chapel Hill: University of North Carolina Press, 1959), 3–12.

41. For an extended discussion of this paradigm, see Mark P. Leone, "Issues in Anthropological Archaeology," in *Contemporary Archaeology,* ed. Mark P. Leone (Carbondale: Southern Illinois University Press, 1972), 19; Schlereth, "Material Culture Studies in America," 46–50.

42. Michael J. Ettema, "History Museums and the Culture of Materialism," in *Past Meets Present: Essays about Historic Interpretation and Public Audiences,* ed. Jo Blatti (Washington, D.C.: Smithsonian Institution Press, 1987), 62–85.

43. Fred Kniffen, "American Cultural Geography and Folklife" in *American Folklife,* ed. Don Yoder (Austin: University of Texas Press), 60, 63.

44. Alf Evers et al., *Resorts of the Catskills* (New York: St. Martin's Press, 1979) was the exhibition catalog.

45. Jared Van Wagener, *The Golden Age of Home Spun* (Ithaca, N. Y.: Cornell University Press, 1953); Henry Chanlee Forman, *Jamestown and St. Mary's: Buried Cities* (Baltimore: The Johns Hopkins University Press, 1938).

46. Schlereth, "Social History Scholarship," 111–43.

47. The Essex Institute, *Life and Times in Shoe City: The Shoe Workers of Lynn* (Salem, Mass.: The Esssex Institute, 1979); Harvey Green, *The Light of the Home* (New York: Pantheon, 1983); Gail Stern, *Freedom's Doors* (Philadelphia: Balch Institute, 1986).

48. Mary Lynn Stevens Heininger, *A Century of Childhood, 1820–1920* (Rochester, N.Y.: Margaret Woodbury Strong Museum, 1984); Martha V. Pike and Janice Gray Armstrong, *A Time to Mourn: Expressions of Grief in Nineteenth-Century America* (Stony Brook, N.Y.: Museums at Stony Brook, 1980).

49. Nicholas Westbrook, "Decisions, Decisions: An Exhibit's Invisible Ingredient," *Minnesota History* 45.7 (Fall 1977): 292–96.

50. Thomas J. Schlereth, "Causing Conflict, Doing Violence," reprinted in this volume as chapter 14.

51. For such exceptions, see Andrew Baker and Warren Leon, "Conflict and Community at Old Sturbridge Village," *History News* 41.2 (March 1986): 6–11; David Crosson, "What's the Risk? Controversial Exhibits Challenge the Romantic Past," *History News* 36.4 (April 1981): 17–19.

52. Richard Hofstader and Michael Wallace, eds., *American Violence: A Documentary History* (New York: Vintage Books, 1971), 4–20.

53. Floyd, "Too Close for Comfort," 8–17.

54. Eugene Genovese and Elizabeth Fox-Genovese, "The Political Crisis of Social History," *Journal of Social History* 10.2 (Winter 1976): 205–20.

55. Dianne Pilgrim, "Inherited from the Past: The American Period Room," *American Art Journal* 10.1: 5–23; Melinda Young Frye, "Charles Wilcomb, Museum Pioneer,"

The Museum of California 1.5; Peter O'Connell, "Putting the Historic House into the Course of History," *Journal of Family History* 6 (Spring 1981): 28–40; Patricia West, "The New Social History and Historic House Museums: The Lindewald Example," *Museum Studies Journal* 2.3 (Fall 1986): 22–26; Roger B. White, "Whither the Urban Row House Exhibit? The Peale Museum's 'Rowhouse,' " *Technology and Culture* (January 1983): 76–90. On Minnesota's installation, see, *A Home of Our Own: An American Dream—An Exhibit Scenario* (St. Paul: Minnesota Historical Society, 1988).

56. Neil McKendrick, John Brewer, and J. H. Plumb, *The Birth of a Consumer Society: The Commercialization of Eighteenth Century England* (Bloomington: Indiana University Press, 1982); Matyas Szabo, "The Use and Consumption of Things," *Ethnologia Scandinavica: A Journal for Nordic Ethnology* (1978): 107–18.

57. On material culture resources for the study of creativity, see Eugene Ferguson, "The Mind's Eye: Nonverbal Thought in Technology," *Science* 197 (1977): 827–36; Roger N. Shepard, "The Mental Image," *American Psychologist* 33 (February 1978): 125–37; Brooke Hindle, *Emulation and Invention* (New York: New York University Press, 1981).

58. Dell Upton, "Material Culture Studies: A Symposium," *Material Culture* 17: 2, 3 (Summer, Fall 1985): 86.

59. *Life and Times in Silk City: A Collaborative Museum Exhibition* (1984); see also John A. Herbst and Catherine Keene, *Life and Times in Silk City. A Photographic Essay of Paterson, New Jersey* (Paterson, N.J.: American Labor Museum, 1984).

60. Jane Powell Dwyer, ed., *Studies in Anthropology and Material Culture,* vol. 1 of the Haffenreffer Museum Studies in Anthropology and Material Culture Series (Providence, R.I.: Brown University, 1975), 5; Miles Richardson, *The Human Mirror* (Baton Rouge: Louisiana State University Press, 1974); Mark Leone, "The New Mormon Temple in Washington, D.C.," in *Historical Archaeology and the Importance of Material Things,* ed. L. Ferguson (Columbia, S.C.: Society for Historical Archaeology, 1977); Grant McCracken, *Culture and Consumption: New Approaches to the Symbolic Character of Goods and Activities* (Bloomington: Indiana University Press, 1988).

61. James Deetz, "Material Culture and Archaeology—What's the Difference?" 11, 66.

62. Harvey Green, "Collecting Collectives: Collaboration in Collecting and Exhibiting," in *A Common Agenda for History Museums: Conference Proceedings,* ed. Lonn Taylor (Nashville: American Association for State and Local History, 1987), 50–53.

63. Charles Phillips and Patricia Hogan, "Who Cares for America's Heritage?" *History News* (September 1984): 12. On the growing tendency for museums to give priority to the conservation of artifacts over the interpretation of material culture, see Charles Phillips, "To Educate or Conserve?" *History News* 40.6 (June 1985): 7–10.

64. Exceptions to this would include Mark P. Leone, "Method as Message: Interpreting the Past with the Public," *Museum News* (October 1983): 35–41; James Deetz, "The Artifact and Its Context," *Museum News* 62.1 (October 1983); Diane Douglas and Bernard Herman, "Theory and Artifact: An Interdisciplinary Approach Reshapes the Mendenhall Story," *History News* 30.3 (March 1983): 32–35.

65. Thomas W. Leavitt, "Toward a Standard of Excellence: The Nature and Purpose of Exhibit Review," *Technology and Culture* 9 (January 1968): 70–75, and "The Need

for Critical Standards in History Museum Exhibits: A Case in Point,'' *Curator* 10.2: 91–94. A recent model review is Richard L. Bushman, ''Regional Material Culture: A Review of 'The Great River: Art and Society of the Connecticut Valley, 1635–1820,' '' *William and Mary Quarterly* (April 1986): 245–51.

66. Wendy A. Cooper, *In Praise of America: American Decorative Arts, 1650–1830,* (New York: Knopf, 1980).

67. Some recent museum catalogs in this class are Kenneth Ames, *Beyond Necessity: Art in the Folk Tradition* (Winterthur, Del.: Winterthur Museum, 1977); Robert Trent, *Hearts and Crowns: Folk Chairs of the Connecticut Coast, 1720–1840, as Viewed in Light of Henri Focillon's Introduction to Arts populaires* (New Haven, Conn.: New Haven Colonial Historical Society, 1977); Barbara Ward, ed., *Silver in American Life: Selections from the Mabel Brady Garvan and Other Collections at Yale University* (New York: American Federation of Arts, 1979); Peter Benes and Phillip C. Zimmerman, *New England Meeting House and Church, 1630–1850* (Boston: Boston University Press, 1979); Herbert W. Hemphill, Jr., *Folk Sculpture, U.S.A.* (Brooklyn, N.Y.: Brooklyn Museum of Art, 1976); Robert St. George, *The Wrought Covenant: Source Materials for the Study of the Craftsmen and Community in Southeastern New England, 1620–1700* (Brockton, Mass.: Brockton Art Center, 1979); John Michael Vlach, *The Afro-American Tradition in the Decorative Arts* (Cleveland: Cleveland Museum of Art, 1978); Howard Wright Marshall, *Buckaroos in Paradise: Cowboy Life in Northern Nevada* (Washington, D.C.: Library of Congress, 1980); Pike and Armstrong, *A Time to Mourn.*

68. Harold Skramstad, ''Interpreting Material Culture,'' 175–76.

69. Westbrook, ''Decisions, Decisions''; Jay Anderson, ''Living History: Simulating Everyday Life in Living History Museums,'' *American Quarterly* 34.3 (Summer 1982): 289–306.

70. Fath Davis Ruffins, ''The Exhibition as Form: An Elegant Metaphor,'' *Museum News* 64.1 (October 1985): 54–59.

71. Barbara G. Carson and Cary Carson, ''Things Unspoken: Learning Social History through Artifacts,'' in *Ordinary People and Everyday Life,* ed. James B. Gardner and George Rollie Adams (Nashville: American Association for State and Local History, 1983), 185–86.

72. James Sims, ''Exhibition as Event,'' presentation at the Seminar on Exhibition Criticism, National Museum of American History, Washington, D.C., 9 November 1988.

73. Brooke Hindle, ''How Much Is a Piece of the True Cross Worth?'' in Quimby, *Material Culture and the Study of American Life,* 20.

Figure 157.
Interior of Reconstructed Dominy Family Woodworking Shop, East Hampton, Long Island, 1790–1870
Winterthur Museum.
(Courtesy The Winterthur Library: Printed Book and Periodical Collection)

Epilogue

In a certain sense, all men are historians.
Most speak only to narrate.
—Thomas Carlyle

Figure 158.
Carpenter with Tools, ca. 1850
Ambrotype, photographer unknown.
(Courtesy Hagley Museum and Library Collections, Wilmington, Delaware)

One Historian's Craft:
Manuscripts, Palimpsests, Artifacts

I hope that the reader who has worked through my works will have found something useful for his or her craft. The diversity of my pieces quickly reveals that my shop is no specialty house; neither is it a single-product enterprise restricted by medium or material. Instead one finds wares of varying quality and in assorted stages of production. Several pieces are as carefully crafted and polished as my skill permitted and my publisher's timetable allowed; others I recognize as still rough-sawn and ill-shaped, much in need of planing and sanding; a few are only templates or prototypes. Others not displayed this collection remain on the shop's back shelves either to be reworked another day or to be tossed to the scrap heap.[1]

Why do I think of historical scholarship as a craft? Why not an art or a science? A discipline or a profession? Why propose the analogue of traditional craftsmanship for modern scholarship?

I cannot claim affinity with traditional artisanry through family heritage, vocational training, or a personal ability to work wood or metal, glass or clay, or any other material in a creative way. Although my father, John Schlereth, was a versatile amateur carpenter who designed and built two homes for his family, my father-in-law, Ralph Clauson, is an expert organ builder and clock maker, and my good friend, James Ferrell, is a machinist and jack-of-all-trades who works wonders with the material "stuff" we salvage from my homestead's barns and outbuildings, I possess no parallel or comparable abilities. Each of these men, however, has served as a model for my artisanry metaphor. My personal ideal has also been expanded and enriched by other craftsmen and craftswomen, past and present, whom I have encountered through material culture studies.

But how is what I do in library and archive, in museum collection and urban landscape comparable with what others do at cordwainers' benches and potters' wheels, in glassworks and cabinetmakers' shops? What do I have in common with Pat Lyon at the forge (see fig. 42) or with any of the *Four Tradesmen* (see fig. 6) by an unknown German folk painter in the early nineteenth century?

Scholars and craftsmen, while not totally self-employed, enjoy an enormous autonomy in their work and workshop. For example, the pace and rhythm of our scholarly work are largely our own—simultaneously a blessing and a burden; as such, it is a style of labor uncommon to the modern office or factory described in chapter 5. As the sociologist C. Wright Mills, writing on scholarship and *The Sociological Imagination* recognized, "one is free to begin his work according to his own plan, and during the activity by which it is shaped, he is free to modify its form in the manner of its creation."[2]

Mills's observation suggests a second affinity of scholarship with craftsmanship. Like the traditional artisan, the scholar often enjoys direct, personal engagement with his product. The scholar, like the artisan, controls, to a degree infrequent in the modern world, many of the components of his or her work. One is, as John Ruskin suggested every true artist should be, an active participant in the three interrelated processes of design, construction, and use.[3] As, for instance, the craftsman of a Midwestern I-house (fig. 159) was usually its architect, builder and inhabitant, so too, the scholar is frequently the originator, verifier, and explicator of an idea. In each case, plan and performance are one. In this volume, I have had the opportunity to control the sequence and pace of the argument, to mold the content and context of the book's separate parts, as well as to integrate its visual evidence with its verbal interpretation.

Such personal independence in creativity is, in part, rooted in an ancient cultural ideal shared by both artisans and authors. Craftsman and scholar William Morris put it thus: "The hope in good work is hope of product and hope of pleasure in the work itself. No ulterior motive (money, reputation, salvation) other than delight in the product being made and in the process of its creation."[4]

While few traditional artisans crafted their wares oblivious to the market place, their shops and stores almost always contained personal exercises of whim or imagination that were not for sale. Likewise, who among us has not wrought much mental labor simply "for the sake of the argument?" Who has not been compelled to read further than first intended in an archive collection or to test an unlikely hypothesis for the sheer fun of it?

In other, perhaps more mundane ways, scholarship is akin to craftsmanship. Like the skilled workers of pre-industrial times, scholars (fig. 160) often own the few tools they need in their trade. This is less so for those in science and engineering, for there researching and testing knowledge often takes massive technologies far in excess of any artisan's chest of tools. Humanities scholars—some philosophers claim they need nothing but con-

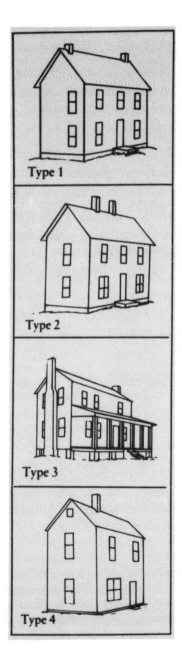

Figure 159.
Midwestern I-House, Typology
From Allen Noble, *Wood, Brick, and Stone*
(Amherst: University of Massachusetts Press,
1984)

Figure 160.
"The Author at His Desk, with Pen in Hand in Study Library"
Woodcut. From Edward Hazen, *The Panorama of Professions
and Trades* (Philadelphia, 1832), p. 117.

sciousness to practice their craft—often take particular solace in their
independence of milieu as well as mind. "The tools that I need for my
trade," William Faulkner once remarked, "are simply pen, paper, food,
tobacco, and a little whiskey."

For a material culture researcher in American Studies, however, not
even a generous supply of the great spirit (bourbon) that America gave
to the world can satisfy the need for "the goods," the artifacts. I could
not have written the previous fifteen chapters without access to the
material culture record saved by various cultural repositories or still extant
on the American landscape.

Writing in some form is, for most scholars, what the act of fabrication is for most craftspeople. Some work in all scholarly media and
materials—book reviews, research abstracts, journal articles, monographs;
others concentrate principally on a single method of communicating their
research; almost all, however, do some writing (fig. 161). Even those much
taken by the meaning of things tell us so by the means of words.

As a student of buildings, I have often been struck by the aptness of
the carpenter's craft (fig. 162) as a metaphor for such writing. Recently
I discovered, at the suggestion of one of my graduate students, that William

Figure 161.
Pen Advertisement, Aikin Lambert and Company, New York, ca. 1870
Chromolithograph.

Figure 162.
Carpenter Portrait, Mid-Nineteenth Century
Tintype.
(Courtesy Harry Rubenstein, Division of Photographic History,
National Museum of American History, Smithsonian Institution,
Washington, D.C.)

Zinsser sees a similar connection. In writing *On Writing Well* (1980), he suggests, "It is first necessary to be able to saw wood neatly and to drive nails. Later you can bevel the edges or add elegant finials, if that is to your taste. But you can never forget that you are practicing a craft that is based upon certain principles. If the nails are weak, your house will collapse. If your verbs are weak and your syntax is rickety, your sentences will fall apart."

An author's exposition often explicates an author's argument. As must be obvious by now, I often use two traditional techniques of the writer's craft: binary opposition and trinary classification. The first frequently structures my visual evidence; the second usually shapes my verbal interpretation. To think and write in threes is an old trick of the trade, traceable in Western thought certainly to Aristotle's *Poetics,* where the fundamentals for narrative discourse are a beginning, a middle, and an end. My penchant for trichotomy pervades this book, perhaps serving as an example in addition to all those surveyed by Alan Dundes in his insightful article, "The Number Three in American Culture."[5]

In one sense, this collection is a triptych, consisting of three sections of five chapters each. Its front matter (acknowledgments, introduction, prologue) form an opening threesome. Nine (3^2) of its chapters argue their points through tripartition. They do so in at least four (alas!) ways: a) by using three artifact assemblages to examine cultural change and continuity (for example, the three world fairs in chapter 10); b) by laying out three research strategies to focus attention on a particular aspect of material culture studies (for example, the three aspects of collecting, exhibiting, and researching childhood in chapter 3); c) by creating three categories both to delimit and to describe a vast topic (for example, the use of typonymy, architecture, and planning in chapter 7; and d) by dividing a historical time period into three chronological phases (for example, the classifying period from 1876 to 1948, the connoisseurship era of 1948 to 1965, and the explanatory era, 1965 to present, that orients chap. 15).

Of course, all these trichotomic schemes are nothing more than other forms of taxonomy or typology—human artifices by which to organize knowledge and understanding of other human artifices. While only tentative constructs, such schemes represent aspiration to culture history synthesis.

Historians devote much shop talk these days to the problems and possibilities of achieving greater synthesis in their work. The debate assumes many forms and is more complicated than specialists versus generalists. It is an important discourse, one I anticipate will have significant ramifications for material culture studies. Simply put, I hope whatever reintegration takes place in American cultural history will take into account material culture as evidence in its explanation. Others like Michael Kammen and Harvey Green agree.[6] In addition to proposals by such practitioners, there are encouraging signs in our trade journals. For example, the *Journal of American History* now includes graphic evidence where such data are vital to an author's historical interpretation; it provides a quarterly listing of material culture scholarship published in other serials; and it now publishes ten history museum exhibition reviews every other issue. I hope these peer reviews of material culture interpretation become a stock item in the history trade, like book reviews or historiographical essays.

I do not wish, however, to romanticize craft, traditional or scholarly. Neither is an idyllic life. Neither is without its acidity or aridity. Neither is without its petty jealousies or its prima donnas. We are, for example, subject to what one eighteenth-century Philadelphia housewright recognized when he referred to the "calling of craft as also one of broken days, slack spells, and dull seasons." While we may no longer need to cope (as did he) with the erratic delivery of materials, vacillating consumer demands, or simply the limited hours of winter's daylight, we have all known research projects that have failed, the depression of writer's block, and the days (nay, the weeks) with no ideas, no hypotheses, no imaginings.

Finally, we must also endure the periodic loneliness of craft life. Never fully knowing the immediate or ultimate destiny of the artifacts we create, scholars, like artisans, must occasionally live on anxiety's edge. We worry whether what we create will be accepted by mentors and colleagues, as craftsmen fret over the opinion of clients and customers. Will what we say or make prove true? Will it have meaning for this generation or, possibly, even future ones? Will our respective artifacts, crafted out of research and reflection, be trash or treasure, hokum or heirloom?

In these dilemmas, however, we have the comfort of craft to assuage us. Scholarship, like craftsmanship, is social as well as solitary. It is a community as well as a calling. It is a world of training and customary performance, of shop talk and canons of excellence, clashes of interpretations and techniques. It is a collective as well as an individual enterprise.

Because the craft of scholarship is communal, books such as this are possible. In a cross-disciplinary field such as material culture studies and in an interdisciplinary program such as American Studies, practitioners share theories and techniques. Hence the plethora of colleague artisans one finds in my acknowledgments, headnotes, and footnotes. Often a tradesman from one guild has the chance to talk of his wares and worries before another craft association. Such is the origin of several of these essays.

"Great nations write their autobiographies in three manuscripts," insisted Ruskin: "the book of their deeds, the book of their words, and the book of their arts. Not one of these books can be understood unless we read the two others; but, of the three, the only trustworthy one is the last." While I would certainly not claim that artifacts possess the only veracity as historical evidence, I do hope I have made a strong case for the potential of such data in cultural research and explanation. I believe, as does Dell Upton, that artifacts are "acts of creation equal to, rather than reflective of, the development of a social system or an intellectual concept. All are part of the human process of signing and symboling that continuously recreates the world by imposing meaning and order on it."[7]

Cultural historians, particularly if they consult material culture evidence as well as statistical, oral, and documentary data, can play a large role in this work of order and meaning. Ideally they address three (what else would you expect?) audiences whether, as historians, their institutional affiliation be within a museum, a historical agency, or the academy. First, like other artisans we do part of what we do to impress, improve, correct, or complement the work of our peers. Hence some of what I include above is specialized research written for professional colleagues. I am convinced that such work is crucial to two other professional responsibilities.

In teaching history in a university, my work reaches a second clientele. Several essays in this collection describe some of my classroom successes and failures. Several were inspired by undergraduate student questions in survey courses or by graduate student inquiries in advanced seminars.

Finally, I think it is important to research, lecture, write, exhibit, and share cultural history for a constituency wider than the artisan guild or the college classroom. As Michael Kammen has eloquently argued, historians have a noble public obligation that might be described as "explaining a culture to itself." Our calling, our vocation, our craft is "to provide society with a discriminating memory."[8]

Notes

1. Mark Block's *The Historian's Craft* (New York: Vintage, 1953; 1964) first prompted me to think of the affinity of scholarship and craftsmanship; see also Lewis P. Curtis, *The Historian's Workshop: Original Essays by Sixteen Historians* (New York: A. A. Knopf, 1970).

2. C. Wright Mills, *The Sociological Imagination* (New York: Oxford University Press, 1959).

3. John Ruskin, *The Stones of Venice* (Boston: Little, Brown, 1858; 1981).

4. William Morris, *Gothic Architecture: A Lecture for the Arts and Crafts Exhibition* (Hammersmith, London: Kelmscott Press, 1893).

5. Alan Dundes, "The Number Three in American Culture," in *Everyman His Way: Readings in Cultural Anthropology* (Englewood Cliffs, N.J.: Prentice-Hall, 1968), 401–24.

6. Michael Kammen, *Selvages and Biases: The Fabric of History in American Culture* (Ithaca: Cornell University Press, 1987); Harvey Green, *The Light of the Home: An Intimate View of the Lives of Women in Victorian America* (New York: Pantheon, 1983).

7. Dell Upton, "Material Culture, A Symposium," *Material Culture* 17.2–3 (1985): 87.

8. Kammen, *Selvages and Biases,* 70.

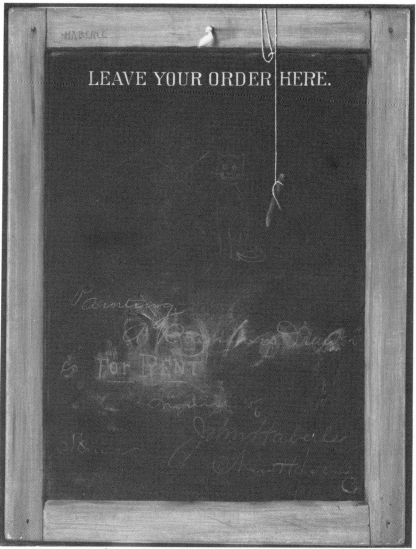

Figure 163.
John Haberle, *The Slate*, about 1895
Oil on canvas.
*(Henry H. and Zoë Oliver Sherman Fund,
courtesy Museum of Fine Arts, Boston)*

Index

Abbott, Bernice, 193
Adams, George H., 149
Adams, Henry, 236, 265, 282
Adams House (Brooklyn, N.Y.), 100
Addams, Jane, 245, 283
Akeley, Robert, 253
Alderson, William, 87, 303
Aldis, Owen, 197, 213
Alexander, Edward, 306, 331, 348
Alotta, Robert, 190
America, Victorian, 7, 13, 87, 90, 168,
    223, 267; embourgeoisement, 9, 30;
    mail order catalogs, 72; middle class, 9,
    219; middle vs. working class, 219–20.
    See also Nineteenth century
American Association of Museums, 11
American Association of Young Museums,
    100
American Historical Association, 11, 285
American history, teaching: function of
    artifacts, 334, 345; text vs. living
    history site, 348, 351, 352; under-
    represented topics, 352, 357; value of
    material culture, 339–42, 344–45, 357,
    427; with museums, 331–44, 387. See
    also Material culture; Museums, history
American Studies Association, 13, 35
Ames, Kenneth, 3, 12, 18, 19, 66, 303,
    308, 390
Anderson, Jay, 49, 347
Andrews, Deborah, 64
Andrews, William, 64
Anthony, Susan B., 275
Anthropology, 19, 101, 318, 335, 342, 378,
    382, 390, 397, 400, 406
Appleton, William, 195
Arbus, Diane, 99
Archaeology: above-ground, 39, 40, 43,
    46, 183, 185, 191, 195, 318, 319, 320;
    commercial, 191; "dingbat," 191;

historical, 183, 379, 400; historical
    associationism, 48; industrial, 191, 320.
    See also Environment; Museums,
    history; Plants; Research; Trees
Architecture, 195, 197, 203, 208, 211,
    215n.17, 236, 246, 265, 266, 320, 397.
    See also Individual fairs; Migration,
    cultural; World's fairs
Art Institute of Chicago, 3, 185, 235, 339
Artifacts, 398. See also American history,
    teaching; Material culture; Museums,
    history
Artisanry, 113–40; actor, 116; artisanry,
    116; artiste, 116; collective identity,
    129–40; communal recreation, 131;
    craft fraternities, 129, 133, 135, 136;
    craft identity, 116, 119, 121–29;
    depictions, 116, 117, 119; economic
    issues, 134; housing, 129, 130;
    individual personality, 116–21;
    mechanization, 129; membership
    certificates, 133–38; nomenclature, 117;
    past/present, 134–35; political activity,
    129, 138–39; portrait, 116, 117;
    production of goods, 121; repair work,
    124; role in history, 116; symbolism,
    139–40; trade card, 121; trade signs,
    125; women, 139
Asher, John R., 149
Axtell, James, 8

Bainbridge, David, 4
Baird, Spencer, 333
Baker, Elizabeth, 64
Banham, Reyner, 189
Barker, Colonel Joseph, 203
Barnard, Charles, 167
Barrick, Mac, 91
Bartholdi, Frédéric, 276
Basalla, George, 91, 396